2

# THE GLIDER SOLDIERS
A History of British Military Glider Forces

*Dedicated to the Glider Pilots,
Gliderborne Soldiers and Tug Crews.*

© Alan Wood 1992
ISBN 0-946771-99-5

First published in the UK in 1992
SPELLMOUNT LTD
12 Dene Way
Speldhurst
Tunbridge Wells
Kent
TN3 0NX

*A catalogue record for this book is
available from the British Library*

Printed in Great Britain by
BIDDLES LTD
Woodbridge Park
Guildford
Surrey

All rights reserved. No part of this publication may be reproduced,
stored in a retrieval system or transmitted in any form or by any means,
electronic, mechanical, photocopying, recording or otherwise,
without prior permission in writing from Spellmount Ltd, publishers.

# THE GLIDER SOLDIERS
A History of British Military Glider Forces.

by Alan Wood

Foreword by
Lt-Gen Sir Napier Crookenden, KCB, DSO, OBE, DL

**SPELLMOUNT LTD**
Tunbridge Wells

In the Spellmount/Nutshell Military list:

The Territorial Battalions - A pictorial history
The Yeomanry Regiments - A pictorial history
Over the Rhine - The Last Days of War in Europe
History of the Cambridge University OTC
Yeoman Service
The Fighting Troops of the Austro-Hungarian Army
Intelligence Officer in the Peninsula
The Scottish Regiments - A pictorial history
The Royal Marines - A pictorial history
The Royal Tank Regiment - A pictorial history
The Irish Regiments - A pictorial history
British Sieges of the Peninsular War
Victoria's Victories
Heaven and Hell: German Paratroop war diary
Rorke's Drift
Came the Dawn - Fifty years an Army Officer
Kitchener's Army - A pictorial history
On the Word of Command - A pictorial history of the
   Regimental Sergeant Major
Marlborough as Military Commander
The Art of Warfare in the Age of Marlborough
Epilogue in Burma 1945-48
Scandinavian Misadventure
The Fall of France
The First Victory: O'Connor's Desert Triumph,
   Dec 1940-Feb 1941
Blitz Over Britain
Deceivers Ever - Memoirs of a Camouflage Officer
Indian Army of the Empress 1861-1903
Heroes for Victoria 1837-1901
The Waters of Oblivion - the British Invasion of the Rio de
   la Plata, 1806-07.
Soldier's Glory - 'Rough Notes of an Old Soldier'
Craufurd's Light Division
Napoleon's Military Machine
Falklands Military Machine
Wellington's Military Machine
Commando Diary
The French are Coming! The Invasion Scare 1803-05
Military Marching - A pictorial history
Sons of John Company - the Indian and Pakistan Armies,
   1903-91

In the Nautical List:

Evolution of Engineering in the Royal Navy,
Vol 1. 1827-1939
In Perilous Seas
Sea of Memories

In the Aviation List:

Diary of a Bomb Aimer
Operation 'Bograt' - Memoirs of a Fighter Pilot
A Medal for Life-Capt Leefe Robinson VC
Three Decades a Pilot-The Third Generation
Bob Doe - Fighter Pilot
The Allied Bomber War, 1939-45

# CONTENTS

ACKNOWLEDGEMENTS 7

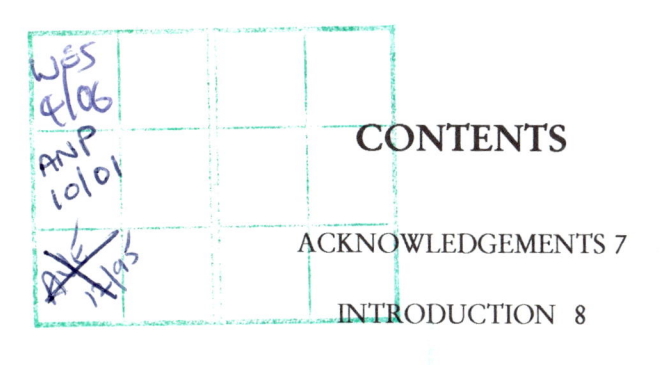

INTRODUCTION 8

FOREWORD 9

GLOSSARY 12

BRITISH MILITARY GLIDER FORCES HISTORY 18

BRITISH MILITARY GLIDER FORCES 35
1st Air Landing Brigade, 6th Air Landing Brigade.
Devonshire Regiment 12th (Airborne) Battalion, King's Own Scottish Borderers 7th (Airborne) Battalion, Border Regiment 1st (Airborne) Battalion, South Staffordshire Regiment 2nd (Airborne) Battalion, Oxford & Bucks. Light Infantry Regiment. 2nd (Airborne) Battalion, Royal Ulster Rifles 1st (Airborne) Battalion, Glider Pilot Regiment 1st & 2nd Battalion, 1st Airborne Reconnaissance Squadron, 6th Airborne Armoured Reconnaissance Regiment.

BRITISH MILITARY GLIDERS 87
Baynes Carrier Wing, GAL 55, Hadrian (CG4A), Hamilcar, Hengist, Horsa, Hotspur, Miles M32, Taylorcraft glider

WEAPONS - GLIDER BORNE 106

ROYAL AIR FORCE - 38 AND 46 GROUP - HISTORY 111

ROYAL AIR FORCE GLIDER TUG SQUADRONS 116

ROYAL AIR FORCE GLIDER TUG AIRCRAFT 125

ROYAL AIR FORCE GLIDER AIRFIELDS 135

ROYAL AIR FORCE OPERATIONAL GLIDER AIRFIELDS 140

BRITISH MILITARY GLIDER TRAINING UNITS 165

## GLIDER SNATCHING 171

## BRITISH MILITARY GLIDER OPERATIONS 174

Operation Freshman 174
Operation Elaborate 194
Operation Thursday 205
Operation Fustian 222
Operation Overlord 232
Operation Deadstick 252
Operation Mallard 272
Operation Dragoon 285
Operation Market 295

Operation Beggar (Turkey Buzzard) 186
Operation Voodoo 200
Operation Ladbrooke 210
Operation Bunghole 228
Operation Tonga 240
Merville Battery 265
Operation Dingson (35A) 281
Operation Molten 293
Megara - Greece 316

Operation Varsity 320

## CONCLUSION 332

## PERSONALITIES 333

## APPENDIX 337

## INDEX 341

# ACKNOWLEDGEMENTS

The author wishes to thank the following persons, museums, government departments, regiments, relatives and friends without whose help and information this book could not have been written. In particular, David Hall, Glider Pilot Regiment, for his painstaking research in glider borne operations: And the Staff at the Museum of Army Flying, Middle Wallop; Lieutenant Colonel Nick Nicholls, MBE. Major Chips Clifton Moore, Major John Cross, Flight Lieutenant Harry Foot, et al. Airborne Forces Museum, Aldershot; Jean Alexander; Major H. Andrews, DFM. Frank Ashton, GPR; Alan Besant, Cartographer; British Broadcasting Service; Lieutenant General Sir Derek Boorman, KCB, Staffordshire Regiment; Dr. P. Boyden, National Army Museum; David Brook, Editor of 'Eagle'; Charles Case, Master Photographer; R. Calder, DFM. GPR; Denis Cason, GPR; Lieutenant Bill Chambers, GPR; Lieutenant Colonel W.R.H. Charley and the Regimental Committee, Royal Ulster Rifles; Major R.K. Cross, GPR; Terence Cuneo, OBE; Ron Driver, GPR; Paula Ellarby; P.J.V. Elliot, Royal Air Force Museum; Roy Eyeions, RAMC Museum; David Fletcher, Tank Museum; Susan and James Francis; W.O.D. Galpin, DFM. GPR; Ray Gough, 38 Group, RAF; Captain A.P.M. Griffith, Gurkha Rifles; Dr. Adrian Groenweg, Arnhem Stichting Museum; James Halley, Air Britain Historian; Major L.W. Halsall, MBE; Major A.G. Harfield, Royal Signals Museum; Major General Joseph H. Harper, US Army; The Controller, Her Majesty's Stationary Office for his kind assistance and permission to use material; Major John Howard, DSO. for much assistance; S/Sgt. Roy Howard, DFM. for his help on 'Deadstick'; Lockheed Aircraft Company USA. (Joe Dabney): Lieutenant Colonel Ralph May, Border Regiment Museum; Joe Michie, GPR; Don Middleton, author; Ministry of Defence (Air) for permission to use material; E.A. Munday, Air Historical Branch, MOD; Museum of Army Transport, Beverly; The Director, Ordnance Survey, Southampton, for permission to use maps. Lieutenant Colonel Terence Otway, DSO, for information and help on Merville. John Potts, GPR; Royal Air Force, Upavon. Harry Rathband, GPR; Alan Richards, DFM, artist; Royal Engineers Museum, Chatham, for photographs; Eric Rowbotham, GPR; Lieutenant Colonel G.J. Rudd, RAOC; Major Ian Toler, DFC. TD; Captain C. Turner and family; Major R.A.J. Tyler, RMP, University of Keele; United States Air Force Historical Branch, for assistance and permission to use maps and material; Lieutenant Colonel K. Vines, RE; Mr. Webb, Devon Regiment Museum; John Willoughby, Oxford & Bucks; Alan Williams and the Imperial War Museum, for permission to use photographs and help given; S/Sgt. Len Wright, DFM. GPR. author; Geoff Yardley for Varsity.

# INTRODUCTION

"The Thin Red Line" is an often used but misquoted British saying which the average listener takes to mean an English Redcoat regiment - not so. "A thin red streak tipped with a line of steel" are the correct words of *The Times*' war correspondent, William Howard Russell, writing at Balaclava in 1854 when the 550 strong 93rd (Sutherland) Highlanders stood two deep against a Russian army of infantry and calvary and won the day. The 93rd (Sutherland) Highlanders were "The Thin Red Line".

In the same way when some hear of airborne forces they immediately think of paratroops - they do not think of the 1st and 6th Air Landing Brigades, The Glider Pilot Regiment, the 1st and 6th Airborne Divisional troops and the glider tug crews of the Royal Air Force.

The main purpose of this book is to put on historical record the valiant part played by 'The Glider Soldiers' - the 'Matchbox Men' - whose name is taken from the glider's intercom and radio callsign, and the fact that a wooden glider weighing seven tons and landing at 70mph could be reduced to matchwood in seconds.

As far as is possible from official and unofficial records this book sets out all the glider borne operations, gliders, glider pilots, tug aircraft, Royal Air Force tug squadrons, Army formations, and airfields, together with histories of the Airborne Regiments and British Glider Forces.

Alan Wood.
Bournemouth, 1992.

# FOREWORD

### by

### Lt-Gen Sir Napier Crookenden, KCB, DSO, OBE, DL

On D-Day and for a year before June 1944 I was lucky enough to be the brigade major of the 6th Airlanding Brigade in the 6th Airborne Division. We were lucky in many ways; in the battalions and the support units, in our brigade commander, Hugh Kindersley, and in being properly launched into a battle for which we had trained for a year. Other Airborne and Glider soldiers and airmen were not so lucky, as Alan makes clear in this monumental account of all the British glider operations of World War II.

He brings back to me some remarkable memories and pays a proper tribute to the pioneers of Airborne Forces. Men like Colonel John Rock, Group Captain Harvey, Squadron Leader Louis Strange, Wing Commander Sir Nigel Norman and Brigadier George Chatterton are too little known to the general public or, indeed, to the airborne soldiers of today.

I was there, on top of the Netheravon control tower, when 74 Horsas made the first ever mass landing by night, an occasion enlivened by some poor briefing, so that half the Horsas landed East to West and half West to East. The great dark shapes came floating in, there was a babble of excited voices from the senior officers on top of the control tower, followed by the sound of splintering wood, as a number of Horsas crashed into each other. Happily nobody was hurt.

I remember our dismay on April 17th 1944 in the glider brigade, when that famous air photograph arrived at our planning headquarters at Old Milston House showing the anti-airlanding poles being erected all over Northern France and general Gale's decision to substitute the 5th Parachute brigade for our own 6th Airlanding Brigade in the first lift.

I can see now Ian Murray's 2nd Bn The Glider Pilot Regiment at Fargo Camp, near Larkhill, drawn up on parade for inspection by Brigadier Hugh Kindersley. My job was to follow him round, doing the detailed inspection of men, arms and equipment - and never before nor since have I seen 400 sergeants paraded together, every man immaculate.

Then Alan Wood describes that amazing ferry of Horsas from Cornwall to North Africa, in which my friend "Babe" Cooper, like me originally from the Cheshire Regiment, got shot down in the Bay of Biscay, picked up by the Navy, and then flew a glider into Sicily, losing his life there in a crash landing.

The whole book is a mine of information and facts as well as being full of stirring history. In the list of RAF aircraft used by Airborne Forces the Whitley comes forcibly to mind, since the whole was so small, that I twice "rang the bell" or in other words, smashed my nose against the far side of it. Then the awful Albermarle took many of my friends to Normandy. Never a popular aircraft, it was extraordinarily uncomfortable and the soldiers all believed that it was only given to Airborne Forces because the rest of the RAF thought the wings might fall off!

When the war was over and I was instructing at the School of Land/Air Warfare, we used to include a glider 'snatch' in our annual demonstration and here Alan Wood's book is the only history I have ever read of this technique. In our last demonstration I accompanied two large, rather stout Egyptian colonels and four United States fighter pilots as passengers in a Waco glider, flown by two sergeants in the Glider Pilot Regiment. A 'snatch' was quite an experience. As the trailing hook of the towing Dakota picked up the tow rope, the glider accelerated from stationary to 100 knots in four seconds. Right over Old Sarum airfield the glider pilots cast off, the jet jockeys looked over the sergeants' shoulders and gave a terrified cry of "Jesus Christ! 30 knots and still flying!" At that moment our glider pilots put the Waco into a vertical dive with full flap, flattened out at what appeared to be the last second and landed in about 25 yards. The Americans reeled away from the Waco, shaken to their boots, but the Egyptians remained stoically unmoved, as they had been throughout the flight.

Alan Wood pays a fitting tribute to the soldiers and airmen who went to war in gliders and their tugs, but has omitted one of the reasons, for which I admired the soldiers. The Horsa was a sovereign cure for a hangover. It not only pitched, rolled and yawed like any other aircraft, but it also surged forward and backward, as the tow rope tightened and slackened. Everybody was sick and in a Horsa full of 25 men, within ten minutes from take-off there was a terrible tide washing too and fro on the glider floor - but of course one must remember, that every man got a shilling a day extra pay.

*Napier Crookenden.*

# FOREWORD

## by

## Maj-Gen Joseph H. Harper, United States Army, Commander 327th/401st Glider Infantry Regiments.

As a WWII Glider Infantry Commander I am pleased to write a foreword to this book. It is dedicated to those gallant Glidermen and Aircrews who did not make it back and whose resting places are on several Continents. It is also a tribute to the brave Glidermen and Aircrews who did make it back. They met and defeated the enemy with courage and gallantry - they flew and stood against flak, tank, artillery, machine-gun and rifle fire but lightly armed as airborne soldiers are on airborne operations. In the line their courage and steadfastness was simply magnificent in the most critical moments. No commander was ever more fortunate or honoured than I, to have the opportunity to command Glidermen in battle.

# ABBREVIATIONS, GLOSSARY, RANKS AND ORGANISATION

| | |
|---|---|
| AAA | Army Air Corps |
| AACC | Army Air Corps Centre |
| AAEE | Aeroplane and Armament Experimental Establishment |
| AARR | Airborne Armoured Reconnaissance Regiment |
| AASF | Advanced Air Striking Force 1939-40 |
| AC | Aircraftman. RAF basic rank |
| ACC | Army Catering Corps |
| ACC | Army Co-operation Command |
| ACK ACK | Anti-aircraft fire |
| AD | Air Defence |
| ADGB | Air Defence Great Britain |
| ADMS | Assistant Director Medical Services |
| ADOS | Assistant Director Ordnance Services |
| AEAF | Allied Expeditionary Air Force |
| AFEE | Airborne Forces Experimental Unit |
| AFS | Advanced Flying School |
| AFTS | Advanced Flying Training School |
| AL | Air Landing |
| ALS | Air Landing School (in India) |
| AM | Air Ministry |
| AMO | Air Ministry Orders |
| Angle of Dangle | Glider instrument to show position of tow rope |
| Anvil | Allied landing South of France |
| AOC | Air Officer Commanding |
| AOCIC | Air Officer Commanding in Chief |
| AOP | Air Observation Post |
| ASR | Air Sea Rescue |
| ASU | Aircraft Storage Unit |
| ATA | Air Transport Auxiliary |
| ATDU | Air Transport Development Unit |
| AW | Armstrong Whitworth |
| BAFF | British Air Forces in France 1939-40 |
| BEF | British Expeditionary Force 1939-40 |
| Blitzkrieg | German 'lightening war' |
| Bunghole | Codename, first daylight glider operation WWII |

| | |
|---|---|
| CASAVAC | Casualty Evacuation Air |
| Cast Off | Disengage glider tow rope by tug or glider |
| Cde G | Croix de Guerre. French etc War Cross |
| CdeM | Coup de Main |
| Chowringhee | LZ north east Burma 1944 |
| CIGS | Chief of the Imperial General Staff |
| CMP | Corps of Military Police |
| Coy | Company - Army Unit |
| CRA | Commander, Royal Artillery |
| CT | Civil twilight. Begins AM when there is enough sunlight to see by. The sun is about 6° below horizon |
| CU | Conversion Unit. From one aircraft type to another |
| DCM | Distinguished Conduct Medal |
| Dingson | Codename, Glider borne SAS operation France 1944 |
| Ditched | RAF slang for landing in sea |
| DFC | Distinguished Flying Cross. RAF Officers decoration |
| DFM | Distinguished Flying Medal. RAF other ranks decoration |
| Dragoon | Allied Invasion South of France 1944 |
| Drink | RAF slang for sea |
| DSC | Distinguished Service Cross |
| DSO | Distinguished Service Order |
| DZ | Dropping Zone - paratroops & containers |
| EFTS | Elementary Flying Training School |
| ETA | Estimated Time of Arrival |
| Eureka | Portable ground homing radio beacon |
| FEAF | Far East Air Force |
| Flak | German anti-aircraft fire |
| Flt | Flight |
| F/Lt. | Flight Lieutenant, RAF rank |
| F/O | Flying Officer. RAF rank |
| FOO | Forward observation Officer |
| FOU. | Forward Observer Unit |
| F/Sgt. | Flight Sergeant RAF rank |
| Freshman | Codename, first British glider operation WWII |
| Fustian | Codename, Allied airborne operation - Sicily, 1943 |
| GIS | Glider Instructors School |
| GOTU | Glider Operational Training Unit |
| GPEU | Glider Pilot Exercise Unit |
| GPR | Glider Pilot Regiment |

| | |
|---|---|
| GPUTU | Glider Pick Up Training Unit |
| GSE | Glider Servicing Echelon |
| GTS | Glider Training Squadron or Glider Training School |
| GRP | Group. RAF/USAAF unit of organisation |
| GP | General Purpose (eg bomb) |
| HE | High Explosive |
| HGCU | Heavy Glider Conversion Unit |
| Holophane | Landing light showing narrow beam |
| Husky | Allied Invasion of Sicily 1943 |
| HXCF | Halifax Conversion Flight |
| IAF | Indian Air Force |
| Jerry | A German: British/U.S slang |
| Kraut | A German: U.S. Slang |
| Ladbrooke | Codename, Allied airborne operation Sicily, 1943 |
| LAC | Leading aircraftman. RAF rank |
| LMG | Light machine-gun |
| Lt/Col. | Lieutenant Colonel |
| Luftwaffe | German Air Force |
| LZ | Landing Zone gliders |
| Mallard | British second airborne operation of D Day, 1944 |
| MAP | Ministry of Aircraft Production |
| Market | Allied airborne operations - Holland 1944 |
| Matchbox | Radio/Intercom. Callsign for British gliders |
| MC | Military Cross - Army Decoration, Officers |
| MM | Military Medal - Army decoration, Other Ranks |
| MU | Maintainance Unit |
| NAAF | Northwest African Air Forces |
| NAAFI | Navy Army & Air Force Institutes |
| NCO | Non-Commissioned Officer |
| Neptune | Assault operations within Overlord D Day, 1944 |
| Nickells | Leaflets |
| OKW | German High Command |
| ORTU | Operational & Refresher Training Unit |
| OTU | Operational Training Unit |
| Overlord | Codename, Allied Invasion of Normandy, 1944 |
| OXBOX | Oxford light twin engined aircraft: nickname |
| Pdr. | Pounder (gun) |
| PGTS | Parachute & Glider Training School |
| PIAT | Projectile Infantry Anti-Tank |

| | |
|---|---|
| Picadilly | LZ North East Burma, 1944 |
| P/O | Pilot Officer. RAF rank |
| POW | Prisoner of War |
| QDM | Magnetic compass bearing |
| QM | Quartermaster |
| RA | Royal Artillery |
| RAF | Royal Air Force |
| RAAF | Royal Australian Air Force |
| RAE | Royal Aircraft establishment |
| RAC | Royal Armoured Corps |
| RAMC | Royal Army Medical Corps |
| RCAF | Royal Canadian Air Force |
| RDF | Radio Direction Finding |
| RE | Royal Engineers |
| REME | Royal Electrical and Mechanical Engineers |
| R/T | Radio telephony |
| RLG | Relief or Reserve Landing ground |
| RMP | Royal Military Police |
| RNZAF | Royal New Zealand Air Force |
| RTR | Royal Tank Regiment |
| RUR | Royal Ulster Rifles |
| SASO | Senior Air Staff Officer |
| SCF | Senior Chaplain to the Forces |
| SEAC | South east Asia Command |
| SF | Station Flight |
| SO | Staff Officer |
| Sqdn. | Squadron |
| S/Ldr. | Squadron Leader RAF rank |
| Sten | British sub-machine gun |
| TAF | Tactical Air Force |
| TCDU | Transport Command Development Unit |
| TD | Territorial Decoration |
| Thursday | Allied airborne operation Burma, 1944 |
| Tonga | Codename, British airborne operation D Day |
| TRE | Telecommunications Establishment |
| Tug | Powered aircraft towing glider |
| U/S | RAF slang for unserviceable |
| U.S. | United States of America |
| USAAC | United States Army Air Corps |

| | |
|---|---|
| USAAF | United States Army Air Force |
| Varsity | Codename, last Allied airborne Operation WWII |
| VC | Victoria Cross |
| VHF | Very High Frequency |
| W/Cmdr | Wing Commander. RAF rank |
| Wimpey | Wellington aircraft - nickname |
| Window | Metal strips dropped to disrupt enemy radar |
| Wing | RAF/USAAF unit of organisation |
| W/T | Wireless telegraphy |

## AIR FORCES. EQUIVALENT UNITS

| Royal Air Force | USAAF | Luftwaffe. |
|---|---|---|
| Air Force | Air Force | Luftflotte. |
| Command | Command | FliegerKorps. |
| N/A | Air Division | Flieger Division. |
| Group | Wing | Geschwader. |
| Wing | Group | Gruppe. |
| Squadron | Squadron | Staffel. |
| Flight | Flight | Schwarm. |
| Section | Element | Kette. |

Note. German airborne forces and anti-aircraft artillery were part of the Luftwaffe. When army infantry were transported by air they were know as air landing (Luftlande) divisions and regiments.

## WWII ARMED FORCES EQUIVALENT/APPROXIMATE RANKS

| Royal Air Force | British Army | US Army & USAAF. | German Army & Luftwaffe. |
|---|---|---|---|
| Marshal of the RAF | Field Marshal | General the Army | General Feldmarschall |
| Air Chief Marshal | General | General | Generaloberst |
| Air Marshal | Lieutenant General | Lieut. General General of | General der Flieger Flieger |
| Air Vice Marshal | Major General | Major General | Generalleutnant |

| | | | |
|---|---|---|---|
| Air Commodore | Brigadier | Brig. General | Generalmajor |
| Group Captain | Colonel | Colonel | Oberst |
| Wing Commander | Lieut. Col. | Lieut. Col. | Oberstleutnant |
| Squadron Leader | Major | Major | Major |
| Flight Lieutenant | Captain | Captain | Hauptman |
| Flying Officer | Lieutenant | 1st Lieutenant | Oberleutnant |
| Pilot Officer | 2nd Lieutenant | 2nd Lieutenant | Leutnant |
| Warrant Officer | Sgt. Major | Master Sergeant | Stabsfeldwebel |
| Flight Sergeant | Staff Sergeant | Top Sergeant | Unterfeldwebel |
| Sergeant | Sergeant | Sergeant | Unteroffizer |
| Corporal | Corporal | Corporal | Hauptgefreiter |
| Leading Aircraftman | Lance Corporal | Airman Ist Cla. | Obergefreiter |
| Aircraftman 1st Class | Private | Airman 2nd Cla. | Schutze or Gefreiter |
| Aircraftman 2nd Class | | | Fleiger |

# BRITISH GLIDER FORCES HISTORY
# 1940-1957

To the Soviet Union falls the distinction of designing and building the world's first military glider - the GN4 - designed by G.F. Gorschev and built by the Moscow Aviation Factory in 1934. The GN4 had a sixty-feet wingspan and could carry a pilot and five troops or 9921lbs of cargo.

The Germans, forbidden by the terms of the Versailles Treaty from producing military aircraft, turned their attention to unpowered glider flight. In the early 1920s they had, with the cooperation of the Russians, established a secret flying training base at Lipetsk near Voronezh in the Soviet Union where the future Luftwaffe began to be trained. Two of Germany's leading proponents of airborne warfare - Generals Kurt Student and Ernest Udet - visited the training base and were influenced by the Russians pioneering use of gliders for military purposes. Opinions differs as to which of the two generals saw the potential of the military glider for silent attack, but what is beyond dispute is the fact the the Germans were the first military power to use gliders in a military combat role in their attack on the Belgian Eben Emael Forts in May 1940.

WWII broke out in Europe in the autumn of 1939 when Germany invaded Poland which resulted in Britain and France declaring war on Germany. A British Expeditionary Force was sent by Britain to France but suffered defeat at the hands of the German war machine. By the 17th June 1940, most of the Continental based British forces together with some Allied troops had been evacuated to Britain - who now stood alone against the victorious Germans with only the English Channel between them. But even in those dark desperate days there were far sighted men in Britain planning for an eventual return to mainland Europe and the carrying on of the offensive war against the enemy.

On the 5th June 1940, before the cross channel evacuation of British troops was completed, Lieutenant Colonel Dudley Clark, a General Staff Officer and Military Assistant to Sir John Dill, Chief of the Imperial General Staff, conceived the idea of forming Special forces to attack and harry the enemy by all means possible - raiding across the North Sea and the English Channel. The same day Sir John Dill - after hearing of Clarke's ideas - broached the subject to the Prime Minister who wholeheartedly gave his blessing and support, subject to the demands of the war on British forces.

On the 7th June 1940, Section MO9 was formed at the British War Office under the command of Brigadier Lund, Deputy Director of Military Operations. Later on the 12th June 1940, Lieutenant General Sir Alan Bourne, Adjutant

*The Glider Soldiers*

General, Royal Marines was placed in command of operations against the enemy. Working with speed and enthusiasm a small sea borne raid was planned and mounted on the French coast on the night of the 23rd-24th June 1940, by the new force - who were to be called Commandos - a name chosen for them by Clarke, Dill and Lund.

The Staff of MO9 decided to form ten Commandos each of ten men and volunteers were solicited from the British Armed Forces - in the face of resistance from some quarters, commanding officers being reluctant to lose their best men to some unknown unit.

On the 22nd June 1940, Prime Minister Churchill had sent a memo to the Army Chief of Staff. "We ought to have a corps of at least 5000 parachute troops. I hear that something is being done to form such a corps but only I believe on a small scale. Advantage must be taken of the summer to train these forces, who can none the less, play their part meanwhile as shock troops in Home Defence. Pray let me have a note from the War Office on the subject"

The War Office on receiving Churchill's memo sent out a call for volunteers to all units of the British Army. The first volunteers were 500 men of Nos.1 and 2 Commando formed earlier in the year and whom it had been originally intended to transport by aircraft then drop by parachute.

Two days later a regular Royal Engineers officer Major John Rock was called to the War Office and placed in charge of British Airborne Forces, but without any specific brief whatsoever. No instructions were given to him as to training, weapons, mode of transport or objectives. Probably because at that time no one knew what was going to happen or had any idea of airborne force operations - except that Britain would never surrender. It was difficult to imagine the Liberation of Europe with the enemy poised to invade over the narrow English Channel.

Major Rock was sent to RAF Ringway near Manchester to commence training and organising Britain's Airborne Forces. Ringway had been selected and named the RAF Central Landing School - with Group Captain L.G. Harvey as Station Commander - as it was considered ideal for training purposes by some, being out of range of German aircraft. Major Rock began his task with the assistance of Squadron Leader Louis Strange, DSO. MC. DFC. and Wing Commander Sir Nigel Norman, CBE. Within three weeks Major Rock had compiled his report on organising and training the airborne forces. It was suggested that some of the airborne forces should be transported by glider - originally it had been thought of purely as a paratroop force. The German ideas had been learned swiftly - parachute troops were scattered over a wide area during their drop and had of necessity only light weapons - but glider borne troops could land in a comparative body with greater firepower available more quickly. When these facts were place before the Prime Minister on the 10th August 1940, he immediately approved them.

At this time there were no British military gliders in being and an appeal went out to the British public for owners of gliders to loan or donate them to the war effort. This appeal was well answered and a mass of civil gliders - including a British owned German one - arrived at Ringway where they were soon in use as trainers for military glider pilots. Winch launch was used when there were no aircraft tugs .

On the 5th September 1940, a conference was held at Air Ministry, London, under the Vice Chief of the Air Staff, Air Marshal Barratt together with representatives of the Royal Air Force and Army, to formulate the future planning, composition and direction of Airborne Forces. It was decided that all airborne soldiers would be under Army command and that the Royal Air Force would provide the aircrews and tug aircraft to transport them but would be under Royal Air Force Command. The point was raised as to who would pilot the proposed military gliders.

New ground had to be broken as the glider pilots, after landing their gliders, would have to fight on the ground as soldiers, but the gliders would have to be on charge to and maintained by the Royal Air Force. It was suggested that the Army would provide the glider pilots and that the Royal Air Force would train them as pilots on light aircraft and forthcoming military gliders. It was also decided that the Air Ministry would issue specifications for troop and tank carrying military gliders capable of transporting the airborne troops to battle.

On the 19th September 1940, a Glider Training Squadron was formed at RAF Ringway with RAF Tiger Moths as glider tugs and ex civilian owned Kirby Kite gliders as trainers. RAF Ringway was renamed the Central Landing Establishment and two Sections for glider training were formed. These two sections later became No. Glider Training School and the Airborne Forces Experimental establishment.

The inter service controversy still raged as to who would pilot the gliders but notwithstanding this fifty-five volunteers: thirty-seven from the Army and eighteen from the Royal Air Force were at Ringway under going training and on the 26th October, staged the first British tug/glider demonstration using two ex civil sailplanes towed by two Avro 504 tugs.

The Royal Army Service Corps had the distinction of providing the first glider pilots to be trained for the Army. Lance Corporal Morris, Lance Corporal Baker and Driver Cooper were the pioneers to be followed by Lance Corporal Harrison. However, senior RAF officers, cast in their own mould of RAF training, shied away from the idea that ordinary soldiers could fly military gliders. To them the deadstick landing of an aircraft was a task for a highly skilled RAF pilot. Later events were to prove them wrong, very wrong. Another anomaly at this time was that the RAF pilots received extra flying pay but the Army pilots did not.

There being no British military gliders in being, the Ministry of Aircraft Production issued Specification X10/40 in late 1940 for an assault and training glider capable of carrying eight troops and a pilot. Influenced no doubt by the German DFS 230 design.

General Aircraft Ltd, (GAL) took up the specification and some four months later the prototype GAL 48 Hotspur Mk 1 glider was flown successfully.

An initial order for 400 Hotspurs was made but the glider, when tested, did not come up to the original requirements as an assault glider and was relegated to a training role. A total of 1012 Hotspurs in its three Marks were made but the glider was never used operationally.

In anticipation of the forthcoming Hotspurs - the Glider Training School was allocated Hawker Hector light aircraft as glider tugs and on the 28th December 1940, the unit moved to RAF Thame. On the 21st February 1941, the first Hector tugs arrived but it was not until the 6th April 1941, that the first Hotspur - serial number BV 125 - arrived and was soon in use on trials on the 9th April 1941.

By the Spring of 1941 Rock's Planning Staff at Ringway had formulated what was to be the WWII role of British Airborne Forces. In addition to the original raiding party role, airborne forces were to be used in tactical and coup de main operations. This far sighted role plan was to be used later in WWII with great success in France and Germany.

A more ambitious airborne exercise was mounted for the Prime Minister on the 26th April 1941, when the Hotspur glider serial number BV 125 and five Kirby Kite ex civil gliders, accompanied by six RAF paratroop carrying converted Whitley bombers, were towed past in a combined glider/paratroop demonstration.

On the 20th May 1941, the Germans attacked and captured Crete with glider borne and paratroops, but suffered such appalling casualties that Hitler forbade any more large scale airborne assaults by German Forces. The British had no such thoughts and on the 10th October 1941, the 31st Independent Brigade Group was reformed as 1st Air Landing Brigade Group with the intention of having therein; the 1st Battalion Royal Ulster Rifles, 2nd Battalion Oxfordshire and Buckinghamshire Light Infantry (52nd), 2nd Battalion South Staffordshire Regiment and the 1st Battalion Border Regiment.

On the 29th October 1941, Major General F.A.M. (Boy) Browning, CBE. DSO. MC. was appointed General Officer Commanding, (GOC) British Airborne

Forces. A few days later on the 1st November 1941, HQ 1st Airborne Division was set up with a small Staff working from offices in London. 1st Air Landing Brigade was to be a brigade of this division and on the 10th December 1941, Brigadier G.F. Hopkinson, OBE. MC. assumed command of the brigade. It was decided that an airborne division would consist of two paratroop Brigades and one gliderborne Brigade plus Signals, Medical Corps and Royal Engineers.

Discussion and argument still carried on as to which Service the glider pilots would belong - the Army or the Royal Air Force. Finally it was decided that the glider pilots would be army personnel but would be trained in flying by the Royal Air Force. The gliders would be on charge to the Royal Air Force and would be serviced and maintained by Air Force ground crews and based at RAF stations.

A Training Programme for 400 army glider pilots was begun which required a much larger training establishment and the Glider Training Unit was divided to become Nos.1 and 2 Glider Training Schools on the 1st December 1941. Later Nos.3, 4 and 5 were formed together with Nos.101 and 102 (Glider) Operational Training Units and a Glider Pilots Instructors' School.

As rather more than half of the Airborne Forces were to be carried to battle in gliders - volunteers were sought for the raising of a Glider Pilot Regiment (GPR) which was duly formed on the 21st December 1941. The now Lieutenant Colonel Rock was appointed Commanding Officer of the 1st Battalion Glider Pilot Regiment and together with forty officers and other ranks was sent to an RAF Elementary Flying School on the 2nd January 1942, to learn how to fly.

Responding to the call for volunteers for the Glider Pilot Regiment was Major (later Brigadier) George Chatterton who had been an RAF pilot with No.1 Squadron, but had suffered injuries in a flying accident which had taken him off flying duties then retirement to the Reserve of Air Force Officers. With the war clouds gathering over Europe Chatterton was recalled to the RAF but posted to ground duties. Not relishing a non active role he transferred to the 5th Battalion of the Queens Regiment - the Royal West Surreys - as a lieutenant then after service in France he was promoted major.

After an interview with General Browning, Major Chatterton was appointed second in command to Lieutenant Colonel Rock, 1st Battalion Glider Pilot Regiment, and posted to Tilshead, near Amesbury, on Salisbury Plain, which was to be the Training Depot for the regiment. The projected establishment of the Glider Pilot Regiment was to be two battalions of six companies of sergeant glider pilots who, apart from being glider pilots, had to be trained soldiers who would fight on the ground after landing their gliders. Flying training on light aircraft would be given under the direction of RAF Instructors at Elementary Flying Training Schools (EFTS) before glider pilot training began.

With the Glider Pilot Regiment coming into being it was found that aircraft and aircrews were needed for glider tug duties on an ever increasing scale so on the 15th January 1942, the Royal Air Force Army Co-operation Command formed No.38 Wing as an airborne forces Wing under the command of Sir Nigel Norman. At first 38 Wing only possessed eight aircrews and it was some time before it reached its establishment of an EFTS, two Glider Training Schools (GTS), two Glider Operational Training Units (GOTUs) and one Glider Exercise Squadron, plus two units for paratroop training.

38 Wing began to take shape and on the 22nd January 1942, 297 Squadron was formed at RAF Netheravon, in the middle of Salisbury Plain, from the Parachute Exercise Squadron and received Whitley MkV aircraft in February for airborne forces duties. The squadron moved to RAF Hurn near Bournemouth on the 5th June 1942.

296 Squadron which had been formed at RAF Ringway on the 25th January 1942, using Hector and Hart light aircraft as glider tugs, moved to RAF Netheravon on the 1st February 1942, as No.296 Glider Exercise Squadron. In June of that year the Squadron received Whitley aircraft as glider tugs and in July was divided into two Flights 296A and 296B with 296A moving to RAF Hurn on the 5th July, leaving 296B at Netheravon as the Glider Exercise Squadron.

Another airborne forces Squadron - No.295 - was formed at Netheravon on the 3rd August 1942, and began duty with Whitley aircraft and engaged in leaflet dropping raids over France. By February 1943, the squadron had converted to Halifax aircraft and moved to RAF Holmesly South near Christchurch on the 1st May 1943.

The Glider Pilot Regimental Depot had now been established at Tilshead eleven miles north of Salisbury and adjacent to RAF Shrewton which had been opened in 1940 as a grass relief landing ground (RLG) and satellite to Netheravon.

Salisbury Plain in winter is a bleak cold windswept place (as the author well remembers on being posted there in winter) but in summer has a character of its own - It has been described as the cradle of civilisation in Britain with its 5000 year old burial mounds and the stones of Stonehenge. It is perhaps symbolic that it became the cradle of British Airborne Forces with the gathering together of the new airborne division and the RAF.

Major Chatterton was tasked with the raising of the Glider Pilot Regiment as Lieutenant Colonel Rock was away learning to fly. Chatterton shrewdly went about his task with nothing but his service experience to guide him. In his own words, "I would have to create a very special dual character - a highly trained fighting soldier as well as a skilful and resourceful pilot - such men could only evolve from a regiment possessed of a strong sense of esprit de corps".

After another interview with General Browning, in which Chatterton requested NCOs from the Brigade of Guards as Instructors, Company Sergeant Major Briody of the Irish Guards and Company Sergeant Major Cowlie of the Coldstream Guards were posted to Tilshead and told of his plan to create the Total Soldier. Chatterton told the two sergeant majors that neither he nor they would be popular in instilling the basic discipline of the parade ground in the glider pilots.

Military training commenced for the volunteer glider pilots under the two sergeant majors who set the highest standards - many of the would-be glider pilots fell by the wayside but the strength of the regiment grew to over 600 men. After four to six weeks military training the soldiers destined to become pilots went to an RAF EFTS for eight weeks flying training - usually on a DH Tiger Moth or other light aircraft - followed by eight weeks flying training at a Glider Training School on Hotspur gliders which were by now in service.

On successful completion of the course a further four weeks was spent converting to the larger Horsa gliders which were by now beginning to come into service. Later (1944) it was decided that 2nd Pilots would have a shorter flying training course of four weeks at an EFTS followed by three to four weeks glider flying training. It had also been decided that the large gliders would need two pilots with the 1st pilot a staff sergeant and the 2nd Pilot a sergeant.

The 1st Pilots would wear a flying brevet of a lion over a crown between two outstretched wings and the 2nd Pilots a brevet with the letter G between two outstretched wings. The flying brevets would be worn on the left breast over the top pocket of uniform. The 1st Pilot would fly the glider on take off and landing and the 2nd pilot whilst on tow but could take over in an emergency.

In October 1942, the Airborne Forces pioneer Colonel John Rock was killed as the result of a night flying accident in a Hotspur glider at Shrewton. The glider tow rope broke in flight and Colonel Rock tried to land the Hotspur in total darkness - the glider struck a telegraph pole and its one ton of sandbag ballast broke loose on landing impact crushing Rock and his co-pilot, who had but recently returned from a GTS. Colonel Rock suffered injuries which proved fatal and he died two days later. His obituary which appeared in the national press read:

> "Lieutenant Colonel John Frank Rock, pioneer of British paratroop and airborne forces, has given his life for his work. After surviving a number of narrow escapes in experimental jumping and glider flying he died in hospital from injuries

received in a glider crash. He always tested the risk himself before asking his men to do it and such was the force of his example that we gladly followed where he had led".

With Colonel Rock dead, Chatterton was appointed to the command of the 1st Battalion of the Glider Pilot Regiment and Lieutenant Colonel Iain Murray assumed command of the recently formed 2nd Battalion of the regiment.

As the HQ of 38 Wing, under the command of the now Air Commodore Sir Nigel Norman, was at Netheravon, premises were required nearby in which the Wing and 1st Airborne Division could work side by side. The choice fell on Syrencot House an old Georgian House standing in its own grounds by the River Avon at Brigmerston on the back road from RAF Netheravon to the Army base at Bulford. Elements of the RAF and Army moved into the closely guarded old house which was given the code name 'Broadmoor' but was known to the people who worked there (including Mrs. Besant - the author's mother-in-law who was a civilian) as the 'Madhouse' as all the windows were barred and there was but one key for the building.

On one occasion the Duty Officer who held the key was delayed and the Planning Staff were unable to gain entry and had to cool their heels for an hour in Milston churchyard which adjoins Syrencot House, until the officer arrived to an indignant reception. (The house still stands little changed and is managed by the Property Service Agency.) At present it is leased to a local firm of builders. A plaque was recently placed to the right of the front door to commemorate the wartime use of the house.

On the 19th November 1942, the first British glider borne operation was made. Operation Freshman was an ill fated attempt to destroy the Norsk Plant at Vemork in German occupied Norway which was producing Heavy Water for use in the German atomic bomb research programme.

Two Halifax bombers of 38 Wing each towing a Horsa glider carrying specialist troops of the Royal Engineers, took off from RAF Skitten, Caithness, Scotland, and flew to Norway. The two Horsas and one of the Halifaxes crashed in bad weather in Norway killing most of the occupants. Those who survived were murdered by the Germans under Hitler's infamous 'Commando Order' which stated that all commando troops were to be killed on capture. (Three of the murderers were tried and executed after the German surrender in 1945).

In May 1943, General Browning was appointed to the post of Major General, Airborne Forces, with a new headquarters, Airborne Forces. Major General Hopkinson assumed command of 1st Airborne Division and Brigadier

P.H.W. Hicks took command of 1st Air Landing Brigade with effect from the 6th April 1943.

6th Airborne Division formed at Syrencot House on the 3rd May 1943, under the command of Major General Richard Nelson Gale. The number 6 had been chosen to mislead the Germans into thinking there were six British Airborne divisions when in fact there were only two.

The 1st Battalion Royal Ulster Rifles and the 2nd Battalion Oxfordshire and Buckinghamshire Light Infantry (The 52nd) were transferred to 6th Air Landing Brigade of the 6th Airborne Division. In September the 12th Battalion Devonshire Regiment, also joined 6th Air Landing Brigade.

Coming into use and still highly secret was a radio homing device known as Eureka/Rebecca which was designed to pin point Lzs and Dzs for glider, paratroop and supply drops on operations. Invented by the British Telephone Research Establishment (TRE) the device was in use by the end of 1942.

The ground Eureka (old Greek for 'I have found it') set was contained in its own packing case measuring 30 inches by 15 inches by 10 inches and weighed 100lb. The apparatus consisted of a five feet long aerial mounted on a seven foot high tripod with the set underneath. Operation was simple - the set was unpacked, tripod and aerial erected and the set switched on to emit 8 watts of power output to the airborne Rebecca set. The Rebecca set in the aircraft sent out a coded signal on 214 megacycles to which the ground Eureka replied on 219 megacycles.

Direction and distance were then shown on the Rebecca set which pin pointed the LZ. As the device was Top Secret an explosive charge was built into the Eureka so that it could quickly be destroyed if in danger of being captured by the enemy. This explosive charge was fitted into the base and operated by a small plunger which was pulled out to fire the explosive after a small delay. This was designed to be simple and fool proof but on the Merville battery operation the Eureka supplied to the paratroops was packed with the plunger out and the impact of the paratroopers landing depressed the plunger and fired the explosive charge thereby destroying the incoming gliders navigational aid so that they were unable to pin point the battery.

With the Germans beaten in North Africa plans were made for the invasion of Sicily. 1st Airborne Division commanded by Major General Hopkinson embarked for Oran in North Africa. Within the division was 1st Air Landing Brigade commanded by Brigadier P.H.W. Hicks and comprised of the 1st Battalion Border Regiment, under Lieutenant Colonel G.V. Britten and the 2nd Battalion South Staffordshire Regiment under Lieutenant Colonel W.D.H. McCardie. Also within the division were two companies of Glider pilots, the first commanded by Lieutenant Colonel Chatterton and the second under Major M. Willoughby.

The remainder of the Glider pilots in the battalion were to follow later. The bulk of the Glider Pilots had but little flying hours in apart from their courses at EFTS and GTS due to chronic shortage of tug aircraft in Britain.

On the 1st April 1943, Colonel Chatterton was sent for by General Hopkinson and informed that 1st Air Landing Brigade had been committed to a glider borne night assault on Sicily on the 9th-10th July 1943, a little over three months away. Chatterton was appalled as his glider pilots had little experience of night flying and the projected LZs were strewn with rocks and had stone walls deadly to a fragile wooden glider. To make matters worse as far as Chatterton was concerned, General Hopkinson stated that the US Army Air Force would supply gliders and tugs. Colonel Chatterton demurred but General Hopkinson was adamant and gave him half an hour to think over his position as commander of the Glider Pilots. Chatterton was told that if he thought the operation too difficult he would be relieved of his position as glider pilot commander. Colonel Chatterton considered the matter and decided to remain with his glider pilots and see the operation through in spite of the difficulties.

An immediate problem arose as to the availability of gliders to transport the air landing troops from North Africa to Sicily. The United States had begun to transport Waco CG4A gliders in crates to North Africa but these gliders were too small to carry both a jeep and a gun so two gliders would have to used. 38 Wing strove to solve this problem by flying out the larger Horsa gliders towed by Halifax aircraft, the 1400 miles from England to North Africa. Operation Beggar, or as it is also known, Turkey Buzzard, was the brainchild of Group Captain Tom Cooper and Squadron Leader A.M.B. Wilkinson and was carried out by 295 Squadron. The first Horsa glider reached North Africa on the 28th June 1943, only twelve days before the Sicily D-Day.

On the 20th May 1943, another pioneer of airborne forces died. Air Commodore Sir Nigel Norman took off from England in a Lockheed Hudson aircraft for North Africa. When in flight the port engine failed and the Hudson crashed and Sir Nigel was killed along with the radio operator. The rest of the aircrew were injured but managed to exit the aircraft before it burst into flames. So another of the founders of airborne forces had gone; first Rock now Norman. Both men had been involved with the air landing forces from the beginning back in the dark days. With Sir Nigel dead his command passed to Air Commodore W.H. Primrose, CBE. DFC. who now took up duty as AOC 38 Wing.

Despite the arrival of Horsa gliders in North Africa there was still not enough gliders to air lift 1st Air Landing Brigade to battle and the US Waco CG4A (Hadrian) glider had to be used in large numbers and were to be towed by USAAF tugs, the aircrews of which had had little glider towing training and no combat experience.

Colonel Chatterton heard that there were Hadrian gliders at Oran airfield and on visiting the airfield found that the Hadrians were still in their shipping crates. Fifty British glider pilots were sent by Chatterton to Oran to uncrate and assemble the US gliders. In a short time and with little help, the glider pilots erected thirty Hadrians which were then towed by the USAAF to US airstrips for training. Colonel Chatterton instituted a glider refresher training programme to give his glider pilots much needed flying practice on the unfamiliar US gliders. All the training was focussed on landing loaded gliders in complete darkness as it would be on the night operation in Sicily.

The task of 1st Air Landing Brigade in the Sicily operation, codenamed Ladbrooke, was to land by glider in moonlight and take the vital Ponte Grande bridge near Syracuse, then capture the town of Syracuse itself on the night of the 9th-10th July 1943. Six Horsa gliders would be released from 4000 feet to land on LZs on either side of the Ponte grande bridge and capture the objective from either end. This would be followed two nights later by another glider assault together with 1st Parachute Brigade to take another vital bridge - the Primosole bridge in the Catainian Plain - and hold it till relieved by the advancing seaborne 8th Army.

In spite of the lack of training which greatly troubled Colonel Chatterton, Operation Ladbrooke went ahead as an Anglo US venture with the glider tugs from the USAAF and the US gliders flown by the British Glider Pilot Regiment. The Six Horsa gliders were included in the operation their role being to capture the vital bridge by a coup de main assault - 130 Hadrian gliders were to land 1st Air Landing Brigade and consolidate the position.

At 1848 hours on the 9th July 1943, the first combinations began to take off from airstrips in Tunisia for Sicily. Adverse weather conditions prevailed en route to Sicily and owing to some tug pilots causing the gliders to release too far offshore many of the gliders fell into the sea with great loss of life. Only one Horsa glider No.133, piloted by Staff Sergeant Galpin of the GPR, was landed on its intended LZ with two more Horsas landing nearby. The limited force of 1st Air Landing Brigade captured their objective with skill and courage and although the enemy re-took the bridge it was again taken by British seaborne forces just an hour later.

On the 13th July 1943, the next Sicily glider operation commenced - Operation Fustian had as its objective the taking and holding of another vital bridge the Primosole - to allow the advance of the ground forces into north east Sicily. A small glider borne force was to carry the guns of the Royal Artillery in

Horsa and Hadrian gliders and the main force of paratroops would be carried in Dakota aircraft of the USAAF.

Unfortunately as the Allied aircraft flew over Allied naval forces they were mistaken for enemy aircraft and the ships opened up with anti aircraft fire causing casualties and damage to the tugs and gliders.

Again as in the first operation, very few gliders reached their intended LZs although a Horsa, piloted by Staff Sergeant White of the GPR, managed to land his glider one hundred yards from the bridge objective. A bitter fire fight ensued round the bridge which was taken, lost, then finally retaken on the 16th July, by the Durham Light Infantry of the ground forces.

In spite of the heavy losses in men and gliders - the Glider Pilot Regiment alone lost fifty-seven pilots - the potential of the glider was still appreciated and the hard won experience was incorporated in planning future gliderborne operations. Plans were laid for the invasion of France in which glider forces would play a crucial role.

The large tank carrying Hamilcar glider was coming into service and 6th Airborne Reconnaissance Regiment, Royal Armoured Corps was formed. For the first time in history tanks would be glider borne to the battlefield as part of 6th Airborne Division.

Great interest was still being shown in the use of the glider in several parts of the world as was shown by the epic glider tow over the North Atlantic by a Royal Canadian Air Force Dakota aircraft towing a Waco CG4A (Hadrian) glider loaded with supplies. The 3500 miles flight was made in stages from Canada to Greenland-Iceland-Scotland in June 1943. The flight, codenamed Voodoo, has never been equalled.

During August and September 1943, 38 Wing and the GPR carried out further long range glider tows. Codenamed Operation Elaborate, Horsa gliders were towed from England to North Africa for use in future glider operations. Again the RAF and the GPR lost men and aircraft to enemy aircraft and bad weather conditions.

By October 38 Wing had expanded so much it was reformed as a Group on the 11th October 1943, with Air Vice Marshal L.N. Hollinghurst in command. By March 1944, ten Squadrons were in being;

| 190 Squadron | Stirling | Horsa | Fairford |
| 196 Squadron | Stirling | Horsa | Keevil |
| 295 Squadron | Stirling | Horsa | Harwell |
| 296 Squadron | Albemarle | Horsa | Brize Norton |
| 297 Squadron | Albemarle | Horsa | Brize Norton |

| | | | |
|---|---|---|---|
| 298 Squadron | Halifax | Hamilcar/Horsa. | Tarrant Rushton |
| 299 Squadron | Stirling | Horsa | Keevil |
| 570 Squadron | Albemarle/Stirling. | Horsa | Harwell |
| 620 Squadron | Stirling | Horsa | Fairford |
| 644 Squadron | Halifax | Hamilcar/Horsa. | Tarrant Rushton |

Another RAF Group - No.46 - had been formed on the 1st January 1944, as an airborne forces group, under the command of Air Commodore L. Darvall, MC. All the squadrons were equipped with C47 Dakota aircraft supplied by the United States. The group had at first five squadrons:

- 48 Squadron  Down Ampney.
- 233 Squadron  Blakehill Farm
- 271 Squadron  Down Ampney.
- 512 Squadron  Broadwell.
- 575 Squadron  Broadwell

but was later joined by 437 (RCAF) Squadron, Blakehill Farm. As the group was equipped with Dakota aircraft it mainly engaged on paratroop dropping but also towed Horsa gliders and engaged in supply dropping.

During the Spring of 1944 training and exercises were carried out on preparation for the forthcoming invasion of France, each exercise getting larger and larger. Mass daylight glider landings were practised - seventy-four gliders landed in twelve minutes on the north and south airfields of RAF Netheravon in one exercise. Night glider landings were less successful with a high rate of accidents. RAF Netheravon was and still is a grass airfield with very little level surface - it is up and down hill in all directions as the author well knows from his RAF service there.

Operation Overlord, the plan to invade France called for 6th Airborne Division to drop by parachute and land by glider during the early hours of D-Day - the 6th June 1944 - and protect the left flank of the invading seaborne forces landing on the Normandy beaches.

Glider borne troops were to play a vital role in the first of the D-Day airborne operations - Operation Tonga - six coup de main Horsa gliders were to land as close as was possible to two bridges and the airborne troops of the Oxford and Bucks. Light Infantry carried in the Horsas, would take and hold the two bridges over the Caen Canal and River Orne (Operation Deadstick) until reinforced by the seaborne forces. Three more Horsa gliders carrying men of the 9th Parachute Battalion would land on the enemy gun battery at Merville as previously dropped paratroops attacked it. Other Horsa gliders would land with support equipment for the lightly armed paratroops attacking the Merville battery.

Another wave of of gliders including four large Hamilcars would land early on the morning of D-Day with heavy equipment for 6th Airborne Division on airstrips cleared of obstruction by the already landed paratroops.

The next glider operation of D-Day - Operation Mallard - was to take place on the evening of D-Day to bring in the troops of 6th Air Landing Brigade carried in 256 gliders, which included 30 Hamilcars carrying tanks, the first in history to be air lifted to battle by military glider.

Both Operations Tonga and Mallard were carried out gallantly and successfully but at a cost of men and aircraft - casualties were heavy but were not as heavy as had been forecast by some.

In Burma the legendary Major General Wingate was fighting the Japanese with troops air landed behind enemy lines. Beginning in February 1944, Wingate's forces using US CG4A (Hadrian) gliders towed by aircraft of the US 1st Air Commando landed behind Japanese lines in fifty-one gliders at remote jungle LZs over a period of time and cleared landing strips for Dakota aircraft to land with more troops. Some of the gliders were recovered by snatching but many were abandoned where they had landed. By the 15th March a strong fighting force had been established deep in enemy territory in difficult terrain for airborne operations. Wingate himself was killed on the 24th March in an air crash but the campaign continued and by the end of April 1944, the main objectives had been achieved by the use of air landed troops and their equipment. For the first time US Sikorsky YR-4 helicopters were used with success, the shape of things to come in later wars.

In Europe glider operations continued to be mounted in Yugoslavia, France and Greece. Operation Bunghole involved pilots of the GPR flying three US CG4A (Hadrian) gliders towed by USAAF tugs carrying a Russian Military Mission from Bari, Italy, to Yugoslavia to meet Marshal Tito the Yugoslav resistance leader.

A small but effective glider operation was Operation Dingson early in August 1944, when ten Hadrian gliders piloted by the GPR and towed by the RAF carried French SAS troopers and jeeps to Brittany to wreak havoc among the Germans and turncoat Russians serving with the German Army, before the arrival of advancing US Forces.

Striking at the supposed soft underbelly of the German Army in the south of France on the 15th August 1944, US and British troops and gliders landed behind the invasion beaches in support of the incoming seaborne forces.

By August 1944, the German Army was retreating to the borders of Germany itself pursued by the Allied Armies. Sixteen airborne operations were planned but had to be cancelled due to the speed of the Allied advance. But logistics prevailed on the Allies as they began to outrun their chain of supplies from the by now distant Channel ports.

General Montgomery decided to land his airborne forces across the river barriers of the Maas, Waal and Lower Rhine and outflank the German Siegfried Line - a chain of formidable static defences - and push into Germany with ground armies who would advance through the airborne troops who would have taken and held the vital bridges over the rivers.

1st Airborne Division was given the task of taking and holding the Arnhem road bridge over the Rhine, the furthest away from the Allied front line and the air landed troops would be in an exposed position until the arrival of ground forces. Such was the scale of the airborne operation, codenamed Market, that the RAF was unable to lift all the airborne troops and supplies in one lift. Three airlifts had to be made to carry the 10,000 troops of 1st Airborne Division to battle. An aerial armada of 692 tug and glider combinations would transport 1st Air Landing Brigade and divisional troops in three daylight landings on three successive days. On the 17th, 18th and 19th September 1944, a total of 692 gliders was towed off from bases in England. 621 gliders reached their LZs making a success rate of 89.74% in the largest glider landings so far in WWII.

In spite of a bitter and hard fought battle by the valiant troops of 1st Airborne division against heavy odds - the position at Arnhem became untenable and the gallant remnants of the division were forced to withdraw as best they could over the Rhine. The name Arnhem - previously unknown - went round the world. On the night of the 25th-26th September the survivors came back across the Rhine - they had stood at the fray but lightly armed for almost ten days instead of the two asked of them. Their comrades of the Royal Air Force had striven to re-supply them and had taken heavy losses without flinching. The Battle of Arnhem has rightly gone down in history as the supreme example of the qualities of the Air Landing Forces and the Royal Air Force.

The GPR was decimated by the loss of 229 glider pilots at Arnhem and many more were wounded so the regiment was re-supplied with 1500 pilots from the RAF who were detached to the strength of the GPR and found themselves flying gliders instead of powered aircraft. They were given military training to enable them to fight on the ground after landing their gliders on the battlefield.

Many of the RAF pilots resented being glider pilots at first but before long they began to feel the esprit de corps of the Glider Pilot Regiment - some began to wear the airborne red beret contrary to Air Ministry orders - some were later to die in action wearing the same beret.

On the 9th October 1944, the pilots of the GPR flew Horsa gliders towed by the RAF to Italy in Operation Molten for possible future use on operations. Thirty-two combinations set out and twenty-seven arrived safely in Italy via France. A week later on the 16th October 1944, twenty USAAF Dakotas towed twenty Hadrian gliders piloted by the GPR to the airfield at Megara, Greece, on Operation Manna with men and equipment for the paratroops who had dropped there on the 12th October.

During the winter of 1944 plans were made for the largest Allied airborne operation yet to be mounted. Operation Varsity would land the 1st Allied Airborne Army over the River Rhine in a single air lift. This would be the first tactical air landing of the war but this time the air landing troops would be covered by the artillery of 2nd Army from the start of the operation. The hard lessons of Arnhem had been learnt and 6th Airborne Division would not be out on a limb without artillery support. Their mission would be to land, take and hold ground whilst behind them the ground divisions would assault across the Rhine, pass through the airborne troops and begin the final drive into the heart of Germany to end the war in Europe.

Before the operation the Allied air forces would pound the enemy defences in a continuous air attack in an effort to eliminate the defensive positions known to be there. As planned the operation began with the preliminary bombardment by Allied aircraft and the guns of 2nd Army artillery. With the enemy reeling from the bombardment the air assault commenced on the morning of the 24th March 1945. From eleven airfields in England an aerial fleet of 386 Horsa and 48 Hamilcar gliders were towed off by 38 and 46 Groups, Royal Air Force, carrying 6th Air Landing Brigade and divisional troops of 6th Airborne Division. Another aerial armada carrying the US 17th Airborne Division took off from Continental base bound for the same battlefield.

Both aerial fleets made an historic meeting over the field of Waterloo and in the greatest air armada ever seen in the history of warfare flew on to the battleground in Germany. At 1300 hours that historic day the first of the gliders began to land amid the fog of war caused by the air and ground bombardment, which reduced visibility and made accurate landings very difficult. But of the 434 British gliders which had been towed off 402 landed successfully. 92% of the British glider force had landed but only 88 were undamaged all the rest were hit by enemy flak and small arms fire.

On landing the glider troops immediately went into action and seized their objectives. By 1000 hours the next day the advancing ground divisions had linked up with the air landed troops. Operation Varsity had been a conspicuous success due to excellent planning and organization which was valiantly carried out by the men of the airborne forces and the RAF. Nevertheless over 1000 casualties were sustained on the first day of the operation. The GPR suffered 101 pilots dead of whom 51 were from the Royal Air Force, many of whom had died wearing their red berets. Their sacrifice was not in vain - the way ahead into Germany lay open and a few weeks later on the 8th May 1945, the Germans surrendered unconditionally and part of a just war had ended.

However the Japanese in the Far East were still fighting and the 44th Indian (Airborne) Division was formed - planning and training went ahead in India to use gliders to transport airborne troops to battle. It had been found that the wooden construction of the Horsa glider was unsuitable for the climate - the bonding glue and plywood came apart in the humid conditions. The steel tube and fabric covered Hadrian proved better and glider training continued on them. But the fanatical Japanese were forced to surrender to the power of the atomic bomb in August 1945 and WWII came to an end.

With end of WWII the need for glider borne troops and glider pilots had gone and the wartime establishments began to run down. By 1948 only two Horsa squadrons were left at Waterbeach and Netheravon and one Hamilcar squadron remained at Fairford. Glider pilot training was carried out at Upper Heyford at No.1 Parachute and Glider Training School. Likewise the wartime RAF airborne forces squadrons were disbanded. No.46 Group was disbanded on March 1950, and No.38 Group in February 1951. By 1950 the GPR had been reduced to a single squadron which continued to fly Horsas but the writing was on the wall for gliderborne warfare and helicopters began to take over the role. On the 31st August 1957, the Glider Pilot Regiment was disbanded and the Army Air Corps assumed responsibility for all Army aviation.

Glider borne forces have lasted but a short time in military use - from the dark days of 1940 through the long years of trail and error to the magnificent Operation Varsity in 1945 - then a slow decline to a redundant end in 1957. The human cost of the glider war was high - a total of 551 glider pilots lost their lives - this total included 55 Royal Air Force glider pilots and two from the Royal Australian Air Force. Their names are recorded .on a Memorial window in Salisbury Cathedral. The names of all the gallant men of the Royal Air Force and the airborne divisions who went to war towing and being carried in gliders are recorded in War Memorials in village, town and city throughout Great Britain.

# BRITISH MILITARY GLIDER FORCES

The Gliderborne Army Forces within the two British WWII Airborne Divisions were selected from some of the oldest units in the British Army while some were newly created, specifically for airborne requirements such as the Glider Pilot Regiment. All the WWII Gliderborne Forces added honour and glory to their unit's histories. Those without history, such as the Glider Pilot Regiment and 6th Airborne Armoured Reconnaissance Regiment, made history.

1st and 6th Airborne Divisions,
1st and 6th Air Landing Brigades,
12th Battalion, Devonshire Regiment. (11th)
7th Battalion, Kings Own Scottish Borderers. (25th)
1st Battalion, Border Regiment. (34th)
2nd Battalion, South Staffordshire Regiment. (38th)
2nd Battalion, Oxfordshire & Buckinghamshire Light Infantry. (52nd)
1st Battalion, Royal Ulster Rifles. (83rd)
1 & 2 Battalions, Glider Pilot Regiment.
6th Airborne Armoured Reconnaissance Regiment. RAC.
1st and 6th Airborne Divisions - Divisional troops.

Many other airborne divisional troops were transported to battle by glider e.g. signals, artillery, medics, security, provost, engineers, and airborne divisional headquarters. All wore the airborne red beret but retained their own regimental or corps cap badge.

1st Light Regiment, Royal Artillery.
1st Air Landing Light Battery, Royal Artillery.
53rd Air Landing Light Regiment, Royal Artillery.
2nd Air Landing Light Anti-Aircraft Battery, Royal Artillery.
1st Forward Observer Unit, Royal Artillery.
9th Field Company, Royal Engineers.
249th Field Park Company, Royal Engineers.
286th Field Company, Royal Engineers.
63rd Company, Royal Army Service Corps.
93rd Company, Royal Army Service Corps.
250th Company, Royal Army Service Corps.
398th Company, Royal Army Service Corps.
716th Company, Royal Army Service Corps.

89th Field Security Company, Intelligence Corps.
317th Field Security Company, Intelligence Corps.
1st Airborne Provost Company, Corps of Military Police.
6th Airborne Provost Company, Corps of Military police.
181st Field Ambulance, Royal Army Medical Corps.
195th Field Ambulance, Royal Army Medical Corps.

The following are abridged histories of the main glider borne units during WWII. Prior to the middle of the 18th century regiments were known by the names of their colonels. Later they were numbered in order of precedence and later still were given a territorial designation.

# 1ST AIR LANDING BRIGADE

The 31st Independent Brigade Group was redesignated the 1st Air Landing Brigade Group on the 10th October 1941, and a few weeks later on the 1st November 1st Airborne Division was formed with Major General F.A.M. Browning as General Officer Commanding. It was decided by the War Office that an airborne division would consist of two parachute brigades, one air landing brigade using gliders and divisional troops from the medical, engineer, signals and artillery corps and regiment plus an HQ staff.

At this time 31st Independent Brigade Group consisted of the 2nd Battalion Oxford and Bucks Light Infantry, 1st Battalion Royal Ulster Rifles and the 2nd Battalion South Staffordshire Regiment. On the 1st December 1941, the 1st Battalion Border Regiment was transferred to the Brigade Group which was stationed around the Harpenden, Hertfordshire area. Other units transferred to the brigade during December 1941, were the 458th Light Battery Royal Artillery and the 1st Air Landing Recce Company. On the 10th December 1941, Brigadier G.F. Hopkinson was appointed to command 1st Air Landing Brigade.

General Browning chose as the emblem of airborne forces a figure from Greek mythology - Bellerphon mounted on the winged horse Pegasus - a symbolic choice as the Corinthian hero Bellerphon was the first airborne warrior who rode the winged horse Pegasus to battle against the fire belching monster Chimaera and slew it. (However he later fell to his death trying to reach Olympus - the home of the Gods). The emblem - the figure of Bellerphon and Pegasus in blue on a maroon background - was designed by Major Edward Seago in May 1942 and authorised to be worn by all airborne soldiers on the upper arm of uniform together with an airborne shoulder flash. The new maroon airborne forces beret was worn by all airborne soldiers with their own regimental or corps cap badges.

In 1942 the title of 1st Air Landing Brigade Group was changed to 1st Air Landing Brigade with Brigadier Hopkinson in command. To form, train and equip the new Air Landing Brigade took time - hard training was endured by all ranks to make themselves physically fit. A high standard was set and those unable or unwilling to meet this standard were posted off strength to other units. Volunteers for airborne forces had to be between 19 years and not more than 40 years of age. No soldier wearing spectacles was accepted and vision had to be 6/12 in each eye. Any volunteer who suffered from persistent air sickness was rejected as was any man whose service character fell below 'Good'. All of these were returned to their original units.

By June 1942 a new experimental establishment of one thousand other ranks and fifty officers had been created for an air landing battalion. The theory was that such a battalion would be able to fight for some time unsupported by reinforcements. To enable it to do this the battalion would have to have their own anti-tank and anti-aircraft guns, their own transport, medical and reconnaissance units: all capable of being air lifted to battle in the larger military gliders then coming into service which could carry two platoons of 6-pounder anti-tank guns and two platoons of Hispano anti-aircraft guns plus troops and equipment.

After three training flights in a glider all ranks were entitled to wear the glider troops badge - a small blue woven glider - on the right sleeve. Extra pay of one shilling (5p) per day was also earned.

Throughout the summer of 1942 intensive training was carried out by the Brigade in all aspects, ranging from learning to drive vehicles to street fighting. Much emphasis was placed on physical fitness which was illustrated by the 2nd Oxford and Bucks who marched 134 miles from Ilfracombe, Devon, to their base at Bulford, Wiltshire, in a heatwave of 90 degrees. Marching by day and sleeping by night the Oxford and Bucks covered the distance in under six days, averaging over twenty-two miles per day.

By the spring of 1943 1st Air Landing brigade was not up to establishment in either aircraft or specialist troops, nevertheless in May 1943, the 1st Battalion Border Regiment, commanded by Lt.Colonel G.V. Britten and the 2nd Battalion, South Staffordshire Regiment, commanded by Lt.Colonel W.D.H. McCardie, embarked for Oran in North Africa for the invasion of Sicily with Brigadier P.H.W. Hicks as Brigade Commander, he having taken over from Brigadier Hopkinson on the 6th April, 1943.

On arrival in North Africa the Air Landing Brigade commanders found that there not enough gliders to air lift them to Sicily. The Royal Air Force 38 Wing had towed out a number of Horsa gliders from England (Operation Beggar/Turkey Buzzard) but in spite of the arrival of the Horsas US Waco CG4A Hadrian gliders would have to be used towed by USAAF aircraft whose aircrews had very little glider towing training and no combat experience.

The objective of 1st Air Landing Brigade was to take and hold (Operation Ladbrooke) the very important Ponte Grande bridge near the city of Syracuse in Sicily, and attack the western side of the city to facilitate the task of the following 17th Infantry Brigade of the 5th Division seaborne assault forces. This was to be the first time an air landing invasion by British troops would be made. The eight Horsa gliders engaged would carry troops of the South Staffords and the men of the Border Regiment would fly in the US gliders.

At 18.48 hours on the 9th July 1943, 1st Air Landing Brigade began their historic flight. The first combinations lifted off from Tunisia and set course for Malta then Sicily. Bad weather prevailed during the flight and on arrival off the coast of Sicily an offshore wind was blowing dust off the hot Sicilian land, making things difficult for the aircrews of both gliders and tugs. Some gliders were caused to be released too far offshore by inexperienced tug aircrews and many gliders fell into the sea with heavy loss of life to their troops.

Both gliders carrying Lt.Colonel Britten and Lt.Colonel McCardie came down in the sea and both commanders had to swim ashore. Three Horsa glider pilots managed to land their gliders near the Ponte Grande Bridge objective. One piloted by Staff Sergeant D. Galpin, DFM and Sergeant Brown, landed by the bridge and the occupants, troops of the South Staffords led by Lieutenant L. Withers MC, stormed the bridge and captured it. About thirty troops of the Border Regiment under Lieutenant Welch were landed within four miles of the objective and quickly moved to reinforce the South Staffords at the bridge.

The troops of 1st Air Landing Brigade held the Ponte Grande bridge against counter attacks throughout the night until, when reduced to fifteen men, they were overran by the enemy who retook the bridge. An hour later the advancing seaborne troops attacked and recaptured the bridge.

General Montgomery sent a message to 1st Air Landing Brigade: "For those responsible for this particular operation I am filled with admiration. Had it not been for the skill and gallantry of the Air Landing Brigade, the Port of Syracuse would not have fallen until very much later".

The second air landing operation (Operation Fustian) involving the brigade was a combined para and gliderborne troop assault on another vital bridge, the Prima Sole, over the River Simeto five miles south of Catania on the east coast of Sicily. After the paratroops had landed eight Waco CG4A and eleven Horsa gliders, piloted by the Glider Pilot Regiment and towed by RAF aircraft, would land ten 6-pounder guns and eighteen vehicles of the Air Landing Brigade Royal Artillery Anti-Tank Battery on two LZs to the south and north west of the bridge.

At 1920 hours on the 12th July 1943, Fustian began from the same bases in Tunisia. As the airborne armada approached Sicily some Allied Naval ships opened fire thinking they were the enemy, some of the aircraft having flown off course into a naval fire zone. As the dropped paratroops were fighting for the bridge the gliders arrived over their two LZs. One Horsa, piloted by Major Alastair Cooper, AFC, and carrying the Royal Artillery Commander Lieutenant Colonel C. Crawford and his staff, crashed into a river bed killing all on board. Only four Horsa glider crews and passengers reached the bridge battle. One piloted by Staff Sergeant White landed on the intended LZ and the gun load was soon in action. The other three landed from half a mile to seven miles away but the occupants managed to join the battle. For their part in the Sicily operation King George VI awarded a Commemorative Scroll to the 9th Airborne Squadron, Royal

Engineers, and an embroidered glider badge to be worn at the top of the sleeve of uniform to the 1st Battalion Border Regiment, 2nd Battalion South Staffordshire Regiment and 1st Battalion Glider Pilot Regiment.

Casualties to 1st Air Landing Brigade were high: The South Staffords suffered 350 men killed, wounded or missing and the Border Regiment 250 men. The Glider Pilot Regiment lost fifty-seven glider pilots. Many of the troops were drowned in the gliders that fell into the sea. One week after the capture of Syracuse 1st Air Landing Brigade was withdrawn to Sousse in North Africa, to reform and assemble the widely scattered surviving troops who had either landed in the sea or far from their intended LZs.

Italy surrendered on the 11th September 1943, and 1st Air Landing Brigade embarked in Royal Navy ships to Taranto, Italy, the brigade becoming part of a special mobile force. They were the first British troops into the town of Foggia and captured the important Foggia airfield.

In October 1943, 1st Airborne Division was relieved in Italy and on the 17th November 1943, returned to Phillipville, North Africa. Embarking for England they landed at Liverpool on the 10th December 1943, then moved to Woodhall Spa, Lincolnshire. As 1st Air Landing Brigade had suffered heavy losses in Sicily they were reinforced by the 7th Battalion, Kings Own Scottish Borderers, commanded by Lt. Colonel R. Payton-Reid.

6th Airborne Division had been formed in May 1943, and the 1st Battalion, Royal Ulster Rifles and the 2nd Battalion Oxford and Bucks were transferred to the new division to form 6th Air Landing Brigade. Together the 1st and 6th Air Landing Divisions formed 1st Air Landing Corps under the command of General Browning. In March 1944, 1st Allied Airborne Army was created under the command of the US General Lewis Brereton, comprising the British 1st Air Landing Corps and the US Air Landing Corps which contained the US 82nd and 101st Airborne Divisions.

1st Air Landing Brigade now consisted of:
1st Battalion, Border Regiment. Lt.Colonel Haddon.
2nd Battalion, South Staffords. Lt.Colonel McCardie.
7th Battalion, Kings Own Scottish Borderers. Lt.Colonel Payton Reid.
1st Air Landing Light Battery. RA. Lt.Colonel Walker.
181st Field Ambulance. RAMC. Lt.Colonel Marrable.
Plus 1st Airborne Divisional troops carried in gliders as required.

6th Airborne Division was engaged in the Normandy D-Day (6th June 1944) operations - 1st Airborne Division's valiant battle came later in September 1944, at Arnhem.

On the 11th June 1944, 1st Airborne Division moved to the Andover, Hampshire, area ready to carry out airborne operations. Sixteen such operations were planned to take place on the Continent but due to the speed of the Allied advance all were cancelled. It took time to plan and execute an airborne operation - the logistics of gathering together troops, aircraft and equipment were immense. By September 1944, the British 2nd Army had advanced into Holland but were beginning to outrun their chain of supplies which stretched back some 250 miles to the French channel ports and the advance came to a halt. Field Marshal Montgomery decided to use his airborne and ground forces to outflank and turn the formidable static defences of the German Siegfried Line. With the line turned his forces could pour into the German heartland and, perhaps, bring a speedy end to the war in Europe. The available airborne troops - 1st Airborne Division, the US 82nd and 101st Airborne Divisions plus the Polish Parachute Brigade - would be air landed in an airborne carpet from Eindhoven to Arnhem and take and hold the vital bridges over the three natural river barriers of the Maas, Waal and Lower Rhine to allow a rapid advance by the following tanks and infantry of the British 2nd Army.

The US airborne troops would be air landed in the area from Eindhoven to Grave and around Nijmegan. 1st Airborne Division and the Polish Parachute Brigade would land at Arnhem to take the road bridge, the furthest away from the Allied front lines. General Browning made the prophetic observation that, perhaps, his forces were "going a bridge too far". 1st Airborne Division was commanded by Major General R.E. Urquhart, CB. DSO. and 1st Air Landing Brigade by Brigadier P.H.W. Hicks, DSO. MC. There were not enough aircraft to carry 1st Airborne Division in one air lift, so it was planned to make three separate air lifts on three successive days by sixteen squadrons of the Royal Air Force 38 and 46 Groups and two Wings of the Glider Pilot Regiment.

At 0940 hours on the 17th September 1944, the first tug/glider combinations began to lift off carrying men of 7th KOSB from Down Ampney airfield. By 1120 hours the last combination had lifted off from Harwell airfield - three hundred and fifty-nine Dakotas, Stirlings, Albemarles and Halifax tugs had towed off three hundred and thirty-six Horsas, thirteen Hamilcars and ten Hadrian gliders from eight airfields in the south of England. 1st Airborne Division was flying to battle and, unknowingly, into the annals of military history.

Arriving over their LZs at 13.25 hours the glider pilots began to cast off their tow ropes and land their gliders amid mostly light enemy fire. 740 men of

7th KOSB rallied on their LZ to the sound of the pipes - the 181st Air Landing Field Ambulance were down at 13.15 hours and by 1600 hours had established their Medical Dressing Station at Wolfhezen. The South Staffords were immediately in action against German machine-guns and took casualties but quickly silenced the opposition. The Border Regiment moved off their LZ with 7th KOSB to take up positions to defend the LZs for the second air lift due in next day.

Low cloud and mist prevailed over the English airfields but nevertheless at 10.45 hours on the 18th September, the second air lift of 1st Air Landing Brigade got under way. Two hundred and seventy-nine Horsa and 15 Hamilcar gliders were towed off by two hundred and ninety-four tugs, carrying troops of the Border Regiment and South Staffords, together with jeeps, guns, scout cars. ammunition and stores. Of the two hundred and ninety-four which had lifted off two hundred and seventy landed on or near their LZs. With the enemy now alerted heavy fighting ensued for 1st Air Landing Brigade who began to take many casualties. Two Victoria Crosses were earned - Lance Sergeant John Daniel Baskeyfield (posthumous) and Major R.H. Cain, both of the 2nd South Staffords, the only battalion so to do in WWII.

On the 19th September the third and final air lift was towed off from seven English airfields. Forty-three Horsa and one Hamilcar gliders were airborne carrying 7th KOSB, Polish troops, RASC, jeeps machine-guns and trailers. Thirty-one Horsas landed at Arnhem amid the fury of battle taking heavy casualties. The other gliders had either broken their tow ropes, ditched at sea or force land away from the battle. In spite of a valiant battle against the odds 1st Airborne Division had to withdraw from the fray, Montgomery giving the order at 0930 hours on the 25th September. 10,000 airborne soldiers of 1st Airborne Division had gone to the battle at Arnhem - some 2163 returned. The rest were killed, missing or taken prisoner of war. 1st Air Landing Brigade had been decimated: the 2nd South Staffords Roll Call revealed that only six officers and one hundred and thirty-three soldiers returned from the battle. 7th KOSB had set our with seven hundred and forty men of all ranks - seventy-six returned. The Glider Pilot Regiment suffered two hundred and twenty-nine pilots killed and four hundred and sixty-nine taken prisoner. It is estimated that 7000 of the enemy died in the Battle of Arnhem.

There was no failure of 1st Airborne Division at the Battle of Arnhem; they had done much more than was asked of them - comparatively lightly armed as airborne troops always are against numerically superior forces with Tiger tanks. The division did not fight again. 21st Army Group crossed the Rhine in the spring of 1945 and the Germans surrendered unconditionally on the 8th May 1945. 1st Airborne Division was disbanded on the 15th November 1945, and some of its troops went to 6th Airborne Division.

## 6TH AIR LANDING BRIGADE

During 1943 with the invasion of Europe drawing closer, it was realised that another airborne division was needed so on the 23rd April 1943, orders were given to form 6th Airborne Division. The title, 6th Airborne Division, had been chosen to confuse the Germans as to the British Order of Battle, the only other British airborne division being 1st Airborne Division.

Major General Richard Nelson Gale was appointed Commanding Officer with General Browning, promoted to Lieutenant General, as General Officer Commanding both 1st and 6th Airborne Divisions. HQ 6th Airborne Division was established at Syrencot House, Brigmerston, Wiltshire, on the 3rd May 1943.

1st Battalion Royal Ulster Rifles, Co Lieutenant Colonel Carson, and the 2nd Battalion Oxford and Bucks Light Infantry, CO Lieutenant Colonel Roberts, were transferred to the new airborne division to form 6th Air Landing Brigade, on the 6th May 1943. On the 14th May 1943, Colonel A.M. Toye took command of the brigade but ten days later on the 24th May Brigadier the Honourable Hugh M. Kindersley assumed command. On 1st June 1943, divisional troops began to be posted to the division:

2nd Air Landing Light Anti-Aircraft Battery, Royal Artillery.
249 Field Company, Royal Engineers.
286 Field Park Company, Royal Engineers.
716 Company, Royal Army Service Corps.
398 Company, Royal Army Service Corps.
63 Company, Royal Army Service Corps.
Ordnance Field Parks, Royal Army Ordnance Corps.
Divisional Signals, Royal Corps of Signals.
Royal Electrical & Mechanical Engineers Workshops.
317th Field Security Section.
Divisional Provost Company, Royal Corps of Military Police
No.1 Wing, Glider Pilot Regiment.
No.2 Wing, Glider Pilot Regiment.

The 53rd (Worcestershire Yeomanry) Air Landing Light Regiment, Royal Artillery, formed within the brigade on the 1st July 1943 and in July 1943, the 12th Battalion, Devonshire Regiment, CO Lieutenant Colonel G.R. Stevens, transferred to 6th Air Landing Brigade. During October 1943, 195th Field Ambulance was posted to 6th Air Landing Brigade and became the 195th Air Landing Field Ambulance, CO Lieutenant Colonel W.M.E. Anderson.

On the 14th January 1944, the Airborne Light Tank Squadron at Larkhill, Wiltshire, was redesignated 6th Airborne Armoured Reconnaissance Regiment, Royal Armoured Corps. The personnel consisted of one troop each from 9th Lancers, 10th Hussars, the Bays, 1st and 2nd Battalions Royal Tank Regiment and a Royal Electrical and Mechanical Engineers Unit. CO Major (later Colonel) Stuart. For the first time in military history tanks were to be flown by glider to the actual battlefield.

Throughout the early months of 1944 intensive training in airborne warfare was carried out, preparatory to the invasion of Normandy, culminating in an exercise on the 4th April 1944, when the entire division was taken into the air by the Royal Air Force and the USAAF. Unknown to most of the troops involved this was a dress rehearsal for D-Day the 6th June 1944, the momentous day in history when the invasion would be launched.

The role of 6th Airborne Division in the invasion was to take and hold ground on the left flank of the invasion beaches during the early hours of D-Day. The task of 6th Air Landing Brigade was to take (intact if possible) and hold the bridges over the Caen Canal and River Orne at Benouville and Ranville, by glider borne coup de main assault (Operation Deadstick) at 00:20 hours on D-Day and land by glider (Operation Mallard) at 21:00 hours the same day, to take and hold ground to provide a firm base from which 6th Airborne Division could prevent the enemy attacking the left flank of the invasion forces.

Operation Deadstick was to be carried out by troops of the 2nd Oxford & Bucks commanded by Major John Howard (DSO) and a detachment of 249 Field Company, Royal Engineers, commanded by Captain Jock Neilson.

Six Horsa gliders towed by the Royal Air Force and flown by pilots of the Glider Pilot Regiment, would carry the troops and would land as close as was possible to the two bridges on fields which the Germans thought were too small for landing zones. Operation Mallard would bring in:

2nd Oxford & Bucks.
1st Royal Ulster Rifles.
6th Airborne Armoured Reconnaissance Regiment with tanks.
211th Light Battery, Royal Artillery.
Headquarters, 6th Air Landing Brigade.
A Company, 12th Devonshire Regiment. (Remainder by sea on D+1)
by Horsa and Hamilcar gliders towed by the Royal Air Force and flown by pilots of the Glider Pilot Regiment.

At 00:16 hours on D-Day the 6th June 1944, the Operation Deadstick Horsa gliders began to land on their LZs. Three Horsas were landed by the Caen Canal bridge and two Horsas by the River Orne bridge - all brilliantly flown by the Glider Pilot Regiment pilots. The first Horsa piloted by Staff Sergeant Jim Wallwork (DFM) landed within yards of the Canal bridge with the other two close behind. The two Horsas with the River Orne bridge assault party also landed close to their objective - the first Horsa piloted by Staff Sergeant Roy Howard (DFM) was on full flap from tow release at 6000 feet to the target. An object lesson in airmanship to those senior RAF officers, who, back in the early days, thought that only trained RAF pilots could fly aircraft.

Both assault parties captured both bridges in spirited aggressive actions - casualties were one officer killed in action and two wounded, and one soldier killed and twelve wounded.

Back in England the vast armada of 256 Horsa and Hamilcar gliders were being loaded for Operation Mallard - twenty tanks were aboard twenty Hamilcars, ready to make history. At 18:40 hours on the evening of D-Day the first gliders were towed off carrying 6th Air Landing Brigade. A few minutes before 21:00 hours they began to land in Normandy, on the LZs prepared by the parachute troops previously dropped. Out of the 256 which had lifted off 246 landed successfully with 6th Air Landing Brigade troops, no mean achievement in airborne warfare. This massive reinforcement dealt German morale a devastating blow at a critical time for the invading armies. The soldiers of 6th Air Landing Brigade were in the line and engaging the enemy from D-Day onwards. The Brigade Commander, Brigadier Kindersley, being wounded on the 12th June 1944. At the end of August and the beginning of September 1944, the brigade was withdrawn and returned to England.

After leave the brigade went through a period of reorganisation and then resumed intensive training but when the Germans made their attack through the Ardennes at Christmas 1944, the brigade was rushed by air and sea transport to stem the German offensive. By the end of February 1945, the brigade was back in England. A short period of intensive training was undertaken and early in March 1945, two large scale divisional exercises were carried out - Mush I and Mush II - designed to practice the division in operating behind the enemy front line. Again, as in the exercises before Normandy, the troops did not know that this was a rehearsal for the crossing of the River Rhine, Operation Varsity. 6th Airborne Division was warned that they would be carrying out a large scale airborne operation before the end of March 1945.

Operation Varsity was to be carried out by the XVIII Airborne Corps commanded by Major General Ridgeway, US Army, and composed the US 17th

Airborne Division and the British 6th Airborne Division, now commanded by Major General E. Bols. 6th Airborne Division would land by glider and parachute at 10:00 hours on the 24th March 1945, over the River Rhine around Kopenhof, Germany, about five miles in front of the ground assault armies, in a tactical air landing. This time however the whole corps would be carried by air in one lift and the artillery of XII Corps of the British 2nd Army would cover the intended battlefield. There was to be no repeat of the Arnhem tactics. A massive airlift of 440 British gliders, including 48 Hamilcars, towed by 38 and 46 Groups, Royal Air Force, would carry 6th Air Landing Brigade, now commanded by Brigadier R.H. Bellamy, who had taken over command on the 19th January 1945, to six LZs on the battlefield in Germany from eight airfields in east Anglia.

The task of 6th Air Landing Brigade was to take and hold the bridges over the River Issel, take and hold the town of Hamminkeln as a bridgehead until the advancing ground assault troops passed through, and to eliminate the enemy in the battlefield area. The Royal Ulster Rifles would take the road bridge over the River Issel at Hamminkeln-Brunen: the 2nd Oxford & Bucks the Hamminkeln - Ringenberg road bridge over the Issel, the Hamminkeln railway station and the road junction to the west. 12th Devons would take the town of Hamminkeln. The whole assault by 6th Air Landing Brigade would be in the nature of a coup de main operation.

At 06:30 hours on the 24th March 1945, the first Horsa gliders carrying the brigade were towed off from England and at 10:21 hours the first 30 Horsas began to land amid heavy German fire and in a thick 'fog of war' caused by the Allied bombing and shelling prior to the assault. By 11:00 hours the last glider was down. The brigade engaged in heavy fighting all day but achieved their objectives. By 14:30 hours most enemy resistance had crumbled and by midnight the advancing ground forces began to pass through 6th Air Landing Brigade.

So ended the largest airborne operation ever mounted in the history of warfare. The cost in lives was great - casualties to the brigade were 25% The Glider Pilot Regiment lost 101 pilots - including Royal Air Force pilots seconded to fly gliders who died wearing their red berets, the wearing of which was officially forbidden by Air Ministry: but Air Ministry did not fly to battle.

There were no more airborne operations for 6th Air Landing Brigade and its soldiers fought on the ground until the end of the war in Europe in May 1945. In the author's view the soldiers of the Air Landing Brigades were second to none, flying to the battle in their fragile wooden gliders, then fighting, only lightly armed, on the ground. A gallant host. 6th Airborne Division was sent to the Middle East after WWII ended and was disbanded in 1948.

# DEVONSHIRE REGIMENT

In 1685 the Marquis of Worcester, son of the Duke of Beaufort, raised a regiment which in 1751 became the 11th Foot then in 1782 the North Devonshire Regiment. The Napoleonic Wars started in 1793 and in 1808 the Peninsula campaign began during which the British Army won nineteen large battles and numerous smaller engagements and drove the French out of Spain and Portugal. During the battle of Salamanca on the 22nd July 1812, the 11th Foot became know as the 'Bloody 11th' as after the battle the regiment had only four officers and sixty-seven other ranks left alive out of a strength of 412 officers and men.

It is recorded that before the battle commenced the 11th, marching to their positions on the battlefield with their band playing the tune 'We've Lived and Loved Together', marched parallel to a French regiment also proceeding to their positions on the battlefield. As the fighting had not commenced both the British and French officers saluted each other but neither side opened fire until they were in their respective places in the lines. The tune played by the band of the 11th became the regiment's regimental march, known to the Devons as 'Turnips' from a line of the march.

In 1881 the regiment's name was changed to the Devonshire Regiment and Exeter Castle was chosen in 1883 to be a device included in the regimental badge. The 'Bloody 11th' lived up to its name during WWI when on the 27th May 1918, as the Devonshire Regiment - the 2nd Battalion under the command of Lieutenant Colonel R.H. Anderson-Morshead, came under a massive German assault north of the River Aisne at Bois des Buttes. Heavily outnumbered and surrounded they stood their ground. They had been ordered to hold up the enemy advance and they did, for seven hours, losing 550 men in the first six hours out of a strength of almost 600. The commanding officer told his men "There is no hope of relief we have to fight to the last". They did. There was no surrender and they fought to the last man. The battalion, 28 officers and 552 other ranks, ceased to exist but their sacrifice enabled reinforcements to form defences south of the River Aisne.

### 12th (AIRBORNE) BATTALION, DEVONSHIRE REGIMENT.

At the beginning of WWII the 12th Battalion, under the command of Lieutenant Colonel R.A.O. Smith, MC, was known as the 50th Battalion: formed from the 12th (Holding) Battalion plus troops from the Higher Barracks Depot, Exeter, and was responsible for the training of recruits to the Regiment at Rawlinson Barracks near Newton Abbot.

In the autumn of 1940 the battalion manned the beach defences at Dawlish then at Budleigh Salterton and Seaton, Devon. In 1941 Lieutenant Colonel R.G. Coates took command and in 1942 Lieutenant Colonel D.D. Rutherford, MC. In September 1942, as part of 214 Infantry Brigade, it moved to the Isle of Wight in a similar role, with sectors at Ventnor, Freshwater and Sandown. In May 1943, under Lieutenant Colonel R.F.B. Hill, it moved as part of the brigade to Truro, Cornwall, for nearly three months. In July, 1943, the battalion came under 6th Airlanding Brigade of 6th Airborne Division, at Bulford Camp, Wiltshire, where it trained in its new airborne role. It became part of 6th Airlanding Brigade officially in October 1943, with Lieutenant Colonel G.R. Stevens taking command in November.

The battalion adopted the red beret of airborne forces with the cap badge of the Devonshire Regiment, a white metal eight-pointed star surmounted by a king's crown, bearing a white metal castle representing Exeter Castle, the motto 'Semper Fidelis' and 'The Devonshire Regiment'. Their shoulder title was 'Devon' in white on red together with the word 'Airborne'. Also, a small blue glider on a kakhi oval was worn on the lower forearm of uniform and the 'Pegasus' patch above the elbow.

On D-Day A Company of the battalion landed in Normandy by glider with the rest of the battalion under the command of Lieutenant Colonel Stevens, following on D+1 by sea. On the 9th June 1944, the 12th Battalion area was attacked by a German infantry regiment supported by Mark IV Panzer tanks - the 12th held their positions. On the 13th June, along with remnants of 12th Parachute Battalion, D Company attacked Breville, Normandy, after two attacks by a battalion of the Black Watch had failed. Company Commander Major J.A.F.W. Bampfylde and twenty-four other ranks were killed in action and three officers wounded with one missing. Breville was taken and held against a strong counter-attack. The 12th was awarded one Distinguished Service Order, two Military Crosses, four Military Medals, and seven Mentioned in Despatches for the Normandy Campaign and their advance to the River Seine.

In August command was taken over by Lieutenant Colonel P. Gleadell, DSO and the battalion returned to England between the 3rd and 7th September 1944. On the 22nd December 1944, the 12th took part with 6th Airborne Division, in the battle of the Ardennes, Belgium, at Christmas 1944, and went into action around the villages of Tellin and Bure, then for a short time in January and February, 1945, the 12th held front line positions at Blerick, Holland. Major W.F. Barrow was awarded the Croix de Guerre and Belgian Order of Leopold and Lieutenant E.D. Nuttal was Mentioned in Despatches.

On the 25th February 1945, the battalion returned to England to prepare for the last great airborne operation of WWII, Operation Varsity, on the 24th March 1945. The battalion had the task of taking the German village of Hamminkeln which they did within three hours of landing by glider.

| Casualties | Officers | Other Ranks | Total |
| --- | --- | --- | --- |
| Killed | 3 | 24 | 27 |
| Wounded | 6 | 26 | 32 |
| Missing | 7 | 74 | 81 |
|  |  |  | 140 |

Two Distinguished Service Orders, four Military Crosses, seven Military Medals, three Mentioned in Despatches and sixteen Commanders in Chief's Certificates were won in the operation.

After Operation Varsity the battalion fought its way to the Baltic coast near Wismar where the met the advancing Russian Army. Lieutenant Colonel Gleadell was awarded the Distinguished Service Order and three Military Crosses, two Military Medals and fifteen Commander in Chief's Certificates were won. The 12th returned to England with the rest of 6th Air Landing Brigade on the 19th May 1945. The battalion, now under the command of Lieutenant Colonel A. Tilly, trained for the invasion of Japan but WWII ended in August 1945 and the 12th battalion was disbanded in November 1945.

The Devonshire Regiment amalgamated with the Dorset Regiment in 1958 but the Devons' WWII soldiers still maintain a strong *esprit de corps*. The 12th (Airborne) Battalion has its own magazine, *The Swedebasher* and is a branch of the Devonshire and Dorset Regimental Association.

# KING'S OWN SCOTTISH BORDERERS

The regiment was raised on the 16th March 1689, at Edinburgh by the Earl of Leven, David Leslie, and was known as Leven's Regiment. Regiments were then known by the names of their colonels - the system of numbering them came later. It first saw action at the battle of Killiecrankie on the 27th July 1689, which resulted in its being awarded the privilege of marching through Edinburgh with bayonets fixed and colours flying, a right which the regiment still possesses.

The first battle honour was won at Namur in 1695 and in 1715 the regiment was in action at the battle of Sheriffmuir then in Flanders in 1743. In 1746, as Sempill's Regiment, it fought in the second line at Drumossie Moor, Culloden, under the Duke of Cumberland against Prince Charles Edward Stuart's Highlanders.

In 1751 the regiment was numbered the 25th Foot. Renamed the Edinburgh Regiment it fought under this title at Minden on the 1st August 1759, when with five other British regiments and seven battalions of Hanoverians and Hessians, they routed 10,000 French calvary and two brigades of infantry. In 1782 the regiment had another change of name when it became the 25th Sussex Regiment and from 1793 to 1794 some of its soldiers served as Marines aboard Royal Navy warships.

The regiment saw service in the West Indies from 1795 until 1799 when it took part in the battle of Egmont-op-Zee in Holland. At the battle of Alexandria in 1801 it won the honour of the Sphinx superscribed 'Egypt'. In 1802 the regiment was designated a Lowland regiment and wore doublets and tartan trews and three years later the regiment was given another title, 'The King's Own Borderers' by King George III and in 1809 was in action at the capture of Martinique. During 1887 the regiment was given the title 'The King's Own Scottish Borderers' and saw service in Burma and South Africa where Lieutenant Coulson was awarded the Victoria Cross.

During WWI the regiment served in Egypt in 1914, Gallipoli in 1951 then France in 1916 were it fought on the Somme and later at Arras, Ypres, Cambrai, Lys and the last battle of Ypres in 1918. During WWI four Victoria Crosses were awarded to members of the regiment: CSM Skinner, CQS Grimbaldeston, Sgt. McGuffie and Piper Laidlaw.

Post WWI saw the regiment in Germany, India, Egypt, Malta and Palestine before returning to Britain in 1936, with battalions being stationed in England and Scotland on the outbreak of WWII in September 1939.

The 7th Battalion was raised early in 1939 and was at full strength by July 1939, under the command of Lieutenant Colonel, The Earl of Galloway. The 1st Battalion embarked for France from Southampton on the 3rd October 1939, and took up station at Lille. On the 9th April 1940, the Germans invaded Norway and a company of the regiment went there with the 52nd (Lowland) Division.

When the Germans unleashed their blitzkrieg attack in 1940 the regiment made a fighting retreat to Dunkirk from where they were evacuated in the immortal armada of 'little ships', the last men leaving on the 3rd June 1940. Two battalions of the regiment returned to France on the 13th June 1940, as part of the Second British Expeditionary Force, in an attempt to retain a foothold in Europe. Disembarking at St. Malo the regiment moved to positions at Le Mans but to no avail having to withdraw to Briquebec, a few miles south of Cherbourg. On the 16th June 1940, the Second BEF was forced to begin its evacuation from France and the regiment formed part of the rearguard. Making a fighting withdrawal to Cherbourg the regiment embarked on SS Manxman on the 18th June, making the regiment the last infantry unit to leave France.

For the next two years the regiment was increased in strength with several more battalions being added and engaged in hard training including mountain training for two battalions in the highlands of Scotland.

## 7TH (AIRBORNE) BATTALION, KOSB.

In November 1943, the 7th Battalion, King's Own Scottish Borderers became an airborne unit. Commanded by Lieutenant Colonel R. Payton Reid the battalion joined the 1st Airlanding Brigade of 1st Airborne Division at Woodhall Spa, Lincolnshire.

On D-Day the 1st and 6th Battalions of the regiment went ashore at Sword beach in Normandy to the sound of the pipes playing 'Blue Bonnets over the Border'. With the 4th and 5th Battalions they were in action until the end of hostilities in Europe. The 7th Battalion, the only Scottish regiment in 1st Airborne Division, went into action by glider from Down Ampney and Blakehill Farm on the 17th September 1944. Lifting off at 1000 hours they were down on their LZs at Arnhem in action at 1330 hours with a strength of 740 all ranks, rallying to the sound of the pipes, again playing 'Blue Bonnets'. By 1500 hours they had assembled were ready to move out to defend the LZs for the next wave of 1st Airborne Division due in next day.

Bitter fighting ensued with the enemy estimated to have two armoured divisions plus artillery and heavy machine guns. Lightly armed airborne soldiers were pitted against 50 ton Tiger tanks. By the 20th September the 7th Battalion, KOSB was reduced to 270 all ranks from the 740 who had landed but they fought on gallantly against the odds.

On the 25th September 1st Airborne Division was ordered to withdraw as the position was untenable. They had been without sleep for a week and constantly at battle, short on food and taking heavy casualties. At 2115 hours on the 25th 7th Battalion began to move out to the Rhine which they crossed at 0200 hours next day. None of the battalion pipers came back. Roll Call of the battalion at Nijmegan showed a Parade State of four officers and seventy-two other ranks out of the seven hundred and forty who had landed on the 17th September.

The 7th Battalion did not fight again - it finished its airborne role in October 1945, and was disbanded in November 1945. The regiment is known to some as the 'KOSBIES' but this nickname is greeted coldly by menbers who frigidly state this title is not known but K.O.S.B. is.

# THE BORDER REGIMENT, 34th & 55th

King William III authorised the raising of several regiments in the eighteenth century in answer to the deposed James II's military attempts to regain the British Throne. Among them was a regiment which became the 34th Foot. The regiment was raised by the Lieutenant of the Tower of London, Robert, Lord Lucas in February 1702, and recruited in East Anglia. The regiment carried out garrison duty at the Tower of London and the Thames estuary for a year then set out to march north, eventually reaching Carlisle Castle which became their Depot.

The regiment first saw action in Spain in the autumn of 1705 during the War of the Spanish Succession when they were in the van at the storming of Barcelona. The regiment returned to England in 1707 but again saw action against the French in 1708 under the Duke of Marlborough until 1713. On its return to England the regiment was disbanded as Britain was no longer at war but with the Jacobite and French threat again looming the regiment was reformed and saw action at Gibralter and Vigo.

At the battle of Fontenoy on the 11th May 1745, under the Duke of Cumberland, the regiment played a distinguished part in the British retreat and this action is commemorated by the laurel wreath of the regiment's badge on the colours. In April of the following year, as Cholmondley's Regiment, they were the front right of the line at Culloden, again fighting under the Duke of Cumberland's command against his cousin, Prince Charles Edward Stuart.

In 1751 the regiment became the 34th Regiment of Foot and another regiment, the 55th, was raised by Colonel George Perry. The two regiments were later to merge as one. The 34th were next in action at Minorca in 1756 and gained their first battle honour 'Havannah' in 1762 against the Spanish in the West Indies. Both regiments saw action in North America and the West Indies with the 55th returning home to England in 1785. The 34th under General John Burgoyne fought in the American War of Independence but due in part to sickness and disease and a lack of supplies were forced to surrender to a larger American force at Saratoga on the 17th October 1777. The few survivors of the regiment did not return to England until 1786 and found that during their absence the 34th had been renamed the Cumberland Regiment and the 55th the Westmoreland Regiment.

In 1794 the 55th were in action against the French in Flanders and in 1803 the Napoleonic Wars began with the 34th in India and the 55th now in the West Indies. In April 1804 the 34th formed a 2nd Battalion which took part throughout the Peninsular War and gained the battle honours 'Arroyo dos Molinos', 'Albuera', 'Vittoria', 'Pyrenees', 'Nivelle', 'Nive', 'Orthes' and 'Peninsula'. At Arroyo dos Molinos the 34th fought and defeated the French 34th Regiment of the Line, capturing the survivors together with their drums and the Drum Major's staff. These battle trophies are now in the Regimental Museum at Carlisle and are trooped annually on Arroyo Day.

After Napoleon was defeated the 2nd Battalion of the 34th was disbanded. The 55th saw action against the French in Holland in 1814 but when the war ended were posted to South Africa and then India, with the 34th seeing service in West Indies, Canada and China.

In 1854 the Crimean War began and the 55th fought at the River Alma taking heavy casualties, then at Inkerman in November 1854, where Private Thomas Beach won the Victoria Cross. The 34th arrived in the Crimea in December 1854, and together with the 55th fought until September 1855, when the war ended. Three more Victoria Crosses were won by the two regiments - one by the 55th's Major Frederick Elton, and two by the 34th's Private William Coffey and Private John Simms, all for gallantry in the face of the enemy.

The 34th next saw action in India during the Indian Mutiny where they remained until 1861. During 1879 they went to South Africa where they fought Cetewayo's Zulus at the battle of Ulundi on the 4th July 1879. The 34th, with four other British regiments totalling 5000 men, formed a hollow square and stood off 20,000 Zulus, killing over a thousand of them. The regiment was in action throughout the Boer War and took part in the Relief of Ladysmith, suffering over 200 casualties. In 1881 the 34th and the 55th regiments were amalgamated as the 1st and 2nd Battalions, Border Regiment.

During WWI the regiment fought in France and at Gallipoli taking heavy casualties of half and two thirds of their strength. During the war the regiment won five Victoria Crosses: Acting Lieutenant Colonel James Robertson, DSO., Private Abraham Acton, Private James Smith, Sergeant Edward Mott and Sergeant Charles Spackman, won the supreme honour on the battlefield. When WWII broke out in September 1939, the 1st Battalion was at Aldershot and the 2nd Battalion in India. Both battalions fought throughout the war on several fronts.

## 1ST (AIRBORNE) BATTALION, BORDER REGIMENT.

The battalion fought in France and during the period 17th to 30th May 1940, and took 250 casualties, killed wounded and taken prisoner of war. Returning to England the battalion reformed at Durham then in September 1940, moved south to the Newbury area. In October 1940, they were stationed in Suffolk on coast defence for the expected German invasion. On the 1st December 1940, the battalion was transferred to 31st Independent Brigade Group and posted to Harpenden, Hertfordshire.

In September 1941, the brigade moved to Barton Stacey, Hampshire, and became 1st Air Landing Brigade, of the 1st Airborne Division, with Lieutenant Colonel R. Bower in command of the Border Regiment. A period of hard training followed for the 1st Battalion in their new airborne role and in December 1942, Lieutenant Colonel G.V. Britten took over command of the battalion. In May 1943, they embarked for North Africa with 1st Air Landing Brigade to take part in the invasion of Sicily. Disembarking at Oran the battalion moved to Mascara and then Sousse to train on USAAF Waco CG4A gliders - there being insufficient Horsa gliders available to transport them.

On the 9th July 1943, the battalion was lifted off from Tunisia in Waco gliders and towed to Sicily in bad weather. The gliders were to be released 3000 yards offshore at 1900 feet. Reaching Sicily the glider/tug combinations met an offshore dust laden wind and heavy enemy flak. The inexperienced tug pilots caused the release of most of the gliders too far offshore and about sixty per cent came down in the sea causing heavy loss of life. Few reached their appointed LZs some were forty miles out.

Both Lieutenant Colonel Britten and his second in command, Major T. Haddon, came down in the sea and both had to swim for shore with Britten and his men under enemy fire. Some thirty men of 1st Battalion under Lieutenant Withers landed about four miles from their target the vital Ponte Grande bridge and struck out for their objective. Reaching the bridge they reinforced "D" Company, South Staffordshire Regiment, who had already taken the bridge. Holding the bridge against assault during the night and for most of the next day the defenders, reduced to only fifteen unwounded, were overrun by the enemy but the bridge was recaptured shortly afterwards by advancing ground forces. The 1st Battalion regrouped with about 150 men and reached Syracuse where north of the town they were joined by another 100 men of their battalion. A Roll Call showed that 250 men of all ranks fell into the sea in gliders - many were rescued but the battalion overall suffered about 250 casualties during the operation.

A week later 1st Air Landing Brigade was withdrawn from Sicily to North Africa where they were joined by more scattered survivors of the battalion. Major T. Haddon, second in command, was appointed to command the 1st Battalion as Lieutenant Colonel Britten was appointed to a Staff Office.

The battalion embarked in Royal Naval cruisers and landed at Taranto, Italy, as part of 1st Air Landing Brigade, after the Italian surrender in September, 1943. The brigade advanced northwards in Italy and the 1st Battalion, Border Regiment took the airfield at Foggia. In October 1943, the brigade was relieved in Italy and returned to North Africa and on the 10th December 1943, 1st Airborne

Division returned to England by sea and were stationed at Woodhall Spa, Lincolnshire, to train for the invasion of France.

1st Airborne Division was not used for Operation Overlord, the invasion of France, and on the 11th June 1944, moved to the Andover, Hampshire, area. Sixteen airborne operations were planned for Allied airborne forces but not carried out owing to the speed of the Allied ground armies advance.

On Sunday, 17th September 1944, the 1st Battalion, Border Regiment, were lifted off in their gliders under the command of Lieutenant Colonel Haddon, bound for Arnhem and a further page in their long history. The task of the battalion was to take and hold the LZs south of Arnhem on the first day to enable reinforcing troop drops to be made on the 18th and 19th September. The battalion achieved its objectives successfully after landing on the 17th but were soon in action next day defending the LZs against strong German attack. The second lift gliders came in six hours late due to fog on the English airfields but were able to land on the defended LZs. The Germans brought up strong reinforcements including tanks and by the third day the position at Arnhem had become serious for the British. A perimeter was formed around the suburb of Osterbeek with the western half of this perimeter held by what was left of the Border Regiment, Royal Engineers and Polish troops, commanded by Major C. Breese.

The 1st Battalion's Commander, Lieutenant Colonel Haddon, on the second day's lift, had one wing of his glider shot off by enemy flak and crash landed in a field near Antwerp. He made his way alone through the enemy to his beleaguered battalion and reached it on the 25th September a few hours before the evacuation. He was then taken prisoner by the Germans whilst trying to find his men. The perimeter was held until Monday, 25th September 1944, when orders to withdraw were received. That night the survivors of 1st Airborne Division withdrew across the River Rhine. Two days later they were at Nijmegan, Holland, and safety. What was left of 1st Airborne Division returned to England to reform but did not fight again. 1st Battalion, Border Regiment, now under the command of Lieutenant Colonel C.F.O. Breese, went to Norway and later to Germany as part of the Army of Occupation.

Post war the Border Regiment was reduced to one battalion - the 1st - and served in various part of the world. On the 1st October 1959, the 1st Battalion, Border Regiment was amalgamated with the 1st Battalion, King's Own Royal Regiment, to form a new regiment, the King's Own Royal Border Regiment. The long proud history of the Border Regiment, nicknamed 'The Cattle Reivers' from earliest times, had ended but the memories live on in the Regimental Museum at Queen Mary's Tower, The Castle, Carlisle, and the new regiment.

# THE STAFFORDSHIRE REGIMENT
# 38TH, 64TH, 80TH, & 98TH FOOT

The 38th is reputed to have been first raised on the 13th February 1702, by Colonel Luke Lillingstone, but other records show April 1705. In 1706 the regiment was sent to Antigua and stayed there for the next sixty years with many of the soldiers dying of tropical diseases. During their sixty year posting no new uniforms were issued and their uniforms were refurbished with cheap brown holland cloth, a piece of which was worn behind the regiment's cap badge.

In 1751 the regiment became the 38th Regiment of Foot and in 1782 was named the 1st Staffordshire Regiment of Foot. In 1881 it merged with the 80th Regiment of Foot to become 1st Battalion, The South Staffordshire Regiment. In 1959 it merged with the North Staffordshire Regiment to form the Staffordshire Regiment (Prince of Wales).

The 64th was raised in 1756 as a second battalion of the 11th Foot (Devonshire Regiment) but became the 64th Regiment of Foot in 1758 and the 2nd Staffordshire Regiment in 1782. The 64th served in India during the Indian Mutiny and took part in General Havelock's first Relief of Lucknow. In 1881 it merged with the 98th Regiment to become the 1st Battalion, North Staffordshire (Prince of Wales's) Regiment and in 1920 became the North Staffordshire Regiment (Prince of Wales's). In 1959 the regiment merged with the South Staffordshire Regiment to become the Staffordshire Regiment (Prince of Wales's).

The 80th was raised in 1793 by Lord Paget at Chatham and was known as the 80th (Staffordshire Volunteers) Regiment of Foot. It served in South Africa during the Zulu War and at Ulundi on the 4th July 1879, with four other regiments, formed the right wall, four ranks deep, of a hollow square to beat off attacks by 20,000 Zulu warriors. Two Victoria Crosses were won during the Zulu War; Private S. Wassal and Colour Sergeant A. Booth, both awards for gallantry in action. In 1881 the regiment merged with the 38th Regiment of Foot to become the 2nd Battalion, South Staffordshire Regiment.

The 98th Regiment of Foot was raised in 1824 and was the sixth regiment to bear the title '98th'. In 1876 the regiment became the 98th (Prince of Wales's) Regiment of Foot and in 1881 merged with the 64th Regiment to become the 2nd Battalion, North Staffordshire Regiment (Prince of Wales's). Both Staffordshire Regiments wore almost identical badges - the Stafford Knot, the armourial crest of Lord Stafford - with the South Staffords' knot surmounted by a crown and the North Staffords' by the Prince of Wales's Feathers.

During WWI the South Staffords expanded to seventeen battalions with the 2nd Battalion being the first to see action at the first Battle of Mons. The regiment fought throughout the war on several fronts: France, Gallipoli, Mesopotamia and in the Caucasus. Seven members of the regiment were awarded the Victoria Cross:

| | |
|---|---|
| Captain J.F. Vallentin. | Ypres. |
| Captain A.F.G. Kilby. | Loos. |
| Lt. Col. E.E.D. Henderson. | Mesopotamia. |
| Private T. Barratt. | Ypres. |
| Sergeant J. Carmichael. | Ypres. |
| Lance Corporal J. Thomas. | Cambrai. |
| Lance Corporal W.H. Coltman. | Sequehart (France). |

Between 1919 and 1939 battalions of the regiment saw service and action in India, Greece, Ireland and Palestine.

## 2ND (AIRBORNE) BATTALION, SOUTH STAFFORDSHIRE REGIMENT.

On the 10th October 1941, the 2nd Battalion was part of 1st Air Landing Brigade Group, 1st Airborne Division, stationed in the Harpenden, Hertfordshire area. Two months later on the 10th December, Brigadier G.F. Hopkinson was appointed Commander. During 1942 the Brigade Group was renamed 1st Air Landing Brigade. By March 1943, the enemy had been cleared from North Africa and the next step was the invasion of Sicily. 1st Air Landing Brigade, consisting of the 2nd South Staffords and the 1st Border Regiment, had not seen action and were brought out from England by sea for the invasion. The coup de main task of the 2nd South Staffords, carried in five Horsa gliders, was to capture the vital Ponte Grande and railway bridges south of Syracuse supported by the Border Regiment.

On the evening of the 9th July 1943, the 2nd Battalion, under the command of Lieutenant Colonel W.D.H. McCardie, were towed off in their gliders from Tunisia and, in bad visibility and amidst enemy flak, reached the Sicily area. Many of the glider pilots were forced to cast off too soon and too far offshore by inexperienced tug pilots and ditched in the sea, some being lost without trace with loss of life. Very few gliders reached their appointed LZs.
The glider carrying Lieutenant Colonel McCardie came down in the sea and he and his men had to swim ashore, the Colonel dressed only in his pants.

Only two out of the five planned Horsa gliders made the Ponte Grande bridge area but one, carrying C Company commanded by Major George Ballinger, blew up killing most of the occupants which left the capture of the bridge to the other Horsa occupants, a platoon of D Company under Lieutenant Withers. The Horsa landed close to the bridge which was stormed, taken, and the demolition charges removed by the South Staffords. The railway bridge was also taken and held. The small party of South Staffords prepared to defend their capture against enemy counter attack and were reinforced by more men from the South Staffords and some from the Border Regiment, so that the defenders totalled some eighty officers and men. For fourteen hours the defenders fought off the enemy until they ran out of ammunition and were overrun and the bridge retaken by the enemy. But three quarters of an hour later the bridge was recaptured by sea landed advancing ground forces before the enemy could blow it.

The South Staffords were awarded three Military Crosses and five Military Medals for the capture and defence of the Ponte grande bridge. Lieutenant Withers was one of the MC winners although he had been recommended for the DSO. The South Staffords had gone into the battle with a strength of 800 men; they took 350 casualties. The Sicily operation gave the South Staffords a rare distinction - it made them the first regiment ever to go into battle by land, sea and air, the regiment having fought at sea in Royal Naval ships during the reign of Queen Anne.

On the 13th July the South Staffords returned by sea to Sousse in Tunisia and for the next few weeks reorganised and gathered together more survivors from the regiment. On the 12th September the battalion moved to Bizerta to travel by sea to Italy. The battalion followed the retreating Germans and took the town of Foggia on the 27th September. Relieved on the 1st October they moved to Brindisi on the 13th leaving there on the 31st October for Taranto then returning to England on the 18th November.

The South Staffords had returned to England as part of 1st Air Landing Brigade but did not go into action again until a year later at Arnhem on the 17th September 1944, commanded by Lieutenant Colonel McCardie. The task of the South Staffords in the first air lift of three was to take and defend the LZs for the next two air lifts during the succeeding two days. The 1st gliderborne air lift of South Staffords comprised Battalion Headquarters, B and D Companies, together with a platoon each of mortars and machine-guns. All but two gliders reached the LZs, one carrying Major Cain, OC B Company, broke its tow rope over Kent and the other carrying a platoon of B Company came down in enemy territory. The South Staffords landed under machine-gun fire which was quickly silenced and then dug in for the night.

Next day, the 18th September, the South Staffords were ordered to try to get through to the hard pressed troops at Arnhem bridge and moved off at 1030 hours. Immediately the South Staffords came under German air attack and sniper fire. Passing through Oosterbeek the troops came under heavy machine-gun and sniper fire but eventually reached the outskirts of Arnhem and made contact with 1st Parachute Battalion which was depleted to about seventy men.

The second gliderborne air lift of South Staffords lifted off from RAF Broadwell at 1030 hours on the 18th September under the second in command Major J.C. Commings; Major Cain lifted off in another glider. All were down safely by 1530 hours but came under enemy fire at once. The second lift South Staffords moved off towards Arnhem and at once came under sniper fire and fixed line machine-gun fire and reached the outskirts of Arnhem at 0530 hours on the 19th and joined 11th Parachute Battalion.

Heavy fighting took place on the 19th and the South Staffords took severe casualties. D Company taking forty per cent losses. Battalion Headquarters was overrun and the CO and second in command were wounded and taken prisoner. Major Cain assumed command of what was left of the Staffords and was forced to withdraw his men in the face of attacking SS Panzers (tanks). A defensive perimeter was formed around the suburb of Oosterbeek and the Staffords established positions to the west of it.

SS Panzers attacked the Staffords who knocked out five of them with their 6-pounder guns. One section commanded by Lance Sergeant Baskeyfield knocked out two Panzers and one self-propelled gun. Baskeyfield himself was badly wounded and the rest of his gun crew killed but he refused to be relieved of his position. The Germans attacked again but were driven off by Baskeyfield, manning his gun alone. The gun was put out of action by enemy fire but Baskeyfield, badly wounded, crawled to another gun whose crew were dead, and fired two more rounds knocking out a self-propelled gun. As he reloaded his gun to fire again, however, he was killed. So died a gallant soldier who was awarded a posthumous Victoria Cross.

The Germans attacked continuously for the next four days and gradually reduced the defensive positions. Major Cain took on a Tiger tank single handed with a PIAT (Projecter Infantry Anti-Tank) and knocked it out. Even after severe concussion he refused to leave his men and when the PIAT ammunition ran out engaged the German tanks with a two inch mortar fired horizontally. He also was awarded the Victoria Cross. Warrant Officer II Class Robinson was awarded the Military Cross for gallantry; Lieutenant Edwards also received a Military Cross and Private Holt the Military Medal.

At 22.00 hours on the 25th September, the order to withdraw commenced and the Staffords began to fall back with honour to the River Rhine. The South Staffords had gone to the battle with 47 officers and 820 other ranks. Only 6 officers and 133 other ranks came back over the Rhine. Further lustre was added to the regiment's history by the fact that they had won two Victoria Crosses in one battle, the only battalion so to do in WWII.

Further recognition came in 1946 when King George VI awarded the 2nd Battalion, the South Staffordshire Regiment, the right for all ranks to wear an embroidered glider badge at the top of the sleeve in battledress and Number 1 Dress. The battalion also won for the regiment the battle honours 'Landing in Sicily' and 'Sicily'.

In 1959 the South Staffordshire Regiment amalgamated with the North Staffordshire Regiment to form the Staffordshire Regiment (The Prince of Wales's).

# THE OXFORDSHIRE AND BUCKINGHAMSHIRE LIGHT INFANTRY REGIMENT, 43rd & 52nd

The 43rd was raised by Colonel Thomas Fowke in 1741 and known as Fowke's Regiment until 1751 when it became the 43rd Regiment of Foot. In 1782 it became the 43rd (Monmouth) Regiment of Foot and in 1803 the 43rd (Monmouthshire Light Infantry) Regiment. During 1881 it merged with the 52nd and became the 1st Battalion, Oxfordshire Light Infantry until 1908 when it was named the Oxfordshire and Buckinghamshire Light Infantry.

During the wars against the French in North America in the 1750s it was found that the British soldier's dress and tactics were unsuited for the terrain and type of warfare and General Wolfe decided to adapt some of his troops to a light infantry role, troops who could march and move faster than ordinary infantry. Part of the 43rd was chosen for the new role which proved to be such a success that a light infantry company was incorporated in each regiment. Later on, whole regiments were converted to light infantry.

In 1808 the 43rd and 52nd, as part of Sir John Moore's Light Brigade, took part in the Peninsular War, serving in the Light Division where they acquired the nickname 'The Light Bobs', winning the battle honours 'Vimeiro', 'Corunna', 'Busaco', 'Fuentes de Oñoro', 'Cuidad Rodrigo', 'Badajos', 'Salamanca', 'Vittoria', 'Pyrenees', 'Nivelle', 'Nive', 'Orthes', 'Toulouse' and 'Peninsula'. At the storming of the fortress of Badajos on the 6th April 1812, the 43rd suffered tremendous casualties. Lieutenant Shaw of the 43rd, at the head of fifty men found himself the only one alive, his men mown down by cannon fire.

In February 1852, the 43rd and the 91st Highlanders were bound for South Africa aboard the troopship 'Birkenhead' when she struck a rock off Simonstown. The soldiers wives and children aboard were put into the ship's lifeboats but there were none for the soldiers. The order to abandon ship was given by the ship's captain but the men stood in disciplined ranks awaiting orders. Lieutenant Giradot of the 43rd and Captain Wright of the 91st asked the soldiers to stand firm as the launched lifeboats were already overloaded. The two regiments stood in ranks until the ship sank under them, not one man moved. 454 soldiers perished.

The 52nd was raised in 1755 by Colonel Hedworth Lambton and was originally numbered the 54th. In 1757 it became the 52nd Regiment of Foot and in 1782 the 52nd (Oxfordshire) Regiment of Foot. During 1803 it was renamed the 52nd (Oxfordshire Light Infantry) Regiment and in 1881 it merged with the 43rd and became the 2nd Battalion, Oxfordshire Light Infantry.

Colonel Sir John Colborne they abandoned their defensive positions and advanced two deep against two columns of Napoleon's best troops, the Imperial Guard, led by Marshal Ney. The 52nd made a bayonet charge and routed one column of the Moyenne Guard, the other column being routed by the Brigade of Guards. These bayonet charges completed the defeat of the French and Waterloo was won.

During the Indian Mutiny the 52nd was in India and at the siege of Delhi on the 14th September 1857, 240 men of the 52nd under Colonel Colin Campbell were preparing to storm the Kashmir Gate. Bugler Hawthorn of the 52nd was with the demolition party which was laying explosives under fire to effect a breach. Most of the sappers were killed or wounded and Bugler Hawthorn attended them under fire. As the explosives were detonated Bugler Hawthorn sounded the 52nd regimental call and the 'Advance', whereupon the 52nd stormed through the breach and into the city. Bugler Hawthorn won the Victoria Cross and a commemorative plaque was placed on the central pillar of the Gate.

During WWI the regiment was in France and Italy and took part in the battles of Cambrai, the Somme, and Ypres as part of 48th South Midland Division. Two Victoria Crosses were won, by CSM Edward Brooks and and Lance Corporal Alfred Wilcox. In 1940 the regiment went to France with the British Expeditionary Force and suffered heavy casualties at St. Omer la Bassee then returned to England to reform and refit.

## 2ND (AIRBORNE) BATTALION, OXFORDSHIRE & BUCKINGHAMSHIRE LIGHT INFANTRY, (52ND).

In October 1941, the 2nd Battalion became part of 1st Air Landing Brigade, 1st Airborne Division, and at the end of the year were stationed at Basingstoke, Hampshire, under the command of Lieutenant Colonel L.W. Giles MC. The airborne beret was adopted and the shoulder flash 'Fifty Second' in regimental colours was worn. On the 9th April 1942, the regiment left Basingstoke for Bulford Camp, Wiltshire, to join 1st Airborne Division quartered there.

On the 4th June Lieutenant Colonel T.G.D. Rowley took command of the regiment which was then re-organised on the new air landing battalion system based on the carrying capacity of the Horsa glider. The regiment engaged in glider training and exercises and seven men were killed on the 26th November at Netheravon when their Hotspur glider spun in after cast off. In December the shoulder title 'Oxf Bucks' was adopted instead of the prized 'Fifty Second' flash.

In March 1943, the regiment was warned for overseas duty (the invasion of Sicily) but owing to a shortage of aircraft and gliders only the South Staffords and Border Regiment went overseas. The Oxford & Bucks were transferred to the newly formed 6th Air Landing Brigade, 6th Airborne Division, and on the 15th December Lieutenant Colonel M.W. Roberts took command of the regiment. For the next few months the regiment trained hard for the invasion of France taking part in ever bigger exercises. From the 25th to 27th March Exercise 'Bizz II' was held when the whole regiment apart from D Company was airlifted in gliders.

On the 2nd May 1944, Major J.Howard, commanding D Company was ordered to effect a plan for the capture by coup de main glider assault on the Caen Canal and River Orne bridges in Normandy in the first part of the invasion of France. On the 25th-26th May, the regiment moved to its take off airfields for the invasion of France: the main body of the regiment under the commanding officer, to RAF Harwell, Berkshire, and the six platoons of the coup de main party under Major Howard, to RAF Tarrant Rushton, Dorset. They were then sealed in the camps until D-Day, 5th-6th June 1944.

At 22.56 hours on 5th June, the six Horsa gliders carrying the coup de main party took off from Tarrant Rushton and at 0016 hours the first of five (one was mistowed by the RAF) Horsa gliders was down on target. The two vital bridges were swiftly taken and held in a spirited action by the coup de main party. Casualties to the coup de main party were one officer killed and two wounded, one soldier killed and twelve wounded. At 0300 hours 7th Parachute Battalion arrived at the bridges and the coup de main party came under their command. The position was held against enemy counter attacks. At noon the sea landed Commandos arrived but the bridge battle continued until 2000 hours. At 2115 hours the position was relieved by the arrival of the 185th Infantry Brigade.

On the afternoon of D-Day the main body of the Oxford & Bucks was airlifted in Horsa gliders from England (Operation Mallard) to occupy the southern flank of 6th Airborne Division's perimeter. The gliders landed successfully and the regiment moved out to its positions east of the Orne River. The regiment went into action and advanced to the River Seine then on the 31st August, began to pull out from the line. On the 2nd September it was back at Bulford Camp. After leave the regiment re-organised and was brought up to strength with replacement troops. Lieutenant Colonel M. Darrel Brown DSO, took command when Lieutenant Colonel Roberts went to Headquarters, 6th Airborne Division Staff.

At Christmas 1944 the regiment was rushed to France to help stem the German offensive through the Ardennes. On Christmas Day they were in position at Givet alongside the US 507th Parachute troops. On the 30th December the regiment handed over its positions to the 12th Parachute Battalion and on the 2nd January 1945, went into reserve at Custinne with C Company detached to Bure to support 13th Parachute Battalion. C Company lost five soldiers killed and one officer and twelve soldiers wounded. On the 21st February the regiment was relieved and arrived back at Bulford on the 28th February.

Early in March the regiment took part in large scale divisional exercises in Suffolk, 'Mush I & II ', which were rehearsals for the next air landing operation, 'Varsity', the crossing of the River Rhine. At 0630 hours on the 24th March, the regiment, carried in Horsa gliders, was towed off from RAF Birch and Gosfield and headed for Germany, their mission to take and hold by coup de main assault the road bridge over the River Issel, a railway bridge two hundred yards north from it, Hamminkeln railway station and a road junction to the west of it.

At 1000 hours they were approaching the battlefield which was shrouded in smoke - the 'fog of war'. Amid heavy German flak the gliders cast off and began to land - many tug and gliders were hit and the regiment lost about half its strength. One glider with its pilots dead at the controls was landed safely by Lieutenant Quartermaster W. Aldworth who had had no flying instruction. Within ten minutes all the gliders were down: despite the heavy casualties the regiment had secured its objectives by 1100 hours in a hard fought confused situation. Sporadic fighting continued all day with the enemy attacking with tanks but the regiment held its positions intact. At dawn next day the regiment's strength was 216 all ranks - less than half strength. Four hundred casualties having been taken. At dusk the forward elements of the ground forces - the 52 Lowland Division - began to arrive and relieve the regiment and by 0200 hours on the 26th March the regiment was relieved and moved to Hamminkeln for rest.

By 1100 hours the same day the regiment was back into action and advanced eastwards into Germany. Fighting several actions they arrived at the Dortmund Ems canal on the 1st April; six hours later the regiment was across and engaged against the enemy losing several men killed and wounded. On the 3rd April the regiment moved towards the River Weser having covered some 105 miles on the march since the 26th and on the 5th April crossed the river under fire, the first British troops so to do. The regiment continued its fighting advance until it reached Bad Kleinen near Wismar as the war in Europe ended on the 8th May.

On the 17th May the regiment began the move back to England and by the 20th May they were back at Bulford. Fourteen days leave was given with another fourteen days for those who were going to the Far East but WWII ended in August 1945. 6th Airborne Division became part of the Strategic Reserve and was sent to Palestine. 6th Air Landing Brigade being stationed at Samaria. Later the brigade was renamed 31st Infantry Brigade and ended its airborne role. In April 1948, 6th Airborne Division returned to England and was disbanded. In 1958 the regiment became 1st Green Jackets (43rd & 52nd) and in 1966 merged with the 2nd and 3rd Green Jackets to form the Royal Green Jackets.

# ROYAL ULSTER RIFLES

The regiment can be traced back to 1793 when the 83rd and 86th Regiments of Foot were raised during the war with France. With the Antrim, Down and Louth Regiments of Militia, which were raised about the same time, all became part of the Royal Irish Rifles and then later the Royal Ulster Rifles.

The 83rd Regiment was raised in Dublin by Colonel William Fitch and saw many years service in the West Indies where many soldiers died from the endemic yellow fever there. The 86th Regiment was originally raised in Shropshire by General Cornelius Cuyler and were know as 'Cuyler's Shropshire Volunteers'. Recruiting was slow and when the regiment moved to Ireland they changed their main recruiting area to Leinster and became known as the 'Irish Giants'. On one occasion two officers sat for the Loyal Toast - they were so tall there was no room for them to stand.

The 86th saw active service as Marines and were involved in actions against the French. A detachment of six companies accompanied an expedition to Egypt and carried out an epic march from Suez to Cairo, a distance of ninety miles in three days under a blazing sun. There were no provisions and little water. The soldiers wore heavy scarlet uniform jackets as they had no tropical kit. The detachment completed the march with only seventeen stragglers of whom eight died. The campaign resulted in the defeat of the French in Egypt and by Royal decree the emblem of the Sphinx inscribed 'Egypt' was added to the crest of the 86th Regiment.

The 83rd Regiment returned to Ireland and raised a 2nd battalion as the British Army was expanding due to the Napoleonic Wars. In 1805 the 1st Battalion 83rd Regiment, landed at Cape Town, South Africa, overcame the local armed resistance and remained in garrison at the Cape of Good Hope until 1818.

The 2nd Battalion 83rd Regiment, went to Portugal in 1809 as part of the Peninsular Expeditionary Force and remained there for five years on campaign in Spain, Portugal and France, gaining twelve battle honours.

They took part in the battle of Talavera where they suffered casualties of over half their strength including their colonel killed. Many were taken prisoner and remained in captivity for five years. Sergeant Major Swinburne was commissioned in the field for gallantry and eventually retired some forty four years later as a lieutenant colonel. A descendant, Major D. Swinburne (later Colonel) served in the regiment as a company commander in 1934.

The 83rd then took part in the battle of Busaco in 1810, the storming of the fortresses of Ciudad Rodrigo and Badajos in 1812, where Sergeant Hazelhurst saved the life of Captain Powys, the first man through the breach, by slashing about him with his sergeant's halberd. Sergeant Hazelhurst served through the Peninsular campaign being awarded twelve battle clasps to his Peninsular Medal. The action at Fuentes de Oñoro (referred to by the soldiers as the Fountains of Horror) was followed by the regiment winning the battle honours of 'Salamanca', 'Vittoria', 'Pyrenees', 'Nivelle', 'Orthez' and 'Toulouse'.

In 1810 the 86th Regiment formed part of a task force sent from India to take the French island of Bourbon (Reunion). During the landing assault in the face of heavy fire from musket and cannon the redoubt covering the landing beach was taken with the bayonet. The halyards of the flag staff had been shot away but Corporal Hall climbed the flagstaff and fixed to it the King's Colour of the regiment. Even the French enemy were impressed with his gallantry and cheered lustily. The island was soon taken. The island's name, Bourbon, was awarded to the regiment as a battle honour together with 'India' in recognition of the regiment's actions in the Mahratta Wars there.

Both the 83rd and the 86th Regiments served from 1819 to 1857 on garrison duty mainly in England and Ireland, but also abroad in Ceylon, Canada and India. Records of the time describe the 83rd Regiment as 'a regiment of 950 efficient soldiers strong and stalwart in form, perfect in discipline and influenced in no ordinary degree by an ardent esprit de corps'. It is also recorded that in 1832 the motto 'Quis Separabit' was adopted by the 86th Regiment and they marched to the tune 'The Kinnegar Slashers' and later to 'St. Patrick's Day'. The 83rd Regiment marched to the tune 'Garry Owen'.

At the outbreak of the Indian Mutiny in 1857 both the 83rd and the 86th Regiments were stationed in India. At the outset they had to fight desperately to hold their own but by the end of 1857 reinforcements began to arrive and mobile forces were formed to capture the mutineers. Many actions were fought all over Rajputana and central India with the most notable being the siege of the fortress of Jhansi, which was defended by 11,000 rebels under a woman leader, the Rani. The British artillery made a breach in the wall of the fortress but before this situation could be exploited a relieving rebel force under the rebel leader Tantia Tope arrived on the scene with 22,000 men and 28 field guns. The British commander, Sir High Rose, decided to deal with Tope and continue the siege of Jhansi at the same time with a force of 1500 troops of whom some 500 were British. In spite of being heavily outnumbered by fifteen to one, the rebel force was at once attacked by a detachment of the 86th Regiment led by Lieutenant Cochrane, who had three horses killed under him, and routed the rebels capturing their artillery.

The siege of Jhansi was renewed and the assaulting troops surmounted the fortress walls with ladders in the face of intense rebel fire of red hot cannon balls and rockets. A ferocious struggle ensued with heavy casualties but the attackers, under Lieutenant Jerome, took the enemy in the flanks and they retired to an inner fort. The fighting went on for a day and a night until an entry was made into the Rani's palace where the attackers engaged her bodyguard in hand to hand fighting. The whole city was taken and the Rani fled. For this action the Victoria Cross, instituted in 1856, was awarded to Lieutenants Cochrane and Jerome and Privates Byrne and Person, all of the 86th Regiment.

The next main event in the regiment's history was the formation in 1881 of the Royal Irish Rifles. The 1st Battalion from the 83rd Regiment, the 2nd Battalion from the 86th Regiment, and the 3rd, 4th, 5th and 6th Battalions from the North Down, Antrim, South Down and Louth Regiments respectively.

Many changes of dress, title, organisation and equipment followed but the greatest of all was the conversion to a Rifle regiment, which was regarded as a signal honour. Both battalions quickly adopted their new role of Riflemen and acquired the characteristics thereof - the alertness, the swift purposeful movement and the exceptional skill at arms.

The Regimental March of the 83rd Regiment, 'Off Said The Stranger', was adopted as the Regimental March of the new regiment. (In 1937 the Durham Light Infantry who used the same tune, relieved 1st Royal Ulster Rifles in Shanghai and the change over took place on the race course when both regiments marched from opposite ends to the same tune.)

No abridged history can do justice to the heroism and selfless devotion to duty displayed by the Royal Irish Rifles in WWI. The 2nd Battalion, as part of the British Expeditionary Force, fought at Mons and in the retreat, then in the later battles of the Marne and Aisne before moving north to Flanders. There in the words of the song, 'Side by side they fought and died as only heroes can, and yez all knows well that Neuve Chapelle was won by an Irishman'.

In the trench war that followed the 1st and 2nd Battalions fought throughout the war, losing many times their strength in casualties. The 6th Battalion formed part of the 10th (Irish) Division and fought at Gallipoli, Macedonia and Palestine. Fifteen more battalions of the Royal Irish Rifles were formed, all but one of which fought on the Western Front (France), mostly in the immortal 36th (Ulster) Division, which suffered so grievously on the Somme but fought on till the end of the war. (The father of Lieutenant Colonel T.B.H. Otway, DSO, of the epic Merville battery assault in 1944, served as a commanding officer in a Royal Engineers Squadron, with 36th Division).

In 1922 the Royal Irish Rifles became the Royal Ulster Rifles - this identified the regiment with the Loyal Province with which it had so long been associated. During 1937 the London Irish Rifles, formed in 1859 as a 'Corps of

Irish Gentlemen at Arms', joined the regiment. The LIR had been a Volunteer Corps and had fought in South Africa, then throughout WWI as part of the London regiment. There had often been contact between the two regiments and they were now welcomed in the Corps of the Royal Ulster Rifles as a Territorial Battalion.

In 1937 the 1st Battalion Royal Ulster Rifles, were in Shanghai, China, where during August to November they came under Japanese shell fire for most of the time, in the hostilities between Japan and China. The outbreak of WWII on the 3rd September 1939, found the 1st Battalion at Razani, on the north west frontier of India fighting the Pathan tribesmen. Lieutenant (later Colonel) B.J. Fitz Donlea, won the Military Cross on a Punitive Expedition against the Pathans. The battalion suffered casualties during its service both in China and India.

On the outbreak of WWII the 2nd Battalion moved to France as part of the British Expeditionary Force and fought back through Dunkirk. The 1st Battalion embarked for England from India on the troopship SS Karanja and when en route a severe fire broke out in the after hold. A volunteer fire fighting party under Captain T.B.H. Otway managed to get the fire under control in four hours. It was found that the fire was deliberate, having been started by incendiary bombs placed by dock workers in Bombay.

On arrival back in England the battalion stood by to defend the beaches as did the 1st and 2nd Battalions of the London Irish which had been embodied on the outbreak of WWII. The 2nd London Irish were the next unit of the regiment to see action, fighting several bloody battles as part of the Irish Brigade in Tunisia. In the invasion of Sicily they were joined by the 1st London Irish who had come the long way round, Africa through Persia and Egypt, as part of the 56th London Division. Both battalions crossed to Italy and fought their way up through the mountains for eighteen months until taking part in the final attacks across the River Po and into Austria.

## 1ST (AIRBORNE BATTALION), ROYAL ULSTER RIFLES.

In December 1940, the battalion was informed of an intended airborne role and Captain T.B.H. Otway was promoted Major and transferred to command 31st Independent Light Armoured Reconnaissance Squadron, with instructions to turn it into an air landing glider borne Reconnaissance Squadron. (There were no gliders available at this time - the War Office was planning ahead).

In November 1941, the 1st Battalion became an air landing unit becoming part of 1st Air Landing Brigade. However in May, 1943, the battalion was transferred to 6th Air Landing Brigade of 6th Airborne Division, at Bulford,

Wiltshire. By June 1943, they were part of 21st Army Group preparing for the invasion of France in 1944. 1st Battalion as a glider borne battalion in 6th Airborne Division and 2nd Battalion within 3rd Division, which was to assault across the beaches.

Both battalions were in action on D-Day, the 6th June 1944, the 2nd Battalion landing from the sea on Sword Beach and the 1st Battalion landing in strength by glider on the evening of D-Day (Operation Mallard). Both battalions were continually in action until the Battle of Normandy was won. The 2nd Battalion fought on through France and Belgium into Holland. The 1st Battalion, as airborne troops, were withdrawn to England to prepare for the next airborne operation but with 6th Airborne Division were called in to 'plug the gap' created by the German offensive through the Ardennes at Christmas 1944.

On the 24th March 1945, the 1st Battalion landed by glider across the River Rhine (Operation Varsity) and secured their objectives. Together with 2nd Battalion they fought on into Germany until the Germans surrendered on the 8th May 1945. In August 1945, the regiment left 6th Air Landing Brigade.

In the immediate post war period both battalions served in Palestine until returning in 1948 to amalgamate as 1st Battalion, The Royal Ulster Rifles, (83rd and 86th). The regiment fought for a year in Korea, for two and a half years in Cyprus and also for nine months in Borneo, as well as normal duty tours in Germany and the Strategic Reserve at home.

Finally in 1968 the Royal Ulster Rifles amalgamated with the Royal Inniskilling Fusiliers and the Royal Irish Fusiliers to form the Royal Irish Rangers, thus preserving the future of the Irish Regiments. 'Quis Separabit'.

# THE GLIDER PILOT REGIMENT

In 1940 Major John Frank Rock was given given the task of organising Britain's non-existent Airborne Forces in the wake of the evacuation from Europe of British Forces. Starting from scratch and with nothing but the example of the German Airborne Forces to guide him, Rock had by 1941 created a plan for British Airborne Forces. As rather more than half of the proposed Airborne Forces were to be carried to battle in gliders, volunteers were sought from the Army and RAF for the raising of a special regiment which would fly the military gliders then fight on the ground as soldiers.

Aptly named the Glider Pilot Regiment, it was formed on the 21st December 1941, and had a projected establishment of two battalions of six companies of NCO glider pilots. A Regimental Training Depot would be established for military training and flying training on light aircraft would be given by RAF Instructors at Elementary Flying Training Schools (EFTS) before glider pilot training began. The now Lieutenant Colonel Rock was appointed Commanding Officer of the 1st Battalion of the regiment and together with forty officers and other ranks was sent to an RAF Elementary Flying School at Derby on the 2nd January 1942, to learn how to fly.

The RAF elementary flying course for Army glider pilots would be the same as for RAF pilots - ab initio training - including navigation, meteorology, night and day take offs and landings, cross country flights and a level of aerobatics.

It had been decided that the large Horsa and Hamilcar gliders would need two glider pilots so flying training was varied. The 1st Pilot was to be a staff sergeant and would undergo an eight week EFTS Course of some 55 hours to be followed by another eight weeks at a Glider Training School (GTS) of about 47 hours. After completing the course successfully, another four weeks with about 14 hours flying time, would be spent converting from the smaller Hotspur gliders used at the Glider Training Schools, to the larger Horsa and Hamilcar gliders.
The 2nd Pilot with the rank of sergeant, would have a shorter flying course as his job would be to fly the glider on tow leaving the take off and landing to the 1st Pilot but given enough training to enable him to land the glider in emergency if anything happened to the 1st Pilot. His course at EFTS would be four weeks with some 20 hours of flying followed by four weeks at a GTS.

The flying brevets of the 1st and 2nd Pilots differed. The 1st Pilot wore a brevet of a Lion over a Crown between two outstretched wings which was introduced on the 11th April 1942. The 2nd Pilot's brevet, introduced later, was a letter G between two outstretched wings.

Responding to the call for volunteers were thousands of personnel among whom was Major (later Brigadier) George Chatterton, who had been an RAF pilot with No.1 Squadron but had suffered injuries in a flying accident which had taken him off flying duties, then retirement to the Reserve of Air Force Officers. When WWII broke out Chatterton was recalled to the RAF but posted to ground duties. Not relishing a non-combat role he transferred to the 5th Battalion, Queens Regiment, the Royal West Surreys, as a Lieutenant, then after service in France he was promoted Major. Many soldiers volunteered for the regiment but very few were accepted. Many more were weeded out by the qualifying tests and the military training which followed. The end result was a regiment of a very high standard - a regiment of sergeants.

Major Chatterton, after an interview with Major General Browning, commanding 1st Airborne Division, was appointed second in command to Lieutenant Colonel Rock and posted to Tilshead on Salisbury Plain, which was to be the Training Depot of the Glider Pilot Regiment. Tilshead Camp was situated on the edge of West Down Artillery Range eight miles west of RAF Netheravon across the bleak inhospitable Salisbury Plain. On arrival there Chatterton found old empty wooden huts with no facilities whatever and very little staff. He was informed that a first batch of soldiers would be arriving in three weeks for military training before being sent to an EFTS for flying training.

With Colonel Rock at Derby learning to fly it fell to Chatterton to organise the military training for the incoming soldiers. He decided that he must create what he called the 'Total Soldier', a soldier who would be both a highly trained glider pilot and disciplined fighting soldier. Such men would form a regiment imbued with *esprit de corps*; there was always competition to join a highly disciplined elite regiment. The new Glider Pilot Regiment had no history to fall back on therefore a sense of pride and belonging would have to be created.

An interview with General Browning, with a request for Instructors from the Brigade of Guards, was made by Chatterton and shortly afterwards two Company Sergeant Majors (CSMs) arrived at Tilshead. CSM Briody of the Irish Guards and CSM Cowlie of the Coldstream Guards when interviewed by Chatterton were told of his plans to create the 'Total Soldier'. The sergeant majors were asked to instil into the men of the new regiment the standards of the Guards on the parade ground and the barrack hut. Only the highest standard of bearing and discipline would be tolerated.

When the first batch of volunteers arrived they were gathered together in the NAAFI and addressed by Chatterton. They were told that they were the first volunteers to form the Glider Pilot Regiment and of his plans to create the 'Total Soldier', a man who could pilot a glider, master all infantry weapons, drive jeeps and trucks, use radio sets; in short there would be nothing that they would not be trained to do. They must instil in themselves the highest form of discipline and esprit de corps. Discipline would be in the hands of Sergeant Majors Briody and Cowlie of the Brigade of Guards. If any volunteer did not like this he could return whence he came.

Many remained and went on to flying training at Royal Air Force EFTS and slowly the Glider Pilot Regiment began to take shape as the soldier trainees began to qualify as pilots. As the strength of the regiment built up the 2nd Battalion, the Glider Pilot Regiment was formed with the now Lieutenant Colonel Chatterton in command. Tragically Lieutenant Colonel Rock died as the result of injuries received in a night flying accident in a Hotspur glider and Chatterton was transferred to command 1st Battalion, Glider Pilot Regiment, and Lieutenant Colonel Iain Murray assumed command of 2nd Battalion of the regiment.

On the 19th November 1942, the Glider Pilot Regiment went to war in gliders for the first time. Two Horsa gliders carrying men of the Royal Engineers were towed by two Halifax tugs from RAF Skitten in Caithness, Scotland, to raid and destroy a plant at Rjukan in southern Norway, where it was thought the Germans were producing heavy water for their atomic bomb research programme. One Horsa was flown by Staff Sergeant M.F.C. Strathdee and Sergeant P. Doig of the Glider Pilot Regiment, the other Horsa by two pilots from the Royal Australian Air Force, Pilot Officer N.A. Davies and Pilot Officer H.J. Fraser. Both Horsa gliders and one Halifax tug crashed in Norway - those gallant men who survived were later murdered by the Germans, under Hitler's infamous order that all Commandos captured were to be executed at once.

Early in 1943 1st Airborne Division was posted to North Africa with Major General Hopkinson commanding, to prepare for the forthcoming invasion of Sicily. Lieutenant Colonel Chatterton was ordered to detail two companies of glider pilots to accompany the division with the rest of his battalion to follow later. All to go by sea to Oran. Chatterton was dismayed as his pilots had but about eight hours flying time in due to lack of tug aircraft to tow the gliders on training in England. Chatterton detailed his second-in-command, Major M. Willoughby, to command the first two companies but General Hopkinson insisted that Chatterton command the two companies.

On arrival in North Africa Lieutenant Colonel Chatterton went to Algiers to confer with US Colonel Dunne, whose USAAF Wing were to train and tow the British glider pilots in US gliders.

On 1st April 1943, Chatterton saw General Hopkinson in Algiers and was told that it had been decided to land 1st Air Landing Brigade by moonlight in Sicily. When shown photographs of the intended LZs Chatterton was aghast - they were strewn with rocks and the fields had stone walls, both deadly to a wooden glider especially at night. He demurred but Hopkinson was adamant, 1st Air Landing Brigade would land by glider on the LZs. Hopkinson gave Chatterton half an hour to consider his position, either to command his glider pilots or resign from command. Chatterton, loyal to his pilots, chose to command.

The next problem was where were the gliders? Hopkinson had stated they would be using US Waco CG4A gliders as there were no Horsas in North Africa. Chatterton found crated US Wacos at Oran airfield and his gliders pilots erected them with the aid of the US glider handbook only.

Chatterton instituted a glider flying training programme to give his pilots day and night flying time on the unfamiliar US Wacos. One problem was the intense heat of North Africa which made the glider's cockpit unbearable during the day. By this time Horsa gliders were beginning to arrive in North Africa, (Operation Beggar/Turkey Buzzard), towed from England in an incredible flying operation by the Royal Air Force and the Glider Pilot Regiment.

Dead on time on the night of the 9th-10th July 1943, the Horsa and Waco gliders were towed off from Tunisia, (Operation Ladbrooke), piloted by the soldier pilots of the Glider Pilot Regiment, and flew towards Sicily via Malta. Adverse weather prevailed and on arriving off the coast of Sicily they were met with a dust storm blowing off the land. Worse conditions could not have been met as the glider pilots struggled to find their LZs. Many of the gliders had to release too far offshore and a great number fell into the sea with much loss of life. Only one Horsa, piloted by Staff Sergeant D. Galpin, DFM, landed on its objective, the Ponte Grande bridge and his load of troops stormed and took it. Another Horsa piloted by Captain J.N.C. Denholm reached the bridge but crashed into a canal bank and the impact exploded part of his load killing him, his co-pilot and passengers. Three more Horsas were landed up to two miles away but their troop loads reached the bridge. The Horsa pilots had been given an almost impossible task, to be released at 4000 feet, fly several miles in darkness, then find a minute LZ and land a hugh loaded glider in darkness. To be asked to do this and carry it out speaks volumes for the calibre of the glider pilots.

The second air landing of the Sicily invasion, Operation Fustian, commenced on the night of the 13th July 1943, when eight Waco CG4A and eleven Horsa gliders piloted by the Glider Pilot Regiment and towed by RAF aircraft, carried the anti-tank guns and vehicles of the air landing battery of the Royal Artillery to land on LZs near another vital bridge, the Prima Sole, near Catania, Sicily, in support of the 1st Airborne Division paratroops who were fighting for the bridge. As the airborne force passed near the Allied naval forces off Sicily, some ships opened fire on them believing they were the enemy. This caused utter confusion in the airborne stream, which was then added to by the enemy opening up with anti-aircraft fire. The tug towing a Horsa flown by Major Alastair Cooper, AFC, was hit by flak and blew up at five hundred feet so Major Cooper had to try and land his heavily laden glider in a river bed but the glider was too low and crashed killing all on board.

Only four Horsa glider crews and passengers contributed to the battle for the bridge, one piloted by Staff Sergeant White, landed on his intended LZ and his gun load was off-loaded and brought into action. Captain Barrie, DFC, Lieutenant Thomas, Staff Sergeant Protheroe, DFM, Sergeants Anderson, Atkinson and Doig took part in the battle with the glider pilots loading and firing the Royal Artillery anti-tank guns and any other weapons they could lay their hands on including a captured German 88mm gun.

By dawn about two hundred and fifty soldiers were defending the bridge against enemy attack. At noon the Germans attacked in force and the defenders had to retire due to casualties and lack of ammunition but the bridge was recaptured at dawn on the 16th July. The cost in lives to the Glider Pilot Regiment in the Sicily Operations was high. The regiment lost fifty-seven soldier pilots.

The first British large scale glider operation ended with many lessons learnt, as Staff Sergeant Galpin observed to the author; "this operation was not really on and was carried out by glider pilots who had far too little experience in night flying", to which the author would add comment that this was not the fault of the glider pilots, brave men who attempted the almost impossible. The faults lay with others.

Following the Sicily operations the Glider Pilot Regiment returned to its base in North Africa then took part in the invasion of Italy at Taranto as infantry soldiers although most were non commissioned officers. Then it was decided to send most of the 1st Battalion back to England but to retain one squadron - to be known as the 1st Independent Glider Pilot Squadron - in the Mediterranean theatre of operations with the British Independent Parachute Brigade.

Back in England the 2nd Battalion of the regiment was beginning to come up to strength under the command of Lieutenant Colonel Murray, with its new Nissen hut base at Fargo Camp (named after a nearby plantation of trees) three miles from Amesbury on Salisbury Plain. The glider pilots were still segregated from the RAF and had to travel to RAF Netheravon for flying practice.

Lieutenant Colonel Chatterton was determined to organize the Glider Pilot Regiment into Royal Air Force type formations and designations not Army titles and the soldier pilots were to live, eat and work alongside the Air Force. He also wanted both battalions of the regiment together, separate from the 1st and 6th

Airborne Divisions. It had been planned that 1st Battalion Glider Pilot Regiment should be under 1st Airborne Division and 2nd Battalion under the 6th Airborne Division.

Chatterton got his way and the regiment was brought together with a Staff Headquarters working alongside No.38 Wing RAF, and new titles of Wing for battalion, Squadron for company and Flight for platoon. 2nd Battalion was renamed No.1 Wing and 1st Battalion No.2 Wing. Chatterton was promoted to full Colonel with the title of Commander, Glider Pilots, with the two Wings under his command.

His Headquarters Staff consisted of:
| | |
|---|---|
| Staff Officer. | Major P. Harding. |
| Operations Officer. | Major K.J.S. Andrews. |
| Staff Officer (3) | Captain I.A. McArthur. |
| Intelligence Officer. | Captain G. Roztorowski |

No.1 Wing was commanded by Lieutenant Colonel I.A. Murray with Major S.C. Griffiths as second in command. No.2 Wing had Lieutenant Colonel J.W. Place in command.

Each Wing had several squadrons, alphabetically listed, and each squadron had several flights, as per the RAF system. Each flight consisted of forty-four soldier pilots - four officers and forty other ranks, armed with revolvers, sub machine-guns, light machine-guns and rifles to enable them to fight on the ground as infantry after landing their gliders.

The Independent Glider Pilot Squadron was now based at Comiso, Italy, and had qualified as glider pilots on the US Waco CG4A (Hadrian) glider.
On the 23rd February 1944, the Squadron successfully carried out the first daylight glider landing of WWII in German occupied Yugoslavia: Operation Bunghole. Three Hadrian gliders piloted by Captain C. Turner, (Commander), Staff Sergeant Newman, Staff Sergeant A. McCulloch, Staff Sergeant Hill, Staff Sergeant W. Morrison and Staff Sergeant McMillen, and towed by the 64th Troop Carrier Group, USAAF, carried a Russian Military Mission to the Resistance leader, Marshal Tito, at his headquarters in Yugoslavia.

During the Spring of 1944 the regiment carried out intensive glider flying training for the forthcoming invasion of France. 6th Airborne Division would land by parachute and glider to protect and hold the left flank of the sea borne invading forces in Normandy. Specific tasks were allocated to the glider crews of the regiment:

OPERATION DEADSTICK (part of Operation Tonga).
The capture of two bridges by glider borne coup de main assault carrying troops of the 2nd Battalion, Oxford & Bucks and engineers.

OPERATION TONGA.
The glider borne landing of troops and equipment.

MERVILLE BATTERY ASSAULT.
The elimination of a coastal gun battery at Merville by landing paratroops and engineers directly on the battery.

OPERATION MALLARD.
The bringing in by glider of soldiers of 6th Air Landing Brigade on the evening of D-Day, the 6th June 1944.

At 22.49 hours on the 5th June, Operation Tonga began when seven Horsa gliders of E Squadron, Glider Pilot Regiment, were towed off by 271 Squadron, Royal Air Force, from Down Ampney. The first British fighting troops of D-Day were airborne into history. A minute later six Horsas of F Squadron were towed off by 233 Squadron, Royal Air Force, from Blakehill Farm carrying equipment for paratroops on their DZ. At Harwell four Horsas of A Squadron, carrying paratroops and Medics, took off at 23.10 hours and headed for Normandy towed by 295 and 570 Squadrons, Royal Air Force.

At 2256 hours on the 5th June 1944, the Deadstick Operation began when six gliders of C Squadron, Glider Pilot Regiment, piloted by Staff Sergeant J. Wallwork, DFM, Staff Sergeant J. Ainsworth, MM, Staff Sergeant O. Boland, CdeG, Staff Sergeant P. Hobbs, DFM, Staff Sergeant G. Barkway, DFM, Staff Sergeant T. Boyle, Staff Sergeant L. Lawrence, Staff Sergeant S. Shorter, Staff Sergeant S. Pearson, DFM, Staff Sergeant L. Guthrie, CdeG, Staff Sergeant R.A. Howard, DFM, Staff Sergeant F. Baacke, CdeG, were towed off from RAF Tarrant Rushton, Dorset, by Halifax tugs of 298 and 644 Squadrons, Royal Air Force, 38 Group, Royal Air Force.

At 0007 the combinations crossed the French coast and the gliders cast off tow. In a magnificent feat of airmanship five of the six gliders landed at 0016 hours without landing aids, in darkness, on target at the two bridges which were swiftly taken by the 2nd Oxford & Bucks under the command of Major J. Howard, DSO. The main Tonga force of sixty-eight Horsa and four Hamilcar gliders led by Lieutenant Colonel Murray, began to be towed off at 0128 hours on D-Day from Brize Norton, Harwell and Tarrant Rushton carrying the Commander of 6th

Airborne Division, General Gale and his HQ, together with artillery, medics and paratroops.

Later, the three Merville battery assault Horsa gliders were airborne at 0230 hours from Brize Norton. One glider tow rope broke over England and the glider landed at Odiham but the other two gliders piloted by Staff Sergeant Kerr, DFM, Sergeant Walker, Staff Sergeant Bone, DFM, and Sergeant Dean, carrying paratroops reached the target and tried to land without landing aids on the battery. Staff Sergeant Bone managed to land his glider three miles from the target and Staff Sergeant Kerr fifty yards from the perimeter wire. Both glider parties engaged the enemy in support of the attacking paratroopers who valiantly took the battery in a splendid feat of arms.

The Operation Mallard armada of two hundred and fifty-six gliders - which included thirty Hamilcars carrying tanks to battle by air for the first time in military history - carrying 6th Air Landing Brigade, were airborne at 1850 hours on the evening of D-Day. Troops of 6th Air Landing Brigade were glider lifted to the battlefield in daylight by seven squadrons of the Glider Pilot Regiment from seven RAF airfields in England. Two hundred and forty-six gliders landed on or near their LZs. At the end of the glider operations the regiment was withdrawn to depot in England. They had suffered thirty-four soldier glider pilots dead but the overall operation had been a success of airmanship.

The small Operation Dingson involved the Royal Air Force 38 Group's 298 and 644 Squadrons from Tarrant Rushton, towing ten Hadrian gliders, piloted by the regiment, carrying French SAS troopers to an LZ near Lorient, on the 5th August 1944, without fatal casualties.

The Independent Glider Pilot Squadron of the regiment did not take part in operations until Operation Dragoon, the invasion of the south of France.
After a recalled take off from Italy the Squadron were again towed off at 1400 hours on the 15th August 1944, and set course for France under the command of Major R. Coulthard, carrying 6-pounder anti-tank guns, ammunition and troops. In spite of anti-glider poles erected on the LZs casualties were slight but Sergeant W.R. Jenner suffered fatal injuries when his glider crashed on landing. He was buried at Frejus.

After Dragoon the Independent Squadron was withdrawn and returned to Italy by ship, the gliders being left where they had landed. The squadron then being largely re-equipped with the US Waco CG4A Hadrian.

To reinforce Horsa glider numbers in Italy, Operation Molten was mounted by the RAF and the regiment. On the 9th October 1944, D Squadron, GPR. under Major J. Lyne, piloted thirty two Horsas, towed by 190 and 620 Squadrons, Royal Air Force, from Fairford, England, to Ciampino, Italy, via

France. Twenty-seven of the Horsas landed next day in Italy in a flight time of ten hours, without casualties to the pilots.

The Independent Squadron's next operation was in Greece on the 16th October 1944. Twenty Dakotas of the USAAF 51st Troop Carrier Wing towed twenty Hadrian gliders piloted by the Independent Glider Squadron with equipment for repairing the airfield at Megara. The glider pilots were later returned to Italy.

Back in England the regiment was preparing for the assault on Arnhem. Six hundred and fifty-four Horsa, twenty nine Hamilcar and fourteen Hadrian gliders would be used to transport 1st Air Landing Brigade and troops of 1st Airborne Division to battle in three air lifts. Ninety per cent of the regiment would be committed and there would be no reserves - all available pilots would be used and retained on the ground after landing in a defensive role. Such was the plan. On the 17th September 1944, three hundred and fifty-nine gliders were towed off from eight English airfields and flew toward Holland into history. The glider landings were successful.

The second lift lifted off next morning, the 18th, and two hundred and ninety-four gliders took to the air. Bad weather prevailed over England next day, the 19th, and the third and final lift was only forty three gliders. Over the three lifts six hundred and twenty-one gliders were recorded as landing successfully, nearly ninety per cent of the total.

The airborne soldiers stood at the battle until the 27th September against the odds but were then ordered to withdraw. The Glider Pilot Regiment suffered a total of six hundred and sixteen casualties. Twenty three officers and one hundred and twenty-four staff sergeants and sergeants killed: Thirty-one officers and four hundred and thirty-eight staff sergeants and sergeants wounded and prisoners of war. The regiment had been decimated and there were no reinforcements. Colonel Chatterton solved the problem by obtaining 1500 RAF pilots from the reserve pool overflow of the Empire Air Training Scheme.

At first most of the officer and NCO RAF pilots objected to being attached to the Glider Pilot Regiment to fly gliders - as RAF aircrew they had volunteered to fly powered aircraft but as the author well remembers there was an order in being in the RAF which required all ranks to fly in any aircraft anywhere in the world at any time.

But before long the spirit of the Glider Pilot Regiment got to them and they began to whiten their stripes with blanco and wear the airborne forces red beret, all contrary to Air Ministry orders as to dress. They also entered into the spirit of military weapon training and tactics.

Plans were now well in hand for the next airborne operation, over the River Rhine and into Germany in a tactical air landing. 6th Air Landing Brigade was tasked with the capture of bridges and the town of Hamminkeln. The regiment would carry them and other divisional troops plus artillery and land them in the centre of the battle zone. This time the tactics would be different - the airborne troops would be covered by the guns of 21st Army firing across the Rhine and there would only be one lift, not three as at Arnhem. Prior to the assault the Allied Air Forces and artillery would pulverise the German defences to ease the task of the airborne soldiers.

On 24th March 1945, the huge formation of three hundred and ninety-two Horsa and forty eight Hamilcar gliders were towed off from eight airfields in East Anglia. Four hundred and thirty-four heavily laden gliders, towed by an equal number of RAF tugs, steered for Brussels to rendezvous over the field of Waterloo with the US 17th Airborne Division. In the greatest aerial armada ever seen in history they arrived over the battlefield and began landing at 1021 hours amid a fog of war caused by the preliminary bombing and shelling. By 1100 hours four hundred and two British gliders were down successfully; 91.36% of the British total. Within a few hours the airborne soldiers had achieved their objectives and the Field was theirs - the gateway into Germany had been opened.

The human cost to the Glider Pilot regiment was high - one hundred and one gliders pilots died, including sixty-one of the Royal Air Force glider pilots attached to the regiment, some of whom died wearing their red berets which they had donned en route to the battle.

Three months later the Germans surrendered unconditionally and the war in Europe was over. However the other enemy, the Japanese, still remained and the regiment was in India under the command of the Royal Air Force. Two Wings, 343 and 344 were formed, using US Waco CG4A Hadrian gliders as the wooden Horsa was unsuitable for the climate. However the Japanese surrendered to the power of the atomic bomb in August 1945, and WWII came to an end.

With the war ended the regiment rapidly ran down until only three squadrons remained in the United Kingdom and one in Palestine. By 1948 the regiment was reduced to a Headquarters and Training Squadron at Aldershot and A and B Squadrons based at RAF Waterbeach and Netheravon. A small Hamilcar Flight, part of B squadron, was based at RAF Fairford and RAF Upper Heyford became No.1 Parachute and Glider Training School with elementary flying training being carried out at RAF Booker.

Late in 1948 glider training stopped as the RAF was engaged on the Berlin Airlift, Operation Plainfare. A Flight of glider pilots was attached to the RAF and flew as second pilots on York and Hastings aircraft of RAF Transport Command.

Glider training resumed when Operation Plainfare ended but the use of military gliders was ending. In 1950 the regiment was reduced to one squadron known as the 1st Independent Squadron flying Horsas and the regiment adopted a new badge, an eagle surrounded by a laurel wreath surmounted by a King's crown and the words Glider Pilot Regiment, the previous badge from 1942, being similar but with the letters AAC (Army Air Corps) thereon. In 1951 the use of gliders ended and the glider pilots were used as Air Observation Post pilots on light aircraft, some of whom served in Korea and Malaya.

The Glider Pilot Regiment was finally closed down under its last Commanding Officer, Major M.W. Sutcliffe, at a parade at Middle Wallop on the 31st August 1957.

The Glider Pilot Regiment had occupied a unique place in the British Army for a comparatively short time but had made its mark with one hundred and seventy-two decorations being awarded and one thousand three hundred and one casualties suffered out of a strength of three thousand - the names of those who made the supreme sacrifice are recorded in a Roll of Honour placed in Salisbury Cathedral.

The surviving soldier pilots of the regiment, whose motto was and is 'Nothing is Impossible', are advancing in years now but maintain a close comradeship in the Glider Pilot Regimental Association of which the author was honoured to be made a member, being qualified through service in 38 Group, Royal Air Force.

# 1ST AIRBORNE RECONNAISSANCE SQUADRON

The squadron was formed in January 1942, as the 31st Independent Reconnaissance Company from the 31st Independent Brigade Anti-Tank Company. In December 1941, the squadron was redesignated as 1st Air Landing Reconnaissance Squadron and came on the establishment of 1st Air Landing Brigade, 1st Airborne Division.

Equipped with jeeps and motor cycles the squadron was intended to be carried in Horsa gliders, but during the campaign in Italy the squadron was seaborne to Taranto where their ship was first into Taranto harbour. The squadron remained in the line along the east coast of Italy until December 1943, when it returned to England to act as reserve for 6th Airborne Division.

On the 1st January 1944, the squadron was renamed 1st Airborne Reconnaissance Squadron (from 1st Air Landing) as they had became a largely paratroop Unit, although their vehicles, which now included Dingo armoured cars, still came in by glider with the drivers and riders.

Making rendezvous after dropping the squadron consisted of Squadron HQ, Reconnaissance Troop HQ, and three Reconnaissance Sections each of one officer, one NCO and nine other ranks using two jeeps landed by glider.
A Support Troop armed with 3-inch mortars and 20 mm Polsten guns completed the squadron, all linked to divisional and squadron HQ by radio.

The reconnaissance troop jeeps were heavily armed with Vickers K machine-guns, 2-inch mortars, Bren light machine-guns, Sten sub machine-guns, rifles, PIAT anti-tank launchers and hand grenades. After taking part in the Arnhem operation the squadron had its last task in Norway in 1945 when it performed duty in connection with the German surrender.

Commanding Officers of the squadron during its existence were:
Major D. Allsop, Captain R.J. Clark, Major C.F.H. Gough MC, and Major T.B.H. Otway. The squadron lost thirty-four men killed in action during WWII and the following nine men were awarded Honours;

| | |
|---|---|
| Sgt. E.K. Haydon, | Mentioned in Despatches. |
| Sgt. G.E. Holderness, | " |
| Sgt. G. Kay, | " |
| Sgt. K.O. Lapper, | British Empire Medal. |
| Sgt. J. Pyper, | Military Medal. |
| Tpr. C.M. Simpson, | Mentioned in despatches. |
| Cpl. J.G. Taylor, | Military Medal. |
| Sgt. H. Venes, | British Empire Medal. |
| Tpr. J.D. Wilkes, | Mentioned in Despatches. |

# 6TH AIRBORNE ARMOURED RECONNAISSANCE REGIMENT

On the 14th January 1944, 6th Airborne Reconnaissance Regiment, Royal Armoured Corps, was formed at Larkhill, Wiltshire, from one of the Special Service Light Tank Squadrons. It was commanded by Major Stewart (13th/18th Hussars) afterwards Lieutenant Colonel, who was to remain in command until the end of WWII. Personnel consisted of one troop each from the following:

9th Lancers.
10th Hussars.
The Bays.
1st and 2nd Battalions, Royal Tank Regiment.
Royal Electrical and Mechanical Engineers Detachment.

The regiment was posted to 6th Airborne Division with an establishment to include one squadron of light tanks, a Reconnaissance Squadron, Headquarters Administrative Squadron, plus Medical, Signals and REME personnel.

The Tank Squadron consisted of five Troops of four Tetrarch tanks each armed with 2 pounder guns adapted for Littlejohn ammunition: a Squadron Headquarters of four Tanks, two of which were armed with 3-inch howitzers and a Regimental Headquarters Squadron with two tanks also armed with 3-inch howitzers.

The Reconnaissance Squadron comprised a Headquarters and four Troops of either two Bren Gun carriers and one Scout car, or two Scout cars and one Bren carrier (according to the carrying Hamilcar glider loading) and a Blitz Troop on motor cycles. All personnel were Royal Armoured Corps. Supplies of petrol and ammunition were carried in nine Rotor trailers towed by Jeeps. There was also a Parachute Harbour Party consisting of one Officer and fifteen other ranks who trained and dropped with the Independent Paratroop Company.

Early on the morning of D-Day the Parachute Harbour Party dropped in Normandy, losing its officer, Lieutenant Belcher, and a complete paratroop stick by enemy fire. On the evening of D-Day the regiment made history when, for the first time in military annals, tanks arrived by air directly onto the battlefield at Ranville (Operation Mallard). The tank engines had been started while airborne in their gliders and on landing the tanks were driven straight out and into action.

The original Plan had been to form an Armoured Group with the 12th Battalion, Devonshire Regiment, but this had to be abandoned as the Devons were required elsewhere.

At dawn on D+1 the regiment joined the 8th Parachute Battalion in the Bois de Bavent and set up a series of observation points overlooking the plain of the Troarn-Caen-Ranville-Escoville area. It also sent bicycle patrols deep into German held territory which gathered intelligence which resulted in successful RAF strikes and naval bombardment from HMS Mauritius lying offshore, on enemy vehicle parks.

The regiment came into reserve after ten days but the Tank Squadron was recalled almost immediately and ordered to dig in its tanks in fire support of the Parachute Battalions which by this time were becoming thin on the ground. When they were eventually pulled out of the line they were sent to a Tank Replacement Unit where their Tetrarchs were exchanged for twelve Cromwells. The tank crews converted to the Cromwells and were back in the line in ten days - a creditable performance.

In the Allied break out from Normandy the Tank Squadron, under Major Barnett, Royal Tank Regiment, consisted of Headquarters with four tanks and two Troops of four Cromwell tanks each. The regiment also had under its command the Independent Parachute Company and the 1st Belgian Armoured Car Squadron and with those Units led the advance until reaching Pont D'Aumer when the Division was withdrawn to England embarking at Graye sur Mer on the 5th September 1944.

Disembarking at Gosport, Hampshire, the next day the regiment returned to its base at Larkhill, Wiltshire. On the 1st October 1944, the regiment was re organized on the basis of the experience gained in Normandy. It now consisted of two Reconnaissance Squadrons (A & B) of four Reconnaissance Troops as before and one Tank troop each. (Locust tanks were now used but could be exchanged for Cromwells when fighting with the main ground armoured element).

A Support Squadron (C) of two medium machine gun troops in Bren Gun carriers, a 4.2 inch mortar Troop, plus a Blitz troop and Headquarters Squadron completed the regiment. Personnel for the Support Squadron came from the Lancashire Fusiliers and the 10th Tank Brigade.

On the 18th October 1944, the entire regimental establishment was fixed at the following:
Regimental Headquarters (2 Scout cars: 3 cars, 5cwt 4 X 4s).

Headquarters Squadron of:
Squadron Headquarters,

Intercommunication Troop,
Administrative troop,
Seaborne Party (including 8 Cruiser Tanks)

Support Squadron of;
Squadron Headquarters
Two troops (each of three Bren carriers).
Mortar Troop (4 cars, 5cwt,4 x 4 each with one 4.2-inch mortar).
Infantry Support Troop (18 motor cycles,1 car 5cwt 4X4)

Two Squadrons each of:
Squadron Headquarters:
Heavy Troop ( 4 light tanks)
Three troops (each) 2 bren carriers, 2 cars 5cwt 4 X 4).
Total strength of personnel.
Officers.        32.
other ranks.     358.

The regiment embarked at Tilbury on the 28th December 1944, for the Battle of the Bulge in the Ardennes, disembarking at Ostend next day.

Operations in the Ardennes and Holland were ideal for shaking down to the new regimental establishment and the Tanks, Mortars and MMGs were given plenty of opportunity to be welded into the Divisional Fire Plan at Bois de Villers, Villers sur Lesse, Voorste, Steeg and Sevenum. Between the 24th to the 28th February 1945, the regiment embarked at Wetterum, Holland, and returned to Larkhill.

Two weeks later on the 16th March 1945, the ground element of the regiment embarked at Tilbury for Europe and landed at Ostend the next day. The gliderborne element took twelve Locust tanks and the 4.2-inch Mortar Troop in by air on Operation Varsity, the 24th March 1945. The regiment, led by the commanding officer, took heavy casualties in the air and on the ground from German flak. Only fifty per cent each of the Tank and Mortar group survived but they gave a good account of themselves in action - one tank though immobilised, outside the perimeter killed over one hundred of the enemy.

The following morning, the 25th, the land element of the regiment arrived and with Cromwell tanks in the van, led the advance across Germany. During the advance the Independent Parachute Company and a Squadron of the Inns of Court Regiment came under command of the regiment.

At Minden, one Squadron Group at the head of 3rd Parachute Brigade, attacked from the south whilst another Squadron, which had taken a crossing some distance back, attempted to storm the main Minden bridge from the north. On the way it became heavily involved with a battery of German 88s hidden in concrete emplacements which opened fire when half the squadron had passed through. The leading half of the squadron pushed on and seized the Minden bridge which it held till 3rd Parachute Brigade linked up. The commanding officer put in an attack on the 88s with the Independent Parachute Company, which in spite of severe casualties captured the strongpoint.

On the 1st May 1945, elements of the regiment crossed the River Elbe and finally, when its standing patrols were five miles in advance of the British line-Wismar to Schwerinsee, met the leading troops of the Russian Stalingrad Armoured Division and became the first British troops to meet the Red Army. On the 24th May 1945, the regiment embarked at Calais for England, arriving next day at Larkhill.

A few weeks later an advance party left for a School of Jungle Warfare in the Far East to prepare for the regiment's arrival there. However 6th Airborne Division and the regiment embarked for Palestine where on the 22nd October 1945, they disembarked at Haifa. In Palestine the regiment served alongside the 3rd Royal Hussars with whom it amalgamated on the 1st February 1946.

# BRITISH MILITARY GLIDERS

At the outbreak of WWII British armed forces had no military gliders - the concept was undreamt of then - but the German use of military gliders in 1940 brought a swift response from the Air Ministry with specifications being issued for training gliders, troop carrying and tank carrying gliders. The main specifications between 1940 and 1944 are listed below together with the resulting gliders produced, developed or experimented with.

| | | |
|---|---|---|
| X10/40 | Assault/Training glider. | Hotspur.Mk. 1 |
| X22/40 | Hotspur development. | Hotspur Mk.11 |
| X23/40 | Hotspur production. | Hotspur Mk II |
| X25/40 | Troop carrier. | Hengist Mk. I |
| X26/40 | Troop carrier. | Horsa Mk. I |
| X27/40 | Tank carrier. | Hamilcar. Miles M32 Project. |
| X3/41 | Bomb carrying glider. | Horsa project AS52 |
| TX3/43 | Training glider. | GAL 55 |
| X4/44 | Powered tank carrier. | Hamilcar X |

"X"   Experimental.
"TX"  Trainer Experimental.

The following gliders were experimented with, produced, projected or used by British Airborne Forces during WWII:

| | |
|---|---|
| Airspeed | Horsa Mk.I & II. |
| Baynes | Carrier Wing. |
| GAL 48 | Hotspur Mk.I & II. |
| GAL 49 & 50 | Hamilcar |
| GAL 55 | Trainer. |
| GAL 58 | Hamilcar X |
| Miles | M32 Project |
| Slingsby 18 | Hengist Mk.I |
| Taylorcraft | "H" Glider. |
| Waco | CG4A Hadrian. |

## THE BAYNES CARRIER WING

During 1941 Mr. L.E. Baynes drew up a design for a flying wing glider which could be attached to a tank to give aerial mobility to battle - a military strategists dream - which was eventually realised on D-Day in Normandy when for the first time in history tanks were flown into battle by Hamilcar gliders.

To test the Baynes theory a one third scale glider was constructed by Slingsby Sailplanes Ltd, and air tested at the AFEE then located at Sherburn in Elmet, Yorkshire, by F/Lt. R. Kronfeld, in August 1943. In appearance the small aircraft looked like a bat as no tailplane was fitted. Flying control was effected by vertical end plate fins and rudders on the end of each wing and, 'elevons', combined ailerons and elevators on the wings. Air operated split bellows type type flaps were fitted on the wings. Single wooden skid undercarriage. The pilots cockpit projected beneath the wing with the transparent cockpit cover above the wing.

The glider performed well on air tests both on tow and in free flight there being excellent flying control of the control surfaces. A speed of 90mph in free flight was attained and an indicated 105mph in a dive. Stalling speed 50mph with flaps up with flaps down 44mph. Landing speed 65mph with flaps up and 55mph with flaps down. Wing span 33 feet. Weight loaded 963lbs. RAF training livery and markings.

As the large Hamilcar tank carrying glider was preferred the Baynes project was abandoned as such the aircraft was used at the Royal Aircraft Establishment at Farnborough for research into tailless aircraft.

## GAL 55.

In response to Air Ministry Specification TX.3/43 for a military training glider General Aircraft Limited (GAL) produced the GAL 55.

The GAL 55 was a midwing two-seat glider with a wing span of 35 feet and a fuselage 25 feet 6 inches long. Built of composite materials it was designed to correspond with the handling characteristics of the large troop carrying Horsa. Single and two point towing points were fitted for single or bifurcated tow ropes. Double bellows flaps and airbrakes were fitted and a tricyle undercarriage. Loaded weight 2407lbs.

The glider tug would have been a single-engined light aircraft such as the Master II but the war ended before trials were completed. The AFEE at Beaulieu carried out acceptance trials on the prototype NP 671 and found that the aircraft was airborne on tow off at 65mph without swinging but when airborne there was a tendency to yaw and after about 120mph the glider became unstable. In free flight the controls were sensitive and a speed of 165mph was attained in a dive. Landing was made at 70mph and with flaps and airbrakes in operation there was a rapid descent. The glider dropped at 1550 feet per minute at this speed and at 100 mph dropped at 3190 feet per minute with a glide angle of 8.4.

The GAL 55 was found to be unsuitable for military training use and the project was abandoned after the trials at AFEE.

# WACO CG4A HADRIAN GLIDER

On the 8th March 1941, the U.S. Government issued USAAF Specification 1025/2 for military gliders to carry two, eight and fifteen troops. Eleven small aircraft manufacturing companies were invited to build prototypes but only Waco Aircraft, Bowlus Sailplanes Frankfort Sailplane Company and St. Louis Aircraft Corporation made positive tenders.

In April 1941, the Waco Aircraft Company of Troy, Ohio, was awarded the U.S. Government contract to build nine and fifteen-place military gliders. Waco's designer and chief engineer A.F. Arcier produced the prototype XCG3, an experimental eight place glider. This glider passed the USAAF tests at Wright Field but none of the other companies glider designs passed the tests.

One of the conditions of the Government's contract with Waco was that they had to furnish designs to other aircraft contractors who would then build the Waco design under licence. The object being large scale production by American industry.

With the need for a larger troop carrying glider contained in their contract Waco designed the XCG4 and built two prototypes. Capable of carrying fifteen troops (including the pilot) the glider was in fact, a larger version of the successful XCG3 with a 83½-feet wing span and a 48-feet long fuselage. A specially made wooden floor could support a quarter ton truck or a 75mm howitzer and crew of three or other combination of load up to 7700lbs all up weight. No flaps were fitted although trim tabs were incorporated in the ailerons.

A lever on the cockpit floor, marked in red Cockpit Release, when pulled allowed the entire nose section, which included the cockpit, to hinge upward allowing direct access to the cargo space in the fuselage.

The trials of the XCG4 being successful the glider was designated the CG4A on the 29th June 1942, and was declared ready for mass production. In July

1942, sixteen companies were awarded contracts to build CG4As with the Waco Company supplying design and manufacturing details. Production costs of the glider were from $15,000 to $26,000 depending on the building company.

At first the CG4A only had one control column fitted which could be swung from pilot to pilot who sat side by side. Later two control columns were fitted. A row of five simple flying instruments: turn and bank indicator, altimeter, rate of climb indicator, compass and airspeed indicator were mounted on a steel tube in front of the pilots. Contact with the tug was by an intercom wire wrapped round the 300-feet long, one inch thick nylon tow rope. Later two way VHF radios were fitted.

CG4A Description.
Wing span 83 feet 8 inches. All wooden structure with two main spars of spruce, wood ribs and mahogany members, all fabric covered. No flaps. Ailerons fitted with trim tabs. Wing area 900 square feet.
Fuselage. Length 48 feet 8 inches. Steel tube structure with fabric covering.
Height. 15 feet 4 inches.
Tail plane. Wooden structure with fabric covering.
Undercarriage. Doughnut wheels fixed to the lower fuselage longerons either side. Long skid under centre line of fuselage - small skid under tail.
Performance. Towing speed 120-125mph. After release a landing space of about 660 feet was needed. Stalling speed 52 to 55mph.

The first CG4A to arrive in Britain was the Voodoo Operation glider serial number FR 556 in July 1943. The rest of the CG4As, renamed the Hadrian I by the RAF, came by sea from the U.S. in crates, some being lost at sea.
The following Hadrians were supplied to the RAF:

Mk.1.
| | | |
|---|---|---|
| FR556-580 | (25) | FR559-60 lost at sea. |
| NP664 | (1) | |
| KK569-789 | (221) | |
| KK792-968 | (177) | |
| VJ120-165 | (46) | |
| VJ198-222 | (25) | |
| VJ239-284 | (46) | |
| VJ313-349 | (37) | |
| VJ368-413 | (46) | |
| VJ735-781 | (47) | |

VJ821-847         (27)
VK573-609        (37)
VK623-655        (33)
VK874              (1)
VK877              (1)
Vk886              (1)
Plus               120 on USAAF Bureau Numbers.
Total              891 Mk.Is.

Mk.IIs.
FR582-778         (198)
KH871-992         (122) Sent to India from the US for 343 and 344 Wings.
KH994-997         (4)   Sent to Canada.
Total.             324.
Both Mks. 1215.

The Hadrian was used on operations by the British in Sicily, Yugoslavia, France, Greece and Holland but the larger Horsa was preferred. A grand total of 13,909 were produced by the U.S. companies with the largest number being made by Ford with 4190 built. A Mk.I Hadrian can be seen at the Museum of Army Flying at Middle Wallop, Stockbridge, Hampshire.

# GAL - HAMILCAR

During 1940 the Air Ministry issued Specification X27/40 for a light tank or cargo carrying glider to meet the needs of airborne forces for tank support or heavy equipment on the battlefield. General Aircraft Company (GAL) of Hanworth Park, Feltham, Middlesex, successfully tendered for the contract and began work in May 1941, on the Hamilcar.

In July 1941, GAL received an order for two prototypes and ten pre-production gliders for evaluation tests. GAL decided to build a half scale test Hamilcar - serial number T-0227 - during the summer of 1941, and the glider, towed off by a Whitley tug, was air tested in September 1941, at RAF Hounslow. The serial number was changed to DP 226 but the glider was wrecked in a heavy landing and written off.

The first prototype DP 206 was built at GAL's factory at Hanworth but the airfield was too small for test flying the large Hamilcar so the glider was taken by an RAF Queen Mary truck to RAF Snaith in Yorkshire, which had a 2000 yard tarmac runway and where it made its successful maiden flight on the 27th March 1942. The second prototype DP210 was completed and further trials were made as to its handling capabilities at Chelveston. In August 1942, DP210 was delivered to RAF Newmarket Heath for load trials and twenty-three flight tests were carried out between the 6th August and the 9th September 1942, most of which were successful.

All ten pre-production evaluation Hamilcars - serial numbers DR851 to 860 - were built by GAL during the winter of 1942 and delivered to various RAF units for assembly instruction at Maintainance Units (MU) and flight trials.

Owing to the size and weight of the Hamilcar a suitably powerful tug had to be found and trials were made with Lancaster, Stirling and Halifax four-engined bombers. It was found during trials in May 1943, using a Stirling I that the tug's engines overheated on climb out. More tests were conducted using a Stirling IV which were better but not satisfactory when the glider was loaded. Lancaster II tug tests were satisfactory but Bomber Command could not spare aircraft for glider tugs. Eventually it fell to the Halifax to tow the Hamilcar on operations. In a bid to get the heavy Hamilcar off the runway more easily trials were conducted in January 1943, to investigate the feasibility of rocket assisted take off for the glider.

The Royal Aircraft Establishment at Farnborough designed 25-inch diameter welded steel cylinders each containing twenty-four 3-inch rockets which were fired in pairs at 1.2 second intervals giving a mean thrust of 2000lbs for twenty-nine seconds. One rocket cylinder was fitted under each wing, well clear of the fuselage, giving a total thrust of 4000lbs. Once airborne the rocket cylinders could be jettisoned and returned to the ground by parachute.

Trials were conducted at RAF Hartford Bridge, (Blackbushe), when two rocket cylinders were fitted beneath the wings of Hamilcar DR854. Towed off by a Halifax tug, the glider pilot waited until a speed of 70mph had been reached then fired the rockets until a height of about 100 feet had been achieved. At 300 feet the rocket cylinders were jettisoned. The tests were successful, reducing the take off run from 1700 yards to 1300 yards but the system was not used as more powerful tug aircraft became available.

GAL built the first twenty-two Hamilcars, comprising the two prototypes, ten evaluation and ten production gliders, serial numbers being HH921 to HH930. The bulk orders were manufactured as sub assembly parts by:

Birmingham Railway Carriage & Wagon Company,
Co-operative Wholesale Society Ltd.,
AC Motors Ltd.

The sub assembly parts were erected as Hamilcars at RAF Lyneham, Wiltshire, and RAF North Luffenham, Rutland.

Description. Hamilcar Mk.I.
High wing monoplane heavy transport military glider.
Wooden construction with plywood and fabric covering.
Fuselage. Square in section of semi monocoque construction. 68 feet long with usable interior dimensions of 27 feet long, 8 feet wide by 6 feet 8 inches high. Front loading - unloading door hinged to starboard - operated manually from inside or outside or by the driver of the vehicle being carried merely driving forward which actuated a push rod which opened the door automatically.

The two pilots sat in tandem in the cockpit which was on top of the fuselage, access being gained from inside the glider by a fixed ladder and a hatch on top of the fuselage. Height with tail down 20 feet 3 inches - with tail up 26 feet 6 inches. Unladen weight was 18,400lbs with a military load of of 17,600lbs to 19,000lbs depending on towing aircraft. The cargo space could take a variety of loads and the following were officially approved:

Tetrarch Mk.IV tank.
Locust T9 tank. (U.S.)
Two Bren gun carriers.
Three Rota Trailers.
Two armoured scout cars.
One 17-pounder gun with tractor.
one 25-pounder gun with tractor.
Self propelled Bofors gun.
One Jeep and carrier.
One carrier for 3-inch mortar and eight motor cycles.
48 Stores panniers.
D4 tractor with angledozer.
Scraper with Fordson tractor.
Grader.
HD10 or HD14 bulldozer (in three Hamilcars)

Towing speed. 130 to 150mph.
The two wheeled undercarriage could be collapsed for unloading and loading cargo by releasing the pressure in the shock absorbers which allowed the fuselage to rest on the ground on its four wooden skids.

Wingspan. 110 feet of wooden construction plywood covered with fabric covered flying control surfaces. Slotted type flaps in two sections to each wing. Slotted ailerons. Wing loading maximum 34.3lbs per square foot - high for a glider.
The Hamilcar Mk.I was used on Operations Tonga, Mallard, Market and Varsity.

TONGA.
Four towed off from RAF Tarrant Rushton, Dorset, by Halifaxes of 299 and 644 Squadrons, 38 Group. One returned to Dorset due to tow rope breakage - the other three landed on their LZ.

MALLARD.
Thirty towed off by Halifaxes of 298 and 644 Squadrons - all reached their LZs but one made a heavy landing and the tank carried was driven from the wreckage and into action for the first time in military history. Due to recovery difficulties all the Hamilcars were written off. Serial numbers of those historic gliders used in Tonga and Mallard were HH923, 924, 926,927,928,929, 930,932, 934, 935, 957, 959, 960,962, 963, 964, and 970.
LA 636, 637, 638, 639, 640, 641, 644, 645, 645, 650, 651, 652, 653, 655, 669, 670, and 671.

MARKET.
Thirty used - towed by Halifaxes of 298 and 644 Squadrons from Tarrant Rushton. Fourteen were towed off on the first lift and all made the LZ. The next lift saw fifteen towed off on on the third and final lift only one but its tow rope parted and it landed near Ghent. The known serial numbers of Hamilcars used are:
HH931, 933, 958, 971.
LA 654, 672, 673, 674, 675, 676, 677, 679, 680, 682, 688, 691, 705,706, 710, 711, 712, 714, 717, 718, 720, 721, 722 and 724.
All the Hamilcars were written off- it was a one way trip - the original airframe life had been estimated at ten hours with this in mind.

VARSITY.
Forty-eight Hamilcars were scheduled to be used, towed off by 298 and 644 Squadrons out of RAF Woodbridge, Suffolk, landing at three per minute on their LZ. Records are not certain as to the Hamilcars used but the following are believed to have been used.
LA685, 689, 690, 707, 708, 709, 715, 719, 723, 729, 730, 731, 733, 734, 735, 738, 740, 743, 744, 745, 747, 748, 750.

NX805, 808, 809, 810, 811, 812, 813, 814, 814, 818, 819, 820, 821, 822, 823, 825, 826, 827 and 875.
All these Hamilcars were written off on the 7.4.45.

Operation Varsity was the last time Hamilcars were used on operations and the remaining gliders were used for training. The author flew in NX 868 from RAF Fairford in 1947 whilst serving in 38 Group and found it an interesting experience but noiser than a Horsa flight especially on landing.

GAL Hamilcar X.
Air Ministry Specification X4/44 called for a powered version of the Hamilcar I for use in the Far Eastern theatre of operations, the idea being to assist the tug on take off and reduce the strain on towed flight.

Designated the GAL 58 Hamilcar X - the prototype LA728 first flew in February 1945, at Feltham, after conversion by strengthening the wings to take two 965 hp Bristol Mercury engines and increasing the track of the landing gear to twenty feet. Apart from this the glider was the same dimensions as the Mk.I. Load carrying ability was increased to a towed maximum of 21,490lbs. On powered flight the load dropped to 6990lbs. Maximum speed was 145mph, Range of 705 miles or 1675 miles with additional fuel tanks. Known conversions to Mk.Xs were:
LA 728 and LA704 prototypes.
RR948, 949, 953, 956, 986.RZ 413, 430, 431.TK722, 726, 735, 736, 737, 738, 741, 742, 742, 744, 746, and 747.
Total 22.

The war being over in August 1945 there seemed no further use for the Hamilcar X but in August 1947, LA728 was used at RAF Defford for testing airborne warning installations.

The Telecommunications Research establishment fitted radar in the redesigned nose of the Hamilcar and successful tests were carried out. The tests were concluded in January 1948 and LA728 was scrapped. As far as can be ascertained from records, 369 Hamilcars were delivered to the RAF, 22 were converted to Mk.X and 74 were cancelled orders.

# SLINGSBY TYPE 18 - HENGIST I

British Air Ministry Specification X25/40 was for a military transport glider capable of carrying fifteen fully equipped troops and two pilots.

The well known firm of civilian glider makers, Slingsby Sailplanes Ltd. of Kirbymoorside, Yorkshire, took up the specification and their Chief Designer Mr. F.N. Slingsby, MM, AFRAeS, began the firm's design for the new glider, to be called the Slingsby Type 18 and later the Hengist I.

Work on the prototype began in January 1941, and by October 1941, a confirmed order was made by Air Ministry for eighteen gliders, the first four to be prototypes. Main delivery of the Hengist was planned for the summer of 1942.

A year later in January 1942, the first of the four prototypes - serial number DG 570 - was air tested at RAF Dishforth. A Whitley aircraft Z6640 towed the Hengist which was piloted by Group Captain H.J. Wilson. (who some three years later on the 7th November 1945, captured the world's air speed record for Britain flying a Gloster Meteor IV at a speed of 606.38mph)

The other three prototypes, DG571, DG572 and DG573 were built and two - DG572 and DG 573 - were delivered to the Airborne Forces Experimental Establishment (AFEE) during January and February 1943, for trials. DG571 crashed at Dishforth in 1943 due it was reported to overloading. The remaining initial order of fourteen Hengists went into production with serial numbers from DG673 to DG686. In February 1943, DG673 went to AFEE for trials to be followed by DG673 in April. By the summer of 1943 all the Hengists on order had been delivered.

The Hengist had originally been intended as a paratroop dropping glider with a tail hook for towing another Hengist behind in a glider train, so that a force of thirty troops could be dropped at the same time. But with the advent of larger transport aircraft which could carry more paratroops, policy changed with the Hengist not being needed in this role.

The Hengist programme was abandoned in 1943, the Horsa glider being preferred, but 38 Wing did try to be allocated three without result. All the gliders were taken to Sherburn in Elmet and crated for storage at Rawcliffe Paper Mills, Yorkshire and were later scrapped in October 1946, as being surplus to requirements.

Description Hengist I.
High wing monoplane of all wood construction and built in sections.
Fuselage. 59 feet 2 inches long of rectangular cross section with plywood skinning. Constructed in two sections - forward for the two pilots sitting side by side - and

Hotspur seating

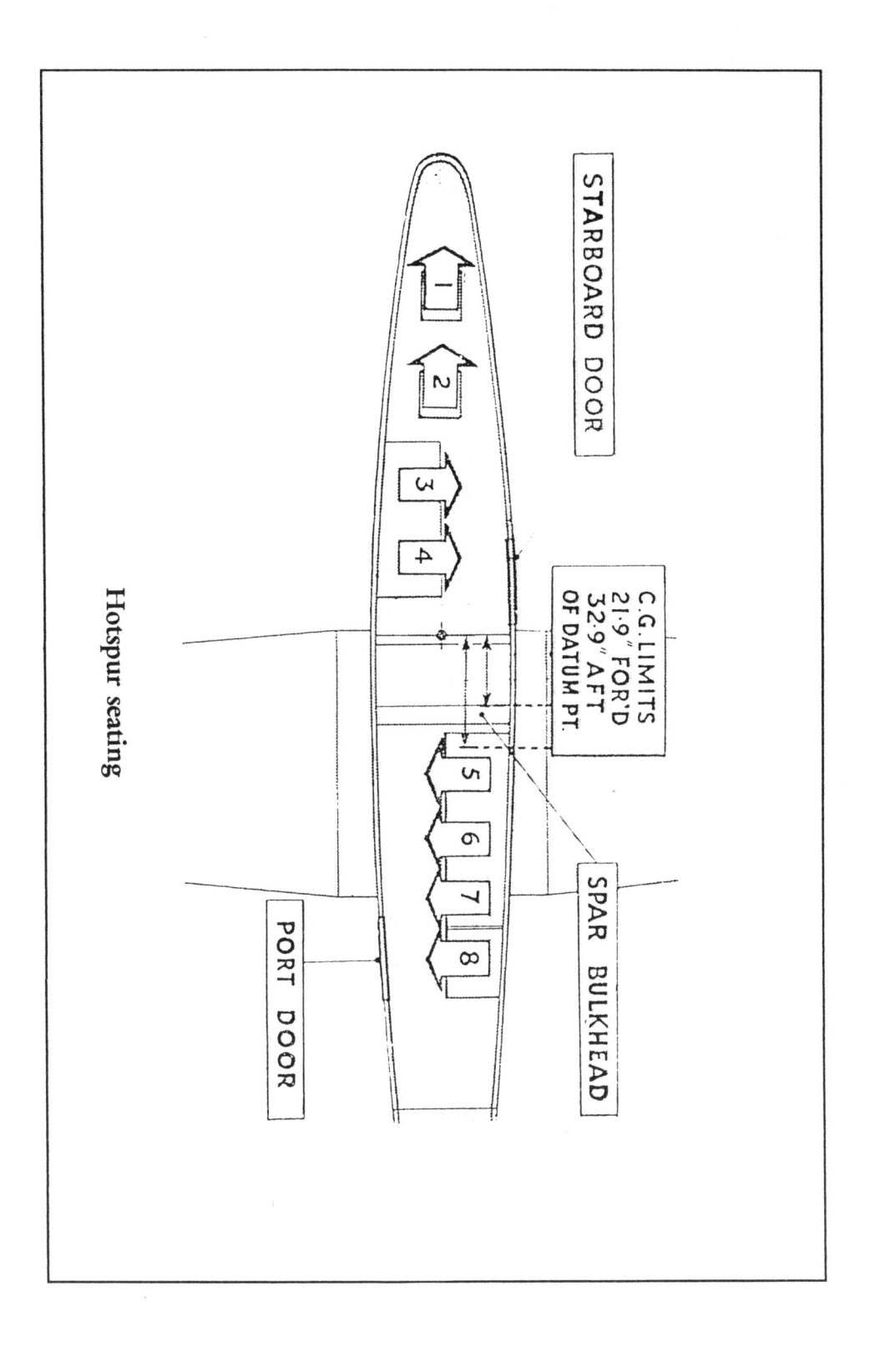

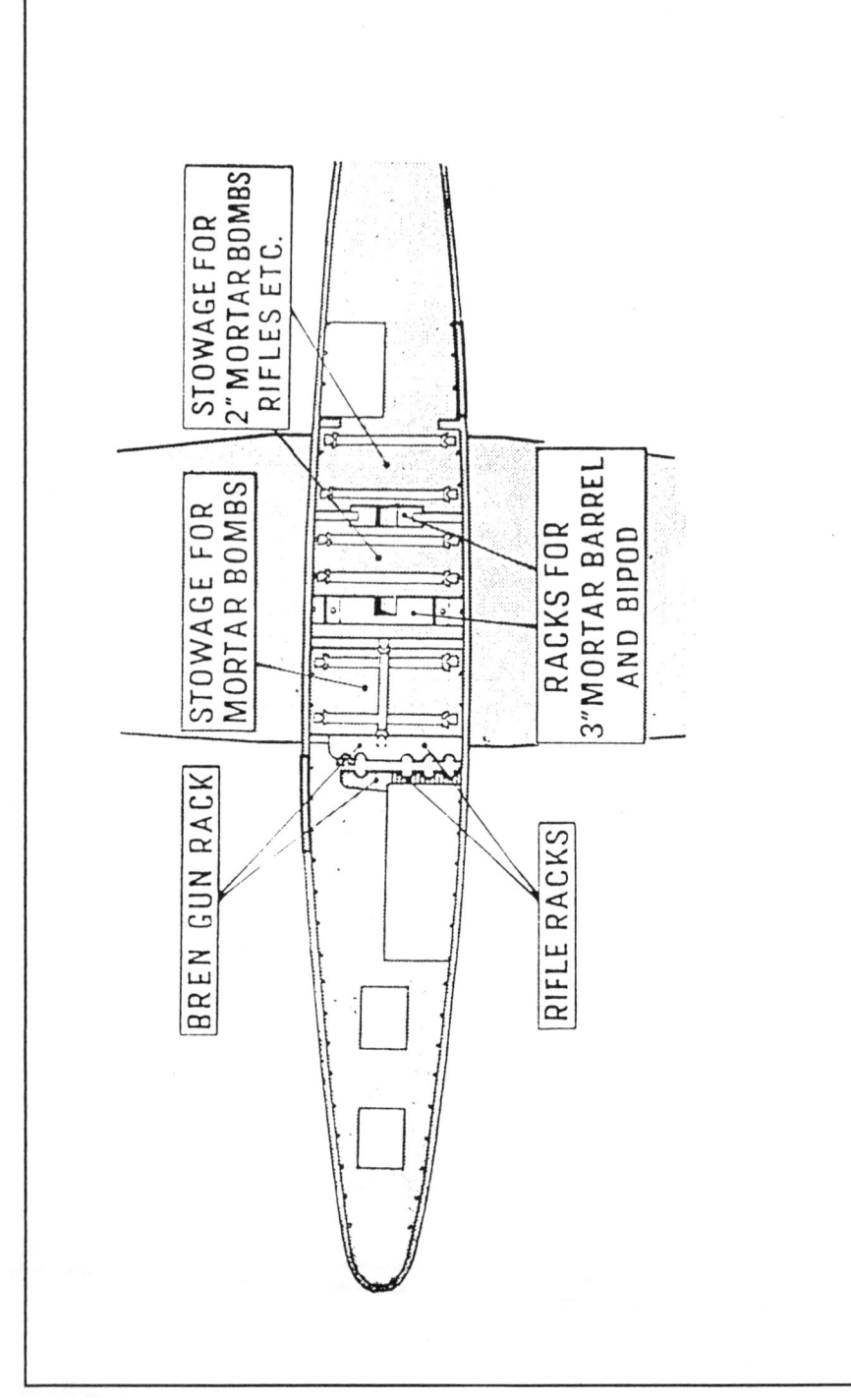

Hotspur weapon storage layout

the load carrying section extending rearwards to level with the trailing edge of the wing. Troops were seated on fifteen tip up seats facing inwards on each side of the fuselage. Access and exit was by two doors in the sides of the fuselage, one forward on the starboard side and one aft on the port side. Provision was to be made for the troops on board to use their light machine guns as defensive armament through holes in the fuselage windows.

The rear fuselage section behind the wing was hinged to reduce travelling length when on a 'Queen Mary' (an RAF truck designed to transport aircraft from airfield to airfield etc.)

Wings. Wooden construction with single main spar, wooden ribs, plywood skinned. 80 feet span with a area of 780 square feet and a loading of 10.7lbs per square foot. Spoilers fitted to upper surface of wings and bellows type trailing edge flaps.

Tail plane. All wooden construction with single fin and rudder plywood skinned.

Undercarriage. Two-wheeled jettisonable after take off. Landing on pneumatic skid under fuselage and another under tail plane. Main skid had twenty feet long inflated bag attached to absorb landing impact and stresses.

Speeds. Towing 130mph. Landing 80-90mph. Stalling 48mph.
Weight. All up 8350lbs. Empty 4629lbs. Payload 3721lbs.
Colour scheme. Operational dark green/dark earth for production gliders. Prototypes - yellow underneath dark green/dark earth on top.

## AIRSPEED HORSA Mk.I AND II

Air Ministry Specification X26/40 was for a military troop carrying glider capable of carrying twenty-five troops and two pilots. The specification was taken up by Airspeed in December 1940 and design work was carried out at Salisbury Hall, London Colney, Herts, under the direction of Airspeed's Technical Director Hessel Tiltman and the Horsa designer A.E. Ellison

The project was brilliantly conceived and carried out in that many firms were involved in building parts of the glider, later to be called the Horsa-Furniture makers, Coach Builders, Motor works and dozens of small firms. Each built component parts of the glider some thirty major sections in total which were then delivered for assembly at RAF Maintainance Units. A total of some 2960 Horsas were built in this way with another 695 being built by Airspeed at its Christchurch, Hampshire, factory.

Two prototypes - serials DG597 and DG603 - were built at Fairys Ltd., Great West Road aerodrome (now London Airport) where DG 597, towed off by a Whitley bomber and piloted by George Errington, made its first flight on the 12th September 1941, some ten months from the design stage.

The Horsa was of almost all wood construction using spruce and laminated plywood for greater strength. Every possible use was made of wood including the three spoked control wheel and column. The wings and tailplane were wooden framed with plywood and doped fabric covering. Mahogany and metal was used for the main spar anchorage points. The cylindrical shape fuselage was of the monocoque type with stressed plywood skin with spruce frames and bulkheads of box construction .

The Horsa Mk.I was a high wing military glider capable of carrying twenty-six equipped troops and flown by two pilots side by side, from the cockpit in the nose. The large perspex-covered cockpit gave excellent visibility with four clear vision panels, one in front of each pilot and one on each side, which could be opened. The instruments were mounted in a central panel; from left to right - Air speed indicator, artificial horizon, rate of climb indicator; underneath these were an altimeter and a turn and bank indicator. Another small panel held, the air pressure gauge - minimum 150lbs on training flights 200lbs for operational flights: when fully charged there was enough air for three complete cycles of flap operation and braking on landing and the the famous 'Angle of Dangle' the Cable Angle Indicator. A VHF TR9 radio was fitted on the right hand side of the 1st Pilot's seat and operated on a frequency of 3.3 to 6.6. megacycles with an air range of five miles and air/ground rage of 15 miles depending on conditions and locale. Communication with the tug pilot was by an intercom line woven into the 350 feet 3-inch diameter tow rope. This intercom frequently went unserviceable due to the stresses of towing and the dropping of the tow rope by the tug after cast off. On training the tow ropes were dropped by the tugs on a DZ and recovered by RAF ground crew. A yoke towing rope fitted to the Horsa's wings was used at first but was superseded by a single tow rope attached to the nose.

Description: Horsa.
Wing span 88 feet with a wing area of 1104 square feet and an aspect ratio of 7. Length 67 feet. MkI. All up weight 15,250lbs. Unladen 7,500lbs.
Tricycle undercarriage with castoring nose wheel and two main wheels on two separate triangular frames of tube construction which pivoted on brackets attached to the fuselage. The undercarriage main wheels could be jettisoned after take off by pulling a jettison release control lever in the cockpit to the right of the flap lever. Landing was then on a wooden metal faced skid under the fuselage and a

small tail skid. An arrester parachute could be fitted behind the tail plane to reduce the landing run.

Normal towing speed 130-140 knots. Depending on tug and load. Landing speed 70-80 depending on load. Large two piece split flaps fitted to the trailing edges of each wing with a maximum depression giving a 45 degree angle on a full flap descent (such as was made by Staff Sergeant Roy Howard, DFM. on the assault on the River Orne Bridge in Normandy on D-Day). The author well remembers when flying in an unloaded Horsa being amazed at the angle of descent followed by a shallow float in landing. The flying controls in free flight were pleasing to use and could be felt in the seat of ones pants. Stall turns, steep turns and dives were amazing for a large glider. When loaded the Horsa controls felt heavier but still positive and responsive. Normal flying control surfaces of rudder, ailerons and elevators were fitted with trim tabs.

Three compressed air bottles in the cockpit supplied pressure to the flaps, wheel brakes and the undercarriage jettison release. Four equipment containers could be fitted under each wing released by two pull handles inside the fuselage. Each handle released four containers on one side only.

Sanitary arrangements consisted of a bottle in the cockpit for the two pilots and a tube in the main cabin for the passengers. Entry to the Horsa was by an upwards sliding door on the port side aft of the cockpit. This door formed part of a larger door which opened outwards on a bottom hinge to form a ramp for entry/exit of cargo. Another upwards sliding door was provided on the starboard side aft of the wing. The Mk.II Horsa had a hinged nose/cockpit section which could be swung open to allow direct entry/exit to the fuselage payload compartment. Weight increased to 15,750lbs.

Passenger cabin seating consisted of plywood benches for twenty-three troops facing inwards, fitted with quick release safety straps. Three more seats faced forward at the rear of the compartment making a total of twenty-six. Three more seats could be fitted on the starboard side of the fuselage opposite the forward loading door, making a total of thirty-one troops carried depending on the weight of their equipment. Two gun hatches for defensive fire were fitted. One in the fuselage roof the other in the floor before the tailplane.

Other equipment carried was a Signal pistol and twenty five cartridges which fitted into a discharge tube on the cockpit floor outboard of the port pilot's seat: four torches, thermos flask, first aid kit, map case and loading charts.

It was considered at first that the glider could be used for paratroop dropping and two rails were provided over the doors for parachute static lines to be clipped onto. This idea was not pursued.

At one time in 1941 it was even considered that the Horsa could be used as a glider bomber. Horsa AS52 project (Air Ministry Specification X3/41) converted a Mk.I by cutting a bomb bay under the fuselage to enable a 12,000lbs armour piercing bomb to be carried. Although a prototype was flight tested in 1941 the idea was abandoned. Other ideas were to fit engines and rocket motors. Trials were made on the rocket assisted take off idea using Horsa DG597 towed by a Whitley aircraft but again the idea was not proceeded with.

With the need to off load equipment quickly on the battlefield experiments were conducted in removing the tail section by fitting a ring of Cordtex explosive around the rear bulkhead. When fired the explosive charge cut the fuselage neatly and it dropped to the ground. Then it was realised that enemy fire could detonate the explosive in flight, or on the ground, with disastrous results and the idea was quickly abandoned. The explosive charge could also damage the cargo or injure the occupants. However it was discovered that the tail section could be unbolted from the fuselage so a large spanner was included in the glider's equipment for this purpose.

A grand total of 3655 Horsa gliders were made - 695 at Christchurch and 2960 elsewhere. The Horsa was used operationally by Allied Forces from the 19th November 1942, (Operation Freshman) to the end of hostilities in Europe. It was not used in the far east due to its construction being unsuitable for the climate. Post war training was carried out with the Horsa until the late 1950s.

## GAL 48 HOTSPUR MK.I

In June 1940, prompted by the successful German gliderborne attack of May 1940, on Belgium, the Air Ministry put out Specification X10/40 for a military assault glider capable of carrying eight men and using the method of a high altitude tug release and a long silent descending glide approach to the intended target. The glider was to be cheap and expendable and and for use on one mission only. The specification called for a free flight glide of 100 miles from a 20,000 feet release.

General Aircraft Company of Feltham, Middlesex: Chief Designer F.F. Crocombe, took up the specification with their Designation GAL 48 Hotspur glider Mk.I. A first order of 400 was placed by Air Ministry and three prototypes, serial numbers BV134, 135 and 136 were built with the first glider flying some four months later on the 5th November 1940.

**Horsa seating layout**

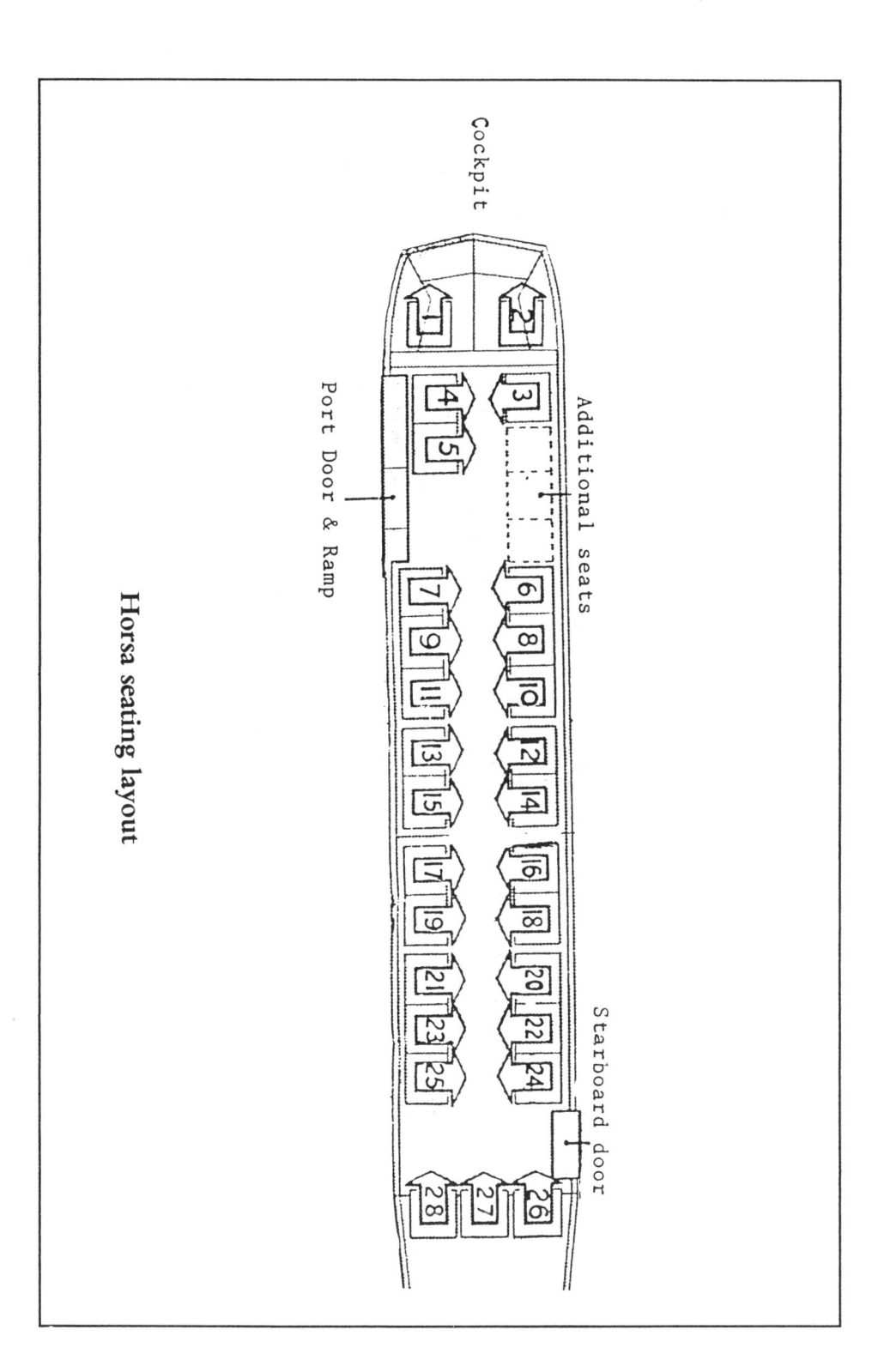

Miles Aircraft Company - M32 Project Glider

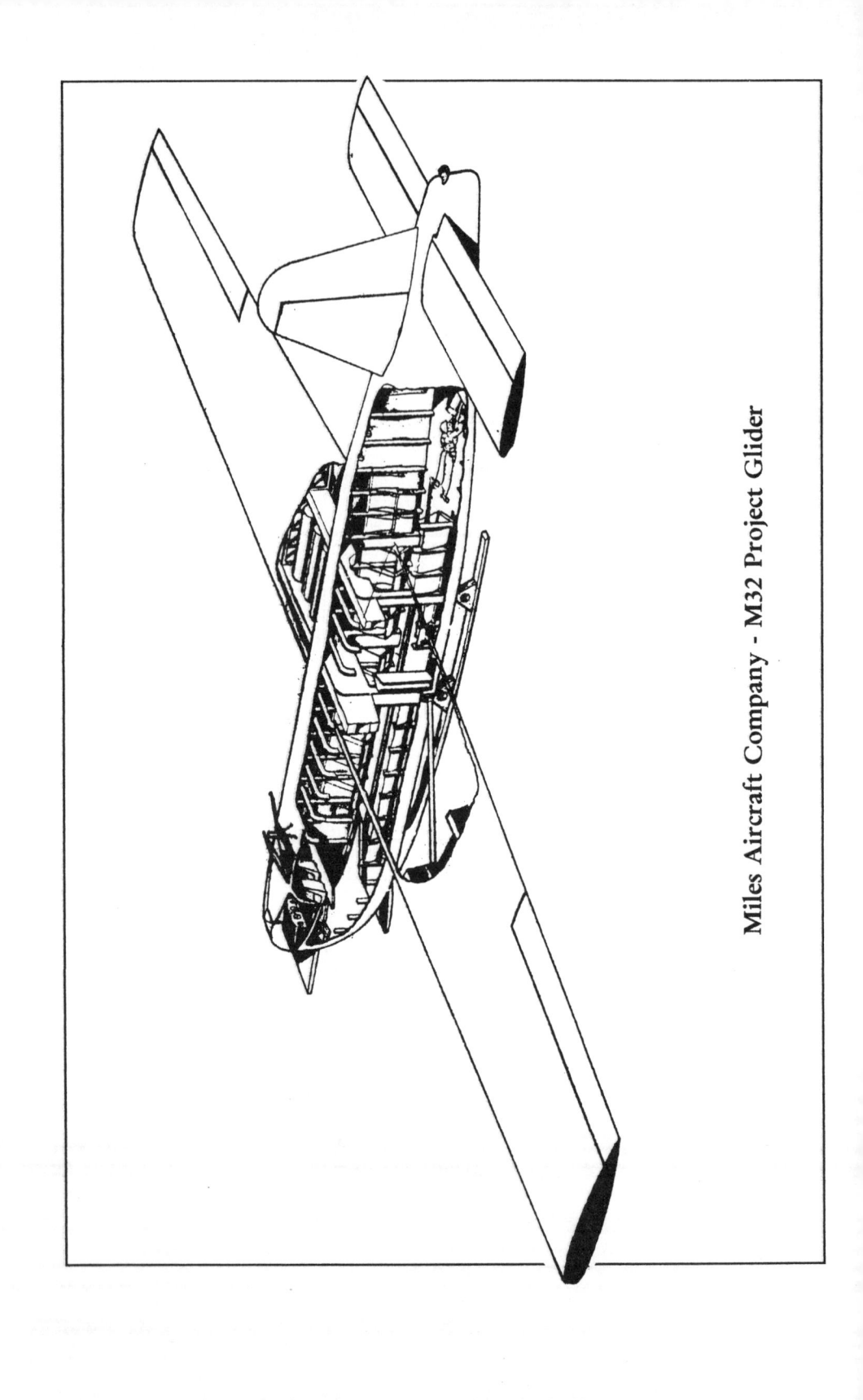

Description Hotspur Mk.I.
Wing Span 61 feet 11 inches. Aspect ratio 12. Wing area 272 square feet. Split trailing edge flaps.
Fuselage 39 feet 3½ inches. Height.10 feet 10 inches.
Weights. Loaded 3598lbs. Unloaded 1661lbs.
Capacity. Eight troops including pilot with light weapons in two compartments in the fuselage. Two in tandem in nose compartment one of whom was the pilot, two more on the port side facing inwards, four in the aft compartment also facing inwards.
Performance. Towing 135mph. Gliding 90mph. Gliding range from 20,000 feet release - 83 miles.
Construction. Mid wing monoplane of all wood construction with normal aircraft control surfaces. Twin wheel landing gear on struts under each wing which could be jettisoned with landing on a long centre and small tail skid. Removable fuselage lid for entry/exit by the occupants. Towing hooks front and rear - as at first it was thought two gliders could be towed in a glider train. A total of twenty-four Hotspur Mk.Is were built as follows:

BV134 - 140  (7) Slingsby.
BV146 - 151  (6) Slingsby.
BV190 - 199  (10)GAL
BV200        (1) Airspeed.

Trials of the Mk.I showed that the Air Ministry Specification could not be met although when not carrying passengers it glided like a sailplane. BV199 became the Mk.II prototype as the War Office changed its views in October 1940, on the role of gliders from the original thinking. The new concept was that the tug would release the glider at low altitude on a LZ and the glider would land quickly with a steep approach thus reducing the time exposed to enemy fire.

This entailed building a stronger glider and specification X22/40 was issued and taken up by General Aircraft Company who sub contracted to several furniture makers including Harris Lebus, Lawrence Mulliners and Waring & Gillows.

Description Hotspur Mk.II.
Wing span. 45 feet 11 inches. Square tips.
Length. 39 feet 9 inches.
Height. 10 feet 10 inches.
Weights. Loaded 3598lbs. Unloaded 1661lbs.

Construction as for Hotspur Mk.I but with the following differences.

Doors fitted to port side just behind the wing for troop entry to the aft compartment and to the starboard side in front of the wing for the forward compartment. Some Hotspurs had a rack fitted on the forward bulkhead for stowing three rifles and a Bren gun with its spare barrel-all held in position by adjustable straps. By removing seats 5, 6 and 7 in the aft compartment a 3-inch mortar with ammunition could be carried again strapped in position. Cockpit cover hinged to starboard side. Cockpit fitted with air speed indicator, altimeter, compass, turn and bank indicator and nose and tail indicator. Cable operated release knob for tow rope. Other equipment carried was torches, map case, vacuum flasks and four urine bottles. A storage battery provided power for navigation and signalling lamps.

Performance. 90mph on tow. 80mph in free flight.
Mk.II Serial numbers were.
BT479-513   (35)   HH109-153   (45)
BT534-557   (24)   HH167-198   (32)
BT561-579   (19)   HH223-268   (46)
BT594-640   (47)   HH284-333   (50)
BT658-693   (36)   HH346-388   (43)
BT715-755   (41)   HH401-431   (31)
BT769-799   (31)   HH448-493   (46)
BT813-861   (49)   HH517-566   (50)
BT877-903   (27)   HH579-623   (45)
BT916-948   (33)   HH636-674   (39)
BT961-990   (30)   HH688-732   (45)
BV112-129   (18)   HH751-800   (50)
Total       390    HH821-853   (33)
                   HH878-919   (42)
                   Total       597.

Built by Harris Lebus, Lawrence Mulliners, Waring & Gillows.
Grand total 987.

In an effort to increase the load carrying capacity of the Hotspur, GAL built an experimental prototype - serial number MP486 - in 1942. Two Mk.II fuselages were joined together by a new twelve foot wide wing centre section and a similar section between the tailplanes. Two Mk.II wings were added to the outer side of the fuselages giving a wing span of 58 feet. The glider was flown from the left hand cockpit and first flew in 1942, towed by a Whitley. However MP486 later crashed and the project was abandoned.

At first it had been intended to use the Hotspur as an assault glider but it simply was not big enough to carry the large large numbers of troops who would be required on an airborne operation and was relegated to a training role. Training livery of dark earth/dark green top surfaces and yellow/black undersurfaces was assumed.

Specification X23/40P put the Hotspur into production by GAL and fifty two Mk.IIs were converted to Mk.IIIs. The main differences between the Mk.II and Mk.III were that the glider was towed from the nose not the keel, the tailplane was braced, the second pilot had an instrument panel - flap lever and intercom, a Cable Angle Indicator (the famous Angle of Dangle) which showed the glider pilot his glider's position relative to the tow rope on low tow. The following fifty two Mk.IIs were converted to Mk.IIIs:

BT540-735-823
BT566-747-895
BT602-751-917
BT632-777-946
BT663-784.
HH143-330-694-751
HH175-373-698-783
HH180-518-704-784
HH190-526-723-786
HH228-529-724-789
HH231-536-754-835
HH261-555-767-834
HH294-565-774-839
HH323-610-775
HH326-691-776.

Twenty-two Hotspurs were transferred to the Royal Canadian Air Force:

HH418-558-659
HH419-559-667
HH421-560
HH425-561
HH427-562
HH521-564

HH551-579
HH552-580
HH553-646
HH557-647

The Hotspur was never used operationally but extensively on glider pilot training. During training the rear seats were weighted with ballast but at Operational Training Units the glider pilot had a load of troops on board. A total of 1012 Hotspurs were built and it became the standard elementary training glider at the Glider Training Schools.

## MILES M32 - PROJECT

The Air Ministry Specification X27/40 was for a tank carrying glider and the Miles Aircraft Company under took up a design project - the M32 glider. The design was a two pilot high wing monoplane capable of carrying 25 troops, or two guns and 16 troops or a jeep in place of the gun. An upwards lifting door and downwards dropping ramp was fitted in the nose with the pilot's cockpit above it. This allowed easy straight out exit and entry to the fuselage.

Two defensive machine gun position were fitted, one on top of the fuselage behind the pilots cockpit and the other in the rear floor of the fuselage. The large square tipped wings were V braced to the bottom fuselage longerons and could carry supply containers. For tow off a jettisonable trolley undercarriage was to be used with landing on skids. Two pusher detachable engines could be fitted to assist take off. As the larger Hamilcar tank carrying glider gave a better payload and the Horsa glider a larger troop carrying capacity the design was not proceeded with.

## BRITISH TAYLORCRAFT H GLIDER

During WWII the Taylorcraft Aeroplane Company (England) of Thurweston, Leicester, produced a prototype three-seater training glider very similar to the the American Taylorcraft TG-6 (Training Glider No. 6). Basically, the glider was a conversion of a two-seater, single-engined light aircraft with the engine removed and a transparent nose section added together with another seat where the engine had been. The glider could be flown from any of the three seats.

Description: Primary three seat training glider.
High wing monoplane with wing span of 36 feet strut braced. Two laminated wooden mainspars with pressed metal ribs fabric covered.
Fabric covered ailerons and split trailing edge flaps.

Fuselage 24 feet long of welded steel tubular structure with wooden stringers fabric covered.

Tail plane of tubular metal fabric covered with fixed trim tabs on rudder and elevators. Mass balanced rudder.

Undercarriage. Doughnut wheels attached to the lower fuselage longerons. Skid under tailplane.

Only one prototype was built - marked with the 'P' symbol (Prototype) behind the RAF roundel. Training livery of dark green and earth on the upper surfaces and yellow undersurfaces with black diagonal stripes.

# GLIDERBORNE WEAPONS AND EQUIPMENT

Military gliders were specifically designed and built to transport troops, tanks and equipment to battle. Specific gliders to do specific tasks. The huge Hamilcar was designed to carry tanks, guns, vehicles and heavy equipment; the Horsa to carry troops, guns, small vehicles and supplies. The Hadrian (Waco CG4A) to carry a jeep, a gun or troops.

## TANKS

TETRARCH A.17E1. Developed from the British pre WWII A17 and Light Tank Mk.VII which came into production in November 1940, and renamed Tetrarch in 1943. Came into airborne service in 1944 then with 6th Airborne Reconnaissance Regiment who had sixteen on establishment. Made military history on D-Day when eight were transported to the battlefield in Hamilcar gliders. Several were used on Operation Varsity.
Weight. 16800lbs. (7.5 tons)
HP.    165hp. 12 cylinder Meadows MAT engine.
Speed. 34mph average. 40mph on roads. 28 cross country.
Guns.  2-pounder (40mm) QFSA main gun. 1X 7.92mm Besa machine gun.
       Ammunition. 50 rounds AP. 2025 rounds 7.92mm. Some fitted with 3-inch howitzer and called Model ICS (Infantry Close Support) in place of standard 2 pounder.
Crew.  3. Commander, Gunner and Driver.
Length. Overall 14 feet 1½ inches.
Height. 6 feet 11½ inches.
Armour. Front 6-10mm. Sides 6mm. Floor 14mm.
The Tetrarch remained in airborne service (3rd Hussars) at Fairford and Netheravon until the Hamilcar was redundant.

LOCUST. US M22 renamed Locust, entered production April 1943. Only British combat use on Operation Varsity, 1945.
Weight. 16452lbs. Loaded. (7.34 tons)
HP.    162hp. Lycoming 0-435T engine.
Guns.  One 37mm L/37 M6 main gun. One Browning .50 machine-gun.
       Ammunition. 50 rounds 37mm. 2500 rounds .50.
Crew.  3.
Armour. 9mm to 25mm.
Height. 4 feet 1 inch.

Length. 12 feet 11 inches.
Speed. 40mph. with radius of 135 miles.
The Locust was made obsolete in July, 1945 as being surplus to requirements.

UNIVERSAL CARRIER. Open top rectangular hull riveted/welded armoured plated twin tracked vehicle - produced in 1940 and designed to carry three or four troops, weapons or equipment. Nine different Marks were made but the vehicle was basically the same, merely adapted for specific tasks. Popularly called a Bren gun carrier.
Weight 3 - 4¼ tons.
Length 12 feet.
Width 7 feet.
Height 5 feet 3 inches.
Engines - Ford V8 90° L head; 65hp - 85hp - 95hp series.
Speed 30mph governed. Armour plate 4mm to 10mm.
Weapons. Fitted as required. 303 Bren LMG. .303 Vickers HMG. .55 Boys anti-tank gun. .30 and .50 Browning MG. PIAT. 2- and 3-inch mortar German 20mm Solothurn anti-tank gun. Flame thrower.
Manufactured in UK, Canada, Australia, New Zealand. 200 were supplied to Russia.

## TRANSPORT VEHICLES

JEEP. Universally known as the Jeep, from its initial 'GP' for general purpose vehicle, the vehicle began life as a response to the US Government's Command Reconnaissance vehicle programme. Three US companies submitted designs and after trials the Willys Overland design was accepted and put into mass production in 1941 by several US companies.

Some authorities say that the US CG4A (Hadrian) glider was designed round the jeep which fitted exactly into the fuselage. The four-wheel drive four seat Jeep could tow the British 6-pounder anti-tank gun, trailers in train, carry stretchers, radio sets, ammunition, equipment and when fitted with Vickers K or Browning machine guns was used by airborne troops, SAS and the Long Range Desert Group. In its main glider borne role the Jeep was used to tow the 6 Pounder gun and both gun and Jeep could be loaded into a MkII Horsa then driven straight out into action.

## MOTOR CYCLES

Standard British civilian motor cycles in camouflage garb were used but in an attempt to save weight the Welbike scooter was issued. Made by the Excelsior Motor Company, Birmingham, the Welbike (named after its place of design and origin Welwyn, Hertfordshire) was a two wheeled folding scooter with a 98cc Villiers Junior two stroke engine. Weighing 70lbs the machine could be unfolded and started in eleven seconds, had a 90 mile range and a speed of 30mph, and could carry a lightly equipped soldier.

## BICYCLES

A special folding bicycle was devised for airborne troops but was of little practical use - none in battle.

## WEAPONS

17 pounder anti-tank gun. Calibre 3-inch (76mm). Crew eight - sergeant, corporal, five gunners and a driver/gunner. Tow vehicle Morris 30cwt truck. Owing to its size and weight the gun could only be air transported in a Hamilcar glider.

75mm pack howitzer.(US).
Weight 1340lbs.
Range 9475 yards.(maximum) Shell weight 10lb. Rate of fire 6 rounds per minute. Tow vehicle GP Jeep. Carried in Horsa with Jeep.

6 pounder anti-tank gun. Calibre 2.2 inches.
Weight 2240lbs.
Rounds per minute 10. Effective range 1000 yards. Muzzle velocity 2700 feet per second. Tow vehicle GP Jeep. Carried in Horsa with Jeep. Carried in the smaller CG4A on its own.

## MORTARS

2-inch, 3-inch and 4.2-inch firing high explosive or smoke rounds. 4.2 weighed 257lbs. Range 4100 yards. Easily portable.

PIAT. Projecter Infantry Anti-Tank.
Weight 32lbs.
Length 39 inches.
Hollow charge round, weight 3lbs. Muzzle velocity 450 feet per second. Combat range 100 yards. Maximum range 750 yards. Fired by compressing the powerful 32-inch long mainspring and pulling trigger. Penetration depth 75mm of armour.

## MACHINE-GUNS

VICKERS .303 machine-gun. Recoil operated.
Weight 43lbs.
Length 3 feet 8 inches.
Fully automatic with cyclic rate of fire of 500 rounds per minute. Range up to 4000 yards with accurate range 600 yards.

BREN LIGHT MACHINE-GUN. One of the best light machine-guns ever made. Originally made in BRNO, Czechoslavakia, and developed in England at Enfield - hence the name BREN.
Calibre .303 British Service round.
Weight 23lbs.
Single or fully automatic. Muzzle velocity 2400 feet per second. Range up to 2000 yards with accurate range 500 yards. 30 round magazine. Cyclic rate of fire 450 to 550 rounds per minute. Battle rate of fire four magazines a minute. Could be fired from the hip or on a tripod. A deadly accurate and popular weapon.

STEN SUB MACHINE-GUN. Considered to be the cheapest sub machine-gun ever made when it was produced. Designed by R.V. Sheppard and A.A. Turpin and made at Enfield, the name is taken from the designers initials and place of manufacture. Calibre 9mm (.35)
Weight with full magazine 9½lbs.
Length 35 inches.
32 round magazine staggered box type. Backward gas operated. Muzzle velocity 1060 feet per second. Accurate range up to 200 range with rear sight set for 100 yards. Cyclic rate of fire 500 rounds per minute. Deliberately designed to use German 9mm ammunition. Single or automatic fire. With a loaded magazine inserted and the cocking handle forward the Sten was liable to fire if dropped or jarred.

## RIFLES

STANDARD .303 SMLE. (Short Magazine Lee Enfield). No.4 MkI. Bolt action ten round magazine (2 five round clips).
Weight 9lbs 3 ounces.

## PISTOLS

ENFIELD .380, WEBLEY .455, SMITH & WESSON .38 revolvers.
US COLT .45 semi-automatic pistol.

## GRENADES

As well as the Mills grenades two other types were used. The Hawkins No.75 grenade or light mine and the Gammon bomb No.82 grenade designed by Captain R.J. Gammon, 1st Parachute Battalion Parachute Regiment which was basically plastic explosive in a stockinette bag with a detonator in a screw cap at the neck. Dangerous to both user and recipient but effective in trained hands.

## KNIVES

Commando fighting knives of various designs.


In battle the airborne soldier would fight with any weapon he could lay his hands on. In Sicily he fought with captured Italian/German weapons and at Arnhem with captured German weapons.

# ROYAL AIR FORCE AIRBORNE FORCES GROUPS

At the outbreak of WWII in Europe in September 1939, the only Royal Air Force units specifically concerned with Army co operation were No.22 Army C Operation Group composed of thirteen squadrons and the Air Component of the British Expeditionary Force (BEF) in France, who were under the command of British Air Forces, France.

A Training Unit for Airborne Forces had been established at RAF Ringway, near Manchester, on the 19th June 1940, at first named the Central Landing School and later on the 19th September 1940, re-named the Central Landing Establishment, with Wing Commander Sir Nigel Norman in charge of RAF training.

With the rapid expansion of the Royal Air Force after hostilities commenced with Germany it became obvious that an RAF Command for Airborne Forces operations was needed. Accordingly in December 1940, Army Co-Operation Command was formed under Air Marshal Sir Arthur S. Barratt, KCB. CMG. MC. who had been appointed Air Officer Commanding in Chief (AOCIC) of the new command on the 20th November 1940. The Training Unit at RAF Ringway had been under the command of 22 Group but on the 1st December 1940, it was placed under 70 Group and HQ Army Co-Operation Command.

As the Airborne Forces organization began to take shape it was decided by Air Ministry and the Chiefs of Staff to form an RAF Wing solely for ARMY/RAF training and operations. Thus No.38 Wing HQ was formed on the 15th January 1942, under Sir Nigel Norman who was promoted to the rank of Group Captain with his HQ at Syrencot House, Brigmerston, Wiltshire, which was midway on the road from Netheravon, where the RAF Squadrons were, and Bulford Camp where the Airborne troops were.

The first gliderborne operation carried out by the new Wing was the ill fated Operation Freshman when two Halifax tugs towed two Horsa gliders carrying volunteer Royal Engineers to attack the Heavy Water Plant at Rjukan, Norway. One Halifax and the two gliders crashed killing most of those on board, those who survived were murdered by the Germans. One Halifax returned to base.

The next glider borne operation carried out by the Wing was that of ferrying Horsa gliders from Portreath, Cornwall, to North Africa in preparation for the invasion of Sicily in July 1943. The Operations, named Beggar/Turkey Buzzard and Elaborate, were carried out by 295 Squadron using Halifax aircraft as tugs and the Glider Pilot Regiment flying the Horsas. 38 Wing provided tugs for the Sicily invasion in July 1943, but the glider operation was not a 100% success in spite of the valour of the British tug and glider aircrews.

On the 1st June 1943, Army Co Operation Command was disbanded and became Fighter Command, Tactical Air Force. It was decided that 38 Wing should be expanded to a Group and the Commander should be of Air Rank. On the 11th October the expansion began with authorisation for nine squadrons - four Stirling, four Albemarle and one Halifax - of aircraft. With this expansion 38 Wing became 38 Group on the 6th November 1943, with Air Vice Marshal L.N. Hollingshurst, CB. OBE. DFC, appointed as Air Officer Commanding the Group.

HQ Allied Expeditionary Force was created on the 15th November 1943, under the command of Air Marshal Sir Trafford Leigh Mallory, and 38 Group was transferred to AEAF but remained under Air Defence of Great Britain Command for administrative purposes.

Even with its expansion 38 Group was not large enough to carry out the planned airborne invasion of France in 1944 so another Airborne Forces Group - No.46 - was formed under Transport Command on the 17th January 1944, with its AOC Air Commodore L.A. Fiddament, CB. OBE. DFC. with its HQ at Harrow Weald. 46 Group was equipped with 150 Dakotas supplied by the United States. Although the Group was under Transport Command - operational control was vested in HQ 38 Group Commander - therefore it was decided to site the operational HQ of 46 Group alongside HQ 38 Group at Netheravon as the two Groups would be working alongside each other on operations and training. By the 6th June 1944, D-Day, both Groups were ready for their part in the invasion of France.

38 Group.

| | | |
|---|---|---|
| 190 Squadron | Stirling | Fairford |
| 196 Squadron | Stirling | Keevil |
| 295 Squadron | Albemarle | Harwell |
| 296 Squadron | Albemarle | Brize Norton |
| 297 Squadron | Albemarle | Brize Norton |
| 298 Squadron | Halifax | Tarrant Rushton |
| 299 Squadron | Stirling | Keevil |
| 570 Squadron | Albemarle | Harwell |
| 620 Squadron | Stirling | Fairford |
| 644 Squadron | Halifax | Tarrant Rushton |

The by now ten Squadron Group had 264 aircraft, 150 Horsa gliders and 70 Hamilcar gliders ready for operations.

46 Group.
| | | |
|---|---|---|
| 48 Squadron | Dakota | Down Ampney |
| 233 Squadron | Dakota | Blakehill Farm |
| 271 Squadron | Dakota | Down Ampney |
| 512 Squadron | Dakota | Broadwell |
| 575 Squadron | Dakota | Broadwell |

Five Squadrons of 150 aircraft with 200 Horsa gliders available. The two Airborne Groups thus had 414 aircraft plus 420 gliders to lift 6th Airborne Division to Normandy in Operations Tonga and Mallard, code names for the British airborne operations on D-Day. Both Tonga and Mallard were carried out successfully by the two groups. 98 gliders were towed off for Operation Tonga and 59 landed on their appointed DZs. 256 gliders were towed off for the daylight Operation Mallard and 246 landed on their LZs.

During the summer of 1944 the two Groups carried out re-supply missions and SAS Operations in France and elsewhere. On the 16th August 1944, both Groups came under the operational command of 1st Allied Airborne Army commanded by the US Lt. General Lewis H Brereton, for airborne operations. 46 Group was commanded by Air Commodore L. Darvall but HQ 38 Group was to be the HQ for RAF operations.

Preparations and training went ahead for the next large scale airborne operation, Operation Market, and both Groups were to transport 1st Airborne Division to battle by glider and paratroop drop followed by re-supply missions. Ten squadrons of 38 Group and six squadrons of 46 Group (437 RCAF Squadron had by now joined 46 Group) were available for the operation. During Operation Market the two Groups towed off 692 gliders (653 Horsas, 30 Hamilcars and 9 Hadrians, both Groups employing 692 aircraft to tow the gliders of which 621 made successful landings. Both Groups suffered heavy losses in men and aircraft particularly during the re-supply missions when the aircrews were determined to supply their army comrades on the ground. Flight Lieutenant D.S.A. Lord, a pilot of 271 Squadron, won a posthumous Victoria Cross when on a re-supply mission.

On the 22nd July 1944, 46 Group moved its HQ to Harrow Weald prior to its Squadrons moving to East Anglia. On the 9th October 190 Squadron of 38 Group towed 32 Horsa gliders from Fairford to Italy (Operation Molten) for use in future projected airborne operations and continued in clandestine dropping of SAS troops and agents. Also on the 9th October 1944, 38 Group moved its HQ from Netheravon to Marks Hall, Colchester, Essex, in preparation for the next airborne operation into Germany itself, Operation Varsity. To shorten flying time all squadrons of the Groups moved their bases to East Anglia.

## 38 GROUP

| | |
|---|---|
| 190 Squadron | Great Dunmow |
| 196 Squadron | Shepherds Grove |
| 295 Squadron | Rivenhall |
| 296 Squadron | Earls Colne |
| 297 Squadron | Earls Colne |
| 298 Squadron | Woodbridge |
| 299 Squadron | Shepherds Grove |
| 570 Squadron | Rivenhall |
| 620 Squadron | Great Dunmow |
| 644 Squadron | Woodbridge |
| ORTU (Stirling) | Matching |

## 46 GROUP

| | |
|---|---|
| 48 Squadron | Birch |
| 233 Squadron | Birch |
| 271 Squadron | Gosfield |
| 437 Squadron RCAF | Birch |
| 512 Squadron | Gosfield |
| 575 Squadron | Gosfield |

On the 18th October 1944, Air Vice Marshal J.R. Scarlett-Streatfield, CBE. was appointed AOC 38 Group when Air Vice Marshal Hollingshurst was promoted Air Marshal. Air Commodore L. Darvall remained in command of 46 Group.

On the 24th March 1945, the largest airborne operation ever mounted commenced - Operation Varsity - the tactical landing into Germany to open the door for the Allies to pour into the German heartland. 38 and 46 Groups put 120 Dakotas, 194 Stirlings and 120 Halifax tug aircraft into the air towing 386 Horsa and 48 Hamilcar gliders. 434 tugs towing 434 gliders. 402 gliders were recorded as landing successfully (92%) and the two Groups losses were four aircraft shot down and thirty two damaged. The largest airborne operation had been the most successful by the two RAF Groups.

No more glider operations were carried out by the Groups during WWII although forty seven Stirlings of 38 Group dropped Canadian paratroops in Holland (Operation Amherst) during the night of the 7th-8th April 1945. No. 161 (Special Duty) Squadron was now included in 38 Group - this squadron specialised in clandestine landing of agents in occupied territory using Westland Lysanders but was also equipped with Stirling aircraft for supply dropping.

The war in Europe ended on the 8th May 1945, with the Germans surrendering unconditionally. 38 Group engaged in Operation Schnapps to land troops of 1st Airborne Division at Copenhagen to be followed by Operation Doomsday, the transporting of troops to Norway to deal with the surrendered German troops there. Three aircraft crashed during the operation including that of the AOC Air Vice Marshal Scarlett-Streatfield, who with all his aircrew were killed. His place as AOC was taken by Air Commodore N.C. Singer, DSO. DFC.

On the 2nd June 1945, the Special Duty 161 Squadron was disbanded and a reshuffle of airfields, squadron and personnel took place. The remaining enemy was Japan and 298 Squadron was transferred to South East Asia Command (SEAC) at Raipur, India, during August and 38 Group came under Transport Command. 620 and 644 Squadrons were transferred to Aqir and Quastina in Palestine to join 283 Airborne Forces Wing under 216 Group, Transport Command.

With Japan surrendering to the Allies in August 1945, both 38 and 46 Groups were in a further state of flux during the immediate post war period. In September 1947, the two Groups carried out Exercise Longstop at Netheravon (in which the author was involved) which included a gliderborne element. By 1949 it was becoming clear that the days of the glider were nearly over and that helicopters were taking over. Glider training was largely concentrated at RAF Upper Heyford as No.1 Parachute and Glider Training School and Netheravon.

No.46 Group was disbanded at RAF Abingdon on the 31st March 1950. By the 1st September 1950, the Glider Pilot Regiment was reduced to one squadron flying Horsa gliders and by 1951 the glider was officially doomed. The run down of 38 Group continued and on the 1st February 1951, the Group was disbanded. It had been the largest Group in the Royal Air Force at the end of WWII and had air lifted the largest airborne assault force ever seen in the history of war. However 38 Group was re-formed in January 1960, as a specialist transport Group within Transport Command in connection with Army support. On the 18th November 1982, it was almalgamated with No.1 Group with its HQ at RAF Upavon and under the control of Strike Command, High Wycombe.

Thus 38 Group disappeared into history but its motto 'Par Nobile Fratrum' (A noble pair of brothers) symbolised the partnership between the Royal Air Force and the Airborne Forces of the Army. As an Airborne officer said simply to the author, "We would never have got there without you."

# ROYAL AIR FORCE TUG SQUADRONS

A total of sixteen squadrons were used during WWII to tow gliders on operations from the United Kingdom and Tunisia and included one RCAF Squadron. These squadrons came from four sources as follows:

Formed as Airborne Support Squadrons. (7)
295, 296, 297, 298, 299, 570 and 644.
Formed as Transport Squadrons. (4).
271, 437(RCAF), 512 and 575.
Transferred from Coastal Command. (3).
48 and 233 (Formerly Hudson squadrons).
190 Formerly Catalina Squadron.
Transferred from Bomber Command. (2).
196 and 620.
The six squadrons of 46 Group (48, 233, 271, 437(RCAF), 512 & 575 were formed and used as transport squadrons, but trained for airborne support duties as required.

47 Squadron, 38 Group
First formed at Beverley on the 1st March 1916, and began a long history of Army Co Operation at Khartoum in 1927 with DH 9A aircraft and continued in such co operation until 1940. On the 1st September 1946, No.644 Squadron was re numbered 47 Squadron and equipped with Halifax A7 and A9 aircraft and was engaged with airborne forces duties until September 1948.

| | |
|---|---|
| Aircraft: | DH9A. Halifax A7 and A9. Hastings C1 and C2 |
| Airfields: | Fairford 30.9.46. Dishforth 14.9.48. |

48 Squadron.    46 Group
Formed on the 15th March 1916, at RAF Netheravon. In 1944 the squadron was transferred to Transport Command and equipped with Dakota aircraft. On the 6th June 1944, D-Day No.48 provided thirty aircraft for para drops and carried out 22 glider towing sorties. In September 1944, the squadron successfully towed 49 gliders to Arnhem (Operation Market) but suffered heavy losses of one third of its strength in re supply sorties. The squadron took part in the Rhine Crossing (Operation Varsity) with 12 glider tugs then went to India. It was disbanded in

January 1946, but was reformed in February 1946. It later engaged in supply dropping in Malaya. It was finally disbanded on the 7th January 1976.

Aircraft:        Dakota III & IV and C4.
Airfields:       Bircham Newton 21.2.44    Down Ampney 24.2.44.

190 Squadron.    38 Group
Originally formed at Newmarket on the 24th October 1917 and disbanded in January 1919. Reformed on the 1st March 1943 then disbanded again on 31st December 1943. Reformed at RAF Leicester East on the 5th January 1944, as an airborne forces squadron equipped with Stirling aircraft and engaged in glider towing exercises. On D-Day the squadron was engaged in Operation Tonga on Para dropping on the initial DZ then towed eighteen gliders on Operation Mallard. At Arnhem the squadron flew forty missions towing gliders and lost eleven aircraft to enemy flak when on re-supply drops. Twenty-eight Stirlings towed gliders on the Rhine Crossing in Operation Varsity. The squadron was disbanded on the 28th December 1945.

Aircraft:        Short Stirling IV, Halifax III & VII.
Airfields:       Leicester East 5.1.44. Fairford 25.3.44. Great Dunmow 14.10.44.

196 Squadron.    38 Group
Formed at RAF Driffield on the 7th November 1942 then transferred to airborne forces duties on the 18th November 1943. Engaged on glider towing and para drop training with Stirling aircraft. On D-Day for Operation Tonga the squadron's Stirlings carried paratroops to Normandy followed later the same day towing seventeen gliders on Operation Mallard. At Arnhem on Operation Market the squadron towed in fifty-six gliders during the assault. For Operation Varsity thirty one aircraft were employed towing gliders over the Rhine. The squadron was disbanded on the 16th March 1946.

Aircraft:        Short Stirling Mk. III, Iv & V
Airfields:       Leicester East 18.9.43.    Tarrant Rushton 7.1.44.
                 Keevil 14.3.44.            Wethersfield 9.10.44.
                 Shepherds Grove 26.1.45.

**233 Squadron. 46 Group**
First formed at Dover in August 1919. In February 1944, the squadron was equipped with Dakota aircraft and became an airborne forces squadron. On D-Day the squadron supplied thirty aircraft to tow six gliders and drop paratroops followed later the same day by supply drops. Four aircraft were lost. Later it carried out casualty evacuation duties from Normandy. At Arnhem on Operation Market the squadron lost three aircraft during its missions which included towing forty gliders. This was followed by thirty-five re-supply sorties. During the Rhine Crossing operation twenty-four aircraft were used all of which were glider tows.

Aircraft:     Dakota III.
Airfields:    Bircham Newton 1.3.44.  Blakehill Farm 5.3.44.  Birch 24.3.45.


**271 Squadron. 46 Group**
Formed during September 1918, at Otranto, Italy, and disbanded on the 9th December 1918. The squadron reformed on the 1st May 1940, at Doncaster and carried out transport duties. In January 1944, the squadron was re-equipped with Dakota aircraft although it still retained Handley Page Harrow I & II aircraft for casualty flights. In the same month it became an airborne forces unit and provided twenty two glider tugs on D-Day for Operation Tonga. The squadron's Harrow aircraft were used for casevac flights from the Normandy beachhead. During Operation Market the squadron supplied forty-eight aircraft to tow gliders. For Operation Varsity 271 towed twelve Horsa gliders into Germany. Seven of the squadron's Harrow aircraft were destroyed during a Luftwaffe attack at Evere airfield on New Years Day, 1945. The squadron was re-numbered 77 Squadron on the 1st December 1946.

Aircraft:     Handley Page Harrow Mk I & II.  Dakota I, II and IV.
Airfields:    Down Ampney 29.2.44.  Doncaster (Part) 29.2.44.
              Blakehill Farm 31.5.44.  Northolt 20.2.45.  Gosfield 23.3.45.
              Croydon 2.4.45.  Odiham 30.8.45.  Broadwell 5.12.46.


**295 Squadron    38 Group**
Formed at RAF Netheravon on the 3rd August 1942, as an airborne forces unit. Equipped at first with Whitley V aircraft. In February 1943 the squadron received Halifax V aircraft. In June 1943 the squadron was engaged in towing Horsa gliders from Netheravon/Portreath to North Africa (Operations Beggar and Elaborate)

until September 1943, for use in the invasion of Sicily. The squadron converted to Albemarle aircraft in October 1943 and engaged in supplying the Resistance in France whilst awaiting D-Day. One aircraft from each of 295 and 570 Squadrons were the first to drop troops in Normandy on D-Day. Later the same day 295 sent thirteen aircraft towing gliders to the LZs.( Operation Tonga). Twenty-one glider tugs were sent with troop reinforcements (Operation Mallard). At Arnhem (Operation Market) the squadron towed twenty-five Horsa gliders in the first lift and three Horsas on the second lift. Three aircraft were lost on re-supply missions. For Operation Varsity the squadron towed thirty-one Horsa gliders over the Rhine. After the end of the war in Europe the squadron carried British troops to Norway to disarm the Germans there which was followed by other trooping duties until the 14th January 1946, when the squadron was disbanded. Two weeks later on the 1st February 1946, the squadron was again reformed and equipped with Halifax aircraft but was again disbanded on the 31st March 1946. It again reformed at RAF Fairford with Halifaxes on the 19th September 1947, (where the author flew with it) as an airborne forces unit but was finally disbanded on the 1st October 1948.

| Aircraft: | Whitley V | Halifax V | Albemarle I & II |
|---|---|---|---|
| | Stirling IV | Halifax VIII | Halifax A.9 |

Airfields:     Netheravon 3.8.42. Holmesly South 1.5.43. Hurn 30.6.43. Harwell 14.3.44. Rivenhall 7.10.44. Tarrant Rushton 1.2.46. Fairford 10.9.47.

296 Squadron     38 Group

Formed at RAF Ringway on the 25th January 1942, from the Glider Exercise Unit. Moved to RAF Netheravon on the 1st February 1942 on being equipped with Whitley aircraft. In July 1942, the squadron was divided into two parts 296A and 296B Squadron. 296A moved to RAF Hurn and became 296 Squadron and 296B was renamed the Glider Pilot Exercise Unit. In October 1942 the squadron began leaflet dropping flights over France. In January 1943 the squadron began converting to Albemarle aircraft. These were flown to Froha in North Africa in June 1943, to take part in the invasion of Sicily (Operation Husky) and returned to England in October 1943, to RAF Stoney Cross and later to RAF Hurn a short distance away. On the 14.3.44 the squadron moved to RAF Brize Norton and on D-Day for Operation Tonga supplied three aircraft as Pathfinders and sent eight more towing Horsa gliders in the first wave of airborne troops. This was followed later the same day in Operation Mallard by the squadron towing twenty Horsas.

For Operation Market the squadron towed in twenty-one Horsa and seven Hadrian gliders on the first lift to be followed on the second lift by towing in sixteen Horsas and four Hadrians. One Horsa was towed on the third lift. No aircraft losses were incurred. During September 1944, the squadron converted to Halifax aircraft and took part in supply drops to the French Resistance. Operation Varsity saw the squadron tow in thirty Horsa gliders from their base at Earls Colne. When the war ended the squadron was employed in air trooping of British troops to Norway and Denmark and repatriating Prisoners of War to England. The squadron was disbanded on the 23rd January 1946.

| | |
|---|---|
| Aircraft: | Hawker Hector. Hawker Hart  Whitley V |
| | Albemarle I, II, V & VI  Halifax  V, III & VII |
| Airfields: | Ringway 25.1.42. Netheravon 1.2.42. Hurn 25.6.42. |
| | Andover 25.10.42. Hurn 19.12.42. Froha 4.6.43. |
| | Goubrine 24.6.43. Stoney Cross 25.6.43. Hurn 15.10.43. |
| | Brize Norton 14.3.44. Earls Colne 29.9.44. |

297 Squadron.   38 Group

Formed at RAF Netheravon on the 22nd January 1942, from the Parachute Exercise Squadron and was equipped with Whitley aircraft. Leaflet dropping began in October 1942, and by February 1944, the squadron was equipped with Albemarle aircraft. The squadron towed twelve Horsa gliders to Normandy on Operation Tonga, including three for the Merville battery assault of which two reached the target the other Horsa breaking its tow rope over Odiham. Twenty more Horsas were towed in Operation Mallard on the evening of D-Day. During Operation Market the squadron towed in twenty-two Horsa and three Hadrian gliders on the first lift and twenty-two Horsas on the second lift. In October 1944, the squadron converted to Halifax aircraft and provided thirty tugs to tow in Horsa gliders during the Varsity Operation. The squadron continued as an airborne force support unit until the 15th November 1950 when it was disbanded.

| | |
|---|---|
| Aircraft: | Whitley V  Albemarle I, II, V & VI |
| | Halifax III, VII, V & A9. |
| Airfields: | Netheravon 22.1.42. Hurn 5.6.42. Thruxton 25.10.42. |
| | Stoney Cross 1.9.43. Brize Norton 14.3.44. Earls Colne 30.9.44. |
| | Tarrant Rushton, March 1946. Fairford 21.8.47. |
| | Dishforth 17.10.48. Germany 13.12.48. Topcliffe 13.12.49. |

## 298 Squadron.   38 Group

Formed at RAF Thruxton on the 24th August 1942, as an airborne forces squadron equipped with Whitley aircraft. Disbanded on the 19th October 1942 it was reformed at Tarrant Rushton on the 4th November 1943 from A Flight of 295 Squadron and equipped with Halifax aircraft. On D-Day the squadron supplied three tugs to tow the Horsa gliders for Operation Deadstick, the taking of the Caen Canal and River Orne bridges in Normandy before the main assault. Fifteen Horsas and two Hamilcar gliders were towed in for Operation Tonga. For Operation Mallard the squadron towed in one Horsa and fifteen Hamilcar gliders. For the SAS Operation Dingson the squadron towed six Hadrian gliders to Brittany. During Operation Market 298 towed in fifteen Hamilcars and thirty-one Horsas in three lifts. For Operation Varsity the squadron towed in six Horsas and twenty-four Hamilcars. The squadron was disbanded on the 21st December 1946.

| | |
|---|---|
| Aircraft: | Whitley V  Halifax V, III & VII. |
| Airfields: | Thruxton 24.8.42.  Tarrant Rushton 4.11.43. |
| | Woodbridge 21.3.45.  Tarrant Rushton 24.3.45. |

## 299 Squadron   38 Group

Formed at RAF Stoney Cross on the 4th November 1943, from a cadre provided by 297 Squadron and equipped with Ventura aircraft which were soon replaced with Stirling aircraft in January 1944. In April 1944, the squadron began to drop supplies to French Resistance Forces. For D-Day the squadron supplied twenty-four Stirlings to drop paratroops (Operation Tonga) and later for Operation Mallard provided sixteen Horsa glider tugs during which the squadron lost two aircraft. At Arnhem the squadron towed in fifty-four Horsa gliders during the three lifts. Seventy-two aircraft were used in re-supply drops and five aircraft were lost to enemy flak. During the Rhine Crossing the squadron supplied twenty-nine tugs to tow in Horsa gliders without loss. In May 1945 the squadron air trooped British troops to Norway. The squadron was disbanded on the 15th February 1946.

| | |
|---|---|
| Aircraft: | Ventura I & II  Stirling IV |
| Airfields: | Stoney Cross 4.11.43.  Keevil 15.3.44. |
| | Wethersfield 9.10.55.  Shepherds Grove 25.1.45. |

512 Squadron     46 Group

Formed at RAF Hendon on the 18th June 1943, and equipped with Dakota aircraft. Until February 1944, the squadron carried out transport duties to North Africa and Gibralter. It then began training with airborne forces and before D-Day carried out leaflet drops over France. Before dawn on D-Day the squadron carried out paratroop drops followed by towing eighteen Horsa gliders on Operation Mallard. During the Arnhem operation 512 towed twenty-two Horsa gliders in the first lift and twenty-four on the second lift. This was followed by twenty-nine re supply drops in which the squadron lost three aircraft. For the final Operation Varsity the squadron towed twenty-four Horsas. The squadron was disbanded on the 14th March 1946.

Aircraft:     Dakota I & II.
Airfields:    Hendon 18.6.43. Broadwell 14.2.44. Evere 31.3.45.

570 Squadron     38 Group

Formed at RAF Hurn on the 15th November 1943, equipped with Albemarle aircraft as an airborne forces squadron. On D-Day 570 sent twelve tugs towing Horsa gliders in Operation Tonga. Later the same day on Operation Mallard the squadron provided twenty Albemarles to tow Horsas to Normandy. During July 1944, the squadron converted to Stirling aircraft and sent twenty tugs towing Horsas to Arnhem in the first lift. For the second lift ten Horsas were towed in. On the third and final lift the squadron towed in one Horsa. Eleven aircraft were lost during the re-supply missions which totalled fifty-nine. Thirty tugs towed Horsas for the final Operation Varsity. Following the German surrender the squadron engaged in air trooping to Norway. On the 8th January 1946, the squadron was disbanded.

Aircraft:     Albemarle I, II & V. Stirling V
Airfields:    Hurn 15.11.43. Harwell 14.3.44. Rivenhall 7.10.44

575 Squadron     46 Group

Formed at RAF Hendon on the 11th January 1944, equipped with Dakota aircraft. For D Day the squadron towed nineteen Horsa gliders on Operation Mallard and twenty-one aircraft for paratroop dropping. At Arnhem the squadron provided twenty-four Horsa tugs in the first lift and twenty-five Horsa tugs on the second lift. Thirty-eight re-supply sorties were then carried out. For Operation Varsity 575 provided twenty-four Horsa tugs. After performing transport duties the squadron was disbanded on the 15th August 1946.

Aircraft: Dakota IIIs.

Airfields: Hendon 1.2.44. Broadwell 14.2.44. Gosfield 24.3.45. Melbourne 5.8.45. Blakehill Farm 16.11.45. Bari 1.2.46.


620 Squadron   38 Group
Formed at RAF Chedburgh on the 17th June 1943 as a bomber unit equipped with Stirling aircraft. On the 23rd November 1943, it became an airborne forces squadron at Leicester East. During the early hours of D-Day the squadron sent twenty-three aircraft to drop paratroops. Later the same day on Operation Mallard 620 sent eighteen Horsa tugs. At Arnhem six aircraft were engaged in paratroop dropping and nineteen towed Horsa gliders in the first lift. On the second lift twenty-two Horsas were towed and on the third lift one Horsa. During sixty-one re-supply sorties five Stirlings were lost. During the Rhine Crossing 620 provided thirty-one Horsa glider tugs. The squadron was then engaged on air trooping to Norway. In January 1946, the squadron moved to the Middle East (Aqir & Cairo) and acquired some Dakota aircraft. On the 1st September 1946, the squadron was re-numbered No.113 Squadron.

Aircraft: Stirling I, III, & IV. Halifax VII, & IX.
Airfields: Chedburgh 17.6.43. Leicester East 23.11.43. Fairford 18.3.44. Great Dunmow 17.10.44. Aqir 1.1.46. Cairo 3.3.46.


644 Squadron   38 Group
Formed at RAF Tarrant Rushton on the 23rd February 1944, from a cadre provided by 298 Squadron and was equipped with Halifax Aircraft as an airborne forces squadron. On the early morning of D-Day 644 towed eighteen Horsa and two Hamilcar gliders on Operation Tonga (three for Operation Deadstick) to be followed on Operation Mallard by fifteen Hamilcar and one Horsa gliders. For Operation Dingson five Hadrian gliders were towed to Brittany with SAS troops. At Arnhem the squadron provided six Hamilcar and fifteen Horsa tugs in the first lift to be followed on the second lift by towing seven Hamilcar and eight Horsa gliders. On the third and final lift 644 sent one Hamilcar and ten Horsa tugs. On

the Rhine Crossing the squadron provided six Horsa and twenty four Hamilcar tugs. After hostilities ended in Europe the squadron engaged in air trooping to Norway and repatriating Prisoners of War. 644 moved to Quastina Egypt in November 1945 and was re-numbered No.47 Squadron on the 1st September 1946.

Aircraft:     Halifax V, III & VII.
Airfields:    Tarrant Rushton 25.2.44. Woodbridge 24.3.45. Quastina Nov.1945

ORTU.(Operational Refresher Training Unit)
Two Albemarles provided to tow two Horsa gliders from Manston on the first lift (17th September 1944) of Operation Market. For Operation Varsity the unit provided twenty Stirlings to tow twenty Horsa gliders from Matching.

India Squadrons.
Six airborne forces squadrons numbered 668 to 672 were formed in India during 1944 to 1945. Each squadron was to have an establishment of eighty Waco CG4A Hadrian gliders, as the wooden Horsa could not stand up to the climate, and ten light aircraft. Pilots were to be from the Royal Air Force and Glider Pilot Regiment. Two Wings were created with three squadrons in each.

343 Wing:
668 Squadron. Formed Calcutta 16th November 1944. Disbanded 10th November 1945.
669 Squadron. Formed Bikram 16th November 1944. Disbanded 10th November 1945.
670 Squadron. Formed Fatehjang 14th December 1944. Disbanded 1st July 1946.

344 Wing:
671 Squadron. Formed Bikram 1st January 1945. Disbanded 25th October 1945.
672 Squadron. Formed Bikram 16th November 1944. Disbanded 1st July 1946.
673 Squadron. Formed Bikram 27th January 1945. Disbanded 25th October 1945.

None of the six squadrons saw action. Records show that Mk1 Hadrians FR582 to FR600 and Mk2s FR772 and FR774 were on charge to the RAF Glider Service Unit, Chaklala, Rawalpindi, India. FR596 was destroyed beyond repair in a gale on the 26th June 1945, and the other Hardrians were flown to Dhamial satellite airfield, beginning 19th June 1945, due to lack of space at Chaklala. The Glider Service Unit was closed on the 26th March 1945, and all gliders moved to Fatehjang.

# ROYAL AIR FORCE GLIDER TUGS

During WWII many types of RAF aircraft were used as glider tugs mainly due to lack of aircraft due to other commitments and lack of knowledge of airborne warfare. With no experience to guide them the early planners had by trial and error to find the right glider tugs.

The following aircraft were used as glider tugs at various times and places before the choice was found in the Albemarle, Dakota, Halifax and Stirling.

| | |
|---|---|
| Albemarle | Armstrong Whitworth |
| Audax | Hawker |
| Avro 504 | Avro |
| Dakota (C47) | Douglas |
| Halifax | Handley Page |
| Harvard | North American |
| Hector | Hawker |
| Hind | Hawker |
| Hudson | Lockheed |
| Hurricane | Hawker. |
| Lancaster | Avro |
| Lysander | Westland |
| Magister | Miles |
| Master | Miles |
| Oxford | Airspeed |
| Spitfire | Supermarine. |
| Stirling | Short |
| Tiger Moth | De Haviland |
| Wellington | Vickers |
| Whitley | Armstrong Whitworth |

## ALBERMARLE

Originally designed as a twin engined bomber to Air Ministry Specification B 18/38 which was taken up by Armstrong Whitworth as the AW 41. The first prototype crashed but the second - P 1361 - flew on the 20th March 1940. With a view to subcontracting parts to various firms and saving valuable alloys the aircraft was of a composite metal and wood construction. The Albemarle was found to be unsuitable as a bomber and it was decided to use it as a transport - the first Albemarles into RAF service were allocated to 511 Squadron in November 1942, as transport aircraft between Gibralter and Malta. It was also decided to use the Albemarle as a glider tug and 296 Squadron of 38 Wing was allocated a number which were flown out to North Africa in June 1943 for use as glider tugs in the Sicily operation. In July 1943, 297 Squadron of 38 Wing began to receive Albemarles and with 296 Squadron supplied twenty-eight Albemarles for the Sicily operation. In October 1943, 295 Squadron of 38 Wing began converting to Albemarles and in November 1943, 570 Squadron also of 38 Wing, received Albemarles. By now four squadrons of 38 Wing/Group were equipped with Albemarles which took part in the D-Day glider operations. By the time the Arnhem operation took place two of the squadrons had converted to Stirlings. The Royal Air Force received sixty-nine Albemarles MK1 and one hundred and seventeen Albemarles MKV1 as glider tugs. Another 380 were received as transports.

Description.
MKs. 1, 11, V & V1.
Wing Span 77 feet. Length 59 feet 11ins. Height 15 feet 7 ins.
Engines. Twin. 1590 hp Bristol Hercules X1.
All up weight 22600lbs.
Speed. Maximum 265mph at 10500 feet. cruising 170mph. Range. 1300 miles.
Guns. Hand operated twin Vickers K amidships.

AUDAX
The Audax was the Army Co Operation Command version of the Hawker Hart single-engined bomber which came into RAF service in 1930. The Audax was equipped with a message collecting snatch hook under the fuselage for Army purposes - an uncanny forecast of things to come in the shape of glider snatching some years later. To tow the light Hotspur military glider coming into service the Audax with its single 530hp engine was pressed into glider tug service. No.2 Glider Training School at Weston on the Green, Oxford, received an Audax for trials in January 1942, and by March 1942 had another 15 as glider tugs. No.4 Glider Training School, Nos.101 and 102 Glider Training Units formed at Kidlington in 1942 also used the aircraft as a glider tug.

Description
Wing Span. 37 feet. Length 29 feet 7 ins. Height 10 feet 5 ins.
All up weight 4381lb. unloaded 2946lb.
Speed. Maximum 170 mph. at 2500 feet.
Engine Single 530hp Rolls Royce Kestrel 1B or Kestrel X

## AVRO 504K

The first Avro 504 made its debut in 1913 and was widely used during the First World War. After the war the Avro began to be used as the Royal Air Force trainer eventually being retired from service in the Twenties. With the outbreak of war in Europe in 1939 and the German use of gliders in 1940 in Belgium, steps were taken in Britain to form an airborne force. As there were no military gliders in Britain at this time civilians were asked to donate their gliders to the new Central Landing Establishment at RAF Ringway, Cheshire, where the British airborne forces were being born. With the donated gliders and two Avro 504k aircraft as tugs the Establishment was, on the 26th October 1940, able to demonstrate the first British glider/tug combination.

Description.
Single engined bi-plane of wooden structure fabric covered.
Wing Span 36 feet. Length 29 feet 5 ins. Height 10 feet 5 ins.
Engine. 100hp Monosoupape, 110 hp Le Rhone or 130 hp Clerget
All up weight 1829lb. Unloaded 1231lb.
Speed. Maximum 95 mph. Range 250 miles.

## DAKOTA (C47).

Derived from the Douglas DC 3 civilian airliner which first flew in 1935 the Dakota C47 was supplied by the Americans to the RAF in large numbers during WWII. The two RAF airborne forces groups No.38 and 46 had six squadrons - 48, 233, 271, 437(RCAF), 512 and 575 - equipped with Dakotas. During Operation Tonga 233 and 271 Squadrons towed thirteen Horsas to Normandy. For Operation Mallard 48, 271, 512 and 575 Squadrons towed seventy-three Horsas and for Operation Market 48, 233, 271, 437, 512 and 575 towed 251 Horsas. On Operation Varsity 48, 233, 271, 437, 512 and 575 towed 120 Horsas. With the end of WWII and the run down of the RAF and Glider Pilot Regiment, the Dakota was used at Ibsley, Hampshire, and Upper Heyford for glider snatching training and glider towing training.

Description.
All metal construction with alloy skin.
Wing Span. 95 feet. Length 64 feet. Height 16 feet 11 ins.
Engines. Two Pratt & Whitney 1200 hp R 1830-92.
All up weight. Maximum 31000lb. Normal 27000lb. Unloaded 16865lb.
Speed Maximum 230mph. Cruising 185mph. Range 2125 miles.

## HALIFAX

The Halifax was the second four-engined bomber to enter RAF service during WWII having first flown on the 25th October 1939. With the large Hamilcar glider coming into service it was found that the Halifax was the only aircraft capable of towing it satisfactorily. Trials being conducted at Newmarket in February 1942. The Halifax was first used in action as a glider tug on the 19th-20th November 1942, on Operation Freshman, when two Halifax tugs towed two Horsa gliders from Skitten, Caithness, Scotland, to Norway in an ill fated attempt to destroy the German Heavy Water Plant at Rjukan. One Halifax crashed killing all the crew the other returned to base. Both Horsa gliders crashed in Norway in bad weather. Halifax tugs were used to tow Horsa gliders from Portreath, Cornwall, to North Africa in Operations Beggar/Turkey Buzzard and Elaborate by 295 Squadron, 38 Wing for the invasion of Sicily. On the 6th November 1943, 38 Wing had become an Airborne Forces Group and some of its squadrons began to equip with Halifax aircraft. 295 Squadron converted to Albemarles in October 1943. 298 Squadron converted to Halifax aircraft in November 1943, to be followed by 644 Squadron in May 1944. 296 Squadron converted to Halifax aircraft in September 1944 then 297 Squadron in October 1944. Both 298 and 644 Squadrons were engaged in towing Hamilcar gliders - the other squadrons towed Horsas and Hadrians.

For Operation Tonga 298 and 644 Squadrons towed thirty-six Horsas and four Hamilcars. During Operation Mallard 298 and 644 Squadrons towed thirty-two Hamilcars and two Horsas. The small Operation Dingson saw 298 and 644 Squadrons tow ten Hadrians from Tarrant Rushton, Dorset to Occupied Brittany in an SAS operation. At Arnhem during the three lifts of Operation Market 298 and 644 Squadrons towed thirty Hamilcars and sixty-four Horsas. For the final Operation Varsity the Halifaxs of 296 and 297 Squadrons towed sixty Horsas and 298 and 644 Squadrons towed six Horsas and forty-eight Hamilcars.

Description.
Four engined glider tug. MkI & MkVI.
Wing Span.MkI 99 feet. Length 70 feet. Height 21 feet. MkVI 104 feet length 71 feet.
Engines. MkI Four 1280 hp Rolls Royce Merlin X. MkVI Four 1800 Bristol Hercules 100.
Speed. Maximum 265mph. Range 2500 miles with light load.
Weights. Mk1. All Up 58000lbs. MkVI 68000lbs. Unloaded 39000lbs.
Guns. MkI Four .303 in tail turret. Two .303 guns in nose turret. MkVI four .303 guns in tail and dorsal turrets. One .303 gun in nose turret.

## HARVARD II
The North American Harvard II was delivered to the RAF in large numbers as a training aircraft, several being used as glider tugs towing Hotspur gliders. Towing range 270 miles. Take off ground run 850 yds. Operational height 7500 feet.

Description.
Construction all metal stressed skin. Wingspan. 42 feet.
Length 29 feet. Height 11 feet 9 ins.
Engine. Single 550 Pratt & Whitney Wasp R 1340-49.
Speed Maximum 205mph. Cruising 170mph.
Weight. All Up 5250lbs. Unloaded 4157lbs.

## HECTOR
The Hector was derived from the Hawker Hart and made its debut at the RAF Air Display at Hendon in 1934 in the Static Park. By the outbreak of war in 1939 the aircraft was obsolete but did give a good account of itself in France in 1940. It was then relegated to training and Army Co-Operation duties and was used extensively as a glider tug at Nos.1, 2, 4, & 5 Glider Training Schools also at Nos. 101 & 102 Glider operational Training Units and the Glider Instructors School.

Description.
Single engined bi-plane of metal construction with fabric covering.
Wing Span. 37 feet. Length 30 feet. Height 10 feet 6 ins.
Speed Maximum 187mph. Engine Single 805 Napier Dagger IIMS.
Supply containers underneath wings.

## HIND
Developed from the Hawker Hart as a light day bomber the Hind first appeared in 1934 and came into service the next year. Like the Audax and Hind when war broke out the aircraft became obsolete and was relegated to training duties. By 1941 the aircraft was in use as a glider tug at Nos.1, 2, 4, Glider Training Schools and Nos.101 and 102 Glider Operational Training School also the Glider Instructors School.

Description.
Metal construction fabric covered. Two seats.
Wingspan. 37 feet 3 ins. Length 29 feet 7 ins. Height 10 feet 7 ins.
Engine. One 640 hp Rolls Royce Kestrel V.
Weight. All up 5298lbs. Unloaded 3251lbs. Speed. 186 mph. Range 450 miles.

## HUDSON III

The American Lockheed Hudson in its several Mks. first entered RAF service in 1939 and continued all through WWII. As the earlier Mks. became obsolescent they were relegated to transport and glider towing duties. The Mk.III was approved for towing Hadrian gliders after the dorsal gun turret had been removed. Towing range 520 miles with a take off run of 1000 yards and an operational height of 10000 feet.

## LANCASTER

The best known and the most successful of Royal Air Force bombers during WWII the four-engined Lancaster was used for test towing the large Hamilcar glider during 1943. It was found that using the Lancaster III (LM 451) that take off and climb out were too critical. However, using a Lancaster II (DS 819) tests were satisfactory with all loads but the operational needs of Bomber Command prevented this Mark of Lancaster being supplied to the airborne forces squadrons.

Description.
Four-engined heavy bomber. Metal construction with alloy skin.
Wing span. 102 feet. Length 69 feet 6 ins. Height 20 feet.
Speed. Maximum speed 287mph. Cruising speed 210mph.
Range 1660 miles light load.
Weight. All up 68000lbs. unloaded 36900lbs.
Guns. Twin .303 guns nose and dorsal turret. Twin .303 in ventral turret at first later removed. Four .303 guns in tail turret.

## LYSANDER

First flown in 1936 the Lysander was the first monoplane to enter service with Army Co Operation Command mainly as an artillery spotter until late 1940. In June 1942 Lysanders became the standard glider tug at No. 102 Glider Operational Training Unit at Kidlington, Oxford, however when this Unit was renamed No.4 Glider Training School the Lysanders were transferred to No.5 Glider Training School which moved to Shobdon on the 30th July with the Lysanders.

Description.
Single-engined high wing monoplane with two seats.
Wingspan 50 feet. Length 30 feet. Height 11 feet 6 ins.
Engine. Single 890 hp. Bristol Mercury XII.
Speed. Maximum 220 mph. Range 600 miles.
Weight. All up 5900lbs. Unloaded 4060lbs.

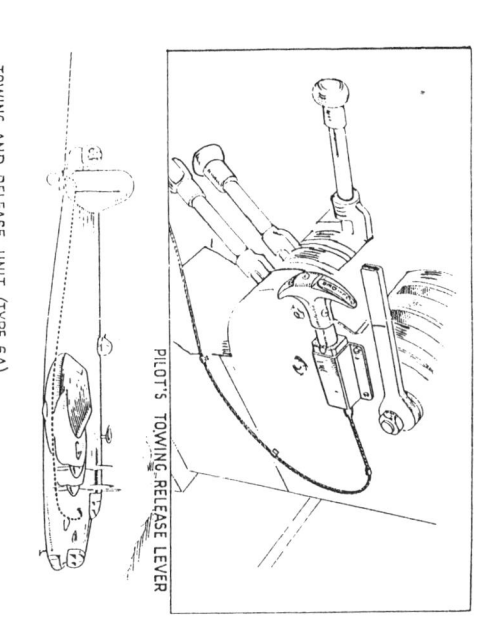

## HALIFAX II & V GLIDER TOWING EQUIPMENT

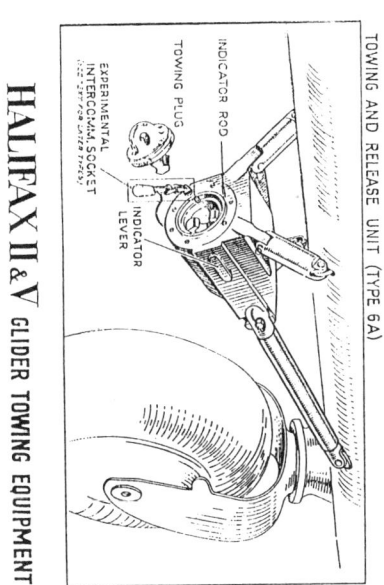

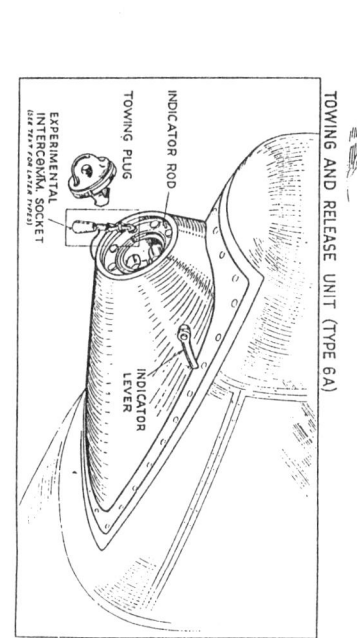

## ALBEMARLE I GLIDER TOWING EQUIPMENT

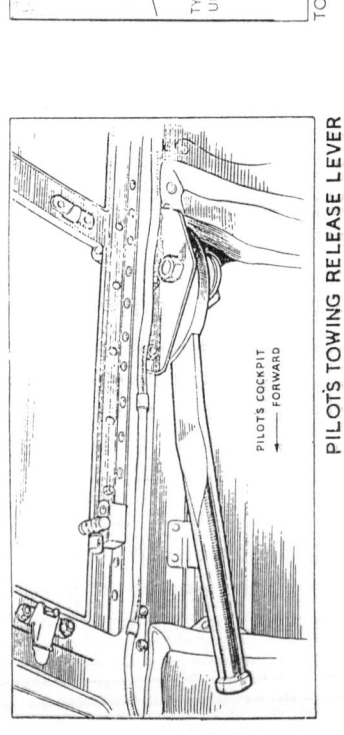

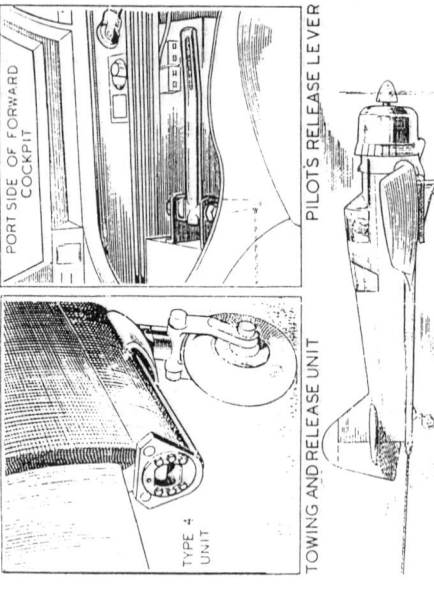

FIG.1 **MASTER II** GLIDER TOWING EQUIPT

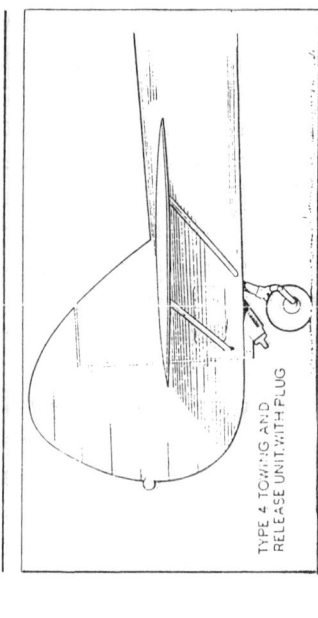

**HECTOR** GLIDER TOWING EQUIPT

**WHITLEY V** GLIDER TOWING EQUIPT

## MAGISTER

The first low-wing monoplane to be used by the RAF as a trainer made its debut in 1937 and was extensively used as a two seat elementary trainer. Known as the 'Maggie' by the thousands who trained on it the two-seat trainer continued in use for much of WWII. Used by No.3 Glider Training School (Serial numbers T9736 and V1067).

Description.
Single-engined two seat elementary trainer of wooden construction with plywood covering.
Wingspan. 33 feet 10 ins. length 24 feet 7 ins. Height 6 feet 8 ins.
Engine. Single 130 hp De Haviland Gipsy Major 1.
Speed Maximum 132. Cruising 123mph. Landing 42mph.
Weight. All up 1900lbs. Unloaded 1286lbs.

## MASTER

The two-seat advanced trainer constructed of wood with a plywood covering was developed from the Miles Kestrel trainer and made its first flight in 1938 and entered service with the RAF in May 1939. Later that year the MkII Master entered service and nearly 1700 were built. With the embryo airborne forces requiring aircraft to tow the Hotspur glider the Master II was taken into use by No.1 Glider Training School. No.3 Glider Training School which was formed at Stoke Orchard on the 21st July 1942, received several Master IIs but by the time the war ended it had 69 Master IIs on strength. No.5 Glider Training School at Kidlington also used the aircraft until the School closed on the 30th November 1945.

Description.
Single-engined two seat trainer.
Wing Span 39 feet. Length 30 feet 5 ins. Height 10 Feet.
Engine. Single 715 hp Rolls Royce Kestrel XXX or 870 hp Bristol Mercury XX.
Speed Maximum 226 mph. Range 500 miles.
Weights. All up 5353lbs. Unloaded. 4156lbs.

## OXFORD

The 'Ox Box' as it was known to all who flew in it first entered RAF service in 1937 as an advanced trainer at the Central Flying School. The aircraft rapidly became a maid of all work ranging from army cooperation to glider towing. A delightful aircraft with few vices apart from a tendency for one of the engines to cut out on landing, which required someone (usually the author) to climb out on the wing and crank start it, always it seemed on a hot day. The Ox Box was used by Nos.1 and 3 Glider Training Schools until the end of the war. It was finally withdrawn from RAF service in 1954.

Description.
Advanced trainer with three seat and of wooden construction with plywood covering.
Wing span 53 feet. Length 34 feet 6 ins. Height 11 feet.
Engine. Two Armstrong Siddley Cheetah X.
Speed Maximum 189 mph. Weight. All up 7600lbs. Unloaded 5380lbs.

STIRLING
The Royal Air Force's first monoplane heavy bomber of WWII which came into service in August 1940. With the advent of the large Hamilcar glider a powerful glider tug was required. Trials were carried out with Stirling I serial number BK 645 in May 1943. With an unloaded Hamilcar the trial take off was long but not too difficult. However, the climb out at 105mph was below the safety limit of the Stirling and the engines overheated. No attempt was made to tow a Hamilcar with an operational load. A MkIV Stirling serial number EF 432 was used on more trials with better results - the climb out speed rose to 140mph but with a training load the overall performance was poor. On the 6th November 1943, No.38 Wing became 38 (Airborne Forces) Group and two of its squadrons - Nos.196 and 620 were equipped with Stirlings MkIV. In January 1944 two more squadrons Nos.190 and 299 were also equipped with Stirlings. For Operation Mallard these four squadrons towed seventy-one Horsa gliders to Normandy from Fairford and Keevil. By July 1944 Nos.295 and 570 Squadrons of 38 Group had equipped with Stirlings for glider towing although 295 Squadron retained some Albemarles for other duties. At Arnhem during the three lifts the six Stirling Squadrons towed 250 Horsa gliders to the epic battle. For the last operation - Varsity - the Stirlings towed 194 Horsas to the Lzs.

Description.
All metal four-engined heavy bomber converted to glider tug.
Wing span. 99 feet. Length 87 feet. Height 22 feet 9 ins.
Speed. Maximum 270 mph. Range 2000 miles,
Engines. Four 1650 hp Bristol Hercules XVI.
Weight. All up 70000lbs. Unloaded. 43200lbs.
Guns. Two .303 guns in nose and upper turrets. Four .303 guns in tail turret.

## TIGER MOTH

Perhaps the most famous elementary flying trainer in the world, certainly so to the Royal Air Force and the Glider Pilot Regiment. First into service in 1932 it continued until the 1950s with various units of the RAF. First used by the RAF Glider Training School at Ringway in 1940 where five were allocated as glider tugs and trainers. No.1 Glider Training School used Tiger Moths serial numbers T5417, N9197 and N9198. No.2 Glider Training School used Tiger Moth T5628 and No.3 Glider Training School used Tiger Moths DE 194 and DE 887. No.102 Glider Operational Training Unit used Tiger Moth DE 304. A delightful aircraft to fly with no vices many are still in use all over the world as private aircraft.

Description.
Bi-plane elementary flying trainer with two seats.
Constructed of composite metal and wood fabric covered.
Wingspan. 29 feet 4 ins. Length 24 feet. Height 8 feet 10 ins.
Engine. Single 130 hp De Haviland Gipsy Major.
Speed Maximum 109mph. Cruising 90mph.
Weight. All up 1770lbs. Unloaded 1115lbs.

## WELLINGTON

Known as the 'Wimpey' to all and sundry, the Wellington prototype first flew in 1936 and served throughout WWII in various roles including the Wellington III which served as a glider tug by adding a towing bridle to the rear fuselage under the rear gun turret similar to that used by the Whitley V. The aircraft was capable of towing one Horsa or two Hotspurs. There is no record of the Wellington being used as a glider tug on operations.

Description.
Twin-engined converted night bomber of metal genetic construction fabric covered.
Wingspan. 86 feet. Length 64 feet 7 ins. height 17 feet 5 ins.
Engines. Twin 1000 hp Bristol Pegasus XVI.
Speed. Maximum 235mph. Range 2200 miles.
Weight. All up 28500lbs. Unloaded 18556lbs.

## WHITLEY

The Whitley as a mid-wing monoplane first flew on 17th March 1936 and entered service with the RAF in March 1937. In 1940 the Whitley II was used at RAF Ringway on experimental parachute dropping. The aircraft was used on the first two airborne operations when paratroops were dropped at Tragino, Italy, and on the Bruneval Raid in 1942. The Mk.V Whitley came into use in 38 Group as a glider tug at RAF Netheravon with 295, 296 and 297 Squadrons and with 298 Squadron at Thruxton during 1942. In 1943 all four squadrons began to convert to other glider tugs although 297 Squadron retained some Whitleys until February 1944. The Whitley was never used on operational glider towing.

Description.
MK.V. Converted night bomber. Wing span 84 feet. Length 70 feet. Height 15 feet. All metal construction.
Engines Two 1145 hp. Rolls Royce Merlin Xs.
Speed 222mph. Range 1250 miles. Towing range 240 miles with Horsa.
Guns. Four .303 machine guns in tail turret (removed for paratroop dropping at Ringway) One .303 in nose turret.
Ventral turret removed for paratroop dropping at Ringway. Glider towing bridle fitted at each side of the fuselage just forward of the rear turret.

*Below: The Royal Air Force Landing Establishment, Ringway, Glider Squadron emblem*

# THE AIRFIELDS
## by David Hall, GPR. Airfield Research Group.

Nearly 120 airfields were used by British air landing forces during and after WWII. The following list gives the name, location and units based there during the airfield's existence.

Abbreviations used in the listing:

| | |
|---|---|
| AFEE | Airborne Forces Experimental Establishment. |
| Det | Detachment. |
| EFTS | Elementary Flying Training School. |
| GIS | Glider Instructors School |
| GOTU | Glider Operational Training Unit |
| GPEU | Glider Pilot Exercise Unit |
| GPUT | Glider Pick Up Training Unit |
| GSE | Glider Servicing Echelon |
| GTS | Originally Glider Training Squadron Ringway. Later Glider Training School |
| HCGU | Heavy Glider Conversion Unit |
| HGMU | Heavy Glider Maintainance Unit. |
| ORTU | Operational & Refresher Training Unit |
| OTU | Operational Training Unit. |
| PGTS | Parachute & Glider Training School |
| RLG | Relief Landing Ground. |
| RTU | Refresher Training Unit |

| | |
|---|---|
| Abbots Bromley, Stafford. | RLG to Burnaston. |
| Aldermaston, Berkshire. | 3 GTS Detachment. |
| Alton Barnes, Wiltshire. | 29EFTS.GPEU.RLG to Clyffe Pypard |
| Andover, Hampshire. | 296 Sqdn. RAF. |
| Ashbourne, Derbyshire. | 38 Group OTU. |
| Balderton, Nottingham. | Horsa test flying. |
| Baginton, Warwickshire. | Horsa testing. |
| Barford St.John, Oxford. | Satellite to Brize Norton |
| Battlestead Hill, Stafford. | RLG to Burnaston. |
| Beaulieu, Hampshire. | AFEE Hamilcar glider Trials |
| Birch, Essex. | Ops. Base Varsity. 48, 233, 437 (RCAF) Squadrons. |

| | |
|---|---|
| Bircham Newton, Norfolk. | 48 Squadron. |
| Blakehill Farm, Wiltshire. | 22HGCU. Ops Base Tonga & Market. 233, 271 437 (RCAF), 575 Sqdns. 11 & 16 GSE. |
| Booker, Buckinghamshire. | 21 EFTS. |
| Bourn, Cambridge. | Horsa storage. |
| Brackla, Nairn. | Horsa storage |
| Brize Norton, Oxford, | GIS. 21HGCU. Ops. Base Tonga & Market. 297 & 296 Squadrons. 7 & 8 GSE. |
| Broadwell, Oxford. | Satellite - Brize Norton. Ops. Base Mallard & Market. 271, 512 & 575 Sqdns. |
| Cambridge, Cambridgeshire. | 22 EFTS |
| Cheddington, Buckingham. | 2 GTS Det. |
| Chelveston, Northampton. | AFEE |
| Chilbolton, Hampshire. | GPEU |
| Christchurch, Hampshire. | Horsa trials and collection from Airspeed. |
| Clyffe Pypard, Wiltshire | 29 EFTS. |
| Cottesmore, Rutland. | Horsa storage. |
| Croughton, Northampton. | 1 GTS. |
| Culmhead, Somerset. | 3 GTS. |
| Darley Moor, Yorkshire. | 38 Group OTU |
| Denham, Bucks. | RLG to Booker. |
| Derby (Burnaston), Derby | 16 & 30 EFTS |
| Down Ampney, Gloucester. | Ops Base. Tonga, Mallard & Market. 48 & 271 Sqdns. RAF. |
| Earls Colne, Essex. | Ops. Base. Varsity. 7 & 8 GSE. 296, 297 Sqdns. RAF. |
| Elsham Wolds, Lincolnshire. | 21 HGCU |
| Errol, Perth. | Horsa storage. |
| Exeter, Devon. | 3 GTs. |
| Fairford, Gloucestershire. | 22HGCU. Ops. Mallard, Market, Molten. 190, 295, 297, 620 Sqdn. 3 & 4 GSE. |
| Feltwell, Norfolk. | Horsa storage. |
| Foulsham, Norfolk. | Horsa storage |
| Fulbeck, Lincoln. | Horsa Storage. |
| Gaydon, Warwickshire. | 3 GTS |
| Gosfield, Essex. | Ops. Base Varsity. 271, 512 & 575 Sqdns. RAF. |
| Great Dunmow, Essex. | ORTU. Ops. Base Varsity. 3 & 4 GSE. 190 & 620 Sqdns. RAF. |
| Grove, Berkshire. | Temporary use whilst Brize Norton resurfaced. |

| | |
|---|---|
| Haddenham, (Thame)Bucks. | 1 GTS. GIS. |
| Hampstead Norris, Berkshire. | ORTU |
| Hartford Bridge, Hampshire. | Hamilcar RATO trials. Hotspur trials. |
| Harwell, Berkshire. | Ops. Base Tonga, Mallard & Market. 295 & 570 Sqdns. 5 & 6 GSE |
| Hatfield, Hertfordshire. | EFTS. |
| Hendon, Middlesex. | 575 Sqdn. |
| Hinton in the Hedges, Norths. | 2 GTS |
| Hockley Heath, Warwickshire. | GTS & 5 GTS |
| Holmesly South, Hampshire. | 295 Sqdn. RAF |
| Honiley, Warwickshire. | Horsa test flying. |
| Hurn, Hampshire. | 295, 296, 297 & 570 620 Sqdns. RAF |
| Ibsley, Hampshire. | GPUTU |
| Keevil, Wiltshire. | 22 HGCU. Ops. base Mallard & Market. 196 & 299 Sqdns. 1 & 2 GSE. |
| Kiddington, Oxfordshire. | Relief Landing Ground Kidlington |
| Kidlington, Oxfordshire. | 2, 4. 5 GTS. 1 GOTU. 101 OTU. |
| Kingston Bagpuize, Berkshire. | 1, 4 GTS. RLG to Haddenham. Satellite to Kidlington |
| Lakenheath, Suffolk. | Horsa storage. |
| Langar, Nottingham. | Horsa storage. |
| Leicester East, Leicester. | 190, 196 & 620 Sqdns. RAF |
| Long Newton, Wiltshire. | 2 GTS Trials only. |
| Lyneham, Wiltshire. | MU glider erection. |
| Manston, Kent. | 296 & 297 Sqdns. RAF. Ops. Base, Market. |
| Marham, Norfolk. | Horsa storage. |
| Matching, Essex. | ORTU. Ops. Base Varsity. |
| Meir, Staffordshire. | 16 EFTS. RLG to Burnaston. |
| Melborne, Yorkshire. | 575 Sqdn. |
| Mildenhall, Suffolk. | Horsa storage. |
| Montrose, Angus. | Horsa storage. |
| Netheravon, Wiltshire. | 1 HGCU. 295, 296, 297 Sqdns. 12 & 13 GSE No1 HGMU. GPEU. |
| Newmarket(Sidehill), Suffolk. | GTS Trials only. |
| North Luffenham, Rutland. | GIS. HGCU. |
| Northleach, Gloucestershire. | 3 GTS (Detachment). |
| Oulton, Norfolk. | Horsa storage. |
| Peplow, Shropshire. | 23 HGCU/RTU. |
| Perth, Perthshire. | Horsa storage. |

| | |
|---|---|
| Perranporth, Cornwall, | Transport Command Staging Post. |
| Portsmouth, Hampshire. | Horsa test flying. |
| Portreath, Cornwall. | Ferry base. Ops. Beggar/Turkey Buzzard & Elaborate. |
| Ringway, Manchester. | Original GTS. 296 Sqdn RAF. |
| Rivenhall, Essex. | 5 & 6 GSE. Ops. Base Varsity. 295 & 570 Sqdns. RAF. |
| Rollestone, Wiltshire. | GPEU. |
| Seighford, Staffordshire. | Satellite to Peplow. 23 HGCU. |
| Sculthorpe, Norfolk. | Horsa storage. |
| Shellingford, Berkshire. | 3 EFTS. |
| Shepherds Grove, Suffolk. | Ops. Base Varsity. 196 & 299 Sqdns. RAF. |
| Sherburn in Elmet, Yorkshire. | AFEE |
| Shobdon, Herefordshire. | 5 GTS. Glider Instructors Flight. |
| Shrewton, Wiltshire. | GPR. GPEU. HGCU. |
| Skitten, Caithness,Scotland. | Ops. Base Freshman. |
| Sleap, Shropshire. | 81 OTU. |
| Snaith, Yorkshire. | Horsa test flights. |
| Snailwell, Suffolk. | 2 HGMU. |
| Southrop, Gloucester. | Glider landing Exercises. |
| Stoke Orchard, Gloucester. | 3 GTS. |
| Stoney Cross, Hampshire. | 296, 297 & 299 Sqdns. |
| Stradishall, Norfolk. | Horsa storage. |
| Tarrant Rushton, Dorset. | Ops. Base. Tonga, Mallard, Dingson, Market. 12, 14 & 15 GSE. 196, 295, 297, 298 & 644 Sqdns |
| Tatton Park, Cheshire. | 38 Wing RLG & DZ. |
| Thorney Island,Hampshire. | Horsa trials. |
| Thruxton, Hampshire. | ORTU. 297 & 298 Sqdns. RAF. |
| Tilstock, Shropshire. | 38 Group OTU. 1665 HGU. |
| Upper Heyford, Oxfordshire. | 1 P&GTS. Post WWII, |
| Wanborough, Wiltshire. | 3 GTS (detachment). |
| Waterbeach, Cambridgeshire. | GPR Squadron Post WWII |
| Welford, Berkshire. | Glider landing Exercises. |
| Wellesborne Mountford, Warwick. | 3 GTS. |
| Weston on the Green, Oxford. | 2 & 4 GTS. |
| Wethersfield, Essex. | GPEU. ORTU 196 & 299 Sqdns, RAF. 1 & 2 GSE. |
| Woodbridge, Suffolk. | Ops Base Varsity. 298 & 644 Sqdns. RAF |
| Woolfox Lodge, Rutland. | Horsa storage. |

Wratting Common, Cambridge. Horsa storage.
Zeals, Wiltshire. 3 GTS Trials. GPUTU.

Overseas Operations:

Bari, Italy. Operation Bunghole.
Kairouan, Tunisia. Operations Ladbrooke & Fustian.
Tarquinina, Italy. Operation Dragoon/Bluebird and Megara, Greece.
Post War training Egypt & Palestine.

# THE OPERATIONAL GLIDER AIRFIELDS
## by David Hall, GPR.
## Airfield Research Group.

The nineteen airfields used for operations by glider towing squadrons were located as far away as possible from the main bomber and fighter stations in the United Kingdom. A single tug/glider on tow was an unwieldy combination; a glider stream flying in loose pairs even more so, necessitating a clear sky for training and eventually for operational purposes. Thus the majority of bases were located in a general area bounded by Oxford-Cirencester-Warminster-Andover. All conveniently near Salisbury Plain where the Airborne Forces were training.

Following the breakout from the Normandy Beachead, bases in Essex, previously occupied by the USAAF, became vacant enabling 38 Group to move into them to be nearer the Continental areas of conflict and providing two advance bases for 46 Group when the Rhine crossing operation took place.

Apart from these two main areas, three airfields, Skitten, Manston and Woodbridge were used as advance bases for single specific operations and one - Portreath - for overseas ferrying to North Africa.

Generally, Tug Squadrons were based in pairs with Glider Pilot Regiment Squadrons alongside them. This excellent arrangement was a great help in overcoming any lingering inter service prejudices and fostered team spirit between tug and glider aircrews.

| | |
|---|---|
| Birch, Essex. | Operation Varsity. |
| Blakehill Farm, Wiltshire. | Operations Tonga, and Market. |
| Brize Norton, Oxfordshire. | Operations Tonga, and Mallard. |
| Broadwell, Oxfordshire. | Operations Mallard and Market. |
| Down Ampney, Gloucester | Operations Tonga, Mallard & Market. |
| Earls Colne, Essex. | Operation Varsity. |
| Fairford, Gloucester | Operations Mallard, Market and Molten. |
| Gosfield, Essex. | Operation Varsity. |
| Great Dunmow, Essex. | Operation Varsity. |
| Harwell, Berkshire. | Operation Tonga, Mallard and Market. |
| Keevil, Wiltshire. | Operations Mallard and Market. |
| Manston, Kent. | Operation Market. |
| Matching, Essex. | Operation Varsity. |
| Portreath, Cornwall. | Operation Beggar (Turkey Buzzard) and Elaborate. |

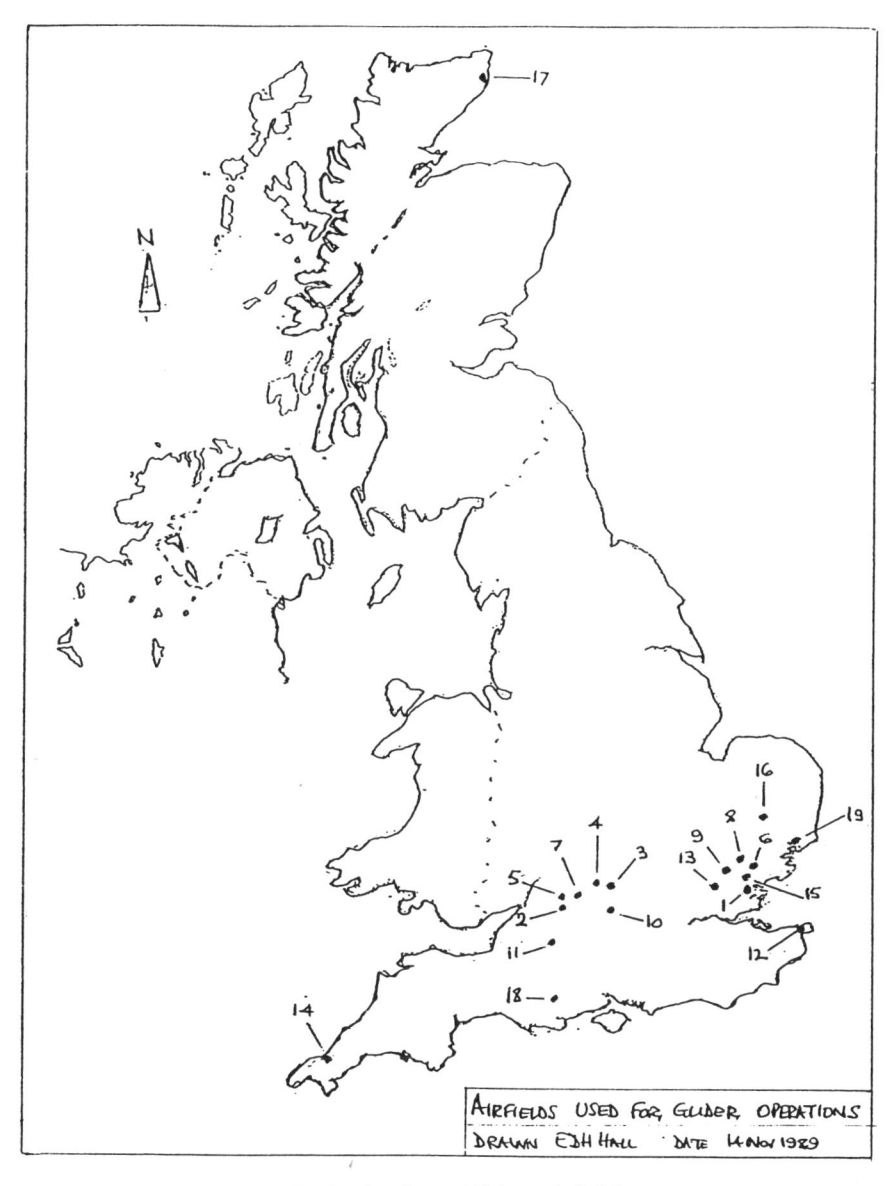

## United Kingdom Glider Airfields

1. Birch
2. Blakehill Farm
3. Brize Norton
4. Broadwell
5. Down Ampney
6. Earls Colne
7. Fairford
8. Gosfield
9. Great Dunmow
10. Harwell
11. Keevil
12. Manston
13. Matching
14. Portreath
15. Rivenhall
16. Shepherd's Grove
17. Skitten
18. Tarrant Rushton
19. Woodbridge

| | |
|---|---|
| Rivenhall, Essex. | Operation Varsity. |
| Shepherds Grove, Suffolk | Operation Varsity, |
| Skitten, Caithness. | Operation Freshman. |
| Tarrant Rushton, Dorset. | Operations Tonga, Mallard Dingson and Market. |
| Woodbridge, Suffolk. | Operation Varsity. |

Overseas:

| | |
|---|---|
| Bari, Italy. | Operation Bunghole. |
| Kairouan, Tunisia. | Operations Ladbrooke and Fustian. |
| Tarquina, Italy. | Operation Dragoon and Megara. |

## BIRCH

Code JB. Location OS Sheet 168 Grid reference TL 915195.
North of B 1022 Tiptree to Colchester road - 8 miles SW of Colchester.

HISTORY.   Built between 1943 and March 1944 by the US 846th Engineer Battalion and was the last airfield completed by US Army Engineers for the

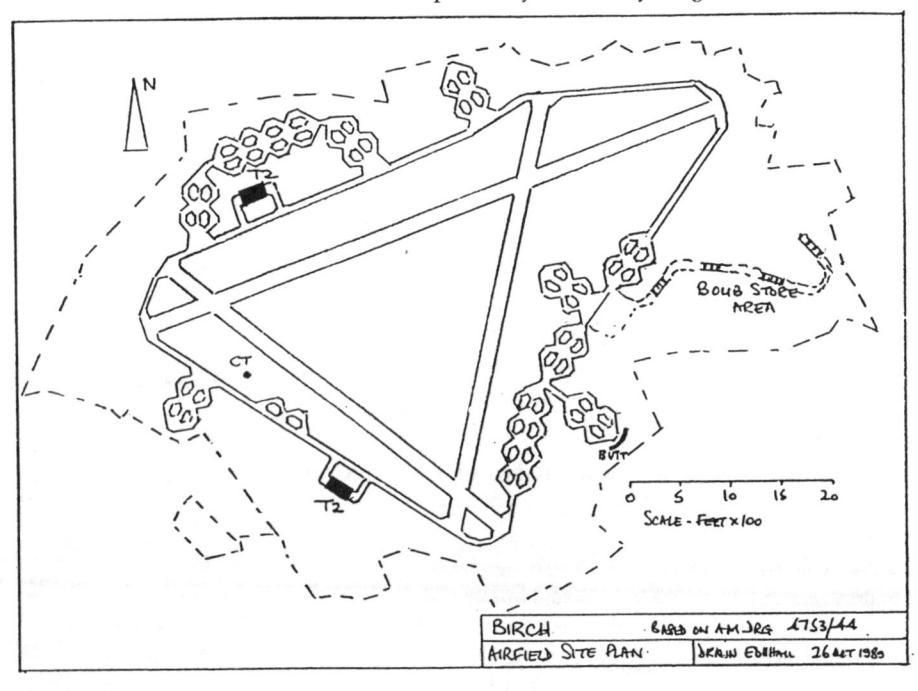

USAAF 8th Air Force. It was transferred to the USAAF 9th Air Force and used briefly as an assembly and storage centre for CG4A and Horsa gliders. Returned to the USAAF 8th Air Force it was held as a reserve airfield for 2nd Air Division but never used by 8th Air Force aircraft.

Birch achieved brief glory as an advance base for Operation Varsity being occupied by detachments from 46 Group Squadrons. It has reverted to agricultural use and a public road uses part of the perimeter track and runways.

Record of glider sorties: Operation Varsity.

| | |
|---|---|
| 48 Squadron | 12 |
| 233 Squadron | 24 |
| 437 RCAF Squadron | 24 |
| Total | 60 |

(All combinations Dakota/Horsa.)

## BLAKEHILL FARM
Code XF. Location. OS Sheet 163. Grid reference SP 075915
2 miles SW of Cricklade; south of B 4040 Malmesbury to Cricklade road.

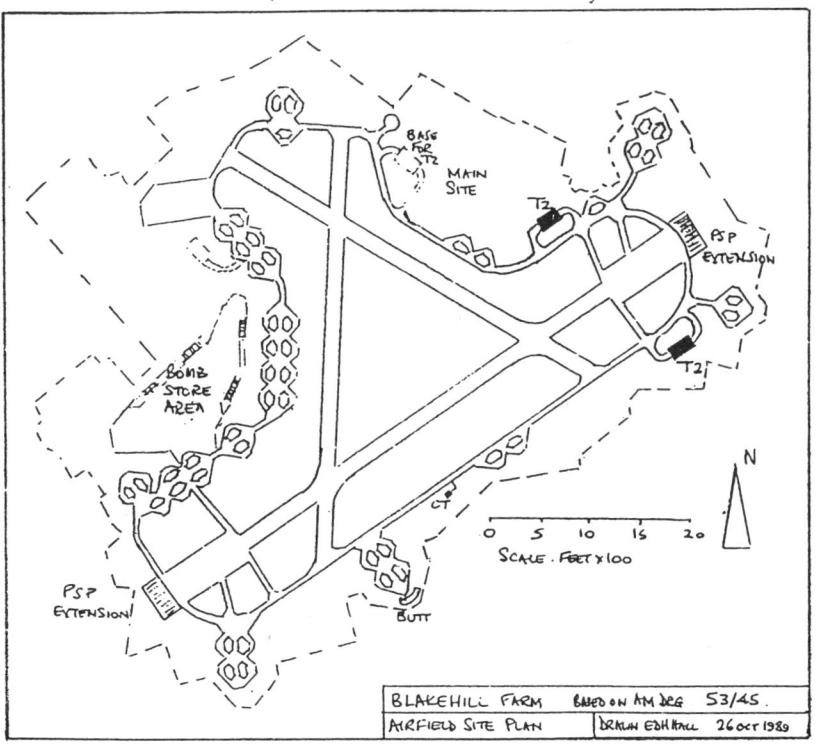

HISTORY.    Built in 1943 and allocated to 46 Group in February 1944. Next month 233 Squadron moved in having previously flown Lockheed Hudsons from Gibraltar. 437 (RCAF) Squadron was formed at the airfield on 4th September 1944, largely by transfers of Canadians from 233 Squadron, and remained until 7th May 1945. Early in June 1945, 233 Squadron left leaving the airfield to 22 Heavy Glider Conversion Unit which engaged in converting glider pilots to Hadrian gliders as well as other duties. (The writer formed part of a live load on a training conversion flight). RAF Transport Command finally left in January 1947 and the airfield became derelict.

| Record of glider sorties: | Operation Tonga. | 233 Squadron | 6 |
|---|---|---|---|
| | Operation Market I. | 233 Squadron | 22 |
| | | 437 (RCAF) Squadron | 12 |
| | Operation Market II. | 233 Squadron | 17 |
| | | 437 (RCAF) Squadron | 6 |
| | Operation Market III. | 233 Squadron | 1 |
| | Total (All combinations Dakota/Horsa.) | | 64 |

Operation Varsity: Both squadrons sent detachments to Birch.

**BRIZE NORTON**
Code BZ. Location. OS Sheets 163/164. Grid reference SP 290060.
3 miles south of A 40 Oxford to Cheltenham road, 4 miles SW of Witney.

HISTORY.    Built under the pre WWII Expansion Scheme. Started in 1935 and first occupied by 2 Flying Training School in August 1937 and Airborne Forces Support in July 1942, first by the Heavy Glider Conversion Unit and later by 296 and 297 Squadrons, who moved to Earls Colne after the Arnhem operation. 21 Heavy Glider Conversion Unit returned and remained until December 1945. Since the end of WWII the airfield has been a main base for RAF transport squadrons.

| Record of sorties. | Operation Tonga. | 296 Squadron | 8 |
|---|---|---|---|
| | | 297 Squadron | 12 |
| | Operation Mallard. | 296 Squadron | 20 |
| | | 297 Squadron | 20 |
| | Total (All combinations Albemarle/Horsa.) | | 60 |

Operation Market: Both squadrons were detached to Manston owing to the limited range of their Albemarle tugs.

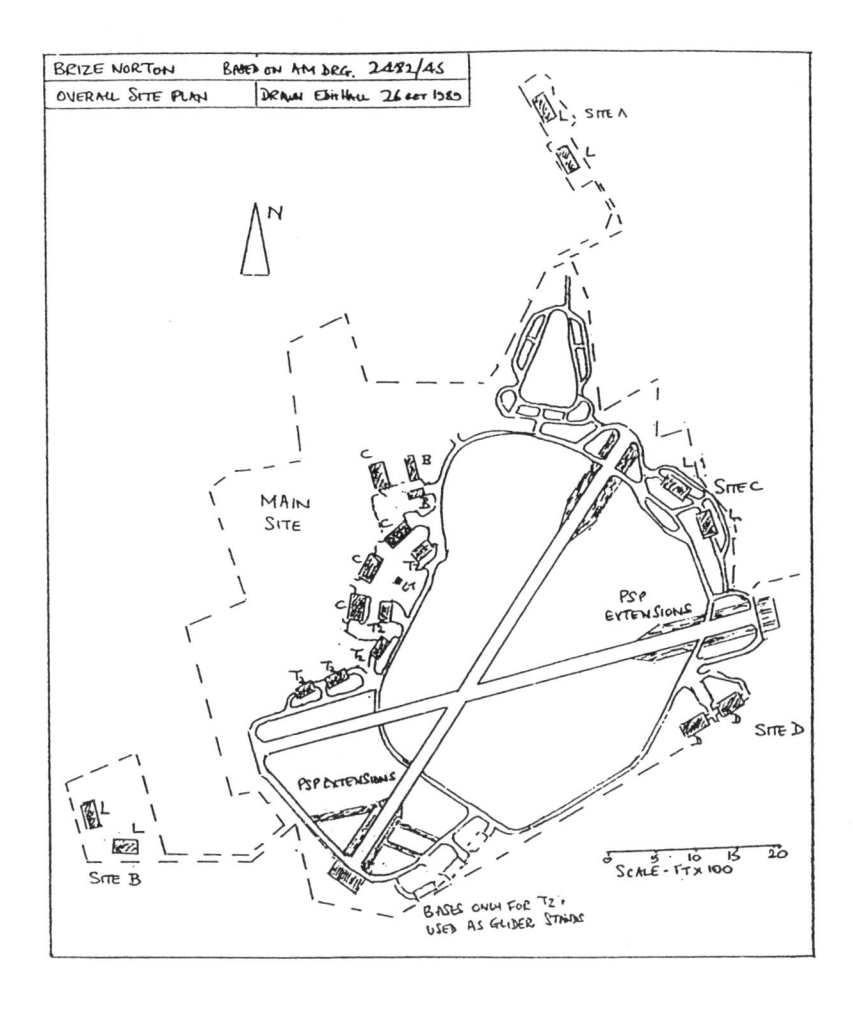

## BROADWELL

Code JR. Location. OS Sheet 163 Grid reference SP248065. East of A 361 Lechlade to Burford road. 2 miles NNE of Lechlade and 2 miles W of Brize Norton airfield.

HISTORY. Built in 1943 the airfield opened 15th November 1943 and was taken over by 46 Group on the 24th January 1944. 512 and 575 Squadrons moved in 6th February 1944, remaining until August 1945. Transport Command continued to use the airfield until the end of 1946. Closed in March 1947. Now reverted to agriculture.

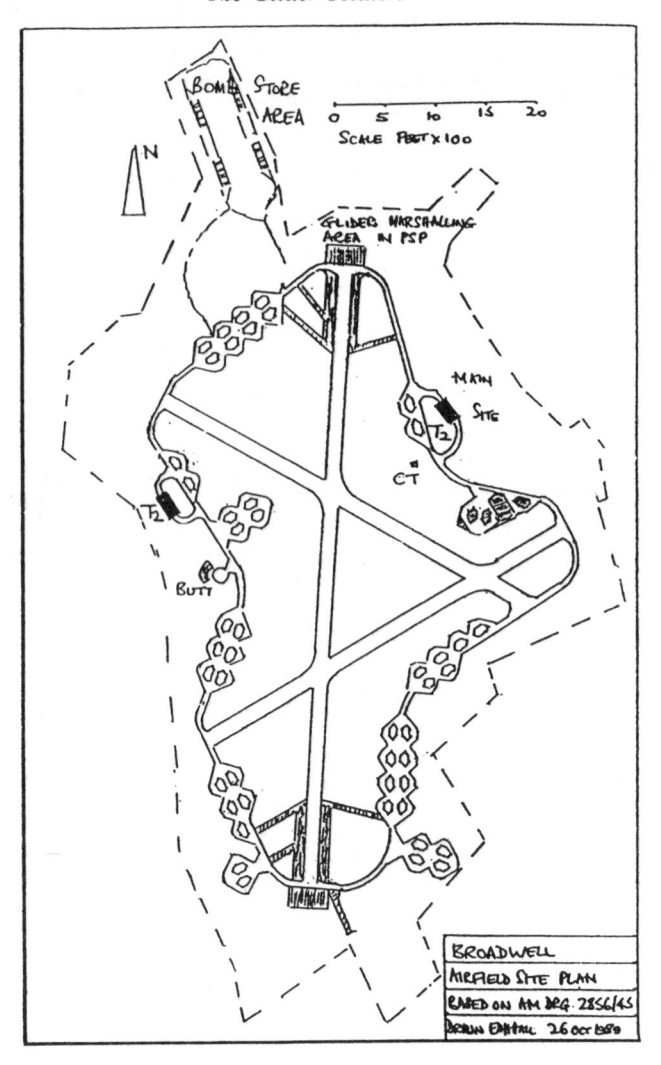

Record of glider sorties:  Operation Mallard.    512 Squadron    18
                                                 575 Squadron    19
                           Operation Market I.   512 Squadron    22
                                                 575 Squadron    24
                           Operation Market II.  512 Squadron    24
                                                 575 Squadron    25
                                                 Total          132
                           (All combinations Dakota/Horsa.)

Operation Varsity: Both squadrons sent detachments to Gosfield.

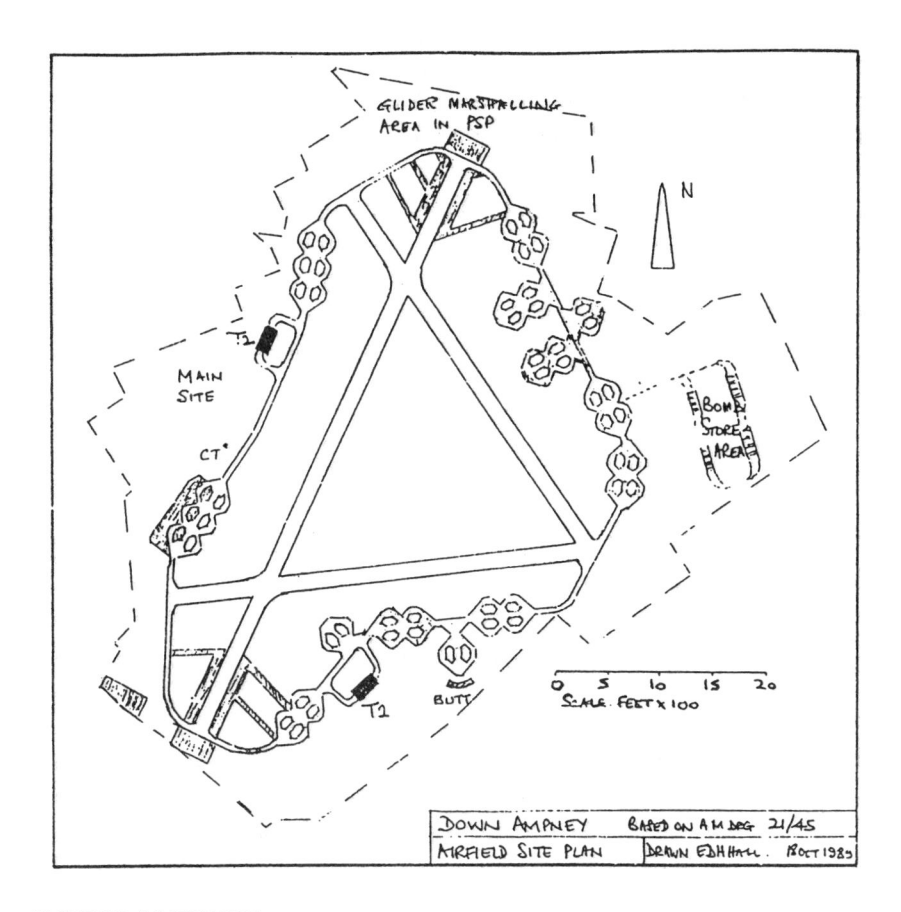

## DOWN AMPNEY
Code XA. Location OS Sheet 163. Grid reference SP 110965.
2 miles N of Cricklade, near the A 419 Cricklade to Cirencester road.

HISTORY. Built in 1943-44 the airfield was occupied by 46 Group on the 7th February 1944. 48 Squadron arrived on 24th February followed by 271 Squadron on the 29th February: both squadrons remaining until after 8th May 1945. The airfield was then used by RCAF Dakota squadrons until April 1946. It reverted to agricultural use and little remains today. There is a flourishing RAF Down Ampney Old Comrades Association.

| Record of glider sorties. | Operation Tonga. | 271 Squadron | 7 |
|---|---|---|---|
| | Operation Mallard. | 48 Squadron | 22 |
| | | 271 Squadron | 15 |
| | Operation Market I. | 48 Squadron | 23 |

|  |  |  |
|---|---|---|
|  | 271 Squadron | 24 |
| On Detachment from Blakehill Farm | 437 (RCAF) Squadron | 2 |
| Operation Market II. | 48 Squadron | 25 |
|  | 271 Squadron | 24 |
| Operation Market III. | 48 Squadron | 1 |
|  | Total | 143 |

(All combinations Dakota/Horsa.)

Operation Varsity: 48 squadron sent a detachment of 12 a/c from Birch and 271 Squadron also sent 12 a/c from Gosfield.

## EARLS COLNE
Code EC. Location. OS Sheet 168 Grid reference TL850270.
3 miles N of Coggeshall and the A120 Bishops Stortford to Colchester road. The B1024 runs just to the E of the airfield.

HISTORY.     Built January to December 1942, and allocated to the USAAF 8th Air Force on the 4th June 1942, the first occupants being the US 94th Bomb Group equipped with B17s who moved in during May 1943. The airfield was allocated in October 1943, to the USAAF 9th Air Force's 323rd Bomb Group equipped with B26s, who remained until 21st July 1944. A number of East Anglian airfields became vacant when the USAAF 9th Air Force moved to the Continent and Earls Colne was one of four taken over by 38 Group to bring the Tug Squadrons nearer to Europe. 296 and 297 Squadrons moved from Brize Norton at the end of September 1944, and converted from Albemarle to Halifax aircraft.
The airfield can still be visited using the perimeter track and disused runways. Essex Flying Club are active and an industrial park occupies much of the former technical site.

|  |  |  |  |
|---|---|---|---|
| Record of glider sorties: | Operation Varsity. | 296 Squadron | 30 |
|  |  | 297 Squadron | 30 |
|  |  | Total | 60 |

(All combinations Halifax/Horsa.)

[Airfield site plan: Earls Colne]

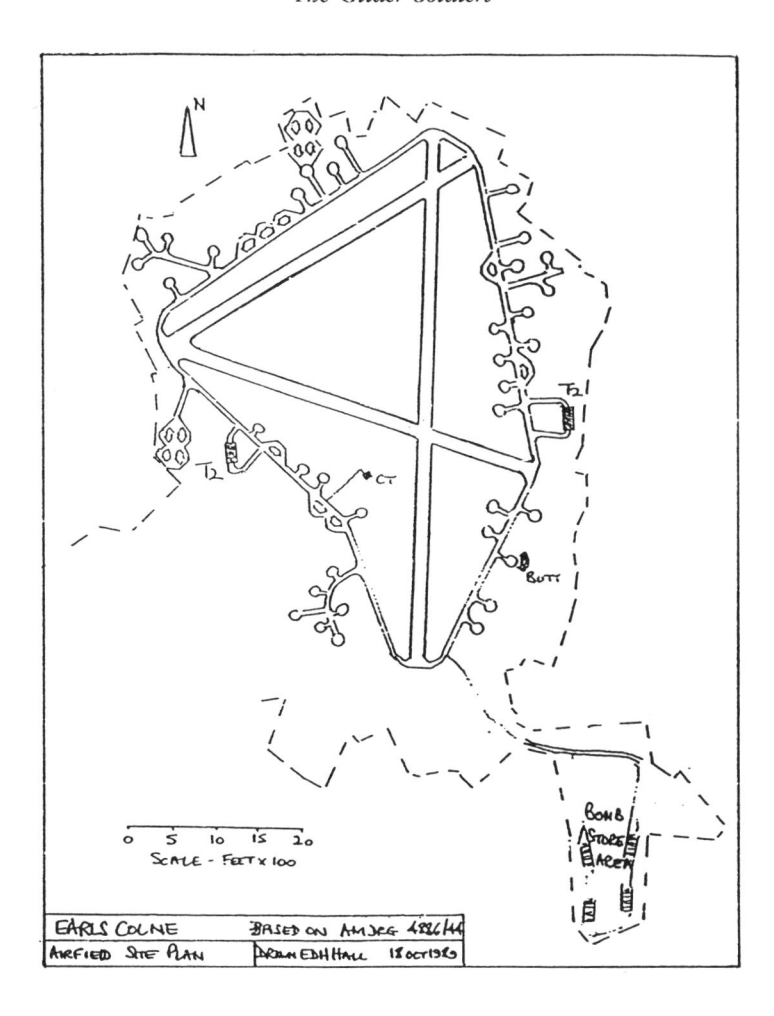

# FAIRFORD

Code FA. Location. OS Sheet 163. Grid reference SP 155985.
9 miles N of Swindon and 3 miles S of the A417 Cirencester to Lechlade road.

HISTORY.  Built in 1943 for the USAAF but not taken up by them. Occupied by 38 Group from the 2nd March 1944. 620 Squadron moved in during March from Leicester East, being joined later in the month by 190 Squadron who were transferred from Bomber Command. Both squadrons moved to Great Dunmow in mid October 1944, and Fairford became a satellite used by 22 Heavy Glider Conversion Unit based at Keevil and Blakehill Farm. Fairford was retained after WWII as a permanent station and enlarged. Main use was and is by the USAF air tanker fleet although the long main runway was used for test flying Concorde.

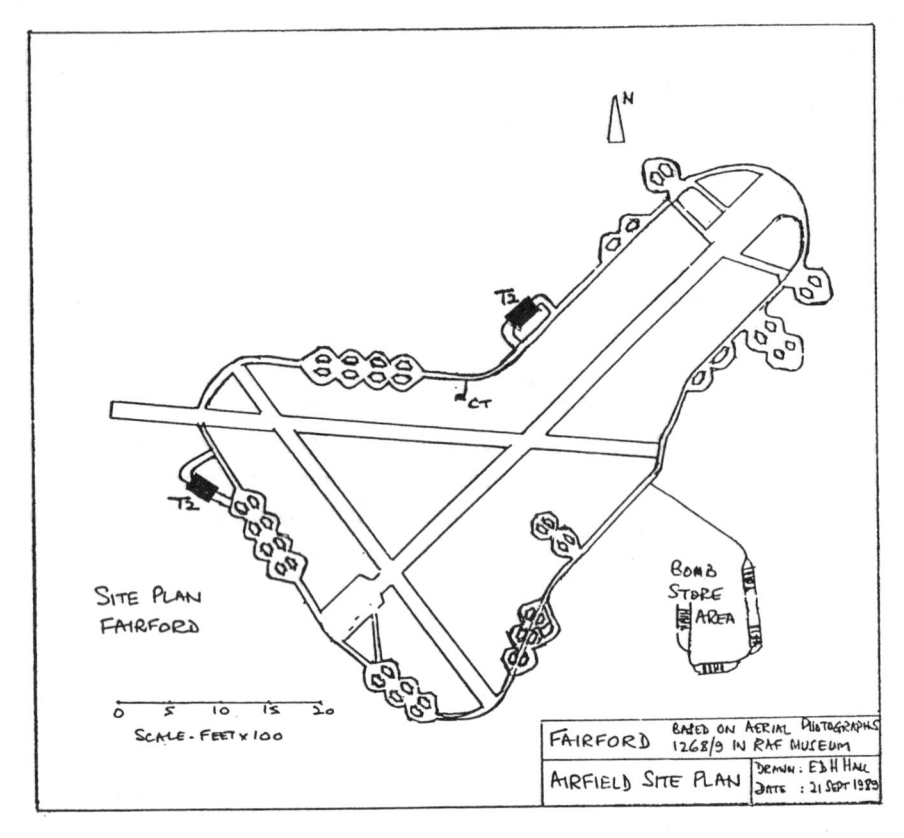

| Record of glider sorties: | Operation Mallard. | 190 Squadron | 18 |
| --- | --- | --- | --- |
| | | 620 Squadron | 18 |
| | Operation Market I. | 190 Squadron | 19 |
| | | 620 Squadron | 19 |
| | Operation Market II. | 190 Squadron | 21 |
| | | 620 Squadron | 22 |
| | Operation Market III. | 190 Squadron | 2 |
| | | 620 Squadron | 1 |
| | Operation Molten | 190 Squadron | 16 |
| | | 620 Squadron | 16 |
| | | Total | 152 |

(All combinations Stirling /Horsa.)

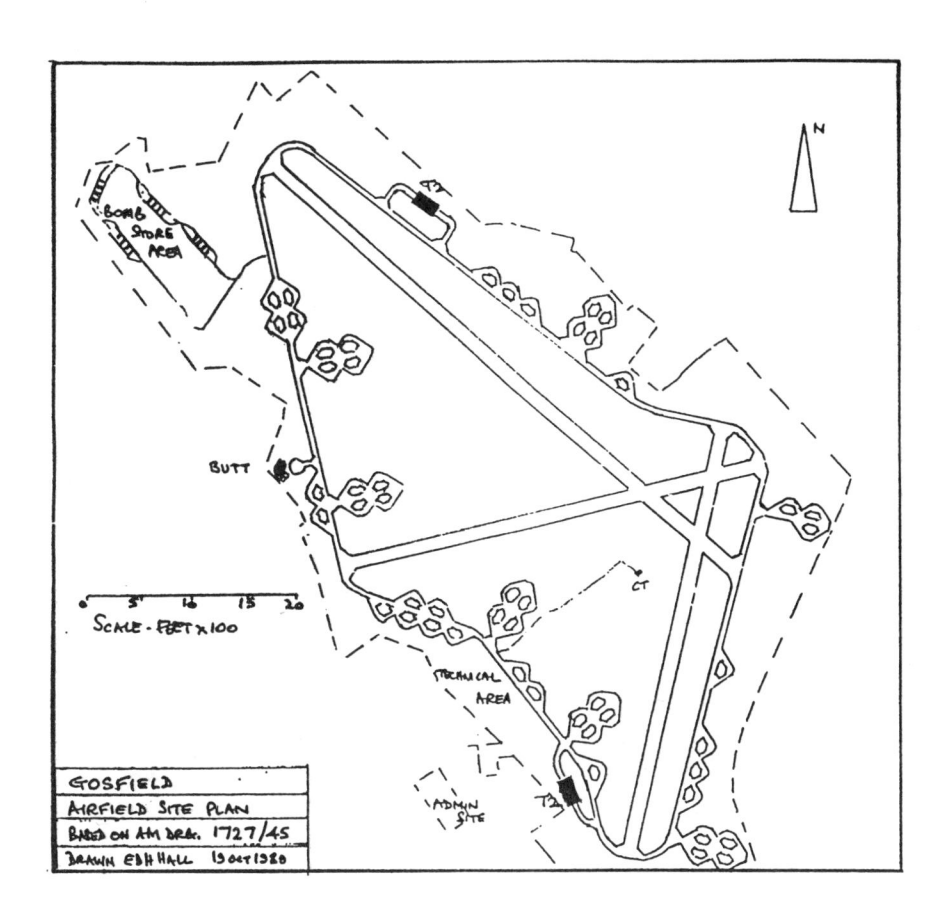

## GOSFIELD

Code GF. Location OS Sheet 167. Grid reference TL 770315.
2 miles W of Halstead, just W of the A1017 Braintree to Haverhill road.

HISTORY. Built in 1943 and allocated to the USAAF 8th Air Force but not used by them. Transferred to the USAAF 9th Air Force and occupied by the 365th Fighter Group equipped with P47 Thunderbolts then the 410th Bomb Group with A20 Havoc aircraft. The USAAF moved to the Continent in September 1944, and the airfield was not used operationally until March 1945, when detachments from three squadrons flew from Gosfield on Operation Varsity.

Post WWII the airfield reverted to agriculture. Part of the perimeter track remains on private land.

Record of glider sorties: Operation Varsity.

| | |
|---|---|
| 271 Squadron | 12 |
| 512 Squadron | 24 |
| 575 Squadron | 24 |
| Total | 60 |

(All combinations Dakota/Horsa.)

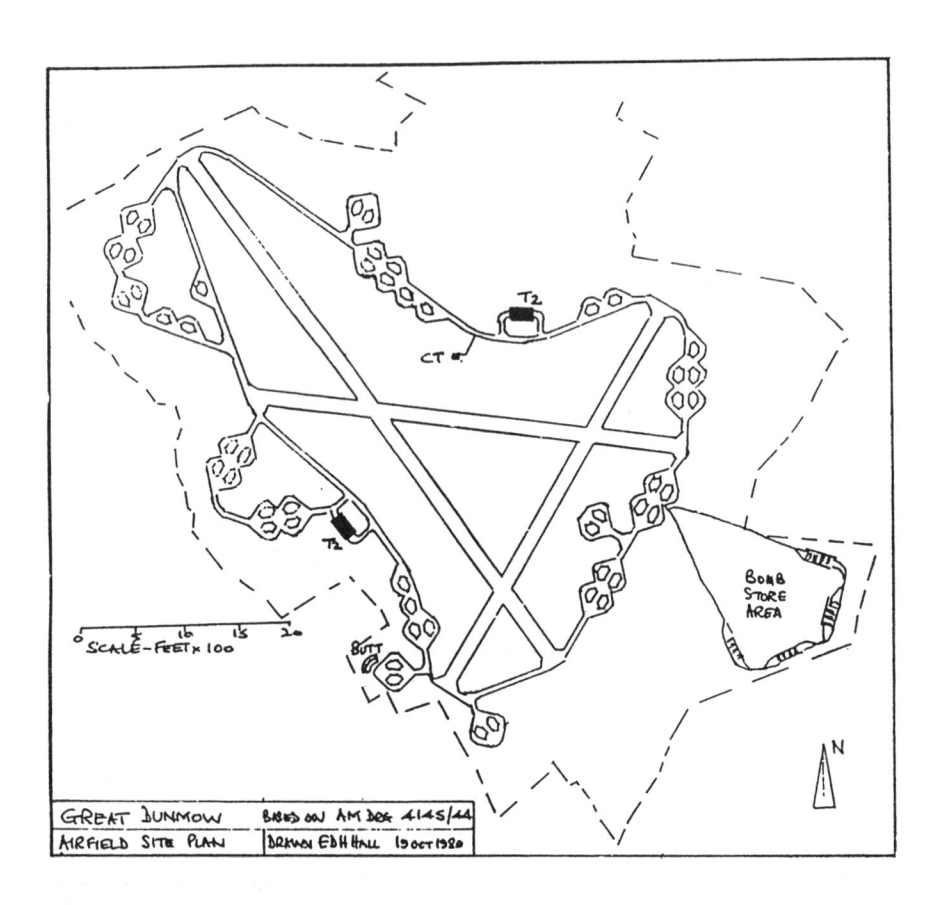

## GREAT DUNMOW
Code GD. Location. OS Sheet 167 Grid reference TL 590235.
6½ miles E of Bishops Stortford, north of the A120 Bishops Stortford to Colchester road.

HISTORY. Built 1942 to June 1943, by the US 818th Engineer Battalion and allocated to the USAAF 8th Air Force. Transferred to the 386th Bomber Group of the USAAF 9th Air Force equipped with B26 aircraft. In October 1944, when the USAAF moved to the Continent the airfield was taken over by 38 Group with 190 and 620 Squadrons moving in from Fairford. Both squadrons took part in Operation Varsity. The airfield reverted to agriculture after WWII. A section of the perimeter track remains on private land.

Record of glider sorties: Operation Varsity.  
    190 Squadron      28  
    620 squadron      31  
    Total      59  
(All combinations Stirling/Horsa.)

## HARWELL
Code HW. Location. OS Sheet 174. Grid reference SU 475865
6 miles S of Abingdon. W of A34 Newbury to Oxford road.

HISTORY. Harwell was developed in the pre WWII RAF expansion programme. Started in June 1935, it opened on 2nd February 1937, as a training station. For the early WWII years it was home for 15 OTU and transferred to 38 Group in April 1944, being occupied by 295 and 570 Squadrons. Harwell went into history on the night of the 5th-6th June 1944, when aircraft from both squadrons dropped the first troops to land in France in addition to glider tug sorties.

The Tug Squadrons moved to Rivenhall in October 1944, and Harwell reverted to hosting 13 OTU. Post WWII the airfield was taken over by the UK Atomic Energy Research Establishment on the 1st January 1946, in whose possession it still remains. Many of the former RAF buildings are still in use.

| Record of glider sorties: | | |
|---|---|---|
| Operation Tonga. | 295 Squadron | 13 |
| | 570 Squadron | 12 |
| Operation Mallard. | 295 Squadron | 21 |
| | 570 Squadron | 20 |
| (Above combinations Albemarle/Horsa.) | Total | 66 |
| Operation Market I. | 295 Squadron | 25 |
| | 570 Squadron | 20 |
| Operation Market II. | 295 Squadron | 3 |
| | 570 Squadron | 10 |
| Operation Market III. | 570 Squadron | 1 |
| (Above combinations Stirling/Horsa.) | Total | 125 |

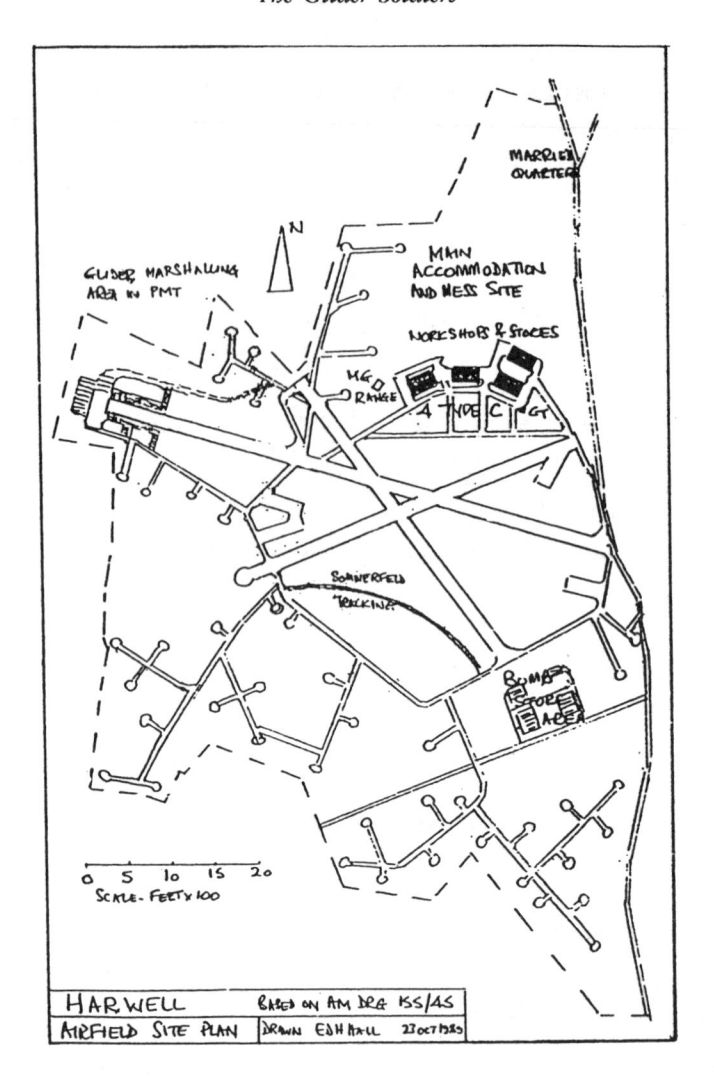

[Map: Harwell Airfield Site Plan, based on AM DRG 155/45, drawn EJH Hall 23 Oct 1989. Labels include: Married Quarters, Main Accommodation and Mess Site, Glider Marshalling Area in PMT, Workshops & Stores, MG Range, A Type, C Type, GT, Sommerfeld Tracking, Bomb Store Area. Scale: Feet x 100.]

## KEEVIL

Code KV. Location. OS Sheet 173 Grid reference ST920570.
4½ miles E of Trowbridge, E of A350 Westbury to Melksham road.

HISTORY.       Built in 1942 for use as a bomber OTU but not used as such. Opened July 1942, and occupied by the 62nd Troop Carrier Group, USAAF 9th Air Force with Dakota aircraft which participated in Operation Torch. Later used by the USAAF 363rd Fighter Group. Vacated by the USAAF in February 1944, and occupied by 196 and 299 Squadrons, 38 Group in March 1944, until 9th October 1944, when the Squadrons moved to Wethersfield and finally to Shepherds Grove. Keevil was then used by 22 Heavy Glider Conversion Unit and later 61 OTU. The airfield is still on charge to the Ministry of Defence and is in use by gliding clubs.

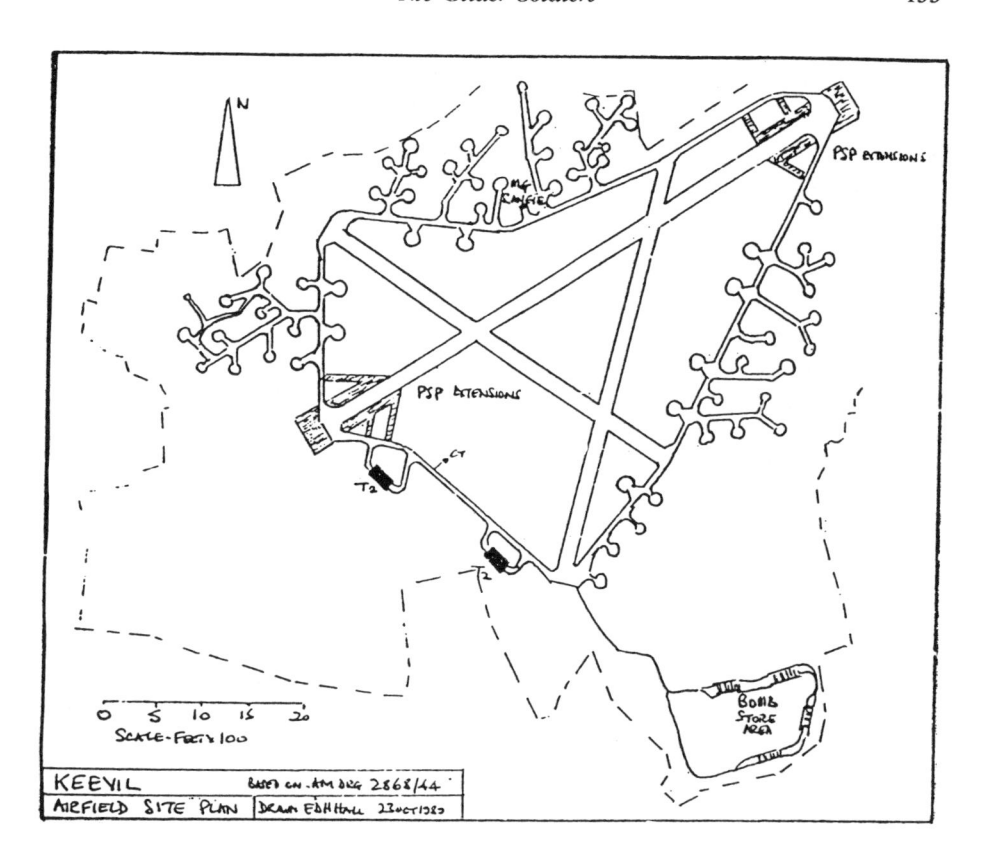

Record of glider sorties:

| | | | |
|---|---|---|---|
| | Operation Mallard. | 196 Squadron | 17 |
| | | 299 Squadron | 16 |
| | Operation Market I. | 196 Squadron | 25 |
| | | 229 Squadron | 25 |
| | Operation Market II. | 196 Squadron | 22 |
| | | 299 Squadron | 22 |
| | Operation Market III. | 196 Squadron | 9 |
| | | 299 Squadron | 7 |
| | | Total | 143 |

(All combinations Stirling/Horsa.)

## MANSTON
Code MQ. (Postwar) Location. OS Sheet 179. Grid reference TR335660
3 miles W of Ramsgate, the A253 Canterbury to Ramsgate road runs along S boundary of airfield.

HISTORY.   A small airfield was sited at Manston during WWI and developed into a permanent RAF Station between the wars. Its position near the south east coast led to selection for development into the first of three Emergency Landing Grounds - with a single (by WWII standards) large runway. Manston was used as an advanced base for Operation Market by the last two Albemarle equipped tug squadrons. Manston is still in use and is being developed for civil purposes as Kent International Airport.

| Record of glider sorties: | Operation Market I. | 296 Squadron | 21 Horsas |
|---|---|---|---|
| | | | 7 Hadrians |
| | | 297 Squadron | 25 Horsas |
| | | | 3 Hadrians |
| | Operation Market II. | 296 Squadron | 16 Horsas |
| | | | 4 Hadrians |
| | | 297 Squadron | 22 Horsas |
| | Operation Market III. | 296 Squadron | 1 Horsa |
| | | Totals | 85 Horsas |
| | | | 14 Hadrians |

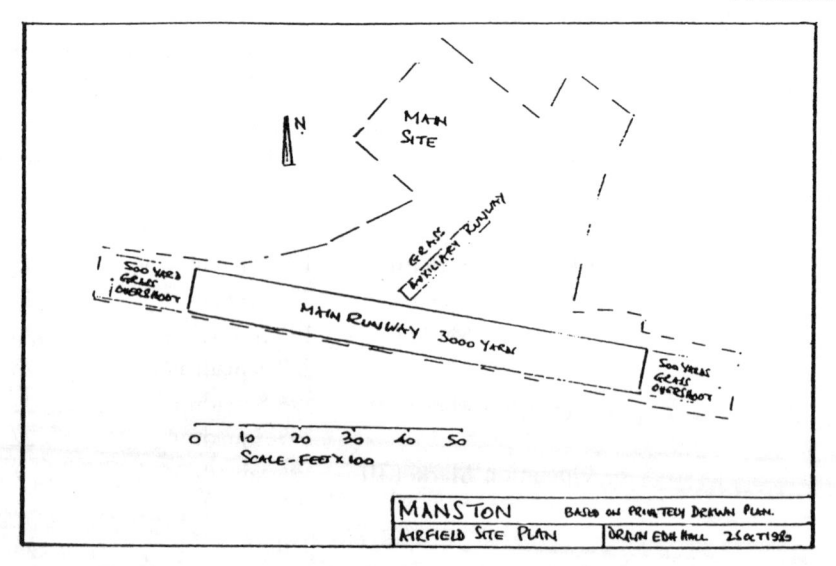

## MATCHING

Code MC. Location. OS Sheet 167. Grid reference TL550110.
5 miles E of Harlow, 2 miles S of A1060 Sawbridgeworth to Chelmsford road.

HISTORY. Built in 1943 by the US Army 834th and 840th Engineer Battalions. Allocated to USAAF 8th Air Force in August 1942, but never used by them. Transferred to USAAF 9th Air Force in October 1943, and used by the 391st Bomb Group with B26 Marauders till September 1944. Taken over by 38 Group in 1944 and the Operational Refresher Training Unit moved in to train aircrews in the techniques of glider towing and paratroop dropping, plus giving refresher training to experienced aircrews. With the need for maximum Group effort for Operation Varsity, ORTU was called on to provide 20 combinations which they did but only 14 gliders were successfully towed to the LZs. Post WWII the airfield reverted to agricultural use but the control tower is still standing and part of the perimeter track is used as a public road.

Record of glider sorties: Operation Varsity: ORTU 20 Stirling/Horsa combos.

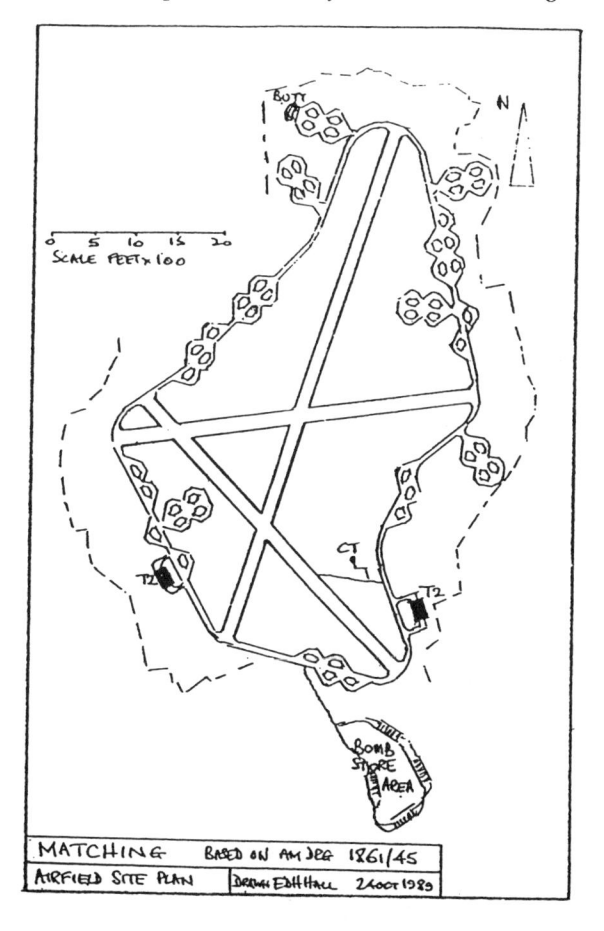

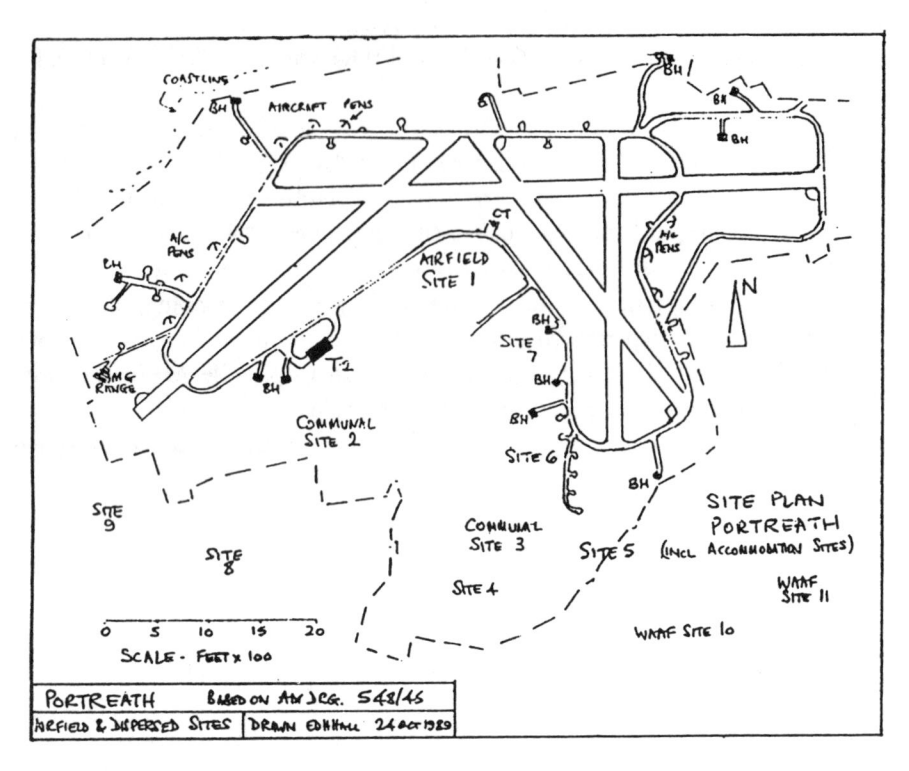

## PORTREATH
Code PA. Location OS Sheet 203. Grid reference SW670460
3½ miles N of Redruth - between B3300 Redruth to Portreath road and the coast.

HISTORY.      Built 1940-41, the airfield was opened in March 1941, being used mainly for fighter operations by 10 Group. For Airborne Forces purposes the only use was ferrying glider operations to North Africa in 1943. Post WWII Portreath was used for some years by the Chemical Defence Establishment then No.1 Air Control Centre.

Record of glider sorties:  Operation Beggar(Turkey Buzzard).      30
                           Operation Elaborate.                    23
                                                          Total    53
                    (All combinations being 295 Squadron - Halifax/Horsa.)

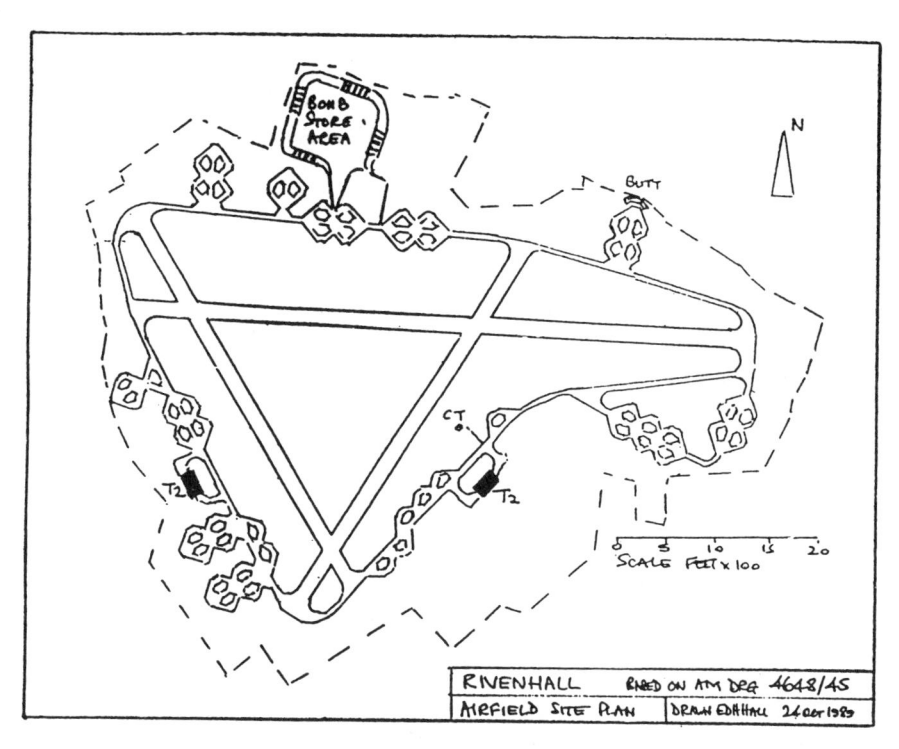

## RIVENHALL
Code RL. Location. OS Sheet 168. Grid reference TL820210
2 miles S of A120 Bishops Stortford to Coggeshall road.

HISTORY.   Built 1943-44 and allocated to USAAF 8th Air Force but never occupied by them, being transferred to the USAAF 9th Air Force in October 1943. First used by the USAAF 363rd Fighter Group with P51 Mustangs then the 397th Bomber Group with B26 Marauders. Vacated by USAAF in September 1944, it was taken over by 295 and 570 Squadrons of 38 Group moving from Harwell on 1st October 1944. Post WWII the airfield reverted to agriculture but many of the building are still in use by Marconi and access is forbidden. The control tower and a hangar are visible from public roads.

Record of glider sorties: Operation Varsity

| | | |
|---|---|---|
| | 295 Squadron | 31 |
| | 570 Squadron | 30 |
| | Total | 61 |

(All combinations Stirling/Horsa.)

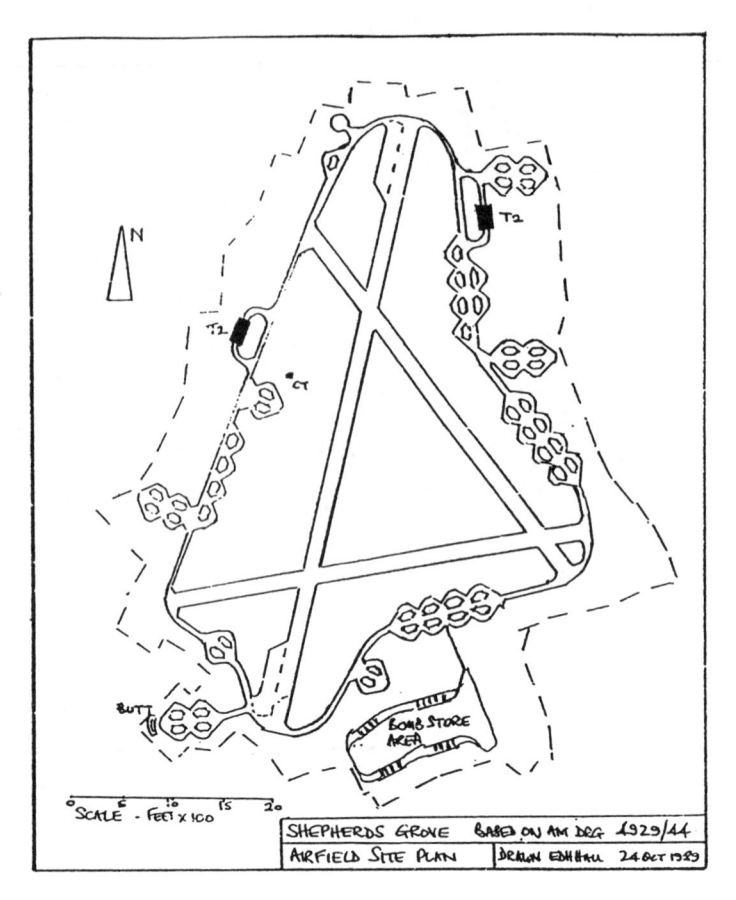

## SHEPHERD'S GROVE
Code HP. Location. OS Sheet 155. Grid reference TM 990730
9 miles NE of Bury St. Edmunds. E of A143 Bury St.Edmunds to Diss road.

HISTORY.   Built 1943-44 and allocated to USAAF 8th Air Force but not used by them. Transferred to RAF Bomber Command being occupied by 1657 HCU. In January 1945, it was taken over by 38 Group with 196 and 299 Squadrons moving from Keevil. Post WWII it was used as a satellite of Watton by the Radar Warfare Establishment, also by various fighter and fighter bomber units of the USAF before becoming a Bomber Command Thor missile site. It is now an industrial site.

Record of glider sorties: Operation Varsity.   196 Squadron      31
                                               299 Squadron      29
                              Total (All combinations Stirling/Horsa)  60

## SKITTEN

Code NS. Location. OS Sheet 12. Grid reference ND 325570
3 miles NW of Wick, Scotland. The A9 Wick to John o' Groats road runs between the airfield and the coast.

HISTORY. Skitten holds a special place in the story of the Glider Pilot Regiment being the airfield from which the first British glider operation was mounted in November 1942. (Operation Freshman). Built in 1940 as a fighter station it later came under Coastal Command and was used as an advanced base by Bomber Command in Norwegian operations. The airfield is now derelict but a few buildings still survive.

Record of glider sorties: Operation Freshman. 2: Both combinations Halifax/Horsa, crews from 38 Wing.

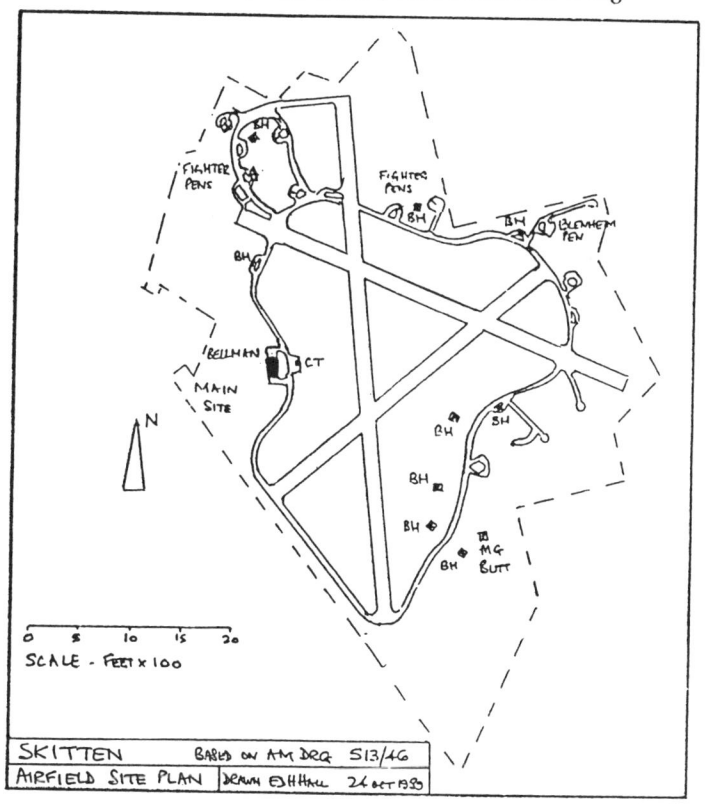

## TARRANT RUSHTON

Code TK. Location. OS Sheet 195. Grid reference ST945055.
4 miles E of Blandford and N of the B 3082 Blandford to Wimborne Road.

HISTORY.     Built 1942-43 and originally allocated to the USAAF 8th Air Force as a transport base but was never taken over by them. It opened in October, 1943, with 38 Group in occupation. 298 Squadron was formed on base on the 4th November followed by 644 Squadron on the 16th March 1944, both squadrons being equipped with Halifax aircraft. Tarrant Rushton is unique in having been the only airfield for the despatch of all three operational glider types used by British airborne forces. After May 1945, the resident squadrons departed and the airfield was used by other squadrons for glider training until September 1946.

In June 1948 the airfield was taken over by Flight Refuelling Ltd. and used by them and for flying training until September 1980. Most of the buildings have been demolished and the airfield has reverted to agricultural use.

Record of glider sorties:

| Operation | Squadron | Horsa | Hamilcar | Hadrian | Total |
|---|---|---|---|---|---|
| Tonga | 298 | 18 | 2 | | 20 |
| | 644 | 18 | 2 | | 20 |
| Mallard | 298 | 1 | 15 | | 16 |
| | 644 | 1 | 15 | | 16 |
| Dingson 35A | 298 | | | 6 | 6 |
| | 644 | | | 5 | 5 |
| Market I | 298 | 13 | 7 | | 20 |
| | 644 | 15 | 6 | | 21 |
| Market II | 298 | 8 | 8 | | 16 |
| | 644 | 8 | 7 | | 15 |
| Market III | 298 | 10 | | | 10 |
| | 644 | 10 | 1 | | 11 |
| Totals | | 102 | 63 | 11 | 176 |

[Airfield site plan: Tarrant Rushton]

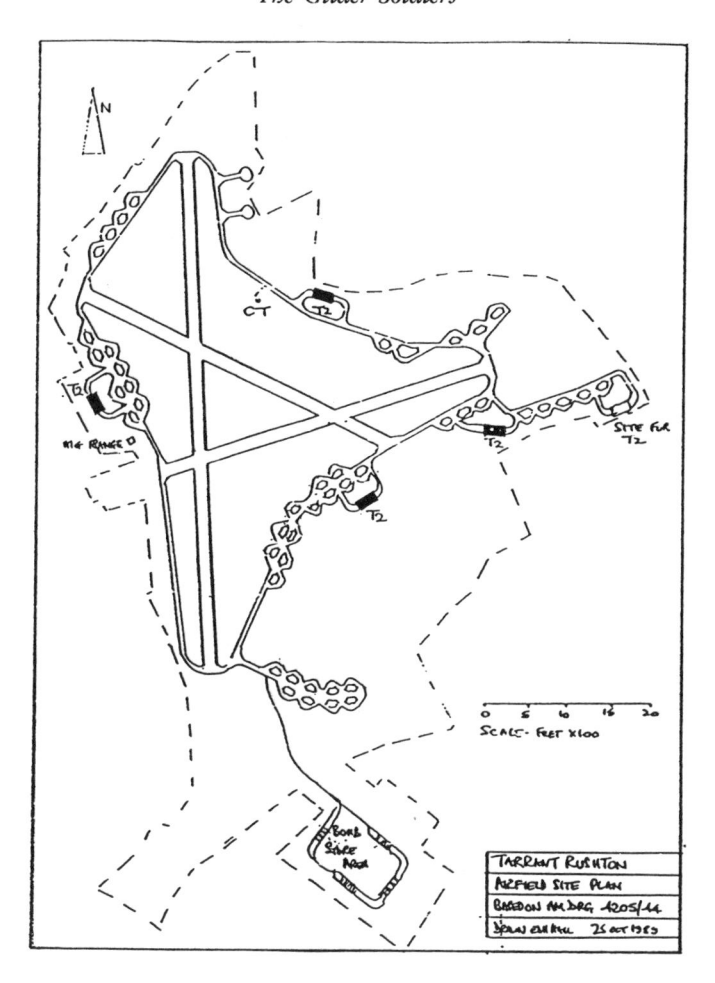

## WOODBRIDGE

Code WX (Postwar). Location. OS Sheet 169. Grid reference TM330485
11 miles ENE of Ipswich and E of the B1083 Woodbridge to Bawdsey road.

HISTORY.   Woodbridge was the second of the Emergency Landing Grounds (ELG) near the east coast to be used on a temporary basis for glider operations. Construction started in July 1942, and its first emergency aircraft -a B17 - landed 18th July 1943. Use as an ELG was interrupted in March 1945, when 298 and 644 Squadrons sent detachments from Tarrant Rushton for Operation Varsity. Post WWII it was used by aircraft taking part in bombing trials and Blind Landing experiments. The RAF left Woodbridge on 15th March 1948 and the USAF assumed occupation on 5th June 1952, using the base for fighter, fighter bomber and helicopter equipped rescue units.

Record of glider sorties: Operation Varsity.

| | | |
|---|---|---|
| | 298 Squadron | 6 Horsas |
| | | 24 Hamilcars |
| | Total | 30 |
| | 644 Squadron | 6 Horsas |
| | | 24 Hamilcars |
| | Total | 30 |
| | | 12 Horsas |
| | | 48 Hamilcars |
| | Total | 60 |

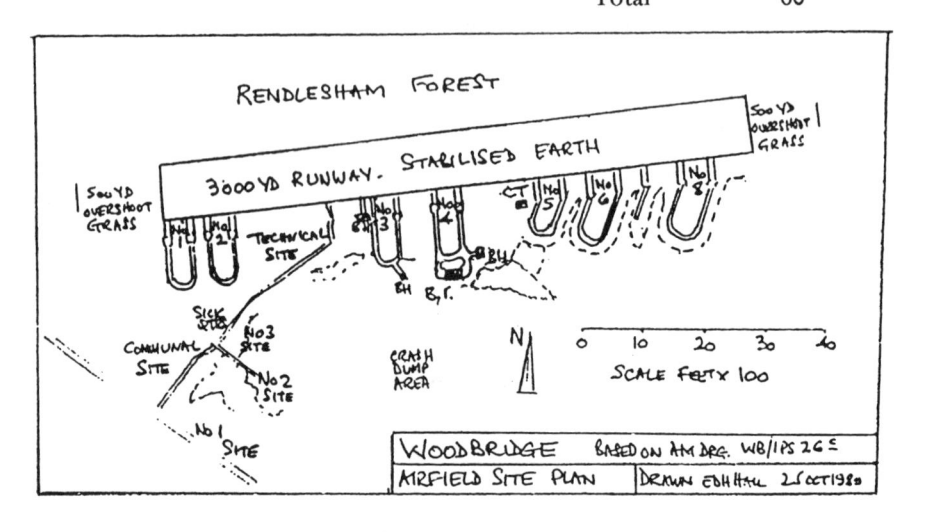

# BRITISH GLIDER TRAINING UNITS

The first British military glider training unit was formed at RAF Ringway, Cheshire, on the 19th September 1940 and designated the Glider Training Squadron - using Tiger Moth and Avro 504 aircraft as tugs and donated sailplanes and gliders for glider training.

On the 28th December 1940, the Glider Training Squadron moved to RAF Thame, Oxfordshire, with five Tiger Moth aircraft as glider tugs. Hawker Hector aircraft were then allocated as glider tugs and began to be delivered on the 21st February 1941.

The first British military glider - the Hotspur - was in production and coming off the assembly line and on the 6th April 1941, the squadron received its first Hotspur glider - serial No.BV 125 - and on the 26th April 1941, a demonstration exercise with the Hotspur and five Kirby Kites gliders was carried out for the Prime Minister Winston Churchill.

As the glider pilot training programme was expanded to train 400 glider pilots, the Glider Training Squadron was divided to become Nos.1 and 2 Glider Training Schools on the 1st December 1941 and transferred from Army Co Operation Command to Flying Training Command.

## NO.1 GLIDER TRAINING SCHOOL.

Airfields used:
RAF Thame.                1-12-41 Reserve landing ground at Kingston Bagpuize.
RAF Croughton.            19-7-41. The School disbanded on the 23-3-43 and all personnel were posted to 20( Pilots) Advanced Flying School. The School was reformed at RAF Kidlington.
RAF Kidlington            1-11-44
RAF Brize Norton          1-6-45 as part of 21 Heavy Glider Conversion Unit.
Aircraft tugs used:       Hawker Hind - serials K5421, K5515
                          Hawker Hector - K8097, K8111, K8119
                          Airspeed Oxford - BF974
                          Tiger Moth - T5417, N9197, N9198
                          Miles Master II - DL484, DM453, EM332

166      *The Glider Soldiers*

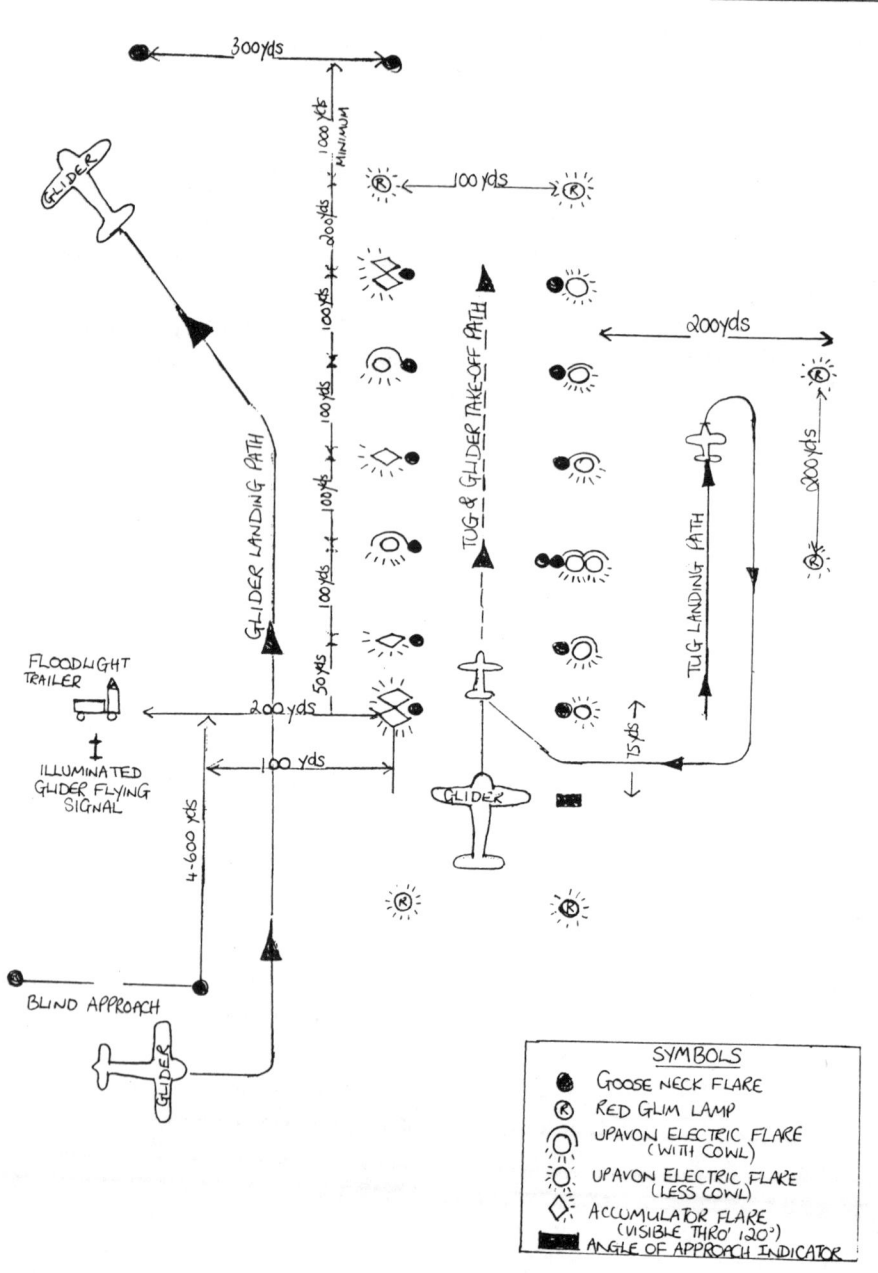

## NO.2 GLIDER TRAINING SCHOOL.

Formed from part of the Glider Training Squadron at RAF Thame and moved to RAF Weston on the Green from the 8th December 1941, with a tug establishment of one Hawker Hind, sixteen Hawker Hectors and two DH Tiger Moths. Glider establishment was thirty Hotspurs divided into two flights - A and B. Personnel establishment was nine tug pilots and twelve glider pilot instructors. Students were to arrive every three weeks for a six week course in glider pilot training.

On the 17th February 1942, No.1 Course had finished training and eight students from No.1 Glider Training School - having completed their glider training - came for tug pilot training. On the 23rd March 1943, No.2 Glider Training School was absorbed into No.20 (Pilots) Advanced Flying Unit.

Tug aircraft used:   Hawker Hind - serial nos. K5450. K7380. K7466
Hawker Hector -K8108, K8111, K8140
DH Tiger Moth - T5628
Hawker Audax - K7328, K8324, K8327, increased to 16 Audax in January, 1942.

## NO.3 GLIDER TRAINING SCHOOL.

Formed at RAF Stoke Orchard on the 21st July 1942, with an establishment of thirty four Miles Master IIs and Airspeed Oxford glider tugs and forty six Hotspur gliders. RAF Northleach was taken over as a relief landing ground.
Detachments from the School were posted to:

RAF Aldermaston, February 1943.
RAF Wanborough, December 1943.
RAF Zeals, October 1944.
RAF Culmhead, December 1944.

On the 16th January 1945, the School was transferred to RAF Exeter and by the 1st February 1945, began to receive AW Albemarles aircraft as glider tugs and Horsa gliders. Total aircraft held on that date was: six Albemarles, seven Horsas,, sixty one Hotspurs, seven Tiger Moths and sixty nine Master IIs. On the 24th July 1945, most of the School moved to RAF Wellesbourne Mountford and used RAF Gaydon as a satellite. The School was finally disbanded on the 3rd December 1947.

Aircraft used (known):    Tiger Moth - serials - DE194, DE887
                          Magister - T9736, V1067
                          Master IIs - DL325, DL373

## NO.4 GLIDER TRAINING SCHOOL.

Formed at RAF, Kidlington on the 13th July 1942, by re-naming No.101 (Glider) Operational Training Unit. Used Kingston Bagpuize as a satellite in January 1943. On the 6th April 1943, the School was disbanded and personnel posted to No.20 (Pilots) Advanced Flying School.

Aircraft used (known):    Hawker Hector - serials K8122, K8136
                          Hawker Audax - K3684, K7331, K7380
                          Hawker Hind - K5450, K5515, K6685

## NO.5 GLIDER TRAINING SCHOOL.

Formed at RAF Kidlington on the 30th June 1942, and moved to RAF Shobdon on the 30th July 1942. Equipped at first with Westland Lysander tugs and Hotspur gliders. In August 1942, Miles Master IIs replaced the Lysanders. RAF Hockley Heath was used as a relief landing ground during July 1944. The School was disbanded on the 30th November 1945.

Aircraft used:            Hawker Hector - serials K8166, Master II DL961, EM291

## NO.20 (PILOTS) ADVANCED FLYING SCHOOL.

Formed on the 10th March 1943, at RAF Kidlington and absorbed the personnel of Nos.1, 2 and 4 Glider Training Schools in late March and early April 1944. On the 1st November 1944, the School became No.1 Glider Training School.

# MARKING OF THE LANDING STRIP FOR GLIDERS OF AIRBORNE FORCES

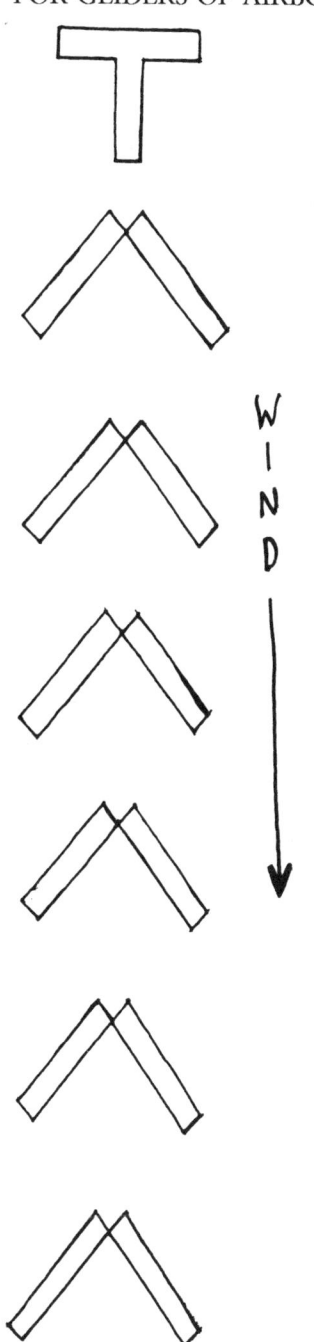

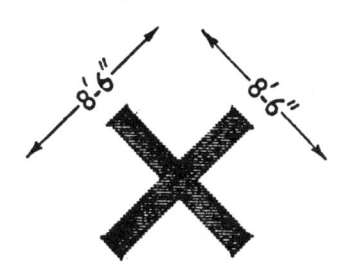

WIND

*A single yellow cross is used to indicate the tow cable dropping area.*

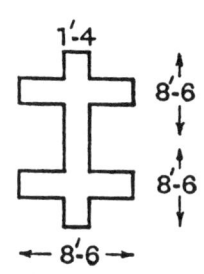

*A double white cross in the Control Tower signal area indicates glider flying in progress.*

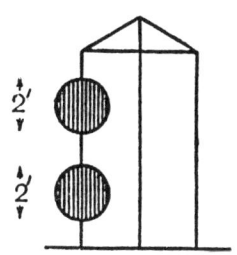

*Two red balls hoisted on the mast, one above the other, indicates glider flying in progress.*

## NO.101 (GLIDER) OPERATIONAL TRAINING SCHOOL.

Formed at RAF Kidlington on the 1st January 1942, using a relief landing ground at RAF Barford St. John. During June 1942, another relief landing ground was taken into use at Kiddington. On the 13th July 1942 the unit became No.4 Glider Training School at Kidlington.

Aircraft used (known):   Hawker Hector - serials K8093, K8099, K8134, K8139
                         Hawker Hind - L7701
                         Hawker Audax - K7468

## NO.102 (GLIDER) OPERATIONAL TRAINING UNIT.

Formed at RAF Kidlington on the 10th February 1942 with training beginning on the 27th February 1942, with Hawker Hind and Audax tugs towing Hotspur gliders. In June 1942, Westland Lysanders replaced the Hinds and Audaxes. On the 13th July 1942, the unit together with No.101 (Glider) Operational Training Unit became No.4 Glider Training School and the Westland Lysanders were transferred to No. 5 Glider Training School.

## THE GLIDER INSTRUCTOR'S SCHOOL.

Formed at RAF Thame for the purpose of teaching glider pilot instructors on the 25th August 1942. The School was disbanded on the 13th January 1943.

## GLIDER SNATCHING

The technique of a low flying powered aircraft tug snatching a stationary glider off the ground had its origins in pre WWII America where a small aviation firm - All American Aviation, Wilkington, Delaware - operated a mail service with light aircraft. To enable the firm's aircraft to pick up mail from inaccessible places, where the aircraft could not land, a snatch off procedure was devised.

A small cable winch fitted with brakes was installed inside the fuselage of their aircraft, with the cable running through guides to an external extended arm and attached to a hook. When the hook engaged a loop on a mailbag on the ground the bag was snatched into the air. The winch cable unwound to absorb the inertial energy of the mailbag weight, then the winch was braked and rewound to retrieve the mailbag into the aircraft. This was the basis of the system later evolved for glider snatching.

With the advent of WWII the technique was adapted to heavier loads by making the winch bigger so that gliders could be retrieved after landing on operations or for casualty evacuation when an aircraft could not land.

The All American Aviation Company produced their Model 40 winch which was successful and later their Model 80 which was developed to snatch the Waco CG4A (Hadrian) glider. Trials were carried out in the United States and Britain with good results.

The evolved technique was for a 220 feet tow cable to be attached to the nose of the stationary glider on the ground with the other end of the cable attached to a triangular loop which was mounted on two 12-foot high poles twenty feet apart. The snatching aircraft, usually a Dakota, flew at about twenty feet above the ground at about 120-130 mph towards the two poles with its snatching hook extended. The glider was placed diagonally to the track of the snatching aircraft to avoid the snatching hook striking the stationary glider.

When and if the snatching hook engaged the triangular loop and took up the tow cable it was pulled away from the offset extended arm to avoid fouling it in flight. The winch cable attached to the snatching hook unwound due to the weight of the glider and absorbed the snatching shock-aided by a friction brake on the winch. The braking capacity of the winch could be increased or decreased as required. The winch operater then re wound the winch cable and the tow cable was secured for normal towing flight.

A weak link was built into the towing cable and broke at a pre-determined load, usually seven tons. An explosive cutter was also provided on the winch so that the winch cable could be cut in an emergency. This of course would leave the glider attached to a heavy steel cable with dire results.

Depending on the terrain surrounding the snatch point a glider could be snatched off an area 600-700 feet long and the glider airborne in as little as 60 feet depending on make and load.

Glider snatching was successfully employed in Europe by the Allies to recover gliders from the glider graveyard in Normandy - some thirty-nine being recovered in this way. Casualties were also evacuated. In the Far East glider snatches were made in the Chindit campaign.

In Britain the RAF set up the Glider Pick Up Flight at RAF Ibsley, Hampshire, where pilots of the Glider pilot regiment and RAF were trained in the technique using Dakota tugs and Hadrian gliders.

The author took part in glider snatching exercises whilst stationed with 38 Group at RAF Fairford - and found it a stimulating experience! To fly at 120mph some twenty feet above the ground heading for between two 12-feet high poles twenty feet apart called for a high degree of airmanship.

Staff Sergeant Joe Michie, Glider Pilot Regiment, a veteran of Normandy and Arnhem, relates an account of the glider snatch course he did at RAF Ibsley:

"In August, 1945, I reported to RAF Ibsley which was three miles north of Ringwood, Hampshire, for a three day glider pick up course on Waco Hadrian gliders. The Glider Pick Up Flight, using C47 Dakota aircraft modified for glider tug snatching and Waco Hadrian gliders - some of which still bore their USAAF serial numbers, had been formed at Ibsley shortly after the end of WWII, to train pilots of the Glider Pilot Regiment in glider snatch technique.

RAF Ibsley had been an 11 Group Fighter Command airfield during the war and lay in a flat part of the River Avon valley. It had three tarmac runways - QDMs (magnetic bearings) 010, 050, and 320 with no flying obstructions. The main runway, 010 was 1600 yards long with undershoot and overshoot extending it to 3600 yards.

On the 18th August I commenced the course which consisted of eight pick ups, four as second pilot and four as first pilot with light and heavy loads. My first pick up was as second pilot on a MkII Hadrian serial number 533075 with Flying Officer Maronoe as first pilot. The nylon tow rope was attached to the nose of the Hadrian and laid out to the two twelve feet high poles twenty feet apart - ending in a loop suspended between the two poles.

The snatching Dakota came thundering in at 125 mph - we could hear it coming but did not see it until it flashed past twenty feet from the deck. The second pilot had to sit with his hand on the tail trim to trim back instantly. The Dakota snatch hook engaged the tow rope between the two poles and our glider shot forward as the tow rope was taken up. There was no jerk but in five seconds we were travelling at 150mph and feeling the "G" force acceleration. The winch operator in the Dakota wound the tow rope in and we were on normal tow. I estimate that we were airborne in about sixty feet from rest.

Casting off tow we circled and pulled the glider's nose up to lose speed and came in about 80mph - the Hadrian having a short landing run using the brakes and putting the nose skid down into the grass. Flying Officer Maronoe and myself repeated the pick up in the same Hadrian later the same day - both flights lasting ten minutes. The course was designed to qualify glider pilots in snatch technique - not on flying the glider itself, we were all qualified glider pilots.

The next day my Instructor Flying Officer Maronoe and myself did another snatch in a Hadrian serial number KK559. On the next pick up the same day in the Hadrian I was to be first pilot in the left hand seat and my second pilot was Sergeant O'Connor. My strongest memory is sitting there in the cockpit, both hands gripping the wheel and sweating blue lights, whilst the Dakota came in on the blind side. Instantly we were off the ground with me shouting to the second pilot to trim back, then in seconds, into normal tow followed a few minutes later by a flashly final side slip approach and landing.

The third and final day of the course I was second pilot to Staff Sergeant East, who had come through Sicily, Normandy and Arnhem. We did a heavy (loaded) pick up in Hadrian Serial number 341049 which was followed by my being first pilot on three more pick ups. Sometimes the Dakota's snatching hook would miss the loop and while the tug thundered by we would sit there like a very wet rag.

On the 23rd August we were certified as having qualified as glider pilots, Hadrian, on snatch pick up by the Squadron Leader CO of the Glider Pick Up Flight. This qualification was entered in our flying log books. Looking back over the years I am surprised at how short the course was - just eight take offs and forty minutes of flying time in three days."

Staff Sergeant Joe Michie is now retired and living in London.

# OPERATION FRESHMAN

The first British glider operation of WWII on the Norsk Hydro Electric Plant at Vemork, Norway, on the 19th-20th November 1942.

The Germans occupied Norway in April 1940, mainly by airborne assault, and took control of the Norsk Hydro Electric company's Plant at Vemork, Rjukan, sixty miles due west of Oslo, Norway and began to produce heavy water (deuterium oxide - $D_2O$) for use in their atomic bomb research programme.

Vemork was a small village two and a half miles west of Rjukan and about sixty miles from the coast. Rjukan is situated in a deep valley the heavily wooded sides of which rise sharply from the bottom to 3000 feet. The Norsk Plant had been built on a plateau of rock 1000 feet above the valley bottom so that gravity fed water turbines could generate electric power. Above the Plant was a sheer 2000 feet high area of thick pines.

British Intelligence discovered that the German atomic programme depended on the Vemork Plant producing heavy water and a Norwegian agent, Einar Skinnerland, who had lived at Rjukan prior to his escape to Britain in 1940, was dropped by parachute early in 1942, onto the Hardanger Plateau relatively near the Plant. Skinnerland surveyed the Plant and the surrounding area, taking photographs and making drawings which he sent back to British Intelligence in London.

The British Government viewed the Intelligence information with grave concern. Both the British and the Americans were working jointly on their own atomic bomb research: if the Germans got the atomic bomb first the results would be disastrous for the Allies. It was immediately decided to put the Plant out of action as soon as was possible.

In the middle of October 1942, Headquarters Combined Operations requested Major General Browning, Airborne Forces Commander, and Group Captain Sir Nigel Norman, 38 Wing, RAF, Commander, to plan an assault on the Plant. The assault plan decided on was for two Horsa gliders towed by Halifax aircraft to glider land a small specialist force of Royal Engineers at an LZ near Mosvatnet Lake about eight miles from Vemork on the night of the 19th-20th November 1942, to assault the Plant guided by Norwegian agents. The LZ would be pinpointed by Norwegian agents using Eureka radio beacons, activated on orders from Combined Operations, responding to the Rebecca receivers in the aircraft. Each glider would carry fifteen engineer troops trained to identify and destroy the heavy water stock and equipment. Escape would be in plain clothes via neutral Sweden some ninety-three miles away assisted by Norwegian agents.

1st Airborne Division would supply the troops and RAF 38 Wing the tug aircraft and Horsa gliders. Combined Operations Headquarters, Special Operations Executive and Military Intelligence would co-operate in the operation, codenamed Freshman. Another operation mounted by Special Operations Executive - codenamed Grouse - would drop four Norwegian agents, Lieutenant Poulsson, Lieutenant Haugland, Sergeant Kjelstrup and Sergeant Helberg on the 18th-19th November 1942, to mark the 700 yard long LZ with Eureka beacons and flares.

To mislead the enemy and cover the reason for the operation, a leaflet dropping sortie would be carried out on Oslo the night before the operation, and by the tug aircraft after the release of the gliders. To camouflage the gliders after landing a roll of butter muslin would be carried in each glider to assist concealment if a landing was made accidentally some distance away from the objective.

The Military forces selected for Operation Freshman were volunteers from the 9th Field Company (Airborne), and the 261st Field Park Company (Airborne), Royal Engineers under the command of Lieutenant Colonel H.C.A. Henniker, MC, Commandant Royal Engineers, based at Bulford Camp, Wiltshire.

The Air Force personnel were air and ground crews from 138 and 161 Squadrons, who were operating as Special Duties Squadrons, RAF Tempsford. Bedfordshire, attached to 38 Wing at RAF Netheravon, Wiltshire, for the operation, under the command of Group Captain T.B. Cooper, DFC. who was to be the Air Force Ground Controller while at the base airfield and who would take the final decision as to the launching of the assault.

Both Army and RAF forces commenced training for the operation, the Army in the use of Arctic clothing and equipment combined with physical training to withstand the rigors of a Norwegian winter and unarmed and armed combat to deal with the sentries at Vemork and possibly the small garrison at Rjukan. The RAF Halifax air crews engaged in night and day Horsa glider towing training from Netheravon, including long range towing, in preparation for the long haul across the North Sea in winter conditions.

To preserve security and give a cover story the troops and airmen were given to understand that they would be pitted against US Forces in a training exercise named the Washington Competition. (As Hedley Duckworth - one of the RAF airmen - says in his account of the operation, "The only Americans we came in contact with were American Rangers at Thruxton").

The base airfield chosen for the operation was RAF Skitten, Caithness, Scotland, some 400 miles from the target. Skitten, commanded by Group Captain N.A.P. Pritchett, was an operational satellite of RAF Wick and used by RAF Coastal Command. The Timetable and Operational Order for Operation Freshman read as follows:

Subject to weather conditions, the following programme will be adhered to.
Saturday, November 14th. Military equipment packed. Royal Engineers Party travels to London and the north.
Sunday, November 15th. First Halifax due at Skitten.
Monday, November 16th. Royal Engineers Party arrives at Skitten airfield.
Tuesday, November 17th. Dinghy drill.
Wednesday, November 18th. First possible day for operation. Ground Controller at Skitten. Horsas to be loaded and party ready for take off. Probable time of take off - 1645 hours.
Thursday, November 26th. Last possible day for the operation.
Limiting Factors.
For the success of the operation weather conditions are needed such that the gliders can be taken off from Skitten in daylight and towed to make and recognise a landfall on the Norwegian coast - one hour after nightfall and thence to the objective area.
In no circumstances must it be necessary to tow the gliders through cloud. Cloud height must be sufficient for towing at not less than 2000 feet above the highest land along the route. The visibility over land must be sufficiently good for map reading and the landing area must be free from mist.

FLIGHT PLAN.
The route from Skitten to the objective will be direct to Egersund on the Norwegian coast and thence to Fliseggen mountain. The take off will be timed so that aircraft do not approach nearer than within 100 miles of the Norwegian coast in daylight. A further limiting factor on timing will be the moon elevation for identifying the coastal RV on making the landfall. Approximately 7 degrees of moon elevation will be necessary to ensure recognition of land marks. This will affect timing during the latter days during which the operation is possible. In the objective area at least 10 degrees moon elevation will be necessary for recognition of the landing zone.

On the outward flight, the height over the sea will be at the discretion of captains, to provide the best flying conditions for glider pilots, but the Norwegian coast will be crossed, if possible, at 10000 feet and this height will be maintained over land. The success of the military plan depends largely upon the glider landings being unobserved by the enemy. For this reason flying by powered aircraft must be restricted to the minimum in the vicinity of the landing zone - and any circling or searching for final land marks should be carried out in the area to the north west which is sparsely populated. The final release should be made from a north westerly direction and tug aircraft should fly on south easterly, turning east for the final part of the flight. If the approach and release of the gliders is carried out successfully, aircraft will proceed to the Oslo district and drop Nickells. (Leaflets)

GLIDER LANDINGS.
Success will depend greatly upon the skill with which the landing is made by the glider pilot. It is desirable that the release should be as high as possible - since by clear moonlight a glider might be distinguished with night glasses when flying at 10000 feet above sea level. The release will be carried out to the west or north of the landing zone and as much as possible of the approach will be carried out north west of the landing point, so that the gliders will not be visible against the moon to enemy guards at Holvik. In seeking the final landing point, glider pilots should be guided by the flare path and signals of the advance party and should only diverge from this in the event of necessity, to avoid a crash.

If, owing to some accidental cause, premature release is made anywhere near the objective area the glider pilots will bear in mind the following points:
1. To be aware as accurately as possible of the pin point at which the landing is made.
2. To get the glider down as far as possible in a position where it will not be visible from roads or habitation. In this connection, a landing in trees may be attempted, since the trees in this area do not normally grow to a height of more than 10 to 15 feet and are not likely to cause serious damage. Particular care will be exercised if a landing has to be made in a precipitous area and if it is on a slope, pilots will conserve considerable surplus speed and will land up the slope.

Royal Air Force Air and Ground Crews detailed per 38 Wing Operational Order No.5 for the operation were:

| Halifax Crew No.1 | Halifax Crew No.2 |
| --- | --- |
| S/Ldr. Wilkinson. | F/Lt. Parkinson. |
| P/O. Kemmis. | P/O. De Gency. |
| Sgt. Jones. | F/Lt. Thomas. |
| Sgt. Otto. | Sgt. Buckton. |
| Sgt. Watt. | Sgt. Falconer. |
| Sgt. Conacher. | F/Sgt. Edwards. |
|  | F/O. Haward. |

Glider pilots:
Staff Sergeant Strathdee.   P/O Davies.
Sergeant Doig.              P/O Frazer.

Engineer officer: F/Lt. Austen. Radio Officer: P/O. Campbell.
Ground Crews:

| | |
|---|---|
| Sgt Gale. | Fitter IIA. |
| Cpl Jackson. | " |
| Cpl Duckworth | " |
| Cpl Lucas. | " |
| LAC Jones. | Flight Mechanic Engines. |
| AC Duffy. | " |
| AC Woodcroft. | " |
| AC Groom. | " |
| LAC Hilton. | Flight Mechanic Airframe. |
| LAC Dawes. | " |
| AC Warburton. | " |
| AC Rigg. | " |
| AC Hobbs Hurrel. | " |
| AC Quinlan. | Electrician. |
| AC Berry. | Wireless Mechanic. |
| LAC Laderoute. | Radar Technician. |
| Sgt Wildgoose. | Fitter IIA. |
| LAC May. | Wireless Mechanic. |
| AC Lancaster. | " |
| AC Caddock. | Fitter II Engines. |
| AC Dorrit. | Fitter II Engines. |

1 Instrument repair mechanic.
Special Radio Party.
Cpl Bidie, LAC Skinner, LAC Stewart, LAC Lyons.
Motor transport drivers. LAC Pepper, LAC Bravery.

On the 14th November, the RAF tugs and Horsas left Netheravon and flew to RAF Waddington, Lincolnshire, staying there overnight and all day the 15th November. On Sunday the 16th November the combinations lifted off for the Fleet Air Arm airfield at Crimond, Aberdeenshire. On the morning of the 17th November the tugs and gliders lifted off for the final leg to RAF Skitten, Caithness.

Reports from the Norwegian agents in Norway stated that all was in order and they were ready for the operation. Their homing beacons had been set up and tested. The crucial factor now was the weather over Norway - it had to be good for navigation over the mountains and locating the LZ. The forecast was good for the 18th November and a successful trial flight of two Halifaxes was made to

Norway. The weather forecast for the 19th November was not satisfactory but reported to be suitable over the LZ so it was decided to go that evening. Operation Freshman was on.

At 1740 hours Halifax A for Able piloted by Squadron Leader A.M.B. Wilkinson, with Group Captain T.B. Cooper aboard (he had decided to go himself as second pilot) took off from Skitten towing Horsa MkI serial number DP349 piloted by Staff Sergeant M.F. Strathdee (320272) and Sergeant P. Doig (3250420), of the Glider Pilot Regiment. Royal Engineers on board were:

| | | | |
|---|---|---|---|
| Lieutenant D.A. Methven, GM. | 2100866 | 20 years. | |
| Lance Sergeant F. Healey | 4385760 | 29 | " |
| Corporal J.D. Cairncross | 2110314 | 22 | " |
| Lance Corporal T.L. Masters | 1872832 | 25 | " |
| Lance Corporal W.M.Jackson | 4537415 | 21 | " |
| Sapper J.F. Blackburn | 1900803 | 28 | " |
| Sapper F. Bonner | 1906932 | 25 | " |
| Sapper W. Jacques | 2114930 | 30 | " |
| Sapper R. Norman | 2110268 | 22 | " |
| Sapper E.J. Smith | 1892979 | 25 | " |
| Sapper J.W. Walsh | 2073797 | 21 | " |
| Sapper T.W. White | 1875800 | 23 | " |
| Driver P.P. Farrell | 2100213 | 26 | " |
| Driver J.G.V. Hunter | 2110332 | 22 | " |
| Driver G. Simkins | 1884423 | 30 | " |

The other Halifax - B for Baker serial number W7801 - took off at 1810 hours, piloted by Flight Lieutenant A.R. Parkinson, RCAF. J5470 aged 26 years with aircrew:

| | | | |
|---|---|---|---|
| Observer: Flt/Lieutenant A.E. Thomas | 101580 | 32 years | |
| Observer: Flying Officer A.T.H. Haward | 115977 | 28 | " |
| 2nd Pilot: Pilot Officer G.W.S. de Gency | 116942 | 20 | " |
| WO/AG: Flight Sergeant A. Buckton | 75116 | 23 | " |
| Air Gunner: Flt/Sergeant G.M. Edwards | 1259259 | 24 | " |
| Engineer: Sergeant J. Falconer | 573120 | 20 | " |

Towing Horsa MKI serial number HS114 piloted by Pilot Officer N.A. Davies, RAAF. 401422, 28 years, and Pilot Officer H.J. Frazer, RAAF. 401601. 28 years.

Carrying Royal Engineers:

| | | | |
|---|---|---|---|
| Lieutenant A.C. Allen | 137173 | 24 | Years |
| Lance Sergeant G. Knowles | 1871585 | 28 | " |
| Corporal J.G.L. Thomas | 2076750 | 23 | " |
| Lance Corporal F.W. Bray | 1884418 | 29 | " |
| Lance Corporal A. Campbell | 1923037 | 24 | " |
| Sapper E.W. Bailey | 1869293 | 31 | " |
| Sapper H. Bevan | 2074196 | 22 | " |
| Sapper T.W. Faulkener | 2115238 | 22 | " |
| Sapper C.H. Grundy | 1886725 | 22 | " |
| Sapper H.J. Legate | 1922713 | 24 | " |
| Sapper L. Smallman | 2068169 | 22 | " |
| Sapper J.M. Stephen | 2010697 | 25 | " |
| Sapper G.S. Williams | 1948916 | 18 | " |
| Driver J.T.V. Belfield | 2016305 | 26 | " |
| Driver E. Pendlebury | 2000197 | 25 | " |

Special Operations Executive and Combined Operations Headquarters were informed by Lieutenant Colonel Henniker at the Operation Room, Wick, that Freshman was under way.

Both Halifax/Horsa combinations set course individually for Egersund on the Norwegian coast - the flight plan being that they would cross the coast at 10000 feet to avoid detection by the Germans - and release their gliders at that height. The operation was flight timed so that the combinations did not approach the coast in daylight but the moon would give sufficient light for the gliders to land assisted by the Eureka beacons and flare path set up by the Operation Grouse advance party.

At 2341 hours on the 19th November the Operations Room at Wick received a radio signal from Halifax Baker (F/Lt. Parkinson) asking for a course to return to Skitten. RDF (Radio Direction Finding) triangulation gave Baker's position as over the North Sea at Latitude 58 degrees 16" North and longitude 06 degrees 17" West. No further signal was received from this aircraft. At 2355 hours Wick received a radio message from Halifax Able (S/Ldr. Wilkinson) stating that their glider had been released in the sea - but RDF bearings gave Able's position as over the mountains of southern Norway; this was later confirmed by a careful navigation check when Halifax Able returned. The glider had been released near the coast many miles from the LZ.

At 0151 hours 20th November Halifax Able returned to Skitten and Group Captain Cooper reported that Able successfully crossed the North Sea but the Rebecca set in his aircraft went unserviceable reducing navigation to map reading only. Thick cloud was met some forty miles north west of Vemork and the combinations could not get out of it. The Halifax was on reserve tanks and fuel was being used up rapidly searching for the LZ. Severe icing was also encountered by the combination which caused it to lose height over the dangerous mountains of Norway. Near Stavanger the iced up tow rope broke and the Horsa glider made a crash landing on snow covered mountains Fylgjedal. The Halifax tug had just enough fuel left to return to Skitten. The failure of the operation was blamed on the Rebecca set going unserviceable and incorrect navigation maps of Norway. Nothing further was heard from Halifax Baker and search and rescue plans were put into action for the daylight hours of the 20th November.

At 1105 hours on the 20th information was received at Wick from a Major Barstow, Combined Operations HQ to the effect that agents in Norway had reported aerial activity during the night but no ground activity. Both Army and RAF personel left Skitten on the 20th November and returned to Netheravon and Bulford, Wiltshire. Operation Freshman, with its unknown result, was deemed a failure. Nothing definite was heard about the aircrew of Halifax Baker and the Royal Engineers carried in the two Horsas, although rumour and counter-rumour abounded in southern Norway about aircraft which had crashed and the survivors being shot by the Germans.

The Vemork Plant was attacked by the Norwegian resistance (Operation Gunnerside) on the 28th February 1943, and partially damaged and the USAAF had bombed it on the 16th November 1943, again without complete success. But on the 20th February 1944, whilst the Germans were transporting the stocks of heavy water by rail ferry over Lake Tinnsjo, the ferry was blown up by the Resistance and the two rail wagons of heavy water cargo lost.

With the end of the war in Europe in May 1945 enquiries were commenced in Norway by the Allied War Crimes Investigation as to the fate of the Operation Freshman British soldiers and airmen. It was found that the Horsa DP349, which had been towed by Halifax Able, had crashed on mountains at Fylgjedal, near Lysefjord, Rogoland Province, killing Staff Sergeant Strathdee, Sergeant Doig, Lieutenant Methven, Lance Sergeant Healey, Driver Simkins, Sappers Norman, Hunter and Jacques. Four soldiers - Corporal Cairncross, Lance Corporal Masters, Sapper Smith and Driver Farrell - had been severely injured in the crash and were take by the Germans to Stavanger Hospital. When the Germans realised that the four soldiers were too badly injured to be questioned they were either poisoned by a Luftwaffe doctor, F.W. Seeling, or shot by three members of the German SD (Security Service), E. Hoffman, F. Feuerlein, and CID Inspector O. Petersen. Their naked bodies were then taken out to sea at night and thrown overboard between Usken and Kvits Island. The bodies were never found. (Their names are recorded on the Brookwood Memorial, Woking, Surrey.)

The other five surviving uninjured soldiers from the Horsa - Lance Corporal Jackson, Sappers Bonner, Blackburn, Welsh and White, were taken prisoner by the Germans and taken across Norway to the Grini Concentration Camp some thirty miles outside Oslo. On the 18th January 1943, they were murdered by a German firing squad in Trandum Forest where their bodies were thrown into a mass grave alongside Norwegians also murdered by the Germans. (The bodies of the British soldiers were exhumed in 1945 and reinterred with Christian ceremony in the Commonwealth War Graves Plot in Oslo Western Civil Cemetery at Vestre Gravlund).

Halifax Baker serial number W7801 crashed into a mountain at Hestadfjell, Helleland, Rogoland Province, at 2445 hours on the 19th November 1942, with the entire seven man crew being killed outright - torn apart by the force of the impact. Their shattered bodies were roughly buried, or rather thrown in pieces, by the Germans into a snow covered marsh - against the wishes of the angry local people, who, when spring came, reinterred the remains in herring boxes. On the arrival of British troops in May 1945 the remains were exhumed and laid to rest in Helleland Church.

The other Horsa glider HS114 crashed in the mountains north of Helleland, some three miles north from where the Halifax crashed. The two glider pilots - Pilots Officers Davies and Fraser were killed by the impact as was Driver Pendlebury. The remaining fourteen soldiers survived the crash - some were injured - and were captured by the Germans. A few hours later all - including the injured - were murdered by the Germans at Slettebo near Egersund. After being shot the bodies were stripped and with the bodies of those killed in the glider crash were taken to the seashore at Brusand, about thirty-five miles from Helleland, where a hole was dug and the bodies thrown in by the laughing Germans who did not know they were being observed by the farmer whose land they were on. In 1945 the remains were exhumed and reinterred properly at Eiganes Cemetery, Stavanger.

With all the airman and soldiers of Operation Freshman being accounted for and some of the persons responsible for their murders being in custody, (some were dead like the local Gestapo chief Wilkens who was killed by the Norwegian resistance on the 4th April 1945; others had committed suicide as it was clear that their war was lost) retribution began on the 10th December 1945, at a Military Court in Oslo. Luftwaffe doctor, Werner Fritz Seeling, Security Service non-commissioned officers Erich Hoffman and Fritz Feuerlein, were indicted and charged with killing four unidentified British prisoners of war in November 1942.

They pleaded not guilty. The Court did not have to prove specifically which of the Operation Freshman British soldiers had been murdered - the facts to be proved were that murder had been done against the rules of war by the accused. One of the murderers, CID Inspector Otto Petersen, committed suicide in Akershus Prison, Oslo, on the 2nd November 1945.

On the 18th August 1942, Hitler had issued Directive No.46 - instructions for intensified action against guerilla units in the East (Russia) where the Russian Partisans were opposing the Germans by all means possible. But Partisan and British Commando action in Europe was becoming a problem for the Germans and on the 18th October 1942, Hitler issued what he called a 'sharp' order to his Forces requiring that 'sabotage troops of the British or their hirelings, whether in uniform or not, whether with not without arms, be 'killed to the last man in battle or flight' and if captured indirectly, to be handed over to the SS. British activities of this kind were merely Russian methods under a different name. Against both these, said Hitler, a war of extermination must be fought.

This infamous order of Hitler's - known in Germany as the Commando Order - and which ran to six paragraphs, was the authority under which the Germans in Norway had acted. The excuse that "Befehl ist Befehl" i.e. "Orders are Orders" was to be trotted out again and again by the Germans accused of War crimes. Each German Officer had sworn an oath of loyalty to Hitler and was presented with a copy of his book "Mein Kampf" (My Struggle) on being commissioned - paragraph six of the Commando order read, "in the case of non compliance with this order, I shall bring to trial before a court martial any commander or other officer who has failed to carry out his duty in instructing his troops about this order or who has acted contrary to it".

The evil order was in complete violation of the accepted laws and customs of war and the Geneva Convention for the Treatment of Prisoners of War. At the date of its issue the Commander in Chief, German Forces, Norway, was General von Falkenhorst, who after receiving the Order added to it by ordering that any man saved for interrogation must not survive his comrades for more than 24 hours.

The Oslo Military Court trial ended on the 13th December 1945, with the three before the court - Seeling, Hoffman and Feuerlein being found guilty as indicted and charged. Seeling was shot at Akershus Prison, Oslo, on the 10th January 1946. Hoffman was hanged on the 15th May 1946. Feuerlein was sentenced to life imprisonment, then handed over to the Russians for crimes committed against Russian prisoners of war. He was no doubt shot for the crimes he had committed.

On the 28th May 1946, at Hamburg, Germany, the War Crime military trial opened of Major General von Behren, Commanding Officer of the Stavanger

District of German Occupied Norway, who was indicted and charged with the war crime of 'murder of fourteen unidentified British prisoners of war at Slettebo, Norway, on or near the 20th November 1942.' He pleaded not guilty. Although von Behren had not been actually present during the murders it did not matter. He was a principal of degree and principals can aid or abet, counsel or procure before or after a crime. After trial von Behren was found not guilty as charged.

The Commander in Chief, German Forces, Norway, General von Falkenhorst, went on War Crimes trial at the British Military Court, Brunswick, Germany,on the 29th July 1946, for indictment and trial on nine counts. He pleaded not guilty to all charges on the indictment, which included the Operation Freshman murders. Falkenhorst was found guilty of eight of the nine counts against him - including all the Operation Freshman charges. He was sentenced by the Court to be shot by firing squad but this sentence was commuted to life imprisonment by the Commander in Chief, British Zone of Germany, Marshal of the Royal Air Force, Sir Sholto Douglas. Falkenhorst was released from prison in 1953 as he was in ill health. He had served but six years of his life sentence: a mere six years for the tortured deaths of many fine young men. Falkenhorst died in 1968 aged 84 years.

There were no more prosecutions brought against any Germans for the murder of the Operation Freshman soldiers. The author, having served for twelve years in the Armed forces and thirty-one years as a real operational (not paper) policeman finds this odd. With the German's well known passion for documentation it would not have been difficult to bring to justice the actual killers - some of whom are probably still alive today.

Printed in every German soldier's pay and record book were 'Ten Commandments'. The first read as follows: 'The German soldier will observe the rules of chivalrous warfare. Cruelties and senseless destruction are below his standard.' Number 3 read: 'No enemy who has surrendered will be killed, including partisans and spies. They will be punished by the Courts. Prisoners of war will not be ill treated.'

Operation Freshman was a failure, a gallant failure of the first British glider operation to be carried out against long odds. A 400-mile hostile sea crossing by night in winter towing gliders which then had to try and land in snowbound unknown country. Hedley Duckworth, Operation Freshman member of the Royal Air Force 38 Wing Detachment, relates his part in Freshman:

Late in September 1942, eight airmen from Nos. 138 and 161 Squadrons, were detached to RAF Netheravon, Wiltshire. All airmen of this detachment were conversant with maintainance and general flight operations of Halifax bombers.

We serviced and crewed the Halifaxes during the initial training, which was to tow two Horsa gliders during day and night training. We were given to understand that we would be competing against an American team but the only Americans we came in contact with were American Ranger parachutists at RAF Thruxton, Hampshire.

Flying continued into October and then into November. On the 14th November (1942) two Halifaxes towing two Horsa gliders - piloted by RAAF pilots and accompanied by one Albemarle - left RAF Netheravon and flew to RAF Waddington, Lincolnshire. We stayed there on Saturday 15th November and left mid-morning of the 16th - a Sunday - and landed mid afternoon at Crimond airfield above Peterhead, (Aberdeenshire). This was a Fleet Air Arm Station - possibly we were the only gliders ever to land their.

On the morning of the 17th Monday - DIs (Daily Inspections) completed we took off and flew to RAF Skitten, satellite to Wick. On Tuesday night the 18th November two Halifaxes without gliders performed a recce over Norway. Late afternoon on the 19th November the Army chaps arrived and the two Army Sergeant pilots (Glider) came out to us. Four glider pilots were in Operation Freshman - two army and two Royal Australian Air Force. The operation took place from RAF Skitten that night, 19th November 1942. Only one Halifax returned. The crew of the other lies in Helleland Church grounds, Norway.

H. Duckworth, 15th May 1989.

# OPERATION BEGGAR/TURKEY BUZZARD

The ferrying of towed Horsa gliders from England to North Africa between the 1st and 28th June 1943, by 295 Squadron, Royal Air Force, and the Glider Pilot Regiment. The operation is known by both code names - Beggar being used by the RAF and Turkey Buzzard by the Glider Pilot Regiment.

During April 1943, 295 Squadron, 38 Wing, was detailed to ferry forty Horsa gliders from England to North Africa by the end of June, for use by air landing forces in the invasion of Sicily, scheduled for the second week of July that year. The distance to be flown was 1300 miles from RAF Portreath, Cornwall, to the USAAF air base at Sale, near Rabat, French Morocco in North Africa. Then another 1000 miles over Africa to Tunisia.

During the first part of the flight - which would be over the open sea - the combinations would be liable to interception by German aircraft operating out of bases in Occupied France. As the flight route passed Cape St. Vincent on the south western tip of neutral Portugal the combinations could be seen by the Germans who had an Embassy in Lisbon.

Owing to the distance involved RAF Coastal Command Beaufighters from St. Eval, Cornwall, would not be able to provide escorts for all of the flight. The 19 Group Beaufighters had had considerable success in downing JU88s over the Bay of Biscay but their endurance was limited. There were no alternative landing airfields, the combinations not being allowed to land at Gibraltar, so it was England to North Africa in one flight. The glider pilots would return to England in the Halifax tugs after having delivered their Horsas.

Such an operation had never been carried out before by the Royal Air Force or the Glider Pilot Regiment so to carry out the commitments aircraft had to be provided, modified and crewed up. Royal Air Force aircrews had to be converted to the Halifax aircraft chosen for the long tow, and trained in towing gliders and dropping paratroops since the aircraft might be needed to do both tasks. Ten of the aircrews and Halifaxes were to be detached to North Africa for use on operations there.

295 Squadron had been formed at RAF Netheravon, Wiltshire, on the 3rd August 1942, as an airborne forces squadron equipped with two Flights of Whitley aircraft. In February 1943, the squadron received Halifax V aircraft and another Flight - "A" - was formed.

RAF Netheravon was, and still is, a hilly grass airfield with no permanent flare path, night flying being carried out on a gooseneck (paraffin lamp) flarepath, so "A" Flight moved on the 13th May 1943, to RAF Holmesly South, near

GAL 55 military training glider. It never went into production - prototype only.

Horsa glider on rocket assisted trials. (*Air Britain, J. Halley*)

*Top:* 12th Devons on training in Horsa. Parachutes were not usually carried. (*Army Museum of Flying*)
*Left:* Interior of Hengist glider looking forward, 1942. (*Army Museum of Flying*)

*Top:* Hengist glider, 1942. Cockpit layout. (*Army Museum of Flying*)
*Right:* Hengist glider, 1942. Cockpit layout and pilot's seat. (*Army Museum of Flying*)

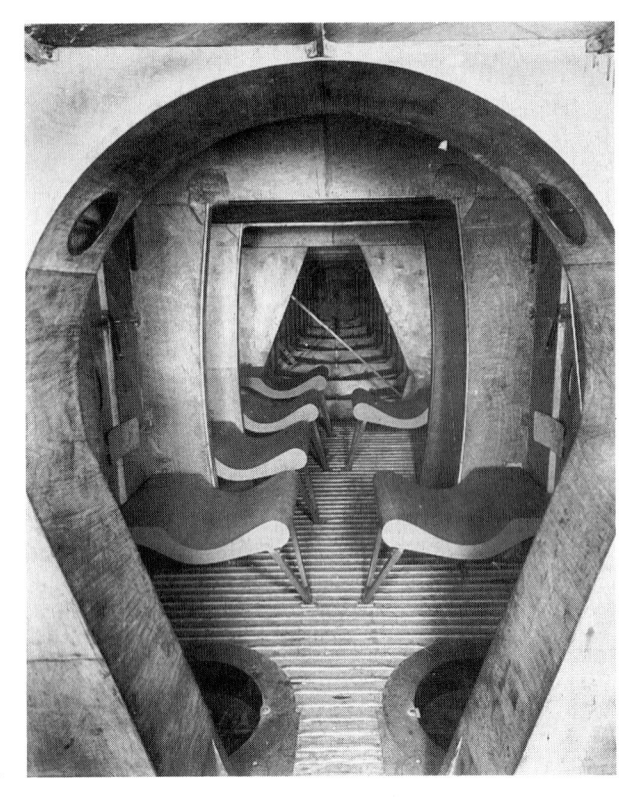

*Right top:* Tank emerging from Hamilcar glider. Undercarriage collapsed for loading or unloading. (*Army Museum of Flying*)
*Right centre:* Hotspur glider, BV 136. (*Imperial War Museum*)
*Right bottom:* Twin Hotspur prototype MP 486G. (*Imperial War Museum*)

*Left:* Interior of Slingsby Hengist Glider, 1942. (*Army Museum of Flying*)
*Below:* Hamilcar glider - prototype. (*Imperial War Museum*)

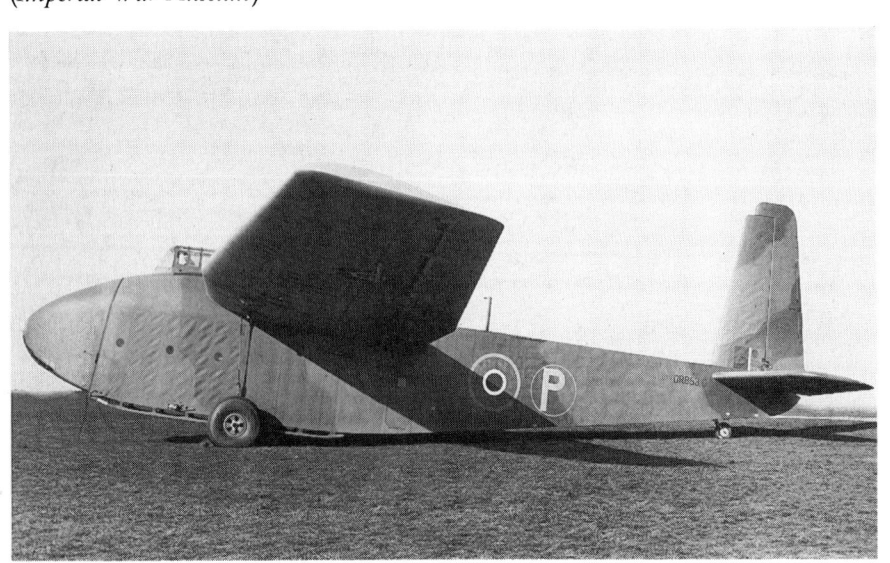

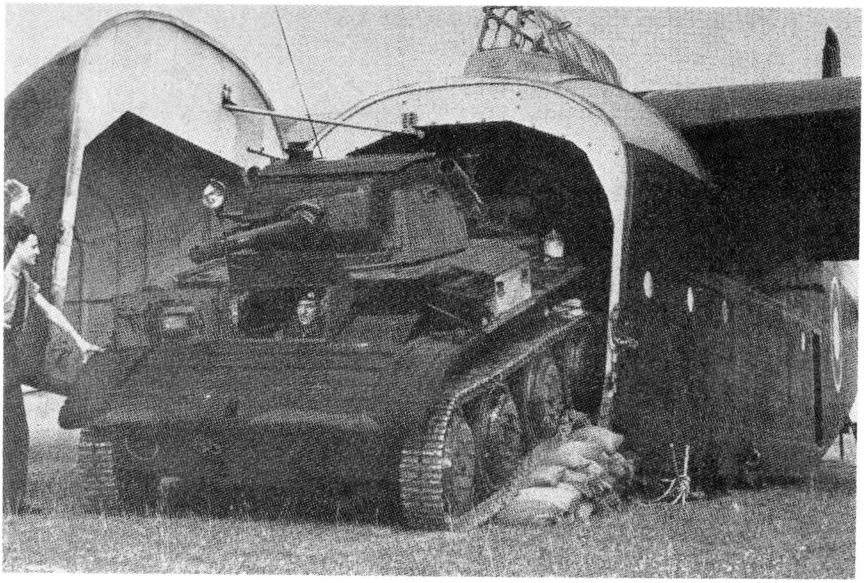

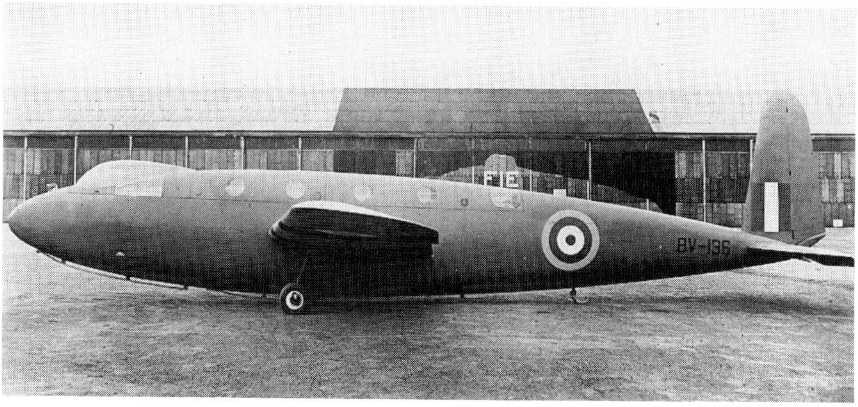
BV-136

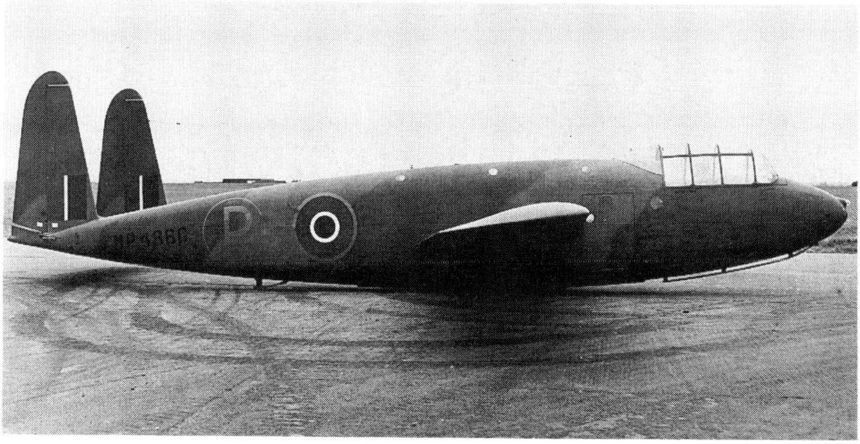

Hotspurs in flight. (*Army Museum of Flying*)

Sicily, 1944. Training flight Horsa near Mt. Etna. (*Frank Ashton*)

The Independent Squadron of the Glider Pilot Regiment. (*Capt. C. Turner, GPR*)

*Above:* Norsk Hydro Plant, Vermok, Norway, target of 'Operation Freshman.' (*Army Museum of Flying*)

*Left:* An electrolysis cell from the Norsk Plant presented to the Royal Engineers Museum, Chatham, in 1982 by the Plant. (*Royal Engineers Museum*)

D-DAY
C47 snatching a CG4A glider. (*Waco Historical Society*)
Horsas tethered together ready for loading, 1944 (*Army Museum of Flying*)

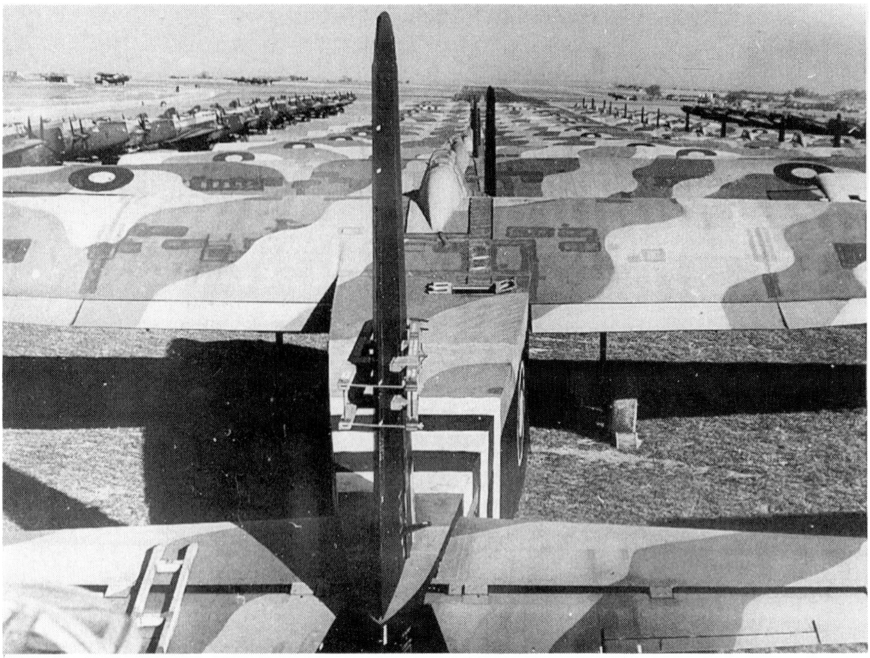

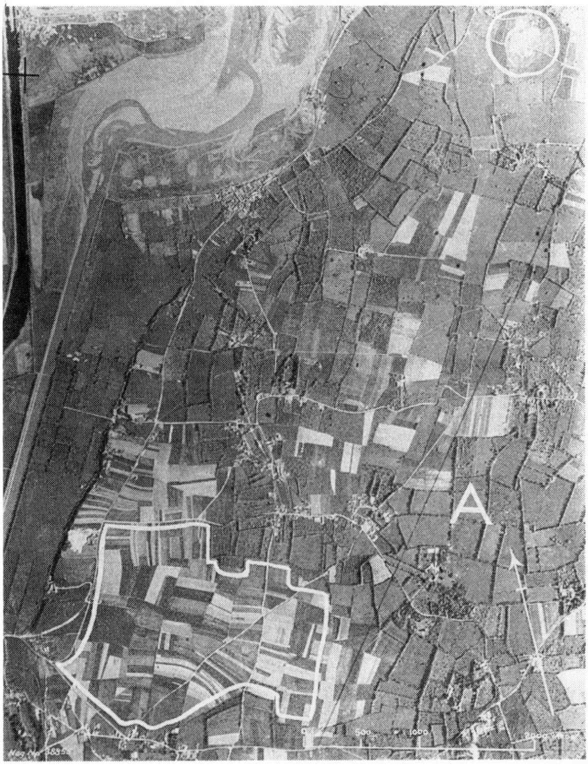

*Opposite page top:* Hamilcars lined up for D-Day, RAF Tarrant Rushton, 1944. (*Army Museum of Flying*)

*Opposite page bottom:* 'Operation Tonga.' D-Day. (*Air photo*)

*Above:* Marker stone showing glider landing spot, Pegasus Bridge, D-Day, 1944. (*Author's photo*)

*Below:* Pegasus Bridge, Normandy, 1944. (*Alan Whittaker was photographer*)

*Opposite page:*
SOUTH FRANCE.
*Top:* Horsa glider landing in South of France invasion, August 1944. (*Captain C. Turner, GPR*)

*Centre:* Horsas landing in South of France invasion. (*Captain C. Turner, GPR*)

*Below:* Horsa glider in which Sgt. Roy Jenner died on landing, South of France, August 1944. (*Captain C. Turner, GPR*)

*Above:* Merville Battery, Normandy, before the assault. The bomb craters are widely scattered. (*Air Ministry*)
*Below:* Merville Battery, 1990. (*Author's photo*)

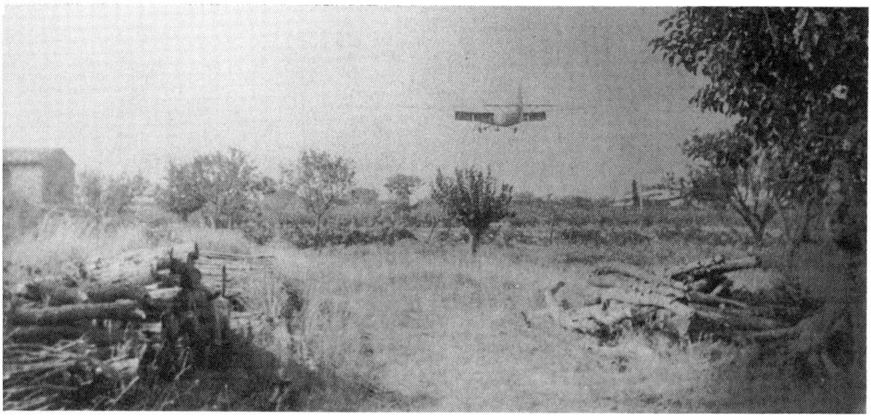
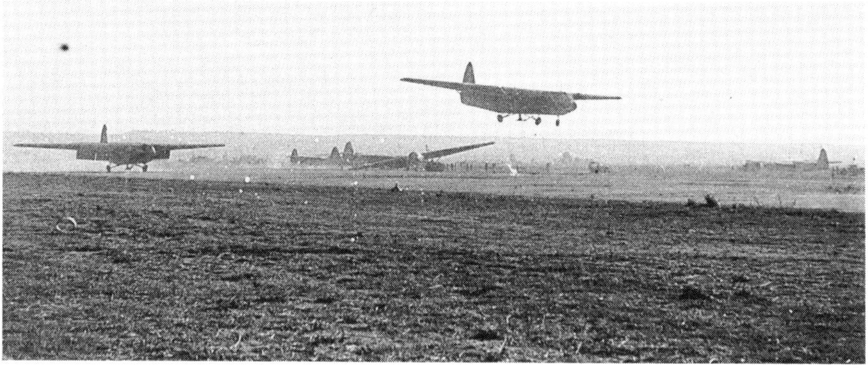
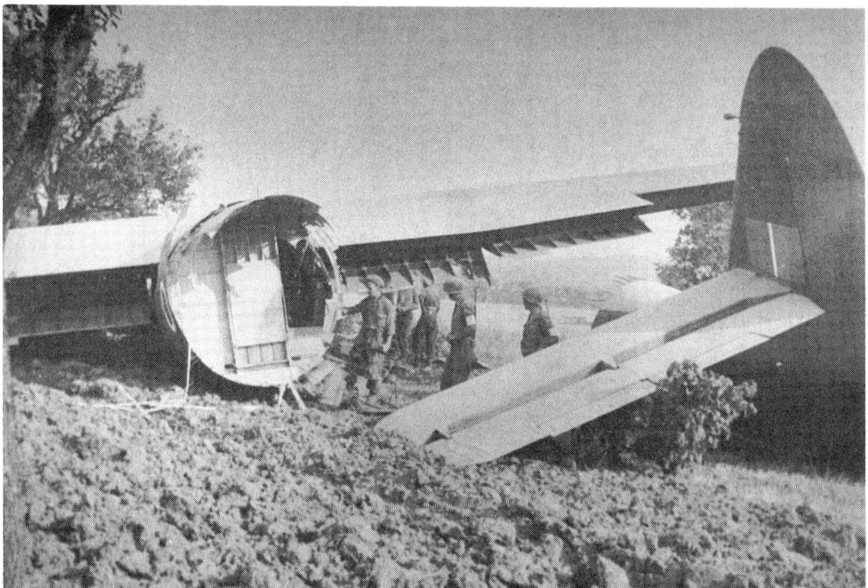

ARNHEM
Lance Sergeant J.P. Baskeyfield VC, South Staffordshire Regiment, at Arnhem, 1944. (*Terence Cuneo OBE*)
Glider pilots decorated by King George VI, December 1944. Left to right; Bruce Hobbs DFM, Stan Pearson DFM, W. Herbert DFM, Jim Wallwork DFM and Tommy Moore MM. (*Eagle*)

Staff Sergeants Fred Baacke and Roy Howard, GPR. (*Roy Howard DFM*)

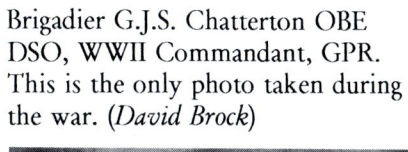

Lance Sergeant John Daniel Baskeyfield VC. (*South Staffordshire Regiment*)

Brigadier G.J.S. Chatterton OBE DSO, WWII Commandant, GPR. This is the only photo taken during the war. (*David Brock*)

Major Robert Henry Cain VC. South Staffordshire Regt. (*South Staffordshire Regiment*)

Dennis Galpin DFM. (*Frank Ashton*)

Major T.I.J. Toler DFC TD, WWII Commander, B Squadron, GPR, now President of the Glider Pilot Regimental Association. (*David Brock*)

Christchurch, Hampshire, with thirteen Halifax aircraft under the command of its Flight Commander, Squadron Leader A.M.B. Wilkinson, pilot of the surviving Halifax tug on the ill-fated Operation Freshman in 1942, and the Squadron Commander Wing Commander McNamara. Major aircraft maintenance was carried out at RAF Hurn, near Bournemouth, with 1st line and minor inspections carried out at Holmesly South, Whitley maintenance being carried out at Netheravon.

Squadron Leader Wilkinson was the only fully converted Halifax pilot on the squadron with two others, Flight Lieutenant Briggs and Flying Officer Tomkins partly converted. (Conversion has nothing to do with religion - in the RAF a pilot has to be converted/trained to fly a particular type of aircraft - a fighter pilot cannot jump into the cockpit and fly a four-engined bomber unless he is qualified so to do). Nine more pilots - Flying Officers Bewick, Blackburn, Collins, Cleaver, Muirhead, Smith, Sizmur and Warrant Officer McCrodden were converted to fly the four-engined Halifaxes. During May, three more pilots - Flying Officers Horne, Norman and Shannon were converted and Flight Lieutenant Grant was lent from the Royal Aeronautical Establishment, Farnborough.

In view of the 1300 mile distance involved the Halifax aircraft had to be modified and petrol endurance tested on 1500 mile ten hour cross country flights around England. The RAF officer with the most experience of long haul glider flights - Group Captain Tom Cooper - who had been engaged on the first long haul glider Operation Freshman in November 1942, and Squadron Leader Wilkinson commenced training aircrews and glider pilots from the 1st Battalion, Glider Pilot Regiment, on the endurance flights. It was found that the Halifax V aircraft could tow for 1500 miles with extra fuel tanks installed in the bomb bays, giving a total of 2400 gallons, and all excess weight removed.

In order to reduce drag the Horsa glider's undercarriage would be jettisoned after take off and the glider would land on its skids in North Africa. This procedure had been evolved on the endurance training flights and on previous tests at RAF Netheravon in January 1943, with the Horsas landing on the grass at RAF Hurn and Netheravon. A spare undercarriage would be carried in the Horsa which would be fitted after landing in Africa for the next 1000 mile flight to the Sicily invasion take off air strips in Tunisia.

As considerable physical effort would be required to fly the gliders on tow, three glider pilots were required in each Horsa. One pilot would do an hour as 1st pilot then an hour as 2nd pilot then an hour on rest. Volunteers were called for from the Glider Pilot Regiment and those who volunteered were detached to RAF Holmesly South, Hampshire, where they were then informed of the long haul operation piloting Horsa gliders from England to North Africa.

As most of the long flights would be over the sea, the glider pilots had to undergo ditching and dinghy drill at Bournemouth Corporation Stokewood Road swimming baths, Bournemouth, in full flying kit and Wellington boots.

The final departure airfield was RAF Portreath near Redruth, Cornwall, where the main runway running east to west ended at the top of 295 feet high cliffs. The method of delivering the Horsas from Netheravon to Portreath was for the Whitleys of 295 Squadron to tow them there to avoid strain to the Halifaxes airframe and engines. As soon as each Halifax had been modified and endurance tested, it was flown to Portreath where, on the 1st June, the first combination took off but because of bad weather was forced to return to Portreath after six and a half hours flying time.

On the 3rd June four combinations took off at first light on a bright clear morning. Of the four, two reached Sale that afternoon. One had to return to base due to bad weather, the forth glider had to ditch in the Bay of Biscay when the tow rope broke some, 200 miles north west of Cape Finisterre. The Halifax tug piloted by Flying Officer Sizmur returned to Portreath after sending out a rescue message. The Horsa flown by Major Alastair Cooper, Staff Sergeant Dennis Hall and Staff Sergeant Antony Antopoulos ditched at 1000 hours and rapidly filled with water. The three pilots escaped through the hatch in the roof of the Horsa with their dinghy which they inflated and scrambled into. The wooden Horsa did not sink but remained awash with the tail and top of the fuselage visible. At 2200 hours the same day the three pilots were picked up by a Royal Navy frigate. As the Horsa was still afloat it was destroyed by the Navy. The three glider pilots were landed in Northern Ireland then flown by 295 Squadron back to RAF Netheravon - all three returned to the ferrying operation. Major Cooper later lost his life on Operation Ladbrooke in Sicily.

On the 14th June Staff Sergeants Hall, Antopoulos and Conway were piloting a Horsa over the Bay of Biscay when the combination was attacked by two German Focke Wulf Condor long range bombers one hundred miles north west of Cape Finisterre. The Halifax tug, piloted by Warrant Officer McCrodden, with aircrew: Sergeant G.R. Hale, Flight Sergeant V.J. Norman, Flight sergeant F.C. Payne, Sergeant A. Selves, and Sergeant H.F. Upperton was shot down after a fierce gun battle. The Horsa pilots were forced to cast off and ditch in the sea. The three glider pilots took to their dinghy but they drifted for eleven days before being picked up by a Spanish fishing boat twenty miles off Oporto, Portugal. Staff Sergeants Antopoulos and Hall were awarded the Air Force Medal.

By the 16th June eighteen gliders had been ferried to Sale and by the 30th June twenty-five. Two more were delivered by the 7th July, bringing the total to twenty-seven. On the 27th June Halifax EB 135 piloted by Flying Officer Horne,

RCAF with aircrew: Sergeant R.B. Minchin, Flying Officer J.A. Smith, Sergeant J. Stretton, Warrant Officer M. Travale, RCAF and Flight Sergeant C.H. West, took off towing a Horsa piloted by Staff Sergeant D.S. Casselden, Sergeant M.A.C. Chandler and Sergeant H. Norris. They were never seen again and are believed to have been shot down over the sea by German aircraft. On the 30th June 295 Squadron moved from RAF Holmesly South to RAF Hurn which had better runways and facilities.

Having reached Sale the combinations were faced with the next 1000 mile leg of their journey to Tunisia. The first stage of this leg was 400 miles from Sale to Froha, then another final leg of 600 miles to Sousse near Kairouan, Tunisia, the operational airborne base for the Sicily invasion. This last 1000 miles was over the inhospitable deserts and the Atlas mountains of North Africa which caused severe turbulence to the combinations and overheating to the tug's engines. Two Horsas had to force land but one was retrieved in time for use in Sicily.

On the 5th July Staff Sergeant Chambers with Sergeants Owen and Ashton did the last Beggar trip towed by a Halifax piloted by Flying Officer Grant. Reaching Sale safely the combination took off next day en route for Sousse to take part in the Sicily operation. When flying at 10000 feet over the desert the Halifax lost two engines - power failing on both. The Horsa had to cast off and land on skids in the desert about 150 miles south of Algiers. The glider was undamaged and the crew uninjured. The Halifax tug landed on two engines in the desert but the crew were uninjured. Both tug and glider crews were picked up three days later by a Hudson aircraft from Maison Blanche and eventually made Sousse - but by then the Sicily operation was over.

The first Horsas reached Air Strip "E" at Kairouan just twelve days before the Sicily assault. Thirty gliders had been towed off from England, three had ditched in the sea but twenty seven had arrived in North Africa.

The official report on the operation refers to the courage and determination of the aircrews and ground crews involved and renders it a splendid achievement in the short time available. The cost was high - two Halifax aircraft with their crews were lost over the Bay of Biscay believed shot down by the German aircraft and one glider crew. Several Halifax aircraft were lost during the pre-operational training - one flown by Flying Officers Collins and Smith crashed killing the entire aircrew. Flying Officer Blackburn was killed while flying and Flying Officers Tomkin's Halifax crashed into a field in Somerset killing four of the crew. In addition to the three glider pilots lost at sea the Glider Pilot Regiment took four more casualties in North Africa on the second leg of the journey. Sergeant J.E. Harrison, Sergeant A. Higgins, Sergeant E.W. Hall and Sergeant F. Wheale. The South Staffords 12 men when a Waco crashed.

Glider Pilot Regiment aircrew who flew on Beggar/Turkey Buzzard:

Lieutenant W.N. Barrie, DFC.
Captain J.N.C. Denholm.
Major C. Line.
Lieutenant R. Walchi.
Lieutenant F.C. Aston.
S/Sergeant A. Antopoulos. AFM.
Sergeant P. Attwood.
Sergeant N. Brown.
Sergeant Baker.
Sergeant J. Brookfield.
Sergeant P. Conway.
S/Sergeant R. Calder, DFM.
S/Sergeant D.S. Casselden.
Sergeant P. Claneghan.
Sergeant R. Desbois.
Sergeant E. England, DFM.
Sergeant H, Flynn.
Sergeant G. Gabbott.
Sergeant P. Hill.
Sergeant D. Hatton.
Sergeant A. Higgins.
Sergeant W.R. Jenner.
Sergeant E. Johnson.
Sergeant C. Lewis.
Sergeant W.B. Morrison.
Sergeant C. Morgan.
Sergeant H. Norris.
SSMajor J.A. Preston.
Sergeant B.H. Patton
S/Sergeant F.W. Simpson
Sergeant L. Ridings.
Sergeant F. Robson.
Sergeant R. Tilling.
Sergeant F. Wheale.
S/Sergeant E.B. Wilkner.
Sergeant Winkle.
Sergeant Waring.

Major A.J. Cooper, AFC.
Lieutenant D.P. Gregg.
Lieutenant McLean.
Lieutenant A.R. Oxenford.

Sergeant F. Ashton.
Sergeant O. Boland.
Sergeant J. Broadhead.
Sergeant J. Barron.
S/Sergeant W. Chambers.
Sergeant C. Coombes.
Sergeant J. Church.
Sergeant M.A.C. Chandler.
Sergeant C. Channel.
Sergeant D. Douglas.
Sergeant Evans.
Sergeant D. Galpin, DFM.
Sergeant D. Hall, DFM.
Sergeant R.B. Hill.
Sergeant J.E. Harrison .
Sergeant E.W. Hall.
Sergeant G. Jenks.
Sergeant A. Kerr.
S/Sergeant McKenzie.
Sergeant P. Mansfield.
Sergeant Nichols.
Sergeant Owen.
Sergeant H. Protheroe. DFM.
Sergeant H.W. Sargent.
Sergeant L. Sanders.
S/Sergeant C. Robinson.
Sergeant K. Roberts.
Sergeant C. Wedgeberg.
Sergeant R. Wedge.
Sergeant T.H. White, DFM.
Sergeant L. Wright, DFM.
Sergeant Waring.

Sergeant White.
Sergeant R.D. Sunter.

S/Sergeant A. McCulloch, DFM.
Sergeant F.J. Davies.

Royal Air Force - Tug pilots:

Wing Commander McNamara.
Squadron Leader Wilkinson.
Flight Lieutenant Briggs, DFC.
Flying Officer Blackburn.
Flying Officer Collins.
Flying Officer Horne.
F/Sergeant McCrodden.
Flying Officer Sizmur, AFC.
Flying Officer Shannon.

Flying Officer Bewick.
Flying Officer Cleaver, DFC.
Flight Lieutenant Grant.
Flying Officer Muirhead.
Flying Officer Norman, DFC.
Flying Officer Tomkins.
Flying Officer Wood.

(The author is indebted to Staff Sergeant Len Wright, DFM. Glider Pilot Regiment, for supplying the above information from his extensive research).

### FROM CORNWALL TO NORTH AFRICA BY GLIDER.

Staff Sergeant (later Lieutenant) Bill Chambers, Glider Pilot Regiment, relates an account of Operation Beggar/Turkey Buzzard.

Early in 1943 the Allies decided to launch an attack on the soft underbelly of Europe and the target selected was Sicily - an admirable jumping off base for the Italian mainland. This presented an opportunity to use the newly formed 1st Airborne Division consisting of paratroops and gliderborne troops plus their equipment. The Americans had already produced a number of Waco CC4A gliders but had very few trained glider pilots - while Britain already had four squadrons of trained pilots.

    A number of Wacos were crated and shipped by sea to North Africa and two squadrons of British glider pilots departed by ship from England. With the aid of a handful of American instructors and technicians, the Waco gliders were assembled and the British glider pilots given all too brief conversion courses.
The Waco glider could carry a Jeep and crew or a 6-pounder anti-tank gun and crew but not both. On the other hand the British Horsa glider could carry a Jeep and a 6-pounder anti-tank gun with the crew and ammunition - so the gun could be in action with ten minutes of landing. It was, therefore, considered desirable to

include a number of Horsa gliders in the forthcoming operation; the problem was to get them to North Africa in time.

Experiments were commenced with 295 Squadron at RAF Netheravon under the command of Wing Commander McNamara to ascertain whether any aircraft was capable of towing a Horsa - wing span eighty eight feet - all the way from Britain to North Africa, a flight of 1400 miles. The Wellington aircraft was quickly discarded as the weight of the glider caused its geodetic framework to stretch and jam the control systems. The final decision fell on the Halifax which, with extra fuel tanks in the bomb bays, could manage a towing duration of around ten hours, giving a safety margin of about half an hour.

Once decided 295 Squadron began converting their pilots from Whitleys to Halifaxes and a nucleus of glider pilots were moved to Netheravon to commence training flights of ten hours duration. The squadron then moved to the newly built airfield at Holmesly South near Bournemouth, and the long training flights continued from this forward base. The Horsa gliders were equipped with a tricycle undercarriage and a skid so in order to decrease drag and therefore increase range, the undercarriage would be jettisoned on four small parachutes - one for each oleo leg and one for each wheel and axle. On the flights from Holmesly the undercarriages were dropped onto the neighbouring airfield at Hurn and later recovered for re-use.

When flying a glider it was essential to keep an accurate station behind the towing aircraft and, bearing in mind the size of the Horsa, this involved considerable physical effort. Three pilots were therefore used on these long flights - the system being one hour as first pilot, one hour as second pilot and one hour resting. The final departure airfield was RAF Portreath near Redruth, Cornwall where the main runway, running east to west, ended at the top of the cliffs. The gliders were not allowed to land at Gibraltar as this consisted solely of one runway and was the main staging post for the Middle and Far East. Gliders landing on a skid would need to be fitted with a new undercarriage before they could be moved from the runway and this was not acceptable.

The selected arrival airfield was the USAAF base at Rabat - Sale in French Morocco where the gliders could land on the sand at the edge of the runway.
On the 31st May the first tug and glider units flew from Holmesly South to Portreath and were briefed for take off at dawn the following morning, after thirty Beaufighters bound for Gibraltar took off.

The day was bright and clear and all the combinations staggered over the cliff edge with only one incident. Staff Sergeant 'Lofty Jenks glider accidently jettisoned the undercarriage while still over the runway and one oleo leg bounced back embedding itself in the wing. The combination flew on however and by taking a short cut over Spain, reached its destination. The other gliders dropped their undercarriages on the next headland, flew on to the Scilly Islands and then set a course well out to sea to avoid detection by German radar based in Western France and Spain. No wireless communication between Halifax and Horsa was allowed but a telephone line incorporated in the towing cable was the only method allowed and this proved rather unreliable.

Half way across the Bay of Biscay the tow rope of the Horsa flown by Major Cooper and Sgts Hall and Antopoulos broke and they were forced to ditch. Their Halifax tug alerted a destroyer which picked them up after a few hours in their dinghy. A second Horsa flown by Lieutenant Walchi, Sgt. Chambers and Owen encountered cloud up to 11000 feet and after several abortive attempts to get through the Halifax tug had used up too much fuel and was forced to return. The remaining four combinations reached Rabat.

On one of the later trips a Halifax tug suffered an engine failure after three hours flight time and returned - with its glider - on three engines after jettisoning all movable objects: spare glider undercarriage. guns, Elsan toilet, etc. into the Bay of Biscay. Shortly afterwards a crew member was 'taken short' and was obliged to use the flare chute as an emergency toilet.

On another trip by the same glider crew (Staff Sergeant Chambers, Sergeants Ashton and Owen) the Halifax tug developed a fuel leak and was forced to return to Portreath. The leak was repaired and the combination took off again later in the day reaching Rabat shortly after dark. The second trip made by Sgts. Antopoulos and Hall also ended in disaster when they were shot down by a German JU88 over the Bay of Biscay. They spent eleven days in a dinghy living on raw fish and were eventually picked up by a Spanish fishing boat and interned.

Altogether about 35 Horsas reached Africa - several being unaccounted for (probably shot down) and most of these, with their crews, took part in the Sicily operation a few weeks later. Two or three crews actually did two trips from Cornwall to Morocco on the operation named Beggar or Turkey Buzzard.

## OPERATION ELABORATE

The further ferrying of Horsa gliders from England to North Africa by 295 Squadron, Royal Air Force, and the Glider Pilot Regiment, between the 15th August 1943, to the 23rd September 1943.

The same take off airfield - RAF Portreath - was used and the same flight route. It was planned to ferry thirty-five Horsas for use in the Mediterranean theatre of operations.

On the 15th August five combinations took off from Portreath:
Halifax DK199 pilot F/O Forster. Horsa LG988 Lt. Oxenford, Staff Sergeants Simpson and Flynn.
Halifax DK198 pilot F/O Clapperton. Horsa LT109 Sergeants White, Waring, Channel.
Halifax DK197 pilot F/Sgt. Doughill. Horsa HG878 Lieutenant Shuttleworth, Staff Sgts. Tilling, Bettridge.
Halifax EB178 pilot F/O Reed. Horsa LH135 Staff Sergeants White, Desbois, Brookfield.
Halifax EB159 pilot F/Sgt. Crossley. Horsa DP 388 Staff Sergeants Johnson, Attwood and Brown.
Four reached Sale successfully. The fifth Horsa, flown by Staff Sergeants Johnson, Attwood and Brown ditched in the sea.

Another combination took off next day:
Halifax DJ 944 pilot Sgt. Evans. Horsa DP329 Sergeants Saunders, Jackson, Wedge. but the Horsa also had to ditch in the sea.

On the 17th August Halifax EB160 flown by F/O Sizmur, towed off Horsa DP 647 piloted by Lt. Davis, Sergeants Gabbott and Lewis and reached Sale successfully.
Two combinations took off on the 21st August:
Halifax DG393 pilot F/O Charter. Horsa LG895 Sergeants Coombes, Hatton Jenks.
Halifax DK199 pilot F/O Forster. Horsa LG947 Lieutenant Telfer, Staff Sergeants Vincent, Humphreys.
Both combinations reached Sale safely but the Halifax piloted by F/O Charter crashed at Sale. The Halifax took off for the next leg of the trip to Tunisia but lost two engines - the Horsa crew (Coombes, Hatton and Jenks) cast off at once to aid

the stricken tug which tried to land on two engines. The Halifax struck the runway undershoot and bounced, causing the rear gun turret to fall off with the gunner inside, then blew up killing all on board. The rear gunner escaped with minor injuries.

On the 23rd August four combinations took off from Portreath:
Halifax EB178 Pilot F/O Reed. Horsa LH309 Staff Sergeants Desbois, Garnett, and England. Had to return to base due to unserviceability.
Halifax EB139 pilot F/O Norman. Horsa DP338 Lt.Prout, Sergeants Hill and Thornton. Successfully reached Sale the same day .
Halifax DK198 pilot F/O Clapperton. Horsa LH122 Staff Sergeants Wright, Ridings and Robinson. The Horsa had to force land in Portugal and the three gliders pilots were interned but eventually made their way back to England.
Halifax DK197 pilot F/Sgt Doughill. Horsa Lt. Oxenford, Sergeants Waring and White. Successfully reached Sale.
Nine gliders had now reached Sale.

Three combinations took off on the 3rd September:
Halifax EB153 pilot F/O Northmore Horsa DP697 Sergeants Baker, Sargent and Barron. Successfully reached Sale.
Halifax EB160 pilot F/O Sizmur. Horsa LH209 Captain Clarke,Sergeants Puckett and Taylor. Reached Sale successfully.
Halifax DK199 pilot F/Sgt. Crossley. Horsa LG671 Sergeants Johnson, Attwood and Sanders. The Horsa had to cast off over the sea but the three pilots were picked up safely. The Halifax returned to Portreath.
Two more combinations lifted off on the 7th September
Halifax EB139 F/O Forster. Horsa DP440 Sergeants Desbois, Lewis and Tilling. Successfully reached Sale.
Halifax EB178 pilot F.O Reed. Horsa DP824 Lt.Shuttleworth, Staff Sergeant Gabbot and Sergeant Garnett. Combination crashed in Portugal south of Lisbon - both tug and glider were destroyed by fire but both aircrews safe.
Twelve Horsa gliders had now made the long haul from England to Sale successfully.
On the 15th September four combinations took off.
Halifax DK197 pilot F/Sgt. Crossley. Horsa DP 691 Sergeants Waite, Brookfield and Bettridge. Successfully reached Sale.
Halifax EB153 pilot F/O Northmore. Horsa LJ945 Lieutenant Telfer, Staff Sergeants Vincent and Humphreys. Successfully reached Sale.

Halifax DG388 pilot F/O Cleaver. Horsa LH130 Lieutenant Aston, Sergeants Brown and Simpson. Successfully reached Sale.
Halifax DK198 pilot F/O Clapperton. Horsa LJ209 Sergeants Channel, James and Thornton. Glider had to land in Portugal.
Fifteen Horsas had now been safely delivered to sale.

At 0740 hours on the 18th September the twenty-third combination took off from Portreath. Halifax DG396 piloted by F/O Norman towing Horsa HS102 piloted by Lieutenant Prout, Sergeant Hill and Sergeant Flynn. At 1100 hours flying at 1000 feet in cloud and rain the combination was attacked by twelve German JU88 aircraft flying in three by four formation. Four of the JU 88s circled while the other eight attacked the combination - Lieutenant Prout ordered Sergeant Flynn to cast off tow to free the Halifax tug to defend itself. Landing their Horsa across the line of waves the glider pilots got into their dinghy which was then fired on by the German aircraft but the glider crew were untouched.

The air gunners in the Halifax engaged the German aircraft and the rear gunner, Sergeant John Grant, shot down one JU88 for which he was later awarded the Distinguished Flying Medal. The Halifax - shot full of holes by enemy fire - managed to reach Sale. The glider pilots were picked up twelve hours later by the sloop HMS Crane, responding to a wireless message from the Halifax giving the position of the downed Horsa. The glider pilots were aboard HMS Crane for a week before being landed at Plymouth.

Tow number twenty-four - Halifax DG384 piloted by F/O Sizmur towing Horsa HF109 piloted by Sergeants Baker, Barron and Sergeant - reached the coast of Portugal. Mystery surround what happened next but the Squadron Operations Record Book states the glider was cast off and ditched in the sea with the tow rope still attached and the three glider pilots were lost. The Halifax returned to Portreath. The other tow off on the 23rd September was the last flight but the combination had to return to base unserviceable.

Out of the twenty-five combinations which had lifted off from Portreath fifteen had reached Sale, one was shot down, two landed in Portugal four ditched, two returned to base and one crashed.

Taken overall the operation was a success and reflects the skill and courage of the aircrews of the Royal Air Force and the Glider Pilots Regiment. To tow a large Horsa glider 1300 miles over the sea through enemy air space with no chance of landing on an emergency airfield, illustrates the qualities of the airmen soldiers and airmen. The author is indebted to Staff Sergeant Len Wright, DFM. Glider Pilot Regiment, for the use of his archives in the compiling of this record.

Report of ditching of a Horsa glider 200 miles NNW of Cape Finisterre on 18th September 1943.

| Crew 176018 | Lieut J.R.Prout. | Tug Pilot |
| --- | --- | --- |
| 5511117 | Sgt Hill P.B. | F/O Norman |
| 969029 | Sgt.Flynn H. | |

We took off at 0740 hours on 18th September 1943, from Portreath. The intercommunication failed immediately after take off and we were unable to contact the tug on the TR 9 (VHF radio). The undercarriage failed to come off at first, but after a time one of the parachutes opened - roman candeled - and beat a hole in the fuselage. The undercarriage then came off and we set course for Sale at 0845 hours.

Owing to a considerable amount of cloud and rain we were flying about 1000 feet, when at 1100 hours we sighted twelve twin-engined aircraft on our starboard beam. I soon recognised them as JU88s. At that time Sergeant Hill was flying the aircraft, Sergeant Flynn was in the second pilot's seat and I was standing in the doorway. The enemy aircraft did not at first come in to the attack, but flew on a course parallel to ours.

As we were in a clear patch the tug pilot increased the speed to 160mph in an endeavour to reach cloud cover, which was about one mile ahead. Owing to the failure of the inter-com we were unable to communicate with the tug. When I saw the first aircraft coming in to the attack from the starboard beam, I decided it was impossible for both the tug and glider to reach the cloud so I gave the order to cast off. Sergeant Flynn carried out my instructions immediately. By this time the attacking aircraft had opened fire on us but the fire passed safely in front of the nose of the glider.

After we cast off Sgt. Hill put on flap and did a series of steep turns in order to evade the enemy attacks. Meanwhile Sgt. Flynn proceeded aft to get the dinghy ready, while I collected together things which I considered we should need in the dinghy. Shortly after casting off we were attacked by another enemy aircraft but the glider again escaped damage. As there was a rough sea Sgt. Hill approached across the line of the waves and made a perfect landing. Sgt. Flynn then climbed onto the wing through the hatch which we had opened on the way down and I passed the dinghy up to him. By this time Sgt. Hill had come back from the cockpit. We all climbed onto the wing taking with us our water bottles, tins of food, groundsheets, compasses, binoculars etc. We inflated the dinghy on the wing, launched it and got in. While we were ditching one JU 88 remained near us the others having gone after the Halifax. When we were getting out of the glider it circled low over us then flew away.

As the roughness of the sea was causing the glider to toss about considerably we cut loose and drifted away. Shortly after cutting loose about six of the enemy returned - the first one diving at us and opening fire. The fire passed just over out heads and left us untouched. For about ten minutes all six aircraft continued diving at us but they did not again open fire.

After the enemy had gone we started to organise ourselves for the stay in the dinghy which I calculated might last several days. The nearest land was at Cape Finisterre about two hundred miles away. I also decided that owing to the roughness of the sea there would be a danger of the dinghy overturning if we erected the sail. Also owing to this danger I gave orders for all loose articles to be lashed to the dinghy. For rope we used the wire from our headsets. Both the Sergeants were very seasick during our stay in the dinghy - Sgt. Flynn being too ill to take part in the bailing etc., which was frequently necessary.

We sighted nothing until a Liberator passed directly over us at 1000 feet at about 1600 hours. We failed to attract its attention. Shortly afterwards a Sunderland passed over us at a greater height. Although we fired our Verey pistols several times we were still unnoticed. After another two hours when we had given up hope of seeing anything more that day and were settling down for the night, the Sunderland returned at a much lower altitude. I again fired the Very pistol and put out a sea marker. The Sunderland turned, circled us and dropped a container of food, flares etc. As the container dropped some distance away Sgt. Hill and I had to paddle the dinghy towards it. This took some twenty minutes to half an hour. The Sunderland continued to circle us for about an hour dropping float flares around us and signalling to us with an Aldis lamp at such a speed that we were unable to decipher his message.

When the Sunderland left us it was getting dark so I came to the conclusion that there was no hope of being picked up until the next morning. The sea, which had showed signs of calming, was now rougher again. With the help of Sgt. Hill I pumped up the dinghy and organised a series of watches to ensure that we did not drift away from the flares. We settled down for the night.

At about 2100 hours we heard an aircraft circling overhead so we fired a Very light to show our position. The aircraft then dropped some more float flares and went away. Eventually we saw it dropping parachute flares some way to the north. The parachute flares gradually came nearer so I fired another Verey light. After a while we heard a ship's siren and saw the ship silhouetted. I fired another Verey light and the ship came alongside and picked us up. It was then about 2230 hours.

We spent a week aboard the sloop HMS Crane which was on anti-U Boat patrol in the Bay of Biscay. We were eventually landed at Plymouth. I cannot speak too highly of the behaviour of my crew, especially Sergeant Hill, on this occasion - nor of the excellence of the Air Sea Rescue. Sergeant Hill and I were on our second and Sergeant Flynn on his third, trip to Africa.

Lieutenant J.R. Prout. GPR.

# OPERATION VOODOO

The first transatlantic towed glider flight from Canada to Britain, from the 23rd June to 1st July 1943.

An airbridge from Canada to Britain had been established since the 10th November 1940, when seven Lockheed Hudson aircraft - flown mainly by civilian aircrews - had made the the 2200 miles flight from RCAF Gander, Newfoundland, to RAF Aldergrove, Northern Ireland, in ten and a half hours. The lead aircraft being flown by BOAC Captain D.C.T. Bennett (later Group Captain 'Pathfinder' Bennett, RAF.)

Under the United States Lease Lend Act passed by the US Government and signed by President Roosevelt on the 11th March 1941, the USAAF was beginning to supply aircraft to the Royal Air Force by flying them to Canada for onward delivery by RAF Ferry Command which was formed on the 20th July 1941, under the command of Air Chief Marshal Sir Douglas Bowhill.

The Canadian Government had built a large new airfield at Dorval, ten miles from Montreal, which became the receiving airfield for lease lend aircraft from the US en route to Britain. Another hugh airfield was built at Goose Bay, Labrador - eight hundred and twenty miles north east of Gander - which had three 7000 feet long runways. With Goose Bay built it was now possible for medium range aircraft to cross the Atlantic with a refuelling stop at Reykjavik, Iceland. The US had also built an airfield in Greenland - Bluie West One - as a refuelling stop between Labrador and Iceland.

With these hugh airfields completed it was possible to establish a firm airbridge over the North Atlantic and on the 11th March 1943, RAF Ferry Command became RAF Transport Command still under the command of Air Chief Marshal Bowhill.

During the hard Canadian winter of 1942 the RAF and the RCAF decided to investigate the feasibility of towing gliders across the North Atlantic from north America to Britain, a distance of 3500 miles. Chosen to carry out the experimental flight were Flight Lieutenant W.S. Longhurst, (tug Captain), a Canadian pilot serving with the RAF, and Flight Lieutenant C.W.H.Thompson,(co-pilot), a New Zealander also serving with the RAF. The glider pilots were Squadron Leader R.G. Seys, DFC. Royal Air Force, and Squadron Leader F.M. Gobiel, RCAF.

Using RCAF Dorval as a base, flying trials were made to select a suitable tug aircraft and glider. Prophetically the combination chosen was a Douglas C47 Dakota and US a Waco CG4A Hadrian glider; this combination later became the US standard tug/glider combination. Flying locally at first the tests soon extended to Gander and Goose Bay airfields, with the glider fully loaded with 1½ tons of freight weight. The test triangular flight route followed by the combination aircraft set up a record for a freight carrying glider of 820 miles on one leg of the route - the previous US held record being 670 miles. The longest test flight was 1177 miles non stop at an average speed of 150mph which took eight flying hours. This flight gave the information and experience required for the transatlantic tow. Tests completed the take off date for the operation was set for the 23rd June 1943.

The tow plane selected - a C47 Dakota II Serial Number FD900 - made by Douglas Aircraft Corporation, California, USA, carried the normal safety equipment for a trans-ocean flight but was also fitted with long range extra fuel tanks which could be jettisoned without danger to the glider on tow behind the tug. Tug Crew for the flight was :

| | |
|---|---|
| 1st Pilot. | F/Lt. W.S. Longhurst. |
| 2nd pilot. | F/Lt. C.H.H. Thompson. |
| Engineer. | F/O. K. Turner. |
| Radio Officer | Mr. H.G. Wightman. |
| Flight Engineer | P/O. R.H. Wormington. |

Glider crew for the flight were;
| | |
|---|---|
| 1st Pilot. | S/Ldr. R.G. Seys, DFC. RAF. |
| 2ns Pilot. | S/Ldr. F.M. Gobiel, RCAF. |

A Waco CG4A Hadrian - serial number FR579 - nicknamed "Voodoo" by Squadron Leader Seys - made by piano makers Pratt Read Company of Connecticut, USA, was to be the glider for this the first transatlantic flight by a towed glider. The steel tube and fabric covered Hadrian was fitted with flotation bags to keep it afloat and give the crew time to get out in case of ditching at sea. A special knife was carried to enable the two man crew to cut their way out of the fabric covered fuselage if necessary. Full survival gear - including an inflatable rubber dinghy - was carried. A 3360lbs freight load of medical supplies, engine and radio spares which were to be sent on to Russia, were carried. The nylon tow rope, made by the Plymouth Cordage Company, Massachussetts, USA, and the towing fixture points on the glider had been designed to take a pull of 20000lbs.

At 1125 hours GMT on the 23rd June 1943, the Dakota towed the Hadrian off from RCAF Dorval and set course in a strong headwind for Goose Bay. Climbing slowly the combination reached an altitude of 9000 feet searching for clear weather above the cumulus clouds. An altitude of 13000 feet was reached but there was no break in the clouds. The cloud cover rendered the tug invisible to the glider pilots and they had to rely on the angle of the tow rope to their glider to judge the towing position relative to the tug. Six hours into the flight the combination ran into bad weather, thunderstorms, ice and snow which forced them down to 1500 feet. At 2325 hours on the 23rd June they were landing at Goose Bay. Flight time had been seven hours for the first leg.

On the 27th June the combination was airborne again heading for Bluie West One - the US airfield in Greenland - the next stop. The weather was reasonably good on this leg and they made the airfield six and a quarter hours later. Total flying time so far 13¼ hours.

Three days later at 1322 GMT on the 30th June the combination took off in favourable weather conditions for the long haul to Iceland. During the whole of the flight so far the two pilots had alternated at the control column as the Hadrian had to be flown all the time. Communication with the tug was by radio but as the glider radio was powered by battery only with no means of recharging, the glider radio had to be kept off most of the time. If they wished to speak to the tug all they had to do was to switch on and transmit. But if the tug crew wished to speak to the glider pilots the tug pilot had to waggle the tug's wings as a signal for the glider pilots to switch on their set.

Both tug and glider landed safely at Reykjavik, Iceland, at 2037 hours on the 30th June with a flight time of 7¼ hours for the leg and making a total flying time of 20½ hours so far. No major problems had occurred, although the nylon tow rope had to be respliced and the steel towing coupling had to be straightened and rewelded due to damage received when the tow rope was dropped by the tug on a rocky surface after releasing the glider.

The final leg of the flight from Iceland to Britain began at 0530 hours on the 1st July 1943, when the combination lifted off in good weather from Reykjavik airfield for the 850 mile flight to Prestwick, Scotland. The crews of both tug and glider were suffering from lack of sleep as good flying weather came before sleep. The weather had mostly been good so they flew. After 7 flying hours the combination broke cloud over Prestwick airfield at 1315 hours on the 1st July - right on their estimated time of arrival. The glider cast off and made a perfect landing on the grass to be followed two minutes later by the tug. So ended a pioneer towed glider flight of 28 hours 15 minutes duration - the first towed glider flight over the North Atlantic.

Part of the nylon tow rope used by the combination can be seen on display at the Army Museum of Flying, Middle Wallop, Hampshire, together with the names of both tug and glider crews.

In connection with his famous flight across the Atlantic Wing Commander Seys, AFC, DFC, gave the following account to the employees of the Waco Factory Troy, Ohio, on the 11th October 1943.

We encountered very bad weather during the early stages of the flight. The turbulence was shocking. The glider was thrown all over the sky. The tug made some dirty lurches too. I had taken over the controls in anticipation of this bad weather before we began to go down through the clouds, and for the next three hours we took a terrific beating. We passed through three belts of thunderstorms, with snow and ice so thick at times I lost sight of the towplane and had only 50 to 100 feet of tow rope before me by which to judge its position relative to the tug. If I allowed the glider to get too low, the tow plane would have been pulled into a climb steep enough to stall it. Had this happened I would have had no alternative but to cut loose and make a forced landing, because a dive resulting from a stall probably would have pulled the wings off the glider through exceeding its designed maximum speed. We got through however and made the first stage - an eastcoast airfield - with a smooth landing only about twenty minutes late. We were dead tired and after sleeping for five hours my shoulders and legs seemed to be a mass of aches and pains from fighting the weather we'd gone through.

An Atlantic glider crossing never had been done before and although we had made many experiments, the sensations were new to me. To be candid, I was more than somewhat frightened at the prospect of the tremendous haul before us. This was soon banished by the thrill of getting away according to plan. The take off was smooth and slow. We had an hour and a half of rough weather, flying under clouds before we were able to climb through them and reach smooth air above at about 6000 feet. By this time the Atlantic, with ice fields and occasional towering icebergs, was visible below. I began to wonder whether, if it was necessary to make a forced landing in the sea, we would be able to land on the icebergs and stay long enough to be picked up. I felt they were much more solid than our rubber dinghy which did not seem at all inviting. I am a bad sailor.

Snatches in a tow rope can be minimized greatly by a skilful glider pilot, but the tow pilot can do little about it. For instance, on seeing the rope getting slack the idea is dive a little just as the tow plane begins to go ahead, so that the glider gets up speed at the same time and the snatch is reduced. Another of the difficulties was the noise. The air rushes past the glider with the sound of a train over rails - an odd rhythmic beat which does not cease until the glider speed drops below 70 knots just before landing. Squadron leader Gobiel, my co-pilot, and I did not talk to each other during the flight. We couldn't. Another strain was watching the tow rope so closely. The effects are hypnotic. In fair weather the average trick at the controls is two hours. If there is no horizon one hour. But in bad weather a spell may last three. Concentration is imperative. Even when the co-pilot takes over the tension does not leave you. You seem to be flying the glider all the time whoever is at the controls. So glider flying is not just sitting in the cockpit and being towed. It is something similar to being towed in a car by a rope from another car - except that the one behind has not brakes and the only way the pilot can slow down to avoid running over the tug or letting the tow rope get slack (which makes a frightful snatch) is to weave about and thereby cover a little more distance than the towing vehicle.

In smooth air everything is delightful. But in bad weather you might as well be in a churn. I remember one particularly rough flight after which I had a tremendous bruise across my stomach and thighs from being thrown against my belt, and I thought my insides would never return to their proper positions. Crossing the Atlantic we were forced below the clouds again about six hours from the North American continent, and for some time we flew less than 1000 feet above the waves. The weather was closing in however and we had to climb to try to get over the top. At 9500 feet we had still not reached the top. It was snowing pretty hard and I was at the controls and pretty busy. Gobiel said afterwards he got absolutely frozen wiping away the snow which came in through the joints in the cockpit. We were wearing the same clothing with US Army parkas and woolens and I had on the red skull cap made from my wife's hat which I wear for luck - but I was working so hard at the controls that I kept warm.

After an hour of this we got into the clear again and had about six hours at 9000 feet, flying between two layers of cloud, where, of course, we could see neither sun nor sea. About thirteen hours from North America, we hit another bad patch. It lasted only about half an hour and from there it was plain sailing at 6000 feet with a layer of cloud covering the sea and the sun shining down on us.

I had taken along a bunch of bananas for the family but they got frostbitten, as did out sandwiches which almost broke our teeth when we tried to eat them. Finally twenty-eight flying hours from Montreal we sighted the coast of Britain - after four false alarms which turned out to be low clouds on the horizon. I never was more glad to see the earth under me and upon receiving the signal from the towplane to cut loose, I did not argue. After a couple of circuits over the landing field we touched down smoothly. Gobiel and I shook hands very solemnly as the machine came to rest. We were very tired. It was quite an effort to submit to the usual interrogation and attend to the unloading of the glider before she was wheeled away and put to bed in the hangar.

(Reprinted by courtesy of the Waco Historical Society, Troy, Ohio.)

# OPERATION THURSDAY

During February, 1943, Lord Louis Mountbatten, Supreme Commander, South East Asia Command, decided to mount an offensive with his forces against the Japanese to regain occupied Burma. General Orde Wingate's six brigades of Chindits would be used, some by moving overland with the 77th Brigade, commanded by Brigadier M. Calvert, and comprising:

1st Battalion, The Kings Regiment.
1st Battalion. The Lancashire Fusiliers.
1st Battalion, South Staffordshire Regiment.
with the 3rd Battalion, Gurkha Rifles flying in by glider.

The USAAF formed a special unit to transport and support the Chindits. In effect, this was a self-contained miniature air force which was at first named the 5318th Air Unit and codenamed 'Project Nine'. It later became known as No.1 Air Commando, and was equipped with one hundred Waco CG4A and seventy-five Aeronco TG-5 gliders, plus B25 Mitchell medium bombers, P51 Mustang long range fighters, C47 Dakota transports, L-1 and L-5 light aircraft and six Sikorsky YR-4 helicopters: the unit had five hundred men to fly and service the aircraft. In command of the Air Commando was US Colonel Phillip C. Cochrane with US Colonel John R. Allison as his deputy. Command of the one hundred US glider pilots was given to US Major William H. Taylor - an experienced glider pilot.

The airborne part of the offensive was to land in two jungle clearings codenamed Picadilly and Broadway - the first wave of glider troops would radio back to base if the clearings were free of the Japanese. If clear the second wave would be flown in and landing strips cleared for the main landing of troops by air. D-Day for Operation Thursday was set for Sunday, 5th March 1944, with eight Waco CG4A gliders assembled at Lalachat and Hailakandi airfields in the valley of Silcher, India. Forty gliders were scheduled to land at Picadilly and another forty at Broadway. All gliders would be on double tow, with one glider on a tow rope of 425 feet and the other on a standard tow rope of 350 feet, giving a 75-feet clearance to avoid collision.

During the afternoon of D-Day Colonel Cochrane sent out a B25 Mitchell of the Combat Camera Unit, flown by a Lieutenant Russhon, to take aerial photographs of Picadilly and Broadway. When Russhon returned with the photographs it was seen that the main LZ Picadilly was obstructed with teak logs laid in rows but that Broadway was clear.

H-Hour for take off was postponed and a hurried conference held which decided to put all eighty gliders down on Broadway. At 1806 hours on the 5th March 1944, the first combinations took off led by Major Taylor, CO of the US Glider Unit, who would act as pathfinder glider followed by four other pathfinder combinations, one of which was flown by Colonel Allison, second-in-command of the Air Commando.

Ten Wacos were now airborne with their tugs straining to climb to 8000 feet to clear the Chin hills. Within two hours six gliders had broken their tow ropes and gone down on the Indian border. The remaining Wacos, led by Major Taylor, flew on to the LZ in severe turbulence and visibility reduced by a thick haze. Due to the turbulence and overloaded condition several more gliders broke their tow ropes and had to force land. Five landed near an enemy headquarters and immediately engaged the Japanese - leading the enemy to believe that the Allies were mounting guerrilla war on them.

As the leading Wacos approached Broadway LZ the haze cleared and the glider pilots could see the LZ in the moonlight. Casting off tow, the Pathfinders began to land without Japanese opposition. Most made heavy landings but the occupants set up a signal beacon to indicate the cast off point and laid a flarepath for the incoming main glider force.

Many of the incoming gliders crashed or made heavy landings on the rutted log strewn LZ - some colliding with other gliders on the ground. Casualties began to mount and about 0230 hours Brigadier Calvert sent out to his India base the code word 'Soyalink', the pre-arranged signal to stop further despatches of gliders.

Eight combinations en route to Broadway were recalled to base and the glider operation was suspended. Of the fifty-four gliders despatched and not recalled thirty-seven reached Broadway. Eight had landed in friendly territory and nine in Japanese held ground. 539 men, 3 mules, and 29972lbs of supplies had been landed during the night.

The US 900th Airborne Engineer Company aided by the Chindits cleared a runway 300 feet wide and 5000 feet long for C47 Dakotas to air land the main body of troops during the evening of the 6th March 1944. With the runway ready the code word 'Porksausage' was sent from Broadway to India - this was the signal for the despatch of the main body of troops to Broadway. During the night of the 6th-7th March, sixty-three C47s landed troops and supplies on Broadway. On the 5th March the 16th British Brigade under Brigadier Fergusson reached the River Chindwin, having marched 360 miles across country. Four Waco gliders landed with equipment for the river crossing and at the same time two Waco gliders landed on the far side of the Chindwin to secure a bridgehead for the 16th Brigade.

*The Glider Soldiers* 207

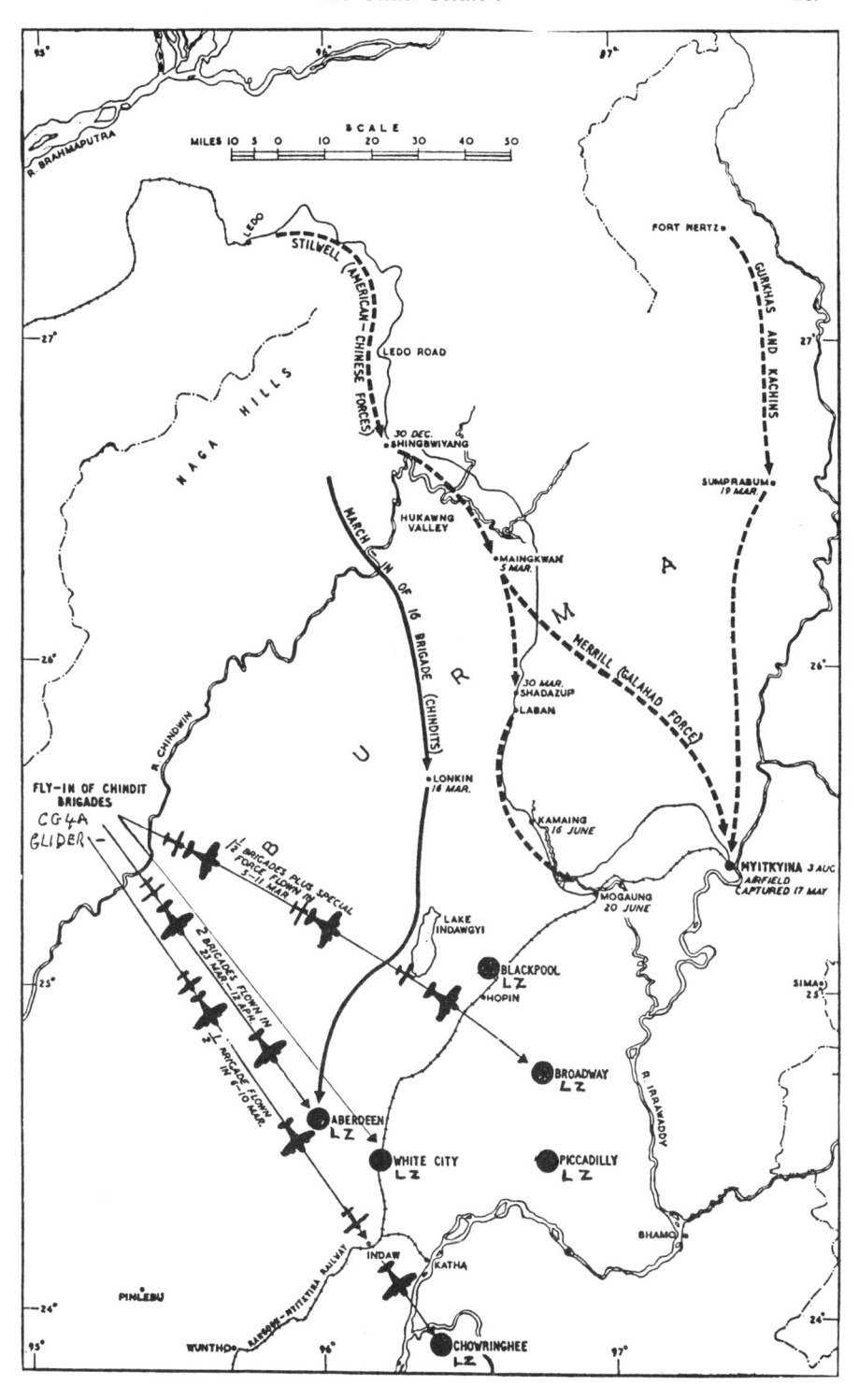

While the main part of the operation was in full swing twelve Waco gliders had been lifted off from Lalachat bound for another Lz, Chowringhee, some seventy-five miles south-west of Broadway. The task of this glider sortie was to act as Pathfinders and lay out a flarepath for later inbound C47 Dakota transports with troops aboard. Carried in the Waco gliders were three Platoons of the 3rd Battalion, 6th Gurkha Rifles and US Engineers with a two ton bulldozer.

This small task force commanded by Lieutenant Clint Gatty had former film star now Flight Officer Jackie Coogan as lead pathfinder glider pilot whose task it was to lay a flarepath for the eleven Waco glider coming in behind his glider. Coogan landed his glider successfully and his Gurkhas fanned out to protect the LZ while the US Engineers cleared a runway. Unfortunately the glider carrying the bulldozer crashed; all the occupants were killed and the bulldozer destroyed.

With the bulldozer out of action it was impossible to create a runway at the LZ so a radio message was sent to the Broadway LZ requesting another bulldozer. At 2100 hours on the 7th March four more Waco gliders - one carrying a bulldozer - began to arrive at Chowringhee and the dozer was quickly at work preparing a 3000 feet long dirt runway. At 0130 hours on the 8th C47 Dakotas began bringing in 111th Brigade under Brigadier Lentaigne. For two night streams of C47s brought in half of the 111th, then Wingate decided that enough troops had arrived and the Chowringhee LZ was abandoned. Two hours later the Japanese began to bomb the LZ - but the Chindits had gone. The USAAF with their snatching equipment pulled out some of the Wacos.

In six days 9052 troops, 175 ponies, 1183 mules and 509,082lbs of supplies had been flown in from India to the LZ - some 150 miles into enemy held territory. Casualties were 121 - all among the glider crews and passengers - 30 men had been killed at Broadway alone with 33 injured. Not one C47 Dakota tug or transport aircraft had been lost.

On the 23rd March, 1944, the second part of the operation began when another Chindit brigade was flown into another LZ - Aberdeen - by Dakota aircraft. By the 12th April two brigades had been flown in but General Wingate did not live to see this. The legendary leader was killed on the 24th March together with his US aircrew when their aircraft crashed into the Naga Hills during a storm. Brigadier W.D.A. Lentaigne took over Wingate's command.

The Japanese counter-attacked the Chindits at a small airstrip nicknamed White City and five Waco gliders - loaded with ammunition landed there. Three of the landed gliders were loaded with wounded Chindits and snatched out by Dakotas but Japanese fire destroyed the other two gliders whose pilots then fought on the ground with the 77th Brigade.

During 16th Brigade's advance on foot through the jungle the CO, Brigadier Fergusson, requested folding boats to carry his soldiers over the River Irrawaddy. 1st Air Commando despatched a Waco CG4A loaded with four boats to the west bank of the river. The Waco landed on a sandbank, offloaded the boats and later the same day was snatched out by a Dakota and flown back to India. During the fighting the air ambulances of 1st Air Commando - nicknamed 'Blood Chariots' engaged in ferrying out wounded Chindits. Some were snatched in Waco CG4A gliders, others in light aircraft and the four small helicopters.

On the 21st March six Waco CG4A gliders landed at Aberdeen LZ with bulldozers and equipment to establish a dirt runway for transport aircraft. When the Dakota transports landed there the next day the gliders were towed back to India. For several weeks the US glider pilots continued to fly re-supply missions to the Chindits and evacuate casualties.

By May the US and Chinese Forces in Northern Burma were closing in on Mykityina. On the 17th May US and Chinese Forces arrived at the airfield near the town - and stormed and took it by noon. The Allied commander, Colonel Charles N. Hunter requested supplies and re-inforcements before the Japanese counter-attacked. Ten Waco CG4A gliders carrying the US 879th Aviation Engineer Battalion lifted off from Shingbwiyang airstrip in Northern Burma and landed under enemy fire at Mykityina airfield. The Engineers immediately went to work preparing the airfield to receive Dakota aircraft. By the late afternoon on the 17th May a battalion of the 89th Regiment arrived by air from Ledo and transport aircraft began landing equipment and supplies.

For the next seventy-nine days the airfield was held against attack and supplies and re-inforcements poured in by air to divisional strength before the town of Mykityina was finally taken on the 3rd August. By the end of August 1944, the Japanese were in retreat and Operation Thursday came to an end with the withdrawal of the Chindits from Burma.

The glider concept had worked well -landing men and equipment to prepare airstrips for the main body troops to be flown in later by transport aircraft. The only way to get a bulldozer to a clearing in the jungle was by glider.

## OPERATION LADBROOKE

During December 1942 whilst the Allied Forces were still fighting the enemy in Tunisia, study plans were being laid for the step - the invasion of Europe. In January 1943 the Casablanca Conference was held and President Roosevelt, Prime Minister Churchill with their military advisors decided that the invasion of Sicily was to be the next step - prior to the invasion of mainland Italy.

The Supreme Commander - General Eisenhower - designated the British General Harold L. Alexander as his Deputy and Commander of all Allied ground forces, and Air Commodore R.M. Foster, Royal Air Force, to head his Air Staff. The task was to plan the Sicily invasion - codenamed Husky - and for this purpose a Headquarters, to be known as Allied Force Headquarters, (AFHQ Force 141) was set up in Algiers. On the 2nd February 1943, AFHQ issued the first Directive on Husky and the next day planning began in earnest. By the 12th February the HQ was able to give its first assessment of the projected invasion.

Various plans were laid and discussed by the Army Commanders but without result so, on the 2nd May, General Eisenhower held a conference at Algiers to resolve the matter. It was agreed that the assault on Sicily would take place on the 9th-10th July 1943, when there was a quarter moon which set at 0030 hours on the 10th July. Order of Battle decided on for the invasion of Sicily was:

Supreme Commander: General Dwight Eisenhower, US Army.
Naval Commander: Admiral Cunningham.
Deputy Commander: General Alexander.
Air Commander: Air Chief Marshal Tedder.

SEABORNE ASSAULT FORCES:

US 7th Army.(Force 343)
General Patton
US 2nd Corps. (General Bradley)
US 1st Division. (General Allan)
US 45th Division. (General Middleton)
US 2nd Armoured Division (Part)
US 3rd Division (General Truscott)

British 8th Army (Force 545)
General Montgomery
13th Corps. (General Dempsey)
5th Division
50th Division
No.3 Commando
30 Corps.(General Leese)
51st Highland Division
231 Independent Brigade
1st Canadian Division
Nos. 40 & 41 Commando

ALLIED AIR FORCES (Troop Carrying):

North West African Air Force (Major General Spaatz).

North African Troop Carrier Command (Brigadier General Williams)
US 51st Wing (Colonel Dunn)             US 52nd Wing (Colonel Clark)
60th, 62nd & 64th Groups                61st, 313th, 314th, 316th Groups
Dakota aircraft, 12 Squadrons           Dakota aircraft, 19 Squadrons

Royal Air Force, 38 Wing. (Wing Commander May).
295 Squadron,   Halifax aircraft (10)    Horsa glider tugs (8)
296 Squadron,   Albemarle aircraft (30)  Waco Hadrian tugs (25)


The British 8th Army would land on beaches of the Gulf of Noto, south of the town of Syracuse, and on both sides of the Pachino peninsula. The US 7th Army would land on a seventy mile beach front along the Gulf of Gela from Licata to Scoglitti, on the left flank of the British Forces.

About the beginning of May 1943, the United States began to ship 500 Waco CG4A (Hadrian) gliders from America, and the Royal Air Force Horsa gliders from England (Operation Beggar/Turkey Buzzard.) The gliders were at first intended for follow up operations or transport only, the planned airborne missions were to be by paratroops.

On the 13th May German resistance in Tunisia ceased and dirt air strips for the invasion aircraft were made near Kairouan. On the 21st May AFHQ allocated two airborne divisions for the invasion. The British 1st Airborne Division (Hopkinson) and the US 82nd Airborne Division (Ridgeway). Two days later General Montgomery published a plan providing that 'Airborne Forces composed of paratroops and possibly gliders will be dropped to the North East of Syracuse shortly before H Hour on D-Day'.

Montgomery and Hopkinson decided that glider forces would be landed at night - before the main seaborne assault - the reasoning being that a glider landing would give the airborne troops the firepower they needed to mount an assault on their objectives. Paratroops on their own would be dispersed on their DZs and lightly armed. The British airborne forces advisor, Group Captain Tom Cooper, Royal Air Force, objected to a night glider assault as he considered the tug and glider aircrews did not have enough experience or training for a night operation. Colonel Chatterton, Glider Pilot Regiment Commander, also objected but both officers were overruled and the plan went ahead.

By the end of May the final assault plan had been decided on. The airborne landing by British Forces - codenamed Ladbrooke - would be by the 1st Air Landing Brigade, 1st Airborne Division, on three landing zones (LZs) south of the town of Syracuse. Some 1500 troops would be involved, one of their objectives being the Ponte Grande bridge over a canal 1½ miles south-west of Syracuse on highway 115, by which the British seaborne 5th Division was to approach Syracuse. It was planned to take the Ponte Grande by coup de main assault using six Horsa gliders carrying men of the 2nd South Staffords.

The Ladbrooke gliderborne forces consisted of:

1st Air Landing Brigade. CO. Brigadier P.H.W. Hicks.

2nd South Staffordshire Regiment. CO. Lt.Colonel W.D.H. McCardie.
1st Border Regiment. CO. Lt. Colonel G.V. Britten.
9th Field Company, Royal Engineers.
181st Airborne Field Ambulance. CO Lt. Colonel G. Warrack.
1st Battalion, Glider Pilot Regiment CO Lt. Colonel G. Chatterton.
Reinforced by nineteen volunteer USAAF glider pilots.

As well as the troops with their personal weapons, the gliders would carry seven jeeps, six 6-pounder guns and ten 3-inch mortars. Each Horsa would carry thirty-two men of the Staffordshire Regiment. The Waco CG4As load would vary according to the equipment carried - the maximum eighteen men the minimum four men and a jeep.

D-Day was fixed for the 9th-10th July 1943, with take off times from 1840 hours on the 9th onwards. By the 3rd June 1943, eighteen airstrips in the Kairouan area of Tunisia had been allocated to the glider training and ground forces. The airstrips - newly constructed by the Allies - were 6000 feet long by 300 feet wide dirt strips which raised clouds of dust on take off by the combinations. The pilots of the gliders were hard put to see their tow planes on take off - the tug disappeared in a cloud of dust which required great flying skill by the glider pilots.

The US 51st Wing and the two squadrons of 38 Wing had been allocated six airstrips south of Sousse near Goubrine and El Djem. No names were given to these strips merely letters: A, B, C, D, E and F. The US 52nd Wing had the other twelve airstrips close to Kairouan from which to carry the US 82nd Airborne on their Husky mission.

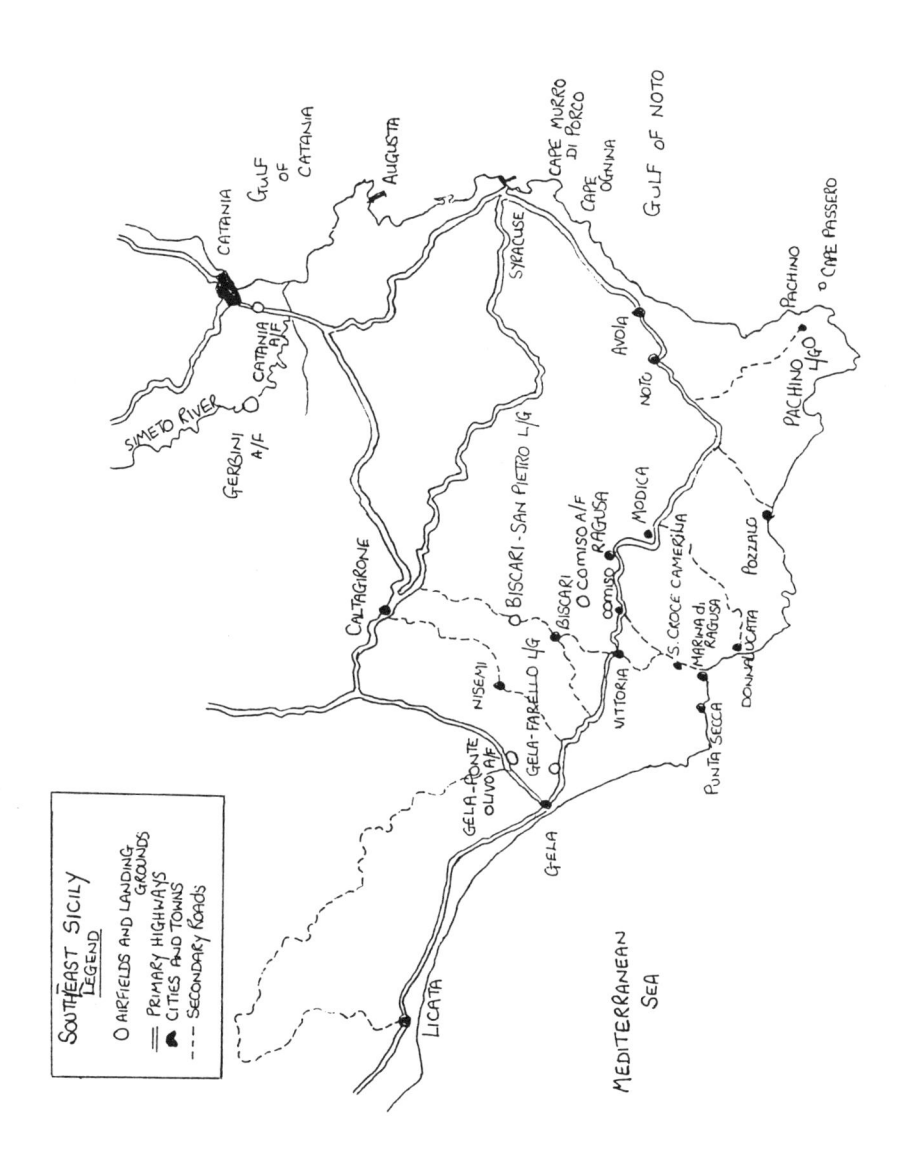

*The Glider Soldiers* 213

The first plan was for the US 51st Wing to work with the American Airborne Forces and the US 52nd Wing to work with the British Airborne Forces. On 6th May the US 52nd Wing - newly arrived in Africa - was ordered to carry the US Airborne Forces and the 51st to work with the British Airborne Forces. The logic behind this reversal was that the 51st Wing had operational experience with the British and the 52nd with the US 82nd Airborne Division. The 52nd had trained in the US on glider towing but the 51st had little or no glider towing training. This change was satisfactory until a glider landing was ordered for the British - the US 51st Wing with little glider towing training were to tow 1st Air Landing Brigade - the glider experienced 52nd Wing would drop paratroops.

On the 29th May, 51st Wing began training its pilots on glider towing - gliders had been in short supply, only Waco CG4A (Hadrians) being available and then in small numbers. By the 13th June 346 Wacos had been delivered more than enough for training and the later operations.

2 and 3 Squadrons of the Glider Pilot Regiment, commanded by Lieutenant Colonel Chatterton, were to pilot the Wacos, reinforced by nineteen US glider pilots who had volunteered for the operation. The British glider pilots, unfamiliar with the US Wacos, began training on them near Oran.

The first glider practice exercise by the Us 51st Wing was held on the 14th June when the Wing towed 54 Wacos piloted by British glider pilots over a 70 mile triangular route, casting them off over Froha airfield. The pilots flew in four aircraft formations spaced out at two minute intervals in daylight.

On the 20th June Exercise Eve was mounted in a similar manner with the Royal Air Force 38 Wing taking part. Again it was a daylight exercise with good results but on Sicily they would be landing in the dark. After Exercise Eve the training period ended and the move to the take off airfields commenced. The British glider pilots on average had been given 4.5 hours flying time on Wacos which included 1.2 hours of night flying. They had made about 16 landings each.

By the 2nd July 38 Wing and the US 60th and 62nd Groups of 51st Troop Carrier Wing had moved to the Sousse area. The British glider pilots with their 140 Wacos were towed from Oran to Kairouan - a distance of 600 miles. One Waco tail plane fell off in flight and the glider crashed killing all on board. 1st Air Landing Brigade and the glider pilots were now established in base camp near the dirt airstrips in Tunisia - the glider pilots naming their camp Fargo II, Fargo I being their base camp in England.

By 4th June Force 141 had decided that the Ladbrooke operation would fly from Tunisia by way of Malta to Cape Passero the southern tip of Sicily. On the 6th July Colonel Clark, Commander of the US 52nd Wing represented the Troop Carriers at a Conference in Malta between General Browning, US Major

General Swing (the US airborne advisor to Eisenhower) and US Admiral Hewitt. The Conference approved troop carrier routes, time schedules and recognition signals for the operation. Fighter protection during the departure of the missions from Tunisia and over Malta was to be provided by the Royal Air Force Air Defence Wing. Hurricane fighters from Malta would attack enemy searchlights in the Gela area on the night of D minus 1 but no fighter escort would be provided between Malta and Sicily.

On the evening of the 9th July, one hundred and nine C47 Dakotas, twenty-eight Royal Air Force Albemarles and seven Halifaxes were ready to tow off one hundred and thirty-six Waco and eight Horsa glider on Operation Ladbrooke. At 1842 hours that evening the first combinations began to take off and set course at 500 feet for the rendezvous point over the Kuriate Islands off the east coast of Tunisia. They continued to take off at one minute intervals until 2020 hours. The US pilots flying in echelon of four to the right (their standard pattern) and the British pilots individually in stream.

Colonel Chatterton with his Adjutant Captain Harding was towed off in a Waco carrying Brigadier Hicks, 1st Air Landing Brigade Commander, and other Staff Officers including the Senior Medical Officer. Six Albemarles of 296 Squadron had to abort the operation for various reason and one C47 Dakota had to force land shortly after take off when its glider jeep load broke loose, leaving one hundred and thirty seven combinations heading for the RV.

Circling over the RV the armada formed into a stream and headed for Malta some 200 miles to the east. The Halifax tugs flew at 145mph at 500 feet with the Albemarles at 125mph at 350 feet and the C47 Dakotas at 120mph at 250 feet. The low height flown was to avoid enemy radar detection - some combinations flew so low they were lashed with sea spray.

The first combinations reached the turning RV off Delimara Point, Malta, at 2122 hours then turned north east for the 70 mile leg to Cape Passero, the south east tip of Sicily. By this time wind speed was about 45mph from the north west making difficult flying conditions for the combinations. The wind moderated to about 30mph as the armada approached Sicily but the quarter moon gave insufficient light to locate the LZs. Four Waco/C47 combinations turned back over the sea and returned unable to locate their LZs. One Waco was accidentally released en route and one Horsa broke its tow rope.

The LZs were: LZ 3 North a mile west of the Ponte Grande bridge and LZ 3 South immediately south west of it - for the Horsas, LZs 1 and 2 some two to three miles south east of the bridge for the Wacos. LZ 2 was close to the sea shore and LZ 1 a mile inland from LZ 2.

216   *The Glider Soldiers*

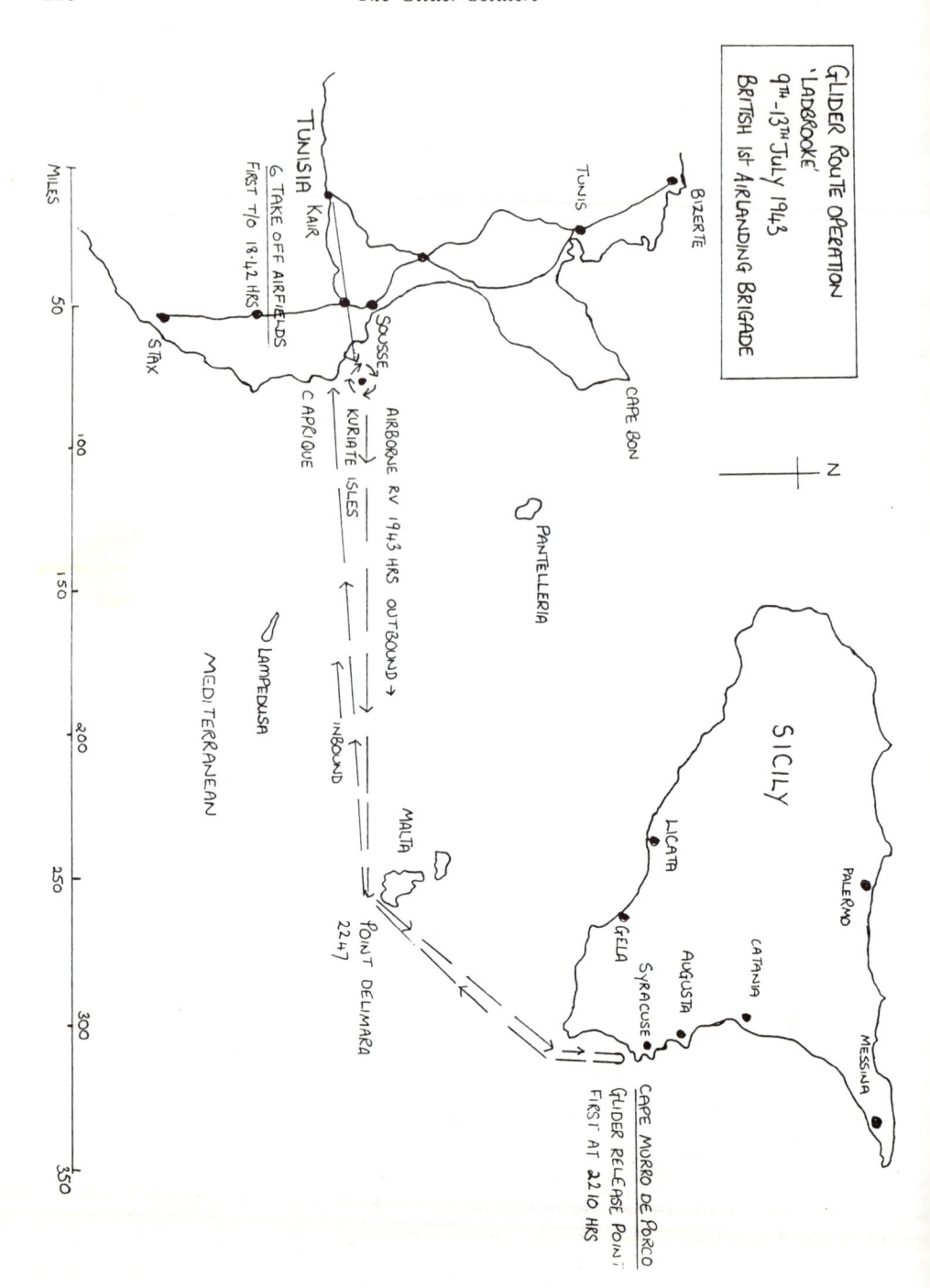

At 2210 the first seven releases were made near Cape Murro di Porco undetected by the enemy. The release point was 3000 yards south east of the shore line nearest to LZs 1 and 2. The Horsas release height was planned for 5000 feet for LZ 3 and the Wacos 1800 feet for LZ 1 and 1400 feet for LZ 2. As this first wave was released the enemy became alerted and opened fire with anti-aircraft guns. Searchlights began to sweep the sky and the combination of flak and searchlights upset the tug pilots - glider No.48 piloted by Lieutenant Steiner was last seen caught in a searchlight beam. Smoke from the flak drifted over the release area making it difficult for the tug pilots to locate their release point. A confused situation developed with the air space full of aircraft and gliders, smoke and gunfire. After cast off - some too far offshore - the tugs dropped their tow ropes and turned south for Malta then Tunisia. The first tug returned to base at 0015 hours. Although five crews lost their way all 137 aircraft returned safely.

Back in Sicily chaos reigned. At least 69 gliders fell into the sea downing 252 men - 7 Wacos and 3 Horsas were missing also believed crashed at sea. Survivors of some of the ditched gliders later complained bitterly that they had been released too far offshore. 49 Wacos and 5 Horsas landed on Sicily.

The glider pilots due to being released too far offshore and disorientated by the confusion and pall of dust whipped up by a gale, could not locate their intended LZs. Only two Wacos landed on LZ 1, one on LZ 2 and only one Horsa on LZ 3. Two more Horsas were landed within a mile of LZ 3.

Colonel Chatterton flying a Waco cast off tow when his tug started to turn and dive and turned the glider towards the direction of the LZs. As he descended into a pall of dust raised by a gale blowing on Sicily he could not locate the LZ - a burst of tracer bullets struck the Waco tearing the fabric and he was forced to land in the sea. The occupants emerged from the Waco and clung to the wings - a searchlight from the shore picked them out and machine-guns fire was directed at them, luckily missing. Chatterton, Hicks and the rest of the party swam to the shore minus their weapons and equipment.

Horsa glider Number 133 piloted by Staff Sergeants Galpin and Brown, Glider Pilot Regiment, towed by a Halifax piloted by Flight Lieutenant Grant was the only one to reach LZ 3. Horsa No.132 piloted by Captain J.W.C. Denholm and carrying part of C Company, 2nd South Staffords, under Major G. Ballinger, crashed into a canal bank only 400 yards from the bridge target, killing all but one of the occupants. Staff Sergeant Galpin landed his glider safely on LZ 3 and the occupants, a Platoon of the 2nd South Staffords under Lieutenant L. Withers, immediately stormed and captured the vital bridge. One of the Platoon - Private Curnock, RAMC, a former miner - helped to remove enemy demolition charges from the captured bridge.

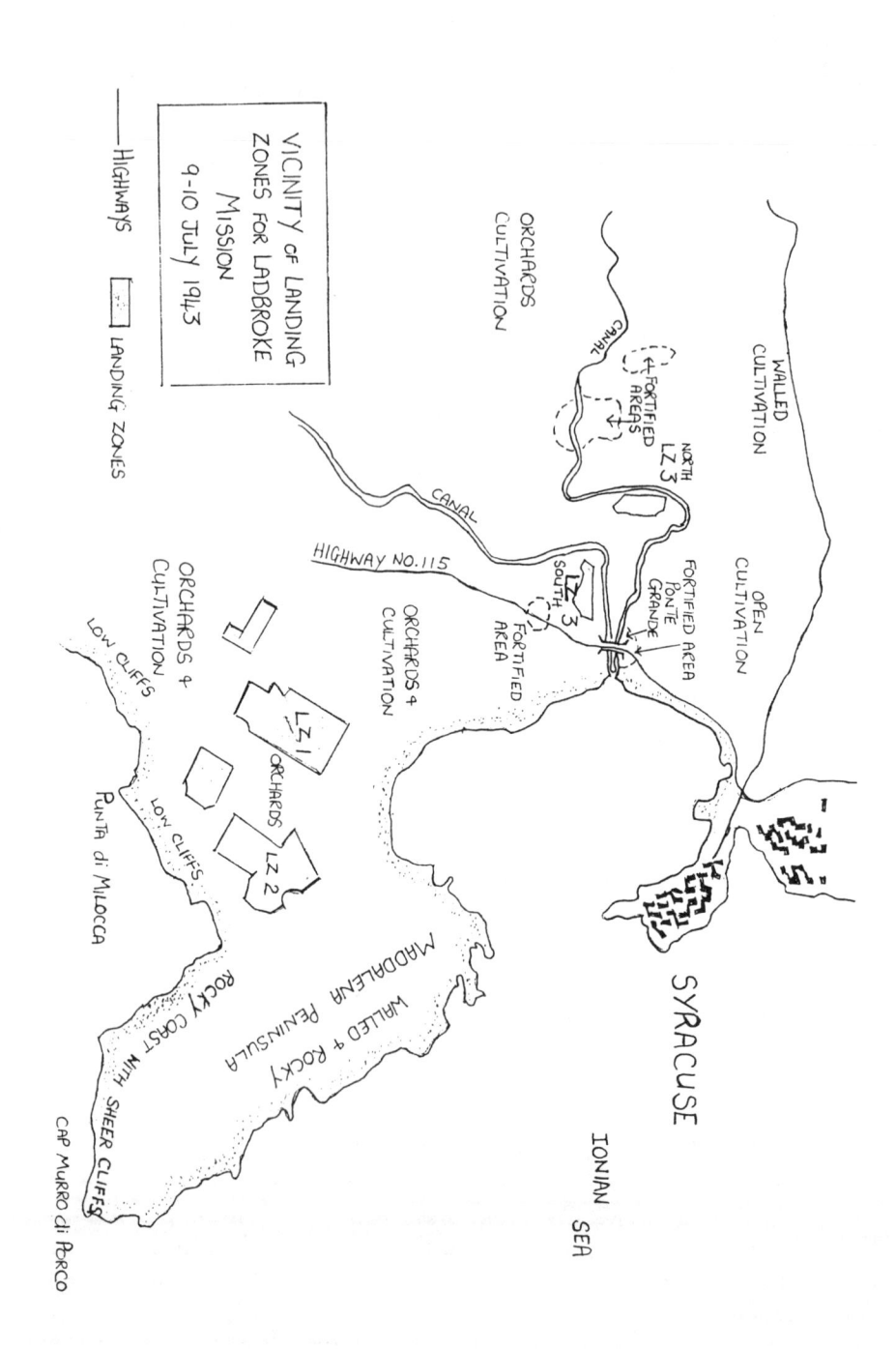

During the night the bridge party was reinforced by thirty men from 1st Border Regiment under Lieutenant Welch and more men from the South Staffords. The senior officer now present - Lieutenant Colonel A.G. Walch - assumed command with Major Breasley, Royal Engineers, as second in command. By morning eighty-seven men were holding the bridge, armed with but two Bren guns, two mortars, sten guns and rifles with ammunition in short supply.

At 0730 hours they were joined by more of the scattered troops including two US glider pilots, Flight Officers Samuel Fine and Russel Parks, from the Waco LZ. Captain A.F. Boucher-Giles and Staff Sergeant Miller pilots of another Horsa which had been landed five miles away, also arrived and two men of the Border Regiment and a platoon of South Staffords. Captain Boucher-Giles was placed in command of the glider pilots, who now included Lieutenant A. Dale, and told to hold the south bank of the canal near the bridge.

At 0800 hours the enemy counter attacked and men of the RAMC armed with captured Italian weapons took part in the defence. Casualties began to mount among the defenders and at 0900 hours Major Breasley was killed on the south bank of the canal by a burst of machine gun fire which also killed one of the glider pilots. By 1530 hours with their ammunition gone the bridge defenders - now reduced to but fifteen unwounded men, were overrun by the enemy and the bridge recaptured. But before the Italians had a chance to blow the bridge a force of the seaborne Royal Scots Fusiliers arrived and in a spirited attack re-took the bridge at 1615 hours.

The glider force landed all over the place but the occupants who survived the crash landings and some who ditched off shore used their initiative and engaged the enemy. Glider no.7 carrying a party of South Staffords landed 250 yards off shore under fire but six of them managed to swim ashore and reached their battalion that evening taking twenty-one prisoners en route. Glider no.10 carrying Colonel O. Jones, Deputy Brigade Commander, and Staff Officers of Brigade Headquarters, was landed near to an enemy coastal battery. At 1115 hours they attacked and overran it though lightly armed. Five field guns and the ammunition store was blown up. Colonel Jones was awarded the DSO for the action. 1st Air Landing Brigade later received this message from General Montgomery:

'For those responsible for this particular operation I am filled with admiration. Others who by their initiative fought isolated actions in various parts of the battlefield, have played no small part in this most successful landing action. Had it not been for the skill and gallantry of the Air Landing Brigade, the Port of Syracuse would not have fallen until very much later.'

General Montgomery later said that the taking of the Ponte Grande bridge saved his forces seven days but the cost was high - 605 men of whom 326 were missing in action, probably drowned in their gliders before reaching the battlefield.

The operation was costly, which could be ascribed to various factors: the dust clouds blowing over the LZs, landing at night without landing aids, but mainly to the fact that most of the gliders had to release too far offshore and too low for the glider pilots to fly to their LZs. Five of the eight Horsas involved reached Sicily all towed by the Royal Air Force.

The 2nd South Staffords earned three Military Crosses and five Military Medals during the capture of the Ponte Grande bridge. Lieutenant Withers was recommended for the Distinguished Service Order,(DSO) but received the Military Cross specifically for the bridge capture. The South Staffordshire Regiment holds the unique distinction of being the first British regiment to go to battle by land, sea and air. Both the South Staffords and the 1st Border Regiment share the distinction of being the first British regiments to be carried to battle in gliders. In recognition of this His Majesty King George VI granted them the distinction of wearing an embroidered glider badge at the top of the sleeve of No.1 Dress and battledress, to commemorate the part played by them on the night of the 9th-10th July 1943, the first occasion in which British gliderborne troops took part in a major tactical operation.

The 2nd South Staffords suffered 350 casualties many of whom perished in the sea. 1st Border Regiment took 250 casualties and 45 British and 13 US glider pilots died, some at sea others in action.

The glider pilots received the following decorations:

Staff Sergeant D. Galpin was awarded the Distinguished Flying Medal for his part in the Ponte Grande assault. Lieutenants (then) Boucher-Giles and Dale were awarded the Distinguished Flying Cross. Captain McMillen and Lieutenant Halsall received the Military Cross. Lieutenant Colonel Chatterton was awarded the Distinguished Service Order. Staff Sergeant Garrat received the Distinguished Conduct Medal and Staff Sergeant Moore the Military Medal. Flight Officer Samuel Fine - the US glider pilot who had been wounded three times during the action at the Ponte Grande bridge - was recommended for the US Silver Star for his actions in battle. The recommendation was turned down by US General Clark, Commanding Officer, 52nd Troop Carrier Wing, who merely awarded the US Purple Heart Medal, which is awarded to any US wounded personnel. Colonel Chatterton awarded Flight Officer Fine the flying brevet of the Glider Pilot Regiment, which the US Officer wore on the right breast of uniform.

Operation Ladbrooke had not been a success in spite of the gallantry of the glider pilots, glider borne soldiers and Royal Air Force tug crews and can best be described in the words of Staff Sergeant Galpin to the author. 'The operation was not really on and was carried out by glider pilots who had far too little experience in night flying'.

# OPERATION FUSTIAN (Marston)

The second airborne operation by British Forces in the overall scheme of the Sicily invasion - codenamed Fustian - was to drop and land troops to take and hold the vital Primosole bridge over the River Simeto, five miles south of Catania on the east coast of Sicily, to allow the British 8th Army to drive through into the Catainian Plain northwards towards Messina.

Fustian was to be a combined paratroop and gliderborne operation by the British 1st Parachute Brigade under Brigadier Lathbury, together with men from the Royal Engineers 1st Parachute Squadron under Major Murray, and 16th Parachute Field Ambulance, Royal Army Medical Corps. A total of 1856 men carried by 116 aircraft of the USAAF and RAF - 105 Dakotas of the US 51st Troop Carrier Wing and 11 Albemarles of 38 Wing, RAF.

After the paratroops had landed eight Waco CG4A (Hadrian) and eleven Horsa gliders towed by twelve Albemarles of 296 Squadron RAF, and seven Halifax aircraft of 295 Squadron RAF, carrying seventy seven Royal Artillery gunners, of 1st Airlanding Anti Tank Battery, ten 6-pounder guns and eighteen vehicles would land on two LZs (LZS 7 & 8) to the south and north west of the Primosole bridge. For the first time paratroops of the 21st Independent Parachute Company would act as Pathfinders and light the LZs for the incoming glider pilots.

The dirt airstrips A, B, C, D, E, and F near Kairouan, Tunisia, used for the previous Operation Ladbrooke, were to be used again, as was the airborne RV over the Kuriate Islands off the coast of Tunisia. A similar flight route to Operation Ladbrooke was planned: east to Malta then north east to Sicily but the run in to Sicily was changed to keep the aerial fleet ten miles off the east coast of Sicily, to avoid Allied naval forces off this coast. Cruising altitude to be 500 feet.

At 1920 hours on the 12th July, 1943, the USAAF 51st Troop carrier Wing began to take off from airstrips A, B, C and D and head for the Kuriate Islands RV. At 2200 hours 38 Wing RAF, began to tow off nineteen gliders. Two Waco and one Horsa gliders had to abort the mission - leaving the remaining sixteen gliders to set course for the RV.

At 1953 hours the paratroop carrying aircraft left the RV for Malta, one Dakota and one Albemarle had to return to base with engine trouble before reaching Malta. One Horsa glider was accidently released over the sea - fifteen gliders were left to continue the operation.

The Dakota aircraft flew at 140mph, the Albemarles towing gliders at 125mph and the Halifaxes at 145mph, all in loose streams of two to eleven aircraft

ROUTE of FUSTIAN MISSION
13-14 July 1943

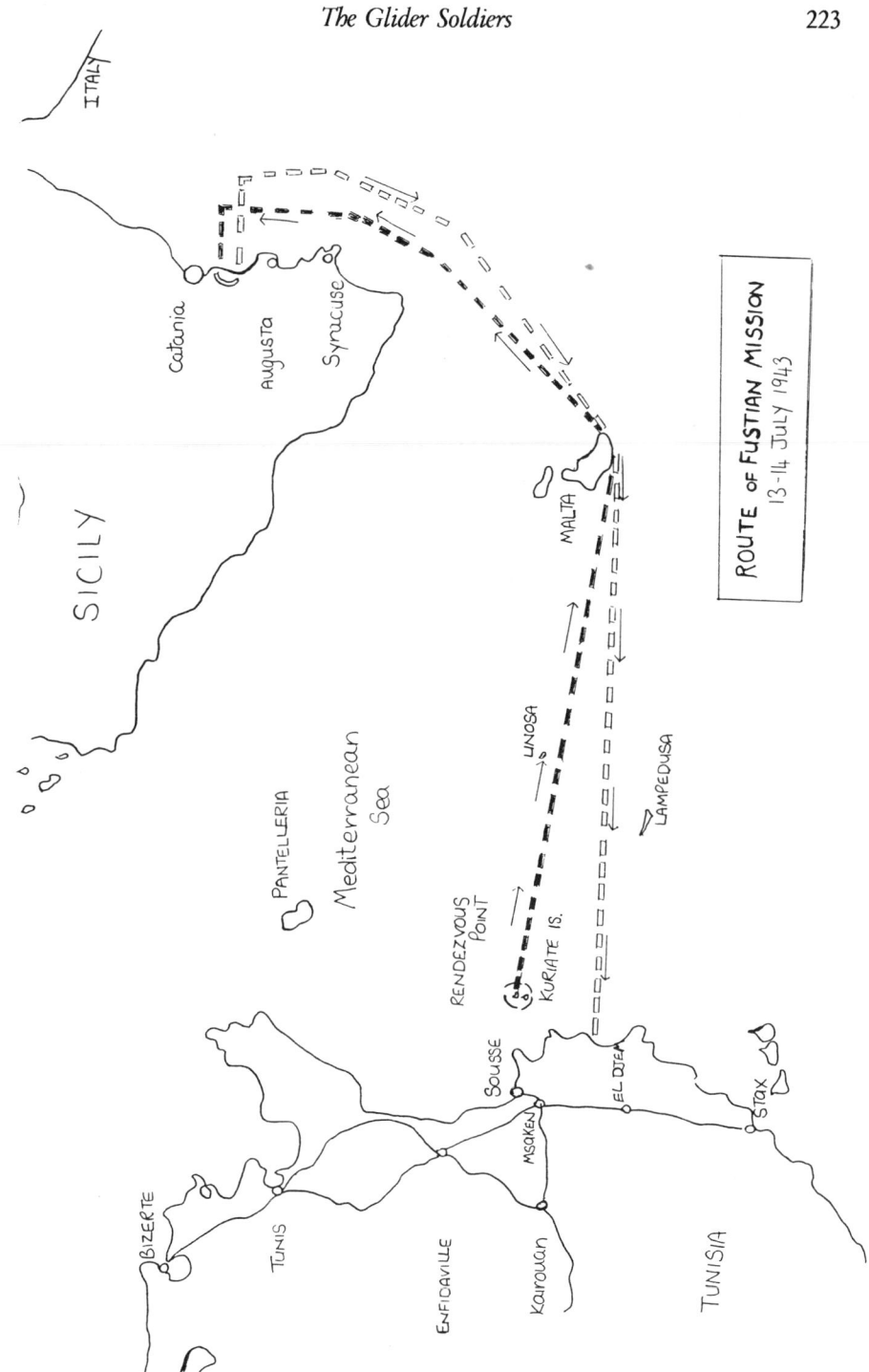

spaced at thirty second intervals. The USAAF pilots were now using the Royal Air Force stream flying pattern instead of their accustomed V formation.

The Naval Commanders of the Allied invasion fleet lying off the eastern coast of Sicily had been informed of the Fustian operation, flight route and schedule as there was a five mile 'no go' area for aircraft off the invasion coast. All the pilots on the Fustian operation had been instructed to keep clear of the 'no go' area.

However as the airborne fleet approached Cape Passero, Sicily, some allied ships opened fire on them. Some of the aircraft, thought to be at least thirty-three, had been flown off course into the danger anti-aircraft fire zone. (Later enquiries revealed that some thirty aircraft had been fired on by Allied naval ships in an area between eight and twenty-three miles off the invasion coast).

Two aircraft were shot down by Allied naval ships and a further nine had to turn back due to damage and injuries. Another six aircraft turned back to base - the pilots later said that they had been so instructed by their Squadron Commander.

The remainder flew on encountering enemy flak between Syracuse and Catania. Nine paratroop aircraft were shot down but most had managed to drop their troops. Four of the nine managed to ditch in the sea. Three glider towing aircraft went missing, believed shot down. Fourteen aircraft in total were shot down, another thirty-four were damaged and one was destroyed by striking the cable of a barrage balloon.

Owing to the flak some paratroops were dropped over a wide area - some were dropped near Mount Etna volcano, twenty miles from their DZ. Dropping began at 2215 hours but it was 0100 hours before Brigadier Lathbury had collected some 100 men to take the Primosole bridge objective. When Brigadier Lathbury's party arrived at the Primosole bridge they found that a fifty-strong party of 1st Parachute Battalion under Captain Rann, had taken it at 0215 hours.

Whilst the battle for the bridge was in progress the glider force began to arrive over the area searching for their LZs which were clearly visible in the light of intense enemy flak. Major A. Cooper, AFC, the veteran of Operation Beggar, with the Royal Artillery Commander, Lieutenant Colonel C. Crawford and his staff aboard glider 127, saw his tow plane hit by flak when they were at 500 feet. Major Cooper and his co-pilot Sergeant C.Morgan, were unable to control the glider and crashed into a river bed losing their lives as did all the other occupants of the glider.

Only four Horsa gliders contributed to the bridge battle. One piloted by Staff Sergeant F.H. White,(DFM), circled over the LZ at 1500 feet amid enemy flak. He successfully landed his Horsa one hundred yards from the bridge on LZ8

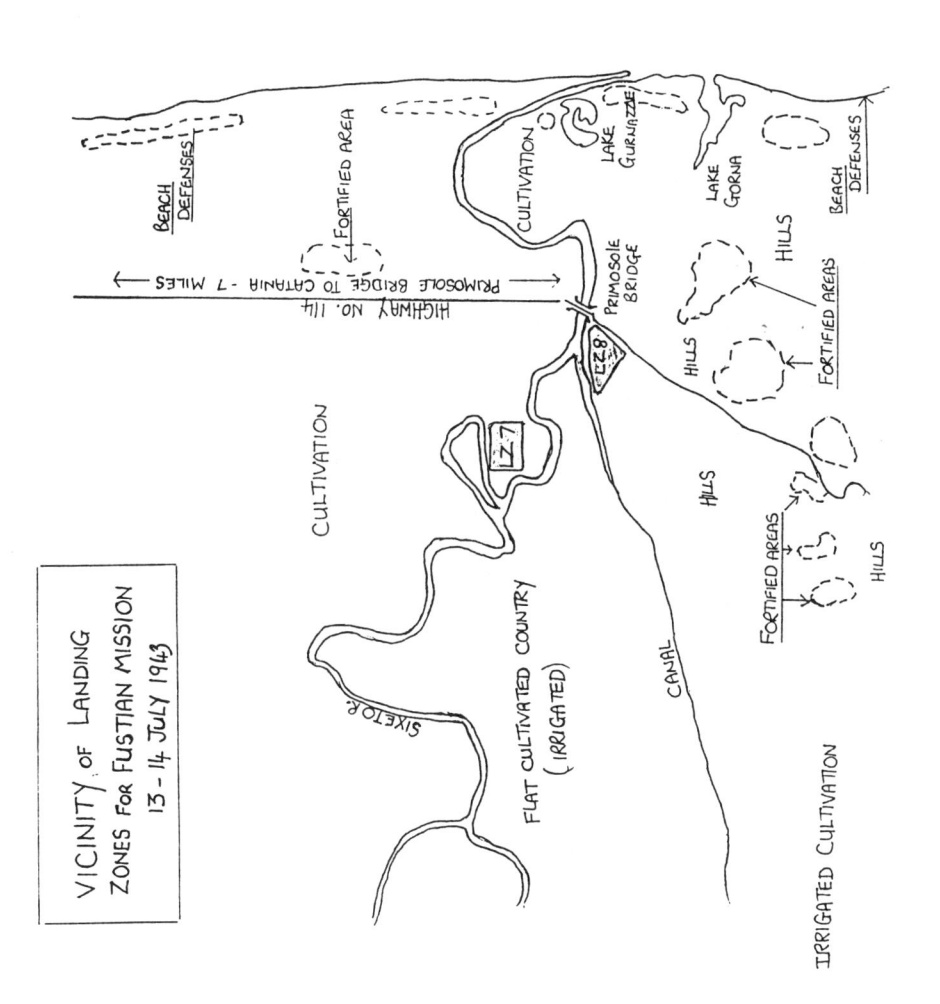

VICINITY of LANDING ZONES FOR FUSTIAN MISSION 13-14 JULY 1943

leaving part of the Horsa's undercarriage actually on the bridge. The glider gun load was off loaded and later brought into action. Another Horsa piloted by Staff Sergeants H.G. Protheroe, (DFM), and Kerr, landed on the LZ south west of the bridge and the occupants came under machine-gun fire from a pillbox on the south west corner of the bridge. The glider load of 6-pounder gun and jeep were extracted from the damaged glider and dug in to protect the bridge. Lieutenant Thomas landed his glider in a ravine some seven miles away from the bridge but managed to get his gun load into action next day at the bridge. Another Horsa landed half a mile west of the LZ. Lieutenant W.N. Barrie (DFC) one of those who had landed his Horsa successfully, fought with his men for three days. (He was later to lose his life at Arnhem).

The glider pilots and men of the Royal Artillery fought alongside the paratroops at the bridge - the glider pilots, after being shown how, fired the 6-pounder anti-tank guns all day. Of the fifteen gliders which approached Sicily four were missing probably shot down by flak, three made fatal crash landings. Staff Sergeant T. Montague and Sergeant F. Street in glider 118 on LZ7 and Sergeant J. Broadheadand WO J. Preston on LZ 8. Four landed among the enemy and most of the occupants were taken prisoner. Only the four Horsa gliders previously mentioned were of effective use in the bridge battle.

Dawn broke the next day with about 200 troops defending the bridge armed with but two mortars, three anti-tank gun and one heavy machine-gun. At 0930 hours radio contact was established for half an hour with 4th Armoured Brigade fighting their way from Syracuse to relieve the airborne troops. The enemy attacked at noon and at 1400 hours in strength but both attacks were repelled. But By 1900 hours the bridge position was becoming untenable for the British airborne troops as the enemy was attacking in strength from the north, east and south. The airborne troops were now running out of ammunition and in spite of using captured enemy weapons, they were forced to withdraw from the bridge.

However, at dawn on the 16th July the Durham Light Infantry counter-attacked and re-took the bridge at their second attempt, the first having being driven back with heavy casualties.

The price paid by the airborne forces was high. The combined casualties of the USAAF 51st Troop carrier Wing and the Royal Air Force 38 Wing were, one known dead, thirty-five missing in action and fourteen wounded. The veteran of Operation Freshman - Squadron Leader A.M.B. Wilkinson, and his crew failed to return to base believed shot down. The Glider Pilot Regiment lost fifty-seven soldier pilots in Operations Ladbrooke and Fustian, 12 pilots alone on Fustian. 1st Parachute Brigade suffered two hundred and ninety-five men killed wounded or missing.

A post mortem on both Ladbrooke and Fustian was dismal, although both objectives were eventually taken. Many lessons were learned and put to good use in later gliderborne operations. The unintended dispersed airborne landings in Sicily confused the enemy and there is no doubt that the Airborne Forces prevented the enemy from driving the first sea borne forces back into the sea.

# OPERATION BUNGHOLE

The first British daylight glider operation of WWII in German occupied Yugoslavia on the 19th February 1944.

When 1st Airborne Division returned to the United Kingdom in October 1944, they left behind parts of the division which were later designated 2nd Independent Parachute Brigade Group - with supporting air landing units and 3rd Squadron, Glider Pilot Regiment, known from January 1944, as the 1st Independent Glider Squadron, Glider Pilot Regiment, commanded by Major Robin Coulthard. The whole formation came under direct command of Commander, Mediterranean, Caserta.

The glider pilots already experienced veterans of the Sicily airborne landings, went into further training at Comiso, Sicily, with 64th Troop Carrier Group of the 51st Wing of the North Africa Troop Carrier Command, USAAF. The 64th TCG had performed well in the Sicily paratroop operations when they had kept formation when dropping their troops. The Americans using C47 Dakota aircraft as glider tugs, gave their whole-hearted support to the training, making all facilities available without stint.

The Pathfinder Company of 2 Parachute Brigade commanded by Captain Peter Baker, was a vital part of this training and co-operation. Together, glider pilots, tug crews and Pathfinders reached standards of competence hitherto unknown. Using Horsa and Waco Hadrian gliders, experimental training was carried out with loads, heights, limits, navigation by day and night and landing with out landing lights.

The US was still delivering crated Waco CG4A Hadrian gliders to Casablanca where, after assembly, they were flown by the Independent Squadron from Tunis to Sicily towed by USAAF tugs. The strained relations between the USAAF and the British Glider pilots improved out of all recognition.

For political reasons the British Government wished to deliver a Russian Military Mission to Marshal Tito at his inaccessible mountain Headquarters at Drvar in Yugoslavia. British Intelligence Force 133 requested the Independent Squadron to carry out the operation using three Horsa gliders. As there were no Horsa gliders available at this time in Sicily Major Coulthard detailed Captain Cornelius Turner and a party of glider pilots to fly to Tunis with the 64th TCG and check the condition of Horsas known to be there.

In Tunsia the Horsa were checked over by a small part of RAF Riggers who had motored from Algiers. The sergeant fitter in charge thought the gliders were serviceable once the glider pilots had shovelled them clean of sand. Trusting to the strength of the wooden Horsas the glider pilots embarked and were towed back to Sicily by the 64th TCG.

Back at Comiso the Horsas were flight tested and doubts were raised by the USAAF as to whether the C47 Dakotas could tow the Horsas over the mountains of Yugoslavia and into the interior so the Independent squadron agreed to use the US Hadrians instead.

The plan of the operation was to deliver by glider in daylight about thirty six senior Russian officers led by Marshal Korneyev, to a point on a mountainside called Mendenapolu, two kilometres north west of the town of Bosan Petrovac, one hundred miles inland from the Yugoslavian port of Split. This would be the first daylight glider operation of the war. An outward escort of twenty-four Spitfires would accompany the glider formation over the sea to the enemy coast when another escort of twenty-four US Mustang long range fighters taking over to the target LZ. Fifty US B17 Flying Fortresses would carry out a diversionary raid on Zagreb at the same time.

The Russian Military Mission took part in the loaded flying trials of the Hadrians, each Russian occupying the place he would take on the operation. They could have been dropped by parachute into Yugoslavia but preferred to take their chances in gliders.

The three Waco glider crews chosen for the hazardous operation - now code named Bunghole - were:

Hadrian No.1.　Captain C. Turner (Commander) and Staff Sergeant Newman.
Hadrian No.2.　Staff Sergeant McCulloch and Staff Sergeant Hill.
Hadrian No.3.　Staff Sergeant Morrison and Staff Sergeant McMillen.

The three towing USAAF C47 Dakotas of 64th TCG commanded by Lieutenant Colonel Duden, had Australian, New Zealand and South African navigators - making the operation inter Allied indeed.

At 1100 hours on the 19th February 1944, the three combinations lifted off from Bari, Italy, and set course due north in clear visibility for their target. Just before the take off a Force 133 Officer handed Captain Turner six suicide phials for use by the pilots if captured by the enemy. The Russian Mission split up into three groups aboard the three Hadrians. Marshal Korneyev sitting on two large cases for some unknown reason. A large Russian OGPU Colonel sat behind Captain Turner clutching a sub-machine gun with the muzzle only six inches from Turner's head. Climbing out over the sea in unlimited visibility they made rendezvous with their fighter escort.

In the clear visibility they could see the towering saw toothed mountains of Yugoslavia from sixty miles away. Passing dead on track over Split - they approached the peaks. Turbulence began and the pilots had to work hard to control their bucketing gliders. The formation passed over the ice tipped mountain peaks with only a hundred feet to spare.

As the interior opened up to the formation the pilots saw that it was covered with a carpet of snow making navigation difficult but then the straw fires marking the LZ were in view. At 3000 feet Captain Turner took over the controls of his glider from Newman who pulled the tow release cable and they were in free flight four or five miles away from the LZ dead ahead. Turner's towing C47 piloted by Captain Wendell C. Little dropped the tow cable and swung round to head back home.

Captain Turner dropped his speed to 70mph and swung to port with the other two gliders below him and going straight on. The escorting Mustang fighters wheeled over the LZ waiting till the three gliders were down. Turner saw that his other two gliders had swung round well above his glider and were overtaking him fast. The three gliders dropped into three feet of snow in perfect landings. The deep snow had had a braking effect on the Hadrians reducing their landing run to about twenty feet and after the gliders had gone nose down into the snow they gently settled back onto an even keel. The gliders had arrived right on target thanks to the USAAF tug crews. With a roar of engines the escorting Mustangs made a mock beat up of the Lz then they were gone.

Getting out of the gliders, everyone embraced everybody else: the Partisans, Drugs (pronounced Droogs) Serbian for Comrade, as they were called, armed to the teeth with cartridge bandoliers on their chests, rifles, knives and grenades, swarmed all over the occupants of the gliders in welcome.

Anchoring the Hadrians with fallen timber the glider occupants were led to sleighs drawn by ponies and taken to the small town of Petrovac nearby. For the next six hours till midnight the glider pilots ate and drank toasts to all and sundry in the 5000 inhabitant town. The secret of Marshal Korneyov's crates was revealed - they contained vodka and caviare which was duly despatched.

The glider pilots McCulloch, Newman, Morrison, Hill and McMillen were billeted together on the northern edge of the town and Captain Turner with the already landed officers of the resident British-American Military Mission under Brigadier Fitzroy Maclean. The Mission's function was to liaise with Cairo and arrange for the collection of downed aircrew, arms drops to the Partisans, and keep the Allies informed as to the state of affairs in Yugoslavia. To this end there was a Sergeant and six signallers to keep in communication with the outside world and operate the homing beacons on the local LZ.

Captain Turner realised that the Germans - who daily machine gunned the LZ from a patrolling JU88 - if they saw the landed Hadrians, might emulate the British example and attack by glider: It was known that the Germans had gliders at Bihac some fifty miles away. Turner asked the Partisans to move the gliders into the cover of trees but without result - therefore he set fire to one of the Hadrians. This had the required effect and the remaining two gliders were towed by ponies under cover of the trees. (On the 25th May 1944, the German SS 500th Parachute Mountain Battalion attacked the LZ by glider).

Five weeks later with the snow melting in the fine March weather the glider pilots were brought out by a C47 Dakota flown by Air Commodore Whitney Straight, a famous Grand Prix racing driver. There was still a foot of snow on the LZ and the Dakota had to be stripped of all unnecessary weight so that it could take off. The Dakota with the glider pilots aboard, engines roaring, bumped over the uneven LZ, still covered in a foot of snow, to successfully lift off at the last second brushing through the tree tops at the edge of the LZ before climbing out and turning south for Italy. Two hours later the glider pilots were back at Bari.

At the debriefing by a Force 133 Officer, Captain Turner was told that Partisans had been angry that he burnt the Hadrian on the LZ as they considered that the glider was theirs. What the Partisans would do with a glider was not stated - they had no glider tugs. Turner was also told that he had been considered for Court Martial because of the incident.

Captain Turner recommended Staff Sergeants McCulloch and Morrison (the first pilots on the other two gliders) for the Distinguished Flying Medal which were duly awarded some two weeks later. Turner did not receive any decoration in spite of being the Operation Commander.

On the 25th May 1944, the Germans attacked Tito's HQ at Drvar and other Partisan strongholds including the LZ used by the British gliders. Tito with the British and Russian Military Mission were escape into the mountains and were later evacuated from Kupresko Polje to Bari by a Russian C47 - one of twelve stationed at Bari. From the British point of view the operation had been a success with the British glider pilots making it possible by landing their gliders in snow on a hillside LZ.

# OVERLORD - THE INVASION OF NORMANDY

Glossary of codenames and terms used:
| | |
|---|---|
| Ct | - Civil twilight. |
| CdeM | - Coup de Main. |
| D-Day | - The actual day, minus before plus afterwards. |
| Eureka | - Portable ground radio beacon. |
| H Hour | - The time of landing of seaborne assault forces. |
| Holophane | - Landing light emitting narrow angle beam. |
| Mallard | - Second British airborne operation of D-Day. |
| Neptune | - The amphibious operations within Overlord. |
| Overlord | - The Allied invasion of Europe (Normandy). |
| Rebecca | - Airborne part of Eureka beacon. |
| Tonga | - First British airborne operation of D-Day. |
| Pathfinder | - Paratroops dropped to mark DZ prior to main drops. |

Planning for the invasion of Europe started in 1940. Even before the last British troops had been evacuated from France to England, the British War Office was at work drawing up plans for the eventual return.

In July 1941, the Inter Services Training and Development Centre produced the first invasion plans which were tried out in the ill-fated British and Canadian raid on Dieppe on the 19th August 1943. Early in 1943 the United States and British leaders had met at Casablanca, North Africa, to plan the future conduct of WWII. High on the agenda was the invasion of Europe - desperately being called for by the Russians to relieve the German pressure on their forces.
But the US and Britain were not yet ready for the invasion - the US had to ship large armies to England and that took time.

One step was agreed on - to appoint Lieutenant General F. Morgan, (British) as Chief of General Staff, to the Supreme Allied Commander, an odd situation as no Supreme Commander had been appointed. General Morgan was instructed to make plans for the invasion of France in the summer of 1944.
In August 1943, the US and British leaders met at Quebec and General Morgan's plans for the invasion - Codenamed Overlord - were approved. In December 1943, US General Dwight D. Eisenhower was appointed Supreme Commander, Allied Expeditionary Force, to carry out the plans with his forces.

The basic plan decided on was for a seaborne assault by Allied Armies landing along the coast of Normandy at 0730 hours on the 6th June 1944. The Allied Airborne troops would be used on the right and left flanks to secure and hold ground and prevent enemy reinforcements counter attacking. 6th Airborne

Division would assault, secure and hold the British left flank, landing in four Phases with specific tasks allocated to units within the division.

Code names for the British airborne operations were:

Operation Tonga - Objectives.
To secure and hold two bridges over the River Orne and Caen Canal by Coup de Main attack. (Operation Deadstick).
To secure a base - including above bridgeheads - east of the River Orne.

To capture or neutralize a German gun battery at Merville.
To prevent enemy reinforcements moving from the south east towards the British left flank.

Operation Mallard: Objectives.
Bring in reinforcements of 6th Air Landing Brigade, tanks and artillery.

Divisional/Gliderborne Plan.
First Phase/down time 0020 hours CT-5 hours.
Coup de Main 2nd Oxford & Bucks. Six Horsa gliders.
The six Horsa gliders would release at 6000 feet and land without landing aids on LZs X and Y. Troops carried would take the bridges over the River Orne and the Caen Canal. The six Halifax aircraft towing gliders will after release, proceed to bomb the cement factory at Caen with 2500lb General Purpose bombs each. The object of this bombing is to distract attention from the glider landings.

Second Phase/down time 0045 to 0103 hours. CT-4.34, 4.30hrs
Seventeen Horsa gliders.

| | |
|---|---|
| HQ 3 Para Brigade | 2 |
| 8 Parachute Battalion | 5 |
| 9 Parachute Battalion | 3 |
| 1 Canadian Parachute Battalion | 3 |
| 224 Parachute Field Ambulance | 2 |
| Det. 4 Airlanding Anti-Tank Battery, RA. | 2 |
| | 17 |

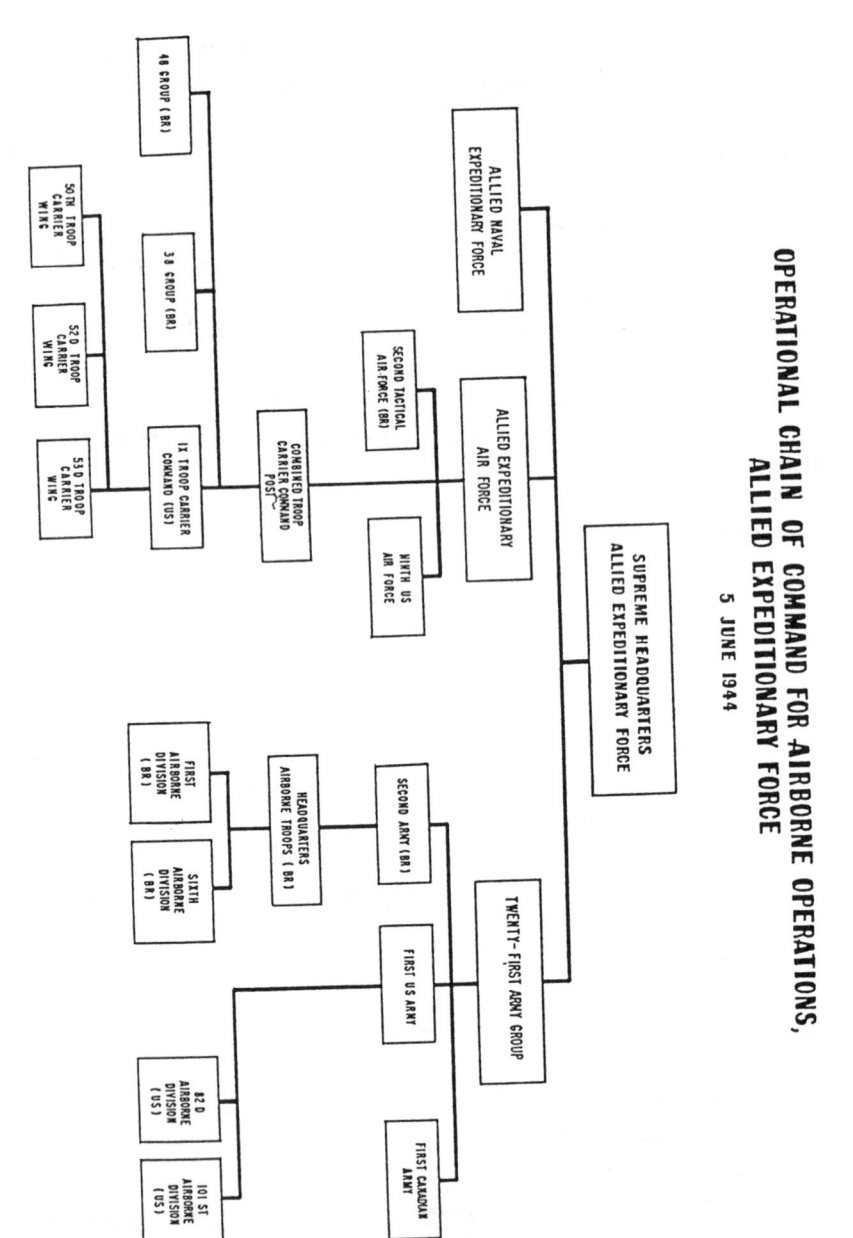

## OPERATIONAL CHAIN OF COMMAND FOR AIRBORNE OPERATIONS, ALLIED EXPEDITIONARY FORCE
### 5 JUNE 1944

```
SUPREME HEADQUARTERS ALLIED EXPEDITIONARY FORCE
├── ALLIED NAVAL EXPEDITIONARY FORCE
├── ALLIED EXPEDITIONARY AIR FORCE
│   ├── SECOND TACTICAL AIR FORCE (BR)
│   ├── COMBINED TROOP CARRIER COMMAND POST
│   │   ├── 38 GROUP (BR)
│   │   │   └── 46 GROUP (BR)
│   │   └── IX TROOP CARRIER COMMAND (US)
│   │       ├── 50TH TROOP CARRIER WING
│   │       ├── 52D TROOP CARRIER WING
│   │       └── 53D TROOP CARRIER WING
│   └── NINTH US AIR FORCE
└── TWENTY-FIRST ARMY GROUP
    ├── SECOND ARMY (BR)
    │   └── HEADQUARTERS AIRBORNE TROOPS (BR)
    │       ├── FIRST AIRBORNE DIVISION (BR)
    │       └── SIXTH AIRBORNE DIVISION (BR)
    ├── FIRST US ARMY
    │   ├── 82D AIRBORNE DIVISION (US)
    │   └── 101ST AIRBORNE DIVISION (US)
    └── FIRST CANADIAN ARMY
```

Eleven Horsa gliders carrying support equipment for the Merville battery assault would land on DZ V. Six Horsa gliders carrying support equipment for parachute troops would land on DZ K. Both groups will land some five minutes in advance of the main paratroop party.

Third Phase/down time 0300 to 0430 hours.CT-2.00hrs.
Seventy-five gliders.
| | |
|---|---|
| HQ 6th Airborne Division (including RE & RA) | 20 |
| Forward Observation Officers. | 8 |
| 5th Parachute Brigade HQ. | 8 |
| 4th Airlanding Anti-Tank Battery. | 24 |
| Royal Engineers Bridge and Mechanical equipment | 8 |
| 9th Parachute Battalion Merville battery assault party | 3 |
| Royal Artillery 17-pdr anti-tank guns and vehicle | 4 Hamilcar |
| | 75 |

Three Horsa gliders will land on the Merville battery which will have been previously attacked by 100 Lancaster bombers - bombing from 8-10,000 feet and which will be under attack by previously dropped paratroops as the gliders land. The gliders will land on the pin point inside the battery defences as briefed. Immediately before landing at a height of 500 feet, the second pilot of the glider will flash three dots on the glider landing light. On this signal the ground forces will illuminate the landing area. Sixty-eight Horsa and four Hamilcar gliders will land on LZ N on three strips which will have been cleared of obstacles by the paratroop force which dropped earlier.

Fourth Phase/down time 2100 hours.
Two hundred and fifty-six gliders.
| | |
|---|---|
| HQ 6th AirLanding Brigade | 15 |
| 1st Royal Ulster Rifles | 74 |
| 2nd Oxford & Bucks. | 65 |
| "A" Company, 12th Devons | 8 |
| 195th Airlanding Field Ambulance | 6 |
| Armoured Recce Regiment | 21 Horsas |
| " " " | 26 Hamilcars |
| 3rd Air Landing Anti-Tank Battery | 4 Hamilcars |
| 211th Air Landing Battery, Royal Artillery. | 27 |
| 716th Light Company Royal Army Service Corps. | 10 |
| | 256 |

Two hundred and fifty-six Horsa and Hamilcar gliders to bring in men, tanks and guns to LZs .

Navigation Aids en Route.
Special Eureka and light beacons will be situated at the points of departure on the English coast at Group RVs in the following positions:

|  | Light Flashing | Eureka Channel |
|---|---|---|
| Group RV1 | Worthing V | CA |
| Group RV2 | Littlehampton K | DC |
| Croup RV3 | Bognor Regis N | ED |

Return Route.
All aircraft will enter UK over Littlehampton at a height of 3000 feet.

Landing Aids at LZs/DZs.
Ground aids will not be available at DZs/LZs for the advance parties which land at the same time as the Pathfinder Force.

      Standard markings are to be be laid out to guide Main bodies. Zone N which is to be used first as a Dz then as a LZ will be appropriately marked for each type of operation i.e. DZ marking for paratroop landings at CT-4.30 hours, will be changed to LZ marking for glider landing at CT-2 hours. The positions of Eurekas on this zone however, will not be changed and, therefore, will be offset from the line of run in of the tug/glider combinations from Target RV to LZ. For glider landings at CT-2 hours, three strips will be cleared of obstacles and lit in accordance with the diagram below. The "T" will show landing directing from south to north for all cases, excepting a wind of over 10mph from 155 degrees to 225 degrees when the "T" will show landing from north to south.

          \*          \*          \*

  \*    \* \* \* \*
Flashing light
Green.
          \*          \*          \*

Clusters of 3 Air Sea Rescue torches on all corners.
"T" to be Green Holophane lights.
Standard markings are to be laid out to guide the main paratroop aircraft to DZs "K" and "V". Glider aircraft landing on these zones will not have standard

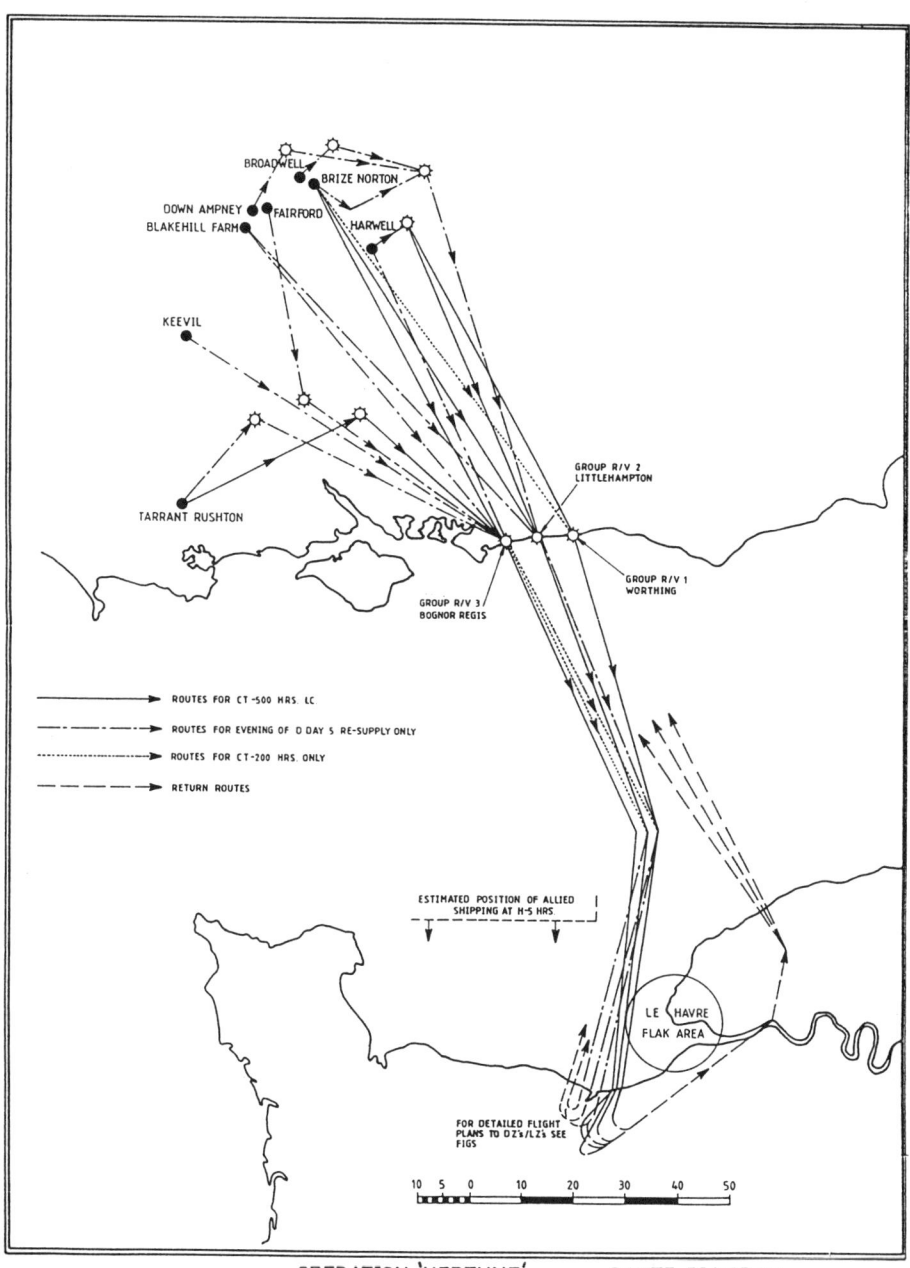

OPERATION 'NEPTUNE' ROUTE DIAGRAM

markings for gliders and glider pilots are to be warned that the normal lighting for paratroops aircraft will be showing at the time of landing. These lights will be laid out on the normal parachute run in from north to south and should be used for area guidance only.

Pathfinders will set up Eureka beacons as near briefed positions as possible. The coding holophane light at the tail of the "T" is to be sited well clear of trees etc. so that it may be clearly seen at a distance by aircraft approaching at low altitudes. Eureka should be set up and working 8 minutes and lights 5 minute before the scheduled time of arrival of the main bodies.

All pilots are to be prepared for variations in, or in the worst cases absence of, lighting as the result of enemy action. Tug and glider crews must use map reading from the coast to locate LZ or DZs where marking lights are absent.

Eureka data at LZ/DZ.

| DZ/LZ | Stream | Position | Channel | Code Letter |
|---|---|---|---|---|
| N | Right hand | 123747 | ED | N |
| N | Left hand | 128741 | AB | N |
| K | | 131699 | DC | K |
| V | | 174759 | CA | V |

Available British glider tug aircraft and gliders: 38 and 46 Groups, Royal Air Force.

| Phase I. | | | | |
|---|---|---|---|---|
| Hour | Station | No of aircraft | Load | LZ/DZ |
| CT-5 | Tarrant Rushton | 6 Halifax | 298 Sqdn.CdeM | X & Y |
| Phase II. | | | | |
| CT-4.35 | Harwell | 4 Albemarle | 295 Sqdn.9th Para. | V |
| CT-4.35 | Down Ampney | 7 Dakota | 271 Sqdn.1st Para. | V |
| CT-4.35 | Blakehill Farm | 6 Dakota | 233 Sqdn.8th Para. | K |
| Phase III. | | | | |
| CT-2 | Brize Norton | 3 Albemarle | 297 Sqdn. Merville battery | |
| CT-2 | Brize Norton | 17 Albemarle | 296 & 5th Para. 297 Sqdn. | N |
| CT-2 | Tarrant Rushton | 34 Halifax | 298 & 3 Para. | N |
| | | | 644 Sqdn Artillery | N |
| CT-2 | Harwell | 21 Albemarle | 295 & HQ6thAB | N |

Totals:
13 Dakotas, 45 Albemarles, 40 Halifaxes, 98 glider tugs.
94 Horsa, 4 Hamilcar, 98 gliders.

Phase IV.
| 2100. | Down Ampney | 37 Dakotas | 48 & 271 Sqdns |
| | Broadwell | 37 Dakotas | 512 & 575 Sqdns. |
| | Fairford | 36 Stirlings | 190 & 620 Sqdns. |
| | Brize Norton | 40 Albemarles | 296 & 297 Sqdns. |
| | Keevil | 33 Stirlings | 196 & 299 Sqdns. |
| | Harwell | 41 Albemarles | 295 & 570 Sqdns. |
| | Tarrant Rushton | 32 Halifaxes | 298 & 644 Sqdns. |

Load 1st Air Landing Brigade
Totals 74 Dakotas.
69 Stirlings.
81 Albemarles.
32 Halifaxes.
256 Tugs
15 Hamilcars.
226 Horsas.
256 gliders.

Overall total for both operations: 708 aircraft.

## OPERATION TONGA

The airlift by 38 and 46 Groups, Royal Air Force, on the night of the 5th-6th June 1944, of part of 6th Airborne Division to Normandy to assault, secure and hold the Allied left flank in the opening of the invasion of France.

6th Airborne Division - objectives and tasks:
1.	To secure and hold two bridges over the River Orne and Caen Canal. Operation Deadstick - Coup de Main.
2.	To secure and hold a firm base, including above bridgeheads, east of the River Orne.
3.	To neutralise a coastal battery at Merville.
4.	To prevent enemy re inforcements moving towards the British left flank from the south east.

Schedule of Operations 38 Group Operational Order 501.
Glider Pilot Orders.
Phase 1.
Coup de Main party.
Six crews of C Squadron, GPR.
Selection by Commander Glider Pilots.
Halifax/Horsa combinations as detailed below.

| Base | Serial nos | Load | Landing areas. |
|---|---|---|---|
| Tarrant Rushton | 91-93 | 2nd Oxford & Bucks | X (099747) |
| Tarrant Rushton | 94-96 | 2nd Oxford & Bucks | Y (104716) |

Release: Height 6000 feet.
Release points at Glider Pilot's discretion. Navigators will check wind speed and direction and pass information to glider crews before release.

Ground Aids: No ground aids will be available.

Landing Plan:
Serial Nos. 91 - 93 (Landing area X).
Direction of final approach and landing - south to north.
All gliders to finish landing run as far into landing area as possible. Landing pattern to be issued at briefing.
Serial Nos. 94-96 (Landing area Y).

Direction of final approach and landing north to south. All gliders to land as far into landing area as possible. Landing pattern to be issued at briefing.
Action after landing:
Military operation orders for glider pilots to be issued by 5 Para. Bde.

Six aircraft would drop Pathfinder paratroops on DZs N, K and V to mark them and establish landing aids for following paratroop drops. Twenty-one aircraft would drop the advance parties of paratroops on DZs N, K and V.

Phase II.
Advance glider party to DZ V. Eleven gliders carrying support equipment for Merville battery assault force. Seven crews of E Squadron, GPR. Selection by CO No.2 Wing.
Four crews of A Squadron, GPR. Selection by CO No.1 Wing.

Dakota/Horsa combinations detailed below:

| Base. | Serial Nos | Load | Landing area. |
|---|---|---|---|
| Down Ampney | 261-262 | HQ 3 Para Bde. | V |
| E Squadron. | 263-265 | 1 Can.Para.Bde. | |
| | 266-267 | 4 A/L A/T Bty. | |

Albemarle/Horsa combinations detailed below:

| Base | Serial Nos | Load | Landing area. |
|---|---|---|---|
| Harwell | 66-68 | 9 Para.Bn. | V |
| A Squadron. | 69 | 224 Para Fld Amb. | |

Releases: Height 1500 feet.
Release points will be detailed at briefing. Navigators will check wind speed and direction and pass this information to glider crews before release.

Ground Aids:
No ground aids will be available except paratroop lighting adjacent to landing area.

Landing Plan:
Definition of landing area to be given at briefing. All gliders to finish landing run as far into landing area as possible.

Action after landing:
Military operations for glider pilots to be issued by 3 Para. Brigade.
Advance glider party to DZ K. Six Horsa gliders carrying support equipment for paratroops.
Six crews of F Squadron, GPR.
Selection by Co No.2 Wing.

Dakota/Horsa combinations detailed below.

| Base | Serial Nos | Load | Landing area |
|---|---|---|---|
| Blakehill Farm | 218 - 222 | 3 Para. Bn. | K |
|  | 223 | 224 Para. Fd Amb. | K |

Release, Ground aids, Landing Plan and Action after landing as per advance glider party DZ V.
Two hundred and thirty-nine aircraft would drop paratroops and containers on DZs N, K and V.

Phase III.
Three Horsa gliders of B Squadron, GPR. would land on the Merville Battery as paratroops - previously dropped - attacked.
Selection by CO No.1 Wing.

| Base | Serial Nos | Load |
|---|---|---|
| Brize Norton | 27. 28. 28a | 9th Para. Bn |
|  |  | RE party. |
|  |  | RAMC party. |

Rebecca and arrester parachute gear all gliders. Star shells would be fired by attacking ground paratroops to illuminate the battery and Eureka beacons switched on.

Glider landing at CT-2 hours.
Sixty-eight Horsa and four Hamilcar gliders would land on LZ N with Divisional HQ and support equipment.
Thirty-four crews D Squadron, GPR.
Twenty-one crews A Squadron, GPR.
Seventeen crews B Squadron, GPR.
Selection by CO No.1 Wing.

Halifax/Horsa combinations detailed below:

| Base | Serial Nos | Load | Landing area |
|---|---|---|---|
| Tarrant R'ton | 97-120 | 4 A/LA/T Bty. | N |
|  | 121-124 | FOOs. Div HQ. |  |
|  | 125-126 | FOOs 3 Para. Bde. |  |
|  | 500-503 | 4 X 17-pdr guns. |  |

Albemarle/Horsa combinations detailed below:

| Base | Serial Nos | Load | Landing area |
|---|---|---|---|
| Harwell | 70-89 | Div HQ. | N |
|  | 90 | FOO 3 Para.Bde. |  |
| Brize Norton | 29-36 | 5 Para. Bde. |  |
|  | 45 | FOO 5 Para. Bde. |  |
|  | 37-44 | RE. |  |

Releases: Height 1500 feet.
Release points will be detailed at briefing. Navigators will check wind speed and direction and pass information to glider crews before release.
LZ N. Three landing strips will be available on this LZ numbered I to III in roman numerals. The holophane light T will show landing in direction from south to north for all cases. (Plan A) excepting a wind of over 10 mph from 155 degrees to 225 degrees when the T will show landing from north to south.

Landing stream.
Left. Harwell and nos. 97-111 Tarrant Rushton.
Right.Brize Norton and nos. 112-503 Tarrant Rushton.

Special Eureka and light beacons would be situated at aircraft RV points of departure on the south coast of England:

| Group RV 1. Worthing | light flashing | V Eureka | CA |
| Group RV 2. Littlehampton | " | K " | DC |
| Group RV 3. Bognor | " | N " | ED |

Return route for all aircraft to UK would be over Littlehampton. All Allied aircraft would be marked on wings and fuselage with three white and two black stripes to identify them to Allied sea, air and ground forces.

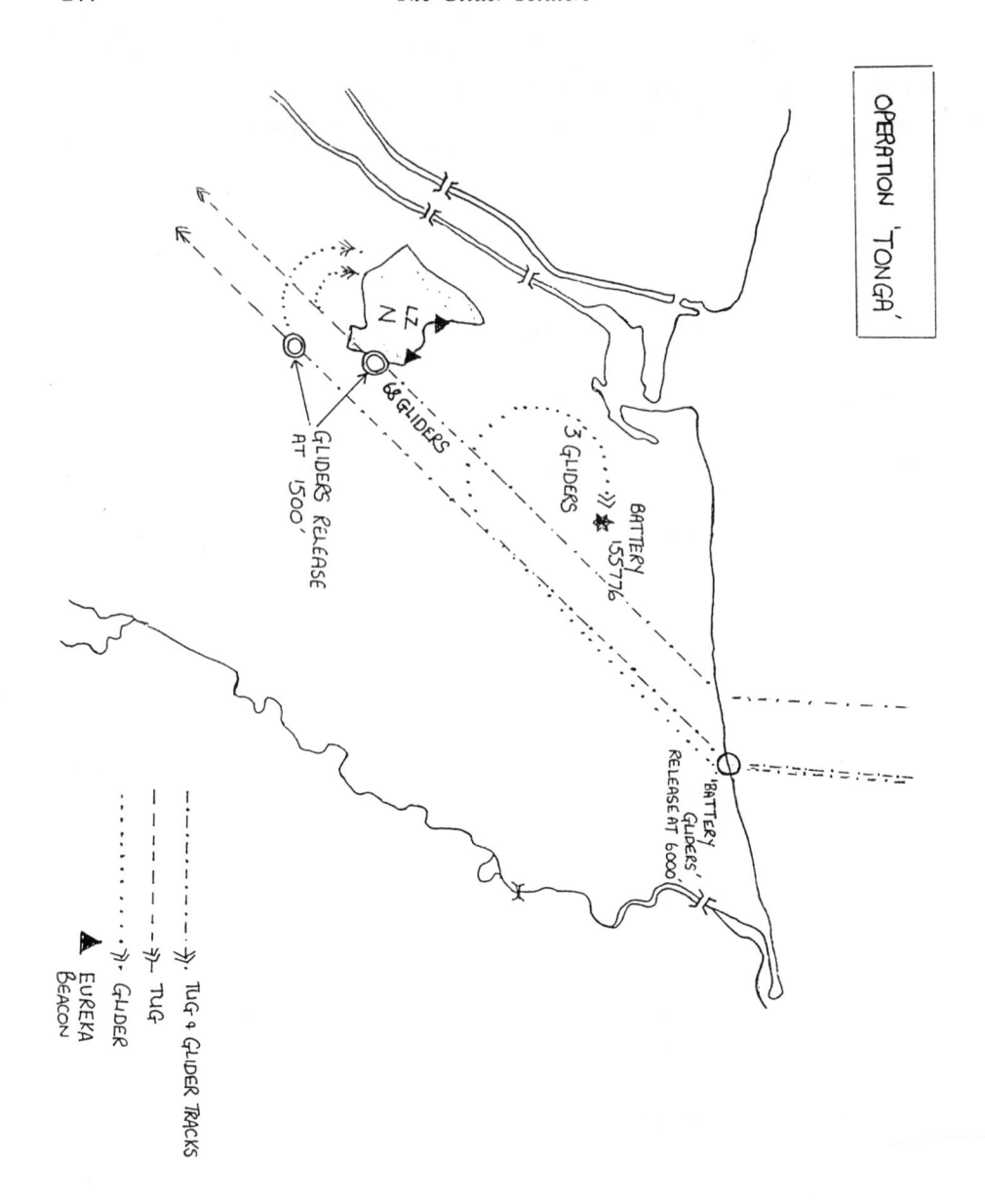

# OPERATION 'TONGA'

Phase IV
Operation Mallard. Would be on the evening of D-Day to airlift by glider 6th Air Landing Brigade, Divisional troops and tanks.

6th Airborne Division and Royal Air Force Groups allocated.
General Officer Commanding 6th Airborne Division.
Major General R.N. Gale, OBE. MC.
Divisional Headquarters.
Commandant Royal Artillery.                    Norris.
Commandant Royal Engineers.                    Lowman.
Divisional Signals.                            Tew.
Royal Army Service Corps.                      Lovegrove.
Assistant Director Medical Services.           McEwan.
Assistant Director Ordinance Services          Fielding.
Royal Electrical & Mechanical Engineers        Powditch.
Senior Chaplain to Forces.                     Hales.
Reconnaissance Regiment.                       Stuart.

3rd Parachute Brigade.
Brigadier S.J.L.Hill, DSO. MC.
8th Parachute Battalion.                       Lt. Col. Pearson
9th Parachute Battalion.                       Lt. Col. Otway
1st Canadian Parachute Battalion.              Lt. Col. Bradbrooke
211th Air Landing Light Battery, RA.
3rd Air Landing Anti-Tank Battery, RA.
3rd Parachute Squadron, RE.
224 the Parachute Field Ambulance, RAMC.

5th Parachute Brigade.
Brigadier J.H.N. Poett, DSO.
7th Parachute Battalion.        Lt. Col. Pine Coffin
12th Parachute Battalion.       Lt. Col. Johnson
13th Parachute Battalion.       Lt. Col. Luard.
212th Air Landing Light Battery, RA.
4th Air Landing Anti-Tank Battery, RA.
591st Parachute Squadron, RE.
225th Parachute Field Ambulance, RAMC.
22nd Independent Parachute Company - Pathfinders.

Glider Pilot Regiment. Colonel G.J.S. Chatterton, DSO.
No.1 Wing. Lt. Col. I.A. Murray.
A Squadron      Harwell         Major H.T. Bartlett.
B Squadron      Brize Norton    Major T.I.J. Toler.
D Squadron      Tarrant R'ton   Major J.F. Lyne.

No.2 Wing. Lt. Col. J.W. Place.
C Squadron      Tarrant R'ton   Major J.A. Dale.
E Squadron      Down Ampney     Major B.H.P. Jackson.
F Squadron      Blakehill Farm  Major F.A.S. Murray

Royal Air Force
Air Vice Marshal L.W. Hollinghurst.   (Both 38 & 46 Groups),
38 Group.
295 Squadron    Albermarle      Harwell, Berkshire.
296 Squadron    Albemarle       Brize Norton, Oxfordshire.
297 Squadron    Albemarle       Brize Norton
298 Squadron    Halifax         Tarrant Rushton, Dorset.
570 Squadron    Albemarle       Harwell, Berkshire.
644 Squadron    Halifax         Tarrant Rushton, Dorset.
46 Group.
233 Squadron    Dakota          Blakehill Farm, Wiltshire.
271 Squadron    Dakota          Down Ampney, Wiltshire.

Aircraft.        Dakota    13.
                 Albemarle 45.
                 Halifax   40.
Total                      98.
Gliders.         Horsa     94.
                 Hamilcar   4.
Total                      98.

Tonga.
At 2249 hours on the evening of the 5th June 1944, seven Horsa gliders of E Squadron, Glider Pilot Regiment, were towed off from RAF Down Ampney by Dakota tugs of 271 Squadron led by Wing Commander Booth in Dakota KG 545 and made for LZ V in Normandy with close support equipment for the 9th Battalion, Parachute Regiment who were to assault and neutralise the coastal gun battery at Merville. A minute later at RAF Blakehill Farm, six Horsa gliders of F

# The Glider Soldiers

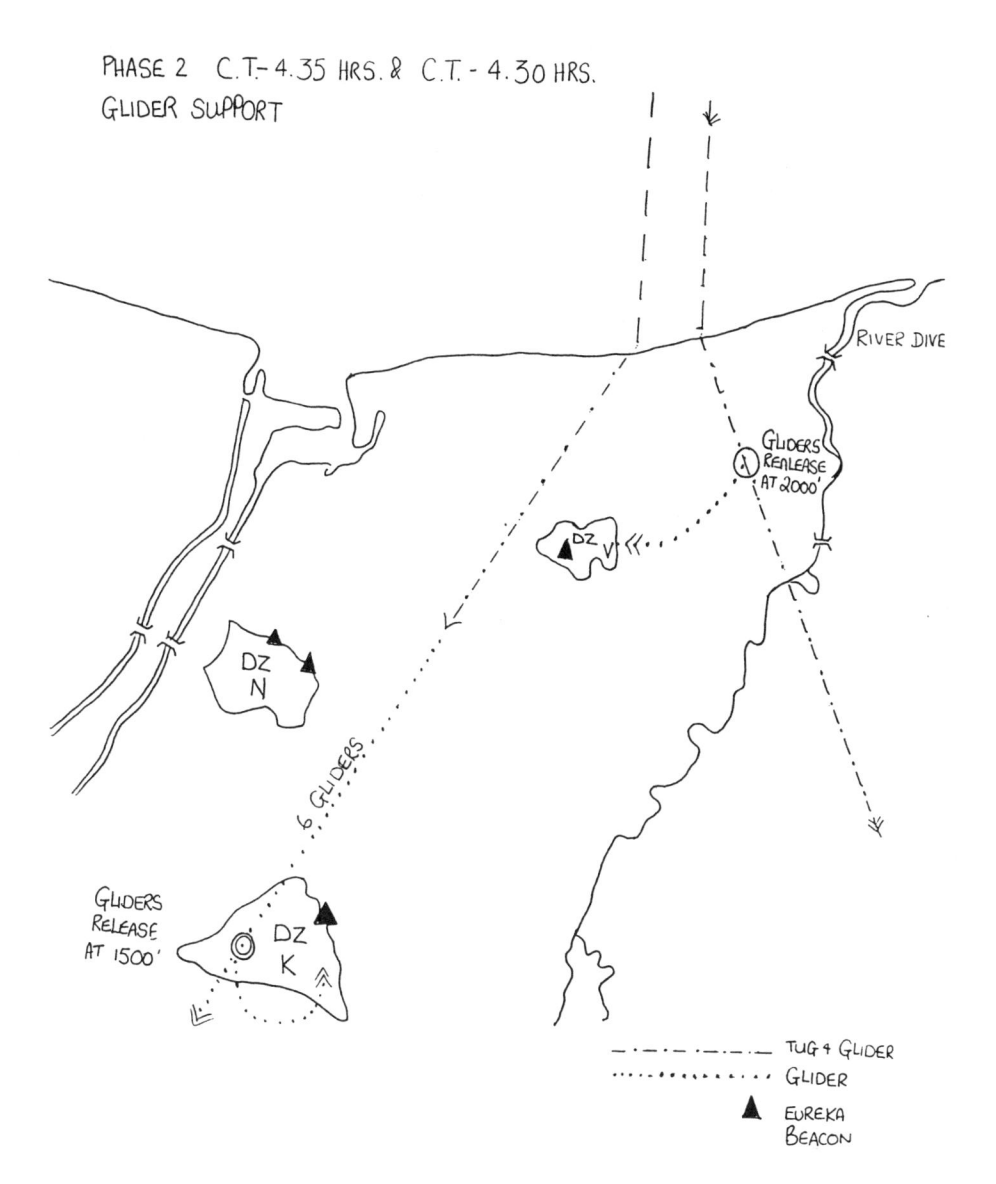

PHASE 2   C.T. - 4.35 HRS. & C.T. - 4.30 HRS.
GLIDER SUPPORT

RIVER DIVE

GLIDERS RELEASE AT 2000'

DZ V

DZ N

6 GLIDERS

GLIDERS RELEASE AT 1500'

DZ K

—·—·—·— TUG & GLIDER
············ GLIDER
▲ EUREKA BEACON

Squadron, Glider Pilot Regiment, carrying equipment for paratroops on LZ K were towed off by Dakota aircraft of 233 Squadron led by Wing Commander Morrison.

The Coup de Main (Deadstick) platoons took off at 2256 hours in six Horsa gliders of C squadron, Glider Pilot Regiment, towed by Halifaxes of 298 and 644 Squadrons, led by Wing Commander Duder from RAF Tarrant Rushton. Four Horsa gliders of A Squadron, Glider Pilot Regiment, carrying equipment for the 9th Battalion, Parachute Regiment's attack on the Merville coastal battery were airborne at 2310 hours en route for LZ V towed by Albemarle aircraft of 295 and 570 Squadrons led by Squadron Leader Grice from RAF Harwell.

At 0230 hours the Merville battery gliderborne assault teams took off from RAF Brize Norton in three Horsa gliders of B Squadron, Glider Pilot Regiment, towed by Albemarle tugs of 297 Squadron led by Flight Lieutenant Thomson. Twenty-six Horsa gliders comprising the first glider waves were airborne and flying into history spearheading the invasion of France.

At RAF Harwell six Albemarles of 295 and 570 Squadrons had loaded with Pathfinder paratroops of 22nd Independent Parachute Company who would drop and mark LZs V, k and N in the area of the Orne with lights and beacons. At 2303 hours the first Albemarle - serial number V1740 - piloted by Squadron Leader Merrick and with AVM Hollinghurst and ten paratroops on board, took off followed by five more Albemarles and set course for Normandy. Another fourteen Albemarle aircraft from 295 and 570 Squadrons next took off with the advance party of 3rd Parachute Brigade to drop in the wake of the Pathfinders.

The Phase I group of Horsa gliders were now being towed up to their cast off points. The Coup de Main (Deadstick) parties in their six gliders made successful landings. Five of the six landing on the minute LZs X and Y in brilliant flying, the other landed some eight miles away but went into action taking a bridge then making for their divisional HQ at Ranville. The Coup de Main troops took their objective in a spirited action.

Eleven Horsa gliders of A and E Squadrons, Glider Pilot Regiment, carrying the Merville battery assault paratroops guns and equipment crossed the French coast at 0030 hours having experienced unfavourable weather en route. They were unable to locate LZ V due to dust and smoke caused by RAF bombing of the Merville battery totally obscuring the area. Three of A Squadron gliders suffered tow rope breakage. Casting off at 1500 feet at about 0045 hours the glider pilots landed as best they could, many amid and striking the anti-glider poles, near their intended LZ. Six glider pilots were killed as were many of the glider occupants, others were taken prisoner others fought their way to British lines. Their equipment did not reach the paratroops at Merville.

The six gliders of F Squadron met adverse weather conditions over the Channel, turbulence being encountered and a westerly wind with 10/10th cloud at 4000 feet over LZ K area. Dust and smoke from the RAF bombing obscured the approach and the LZ. Releasing at heights between 700-1700 feet between 0045 and 0048 hours the glider pilots attempted to land their gliders amid the murk. Three landed on or near LZ N being misled by the LZ N beacon showing K instead of N. Two gliders however managed to reach their correct LZ.

One of the three Merville battery assault Horsas broke its tow rope and landed at RAF Odiham, the other two were towed on in continuous cloud cover. The parachute arrester gear on one glider streamed in mid-channel and the combination stalled losing height but control was regained though the glider tail assembly had been strained. The parachute was jettisoned but the starboard undercarriage was carried away. Crossing the French coast enemy flak was met and both gliders were damaged and four passengers wounded. Over the target weather conditions were 10/10th cloud at 1000 feet with a wind from 300 degrees at 28 knots. Both Horsas made four circuits on tow over the target looking for the ground attack paratroops signals but the attacking ground paratroops had no way of signalling to them and the two gliders circled overhead vainly trying to locate the battery in the bad visibility. The two glider pilots released tow at 0424 and 0425 hours at 1800 feet and 1200 feet and descended amid enemy machine gun fire and with no landing aids put their Horsas down - one only 50 yards from the battery the other three miles away - in a display of magnificent flying in the conditions. The crews of the gliders then came under machine-gun and mortar fire but engaged the enemy while a depleted party of 9th Parachute Battalion gallantly attacked and took the battery. By 0445 hours Operation Tonga's first objectives had been achieved, due to the skill and courage of the men-at-arms in spite of the difficulties.

Back in England seventy-two more gliders were lined up ready to be towed off in Phase III of Tonga. At 0128 hours Wing Commander Macnamara lifted off from Harwell in Albemarle V1749 towing a Horsa piloted by Major S.C. Griffith, with Major General Gale and part of HQ 6th Airborne Division, and set course in low cloud and heavy rain for Normandy, followed by twenty other combinations. By 0144 hours all were airborne, as were the combinations from the other airfields, and heading for the RV exit points on the English coast still in bad weather conditions.

Over Worthing two Horsa gliders had to cast off due to the tug aircraft becoming unserviceable and had to land at Ford and Worthy Down to be followed shortly afterwards by a Hamilcar which had to land at Ford. As the glider stream made landfall on the French coast enemy flak opened up. Twenty-five gliders were hit by flak but no casualties were suffered. Seven gliders tow ropes broke or were shot away by flak between the coast and the LZ.

On LZ N parachute engineers of 5th Parachute Brigade were clearing landing strips for the incoming glider force. Anti-glider poles were blown down by explosive charges and four landing strips prepared. Each strip was 1000 yards long - three were sixty yards wide for the Horsa gliders and one ninety yards wide for the Hamilcars. Fire fights were still raging all round the LZ.

Of the original seventy-two gliders (68 Horsa and 4 Hamilcar) fifty Horsas and two Hamilcars were released over LZ N between 0324 and 0334 hours. Forty-eight Horsas and two Hamilcars landed on or near LZ N. One Hamilcar piloted by Staff Sergeants Ridings and Harris broke its tow rope due to flak one mile short of the LZ but landed. Weather conditions had moderated over the Channel but a strong cross wind was blowing across the LZ making for difficult landings. Many of the gliders collided with obstacles or with other gliders and difficulty was found in offloading the support equipment due to glider damage.

HQ 6th Airborne was established near the LZ and the glider pilots under Major Griffith took up defensive positions round it and were immediately engaged by the enemy. Other glider pilots who had landed away from the LZ made their way towards it. Major J. Lyne Co of D Squadron, Glider Pilot Regiment, with six men from his crashed Horsa glider, took three days to reach Divisional HQ at Ranville, covering some forty-five miles through enemy held ground on foot and fighting two actions with the Germans en route.

With the evening of D-Day came another fleet of gliders carrying reinforcements and tanks (Operation Mallard) - Operation Tonga was over. All the set tasks had been accomplished. Operation Tonga was a success for the Royal Air Force, the Glider Pilot Regiment and the troops of 6th Airborne Division. A total of 364 aircraft and 98 gliders were involved. 4512 parachute troops were carried of which 4310 (95.5 %) were dropped. 59 gliders landed on the LZs (60.2%) carrying 493 troops, 44 jeeps, 55 motor cycles, 15 X 6-pounder guns, 2X17 pounder guns and one bulldozer. The Royal Air Force lost seven aircraft and the Glider Pilot Regiment lost thirty-four pilots killed in action.

## OPERATION TONGA – AIR MOVEMENTS CHART

| Airborne Unit | RAF Unit | A/C | Gpr Unit | Glider | Chalk Nos. | Airfield | T/O | Remarks & Load |
|---|---|---|---|---|---|---|---|---|
| 4th A/L A/T Bty, RA. 1st Canadian Para Battalion 3rd Para. HQ. | 271 Sqdn 46 Grp | Dakota " | E Sqdn " | Horsa " | 261-267 (7) | Down Ampney | 2249 | LZ V. 20 Troops 7 Jeeps 4 Trailers 2x6 PDR Guns 4 Motor Cycles |
| 8th Para Batt. 224 the Para. Field Ambulance | 233 Sqdn 46 Grp | Dakota " | F Sqdn " | Horsa " | 218-223 (6) | Blakehill Farm | 2250 | LZ K. 6 Jeeps 6 Trailers 8 Motor Cycles 12 Bicycles |
| 2nd Oxf & Bucks 249 Coy. RE. I/C Major Howard | 298 Sqdn 644 Sqdn 38 Grp | Halifax " " | C Sqdn " " | Horsa " " | 91-93 (3) 93-96 (3) | Tarrant Rushton " | 2256 " | Caen & Orne Bridges Coup de Main Party |
| 224 Field Ambulance. 9th Para. Battalion | 295 Sqdn 570 Sqdn 38 Grp | Albemarle " | A Sqdn " | Horsa " | 66-69 (4) | Harwell " | 2310 2315 | LZ V.Rope Broke (1) LZ V.Ditched(2) Short of Coast |
| 9th Para. Battalion | 297 Sqdn 38 Grp | Albemarle | B Sqdn | Horsa | 27.28. 28a | Brize Norton | 0230 | Merville Battery Assault Two landed |

### MAIN FORCE

| Airborne Unit | RAF Unit | A/C | Gpr Unit | Glider | Chalk Nos. | Airfield | T/O | Remarks & Load |
|---|---|---|---|---|---|---|---|---|
| 5th Para. Brigade | 296 Sqdn 297 Sqdn 38 Grp | Albemarle | B Sqdn | Horsa | 29-36 (8) 37-45 (9) | Brize Norton | 0141 0110 | LZ N LZ N |
| Gen. Gale+HQ6th 5th Para. Brigade | 295 Sqdn 570 Sqdn 38 Grp | Albemarle | A Sqdn | Horsa | 70-80 (11) 81-90 (10) | Harwell " | 0128 " | LZ N LZ N |
| 4th A/L A/T Bty Div. HQ. 3 Para Brigade | 298 Sqdn | Halifax | D Sqdn | Horsa | 97-111(15) 112-126(15) | Tarrant Rushton | 0130 0130 | LZ N |
|  | 644 Sqdn 38 Grp | Halifax | " | " |  |  |  | LZ N |
| 4 x 17 PDR Guns | 298 Sqdn 644 Sqdn 38 Grp | Halifax | D Sqdn | Hamilcar | 500-501 (2) 503-503 (2) | Tarrant Rushton | 0210 0210 | LZ N LZ N |

TOTALS  Horsas 94  Hamilcars 4  Gliders 98

# OPERATION DEADSTICK

The Coup de Main gliderborne operation to capture and hold the River Orne and Caen Canal bridges in Normandy, during the early hours of D-Day, 6th June 1944, before the main landings.

### FOREWORD

It was obvious at the outset to everyone involved that the success of the bridges coup de main operation primarily depended upon the ability of the glider pilots to land the party near enough to the bridges to achieve full surprise.

In the event, five of the six gliders did exactly that, four of them crash landing their Horsas on the precise spots on the ground where I had hopefully indicated, during my briefing, they should finish up!

As soon as we first met our twelve glider pilots at Tarrant Rushton about D minus 4 we all had complete confidence in their ability to do the job. Their manner and determined outlook was inspiring for us all. Air Chief Marshal Sir Trafford Leigh Mallory, commanding the Allied Air Forces on D-Day, praised the glider landings as the finest feat of piloting in World War II.

I am happy to say that today I still have contact with all but one of the survivors of that group of superb glider pilots

John Howard.

(Major R.J.Howard DSO, was the commander of Operation Deadstick on D-Day)

The object of the operation was to seize the two bridges intact to provide access over the canal and river, between the main seaborne landings by the British 2nd Army and the airborne troops of 6th Airborne Division, dropping and landing east of the canal at Ranville to protect the left flank on the invading forces.

The task of capturing the two bridges by glider borne coup de main assault fell to the 2nd Battalion, Oxfordshire and Buckinghamshire Light Infantry. (The 52nd). D Company, plus two platoons from B Company, of the regiment were selected and placed under the command of Major John Howard, DSO. D and B Companies were part of 6th Air Landing Brigade, commanded by Brigadier the Honourable Hugh Kindersley, which in turn was part of 6th Airborne Division commanded by Major General Richard Gale, OBE. MC. The division was further composed of 3rd Parachute Brigade, commanded by Brigadier J.S. Hill, DSO. MC. and 5th Parachute Brigade commanded by Brigadier N. Poett, DSO. (later KCB).

On the 2nd May 1944, Major Howard went to Syrencot House, Brigmerston, on Salisbury Plain, the Planning Headquarters of 6th Airborne Division and 38 Group, Royal Air Force. The Georgian house codenamed Broadmoor by authority was known to its staff as The Madhouse. Major Howard was given his Operational Orders for the capture of the two bridges by Brigadier Poett. The orders were marked TOP SECRET and BIGOT NEPTUNE - the latter meaning Major Howard was now one one of a select number of officers who had access to D-Day planning but could not reveal any details except to officers similarly classified. The popular name for this classification was Bigoted.

Horsa gliders were to be used for the assault in preference to paratroops as the six gliders could land 180 troops almost at the same time and place instead of widely dispersed paratroops. Silence, surprise and speed were to be the essence of the mission.

The Orders read:

5 PAR BDE OO No.1.
To Maj. R.J. Howard, 2 OXf Bucks.
INTENTION.
Your task is to seize intact the brs over R. Orne and canal at BENOUVILLE 098748 and RANVILLE 104746. and to hold them until relief by 7 Para Bn. If the brs are blown you will est personnel ferries over both water obstacles as soon as possible.
METHOD.
Composition of Force.
Cmd. Maj R.J. Howard, 2 OXF BUCKS.
Tps. D Coy 2 OXF BUCKS less sp Brens and 3" M dets.
Two pls B Coy 2 OXF BUCKS.
Det of 20 Sprs 249 Fd Coy (Airborne)
Det 1 Wing Glider P Regt.
FLIGHT PLAN.
Horsa gliders available 6.
LZ X triangular fd 099745 3 gliders.
LZ Y rectangular fd 104747 3 gliders.
Timing First ldg H minus 5 hours.

GEN OUTLINE.

a. The capture of the brs will be a coup de main op depending largely on surprise, speed and dash for success.
b. Provided the bulk of your force lands safely, you should have little difficulty in overcoming the known enemy opposition on the brs.
c Your difficulties will arise in holding off an enemy counter attack on the brs until you are relieved.

POSSIBLE ENEMY COUNTER ATTACK.
a You must expect a counter attack at any time after H minus 4 hours.
b This attack may take the form of a Battle Gp consisting of one coy inf in lorries, up to eight tanks and one or two guns mounted on lorries, it may be a lorried inf coy alone, or inf on foot.
c The most likely line of approach for this force is down one of the roads leading from the WEST or SW, but a cross country route cannot be ignored.

ORG of DEF POSN.
It is vital that the crossing places be held and to do this you will secure a close brhead on the WEST bank in addition to guarding the brs. The immediate def of the brs and of the WEST bank of the canal must be held at all costs.

PATROLLING.
You will harass and delay the deployment of the enemy counter attack forces of the 736 GR by offensive patrols covering all rd approaches from the WEST. Patrols will remain mobile and offensive.

EMP of RE.
You will give to your Sprs. the following tasks on order of priority;
Neutralizing the demolition mechanisms.
Removing charges from demolition chambers.
Establishing personnel ferries.

RELIEF.
I estimate that your relief will NOT be completed until H minus 3 hrs, ie two hours after your first ldg. One coy 7 Para Bn will however be despatched to your assistance with the utmost possible speed after the ldg of the Bn. They should reach your posn by H minus 3 hrs 30 mins and will come under your command until arrival of OC 7 Para Bn.

GLIDER LOADS.
Outline.
Gliders 1 - 4 One rifle platoon less handcart. 5 Sprs.
Glider 5 - 6 One rifle platoon less handcart. 5 men Coy HQ.

Detailed load tables will be worked out by you in conjunc with the RE and Bde Loading Officer.
TRG.
The trg of your force will be regarded as a first priority matter.

At the end of May 1944, Major Howard and his men moved to RAF Tarrant Rushton, Dorset, near the Channel coast, where they joined with the Royal Air Force glider tug pilots of 298 and 644 Squadrons, and the glider pilots of C Squadron, Glider Pilot Regiment, and began training.

Major Howard divided his force between the six gliders allocated and into two groups of three glider loads. One group to attack each bridge. All of his men were now informed of the mission as they were now confined to a secure section of Tarrant Rushton camp - each man familiarised himself as to his particular part in the mission.

Two landing zones (LZs) had been selected. LZ X was a triangular field SE of the canal bridge and gave landing access right up to the actual target. LZ Y was a rectangular field NE of the river bridge and also gave landing access almost to the target.

Both fields had been considered too small by the enemy for glider landings but on May 30th aerial photographs showed evidence of holes being dug for erection of anti glider poles. However by the 3rd June no poles had been erected.

The enemy garrison at the two bridges was thought to be about fifty men - mainly drafted from occupied countries - but with German NCOs. All were expected to be well armed with sub machine-guns. Other defensive weapons were four light anti-aircraft guns, six light machine-guns, an anti-aircraft machine-gun and two anti-tank guns. The main body of troops in the area was a battalion of the 736th Grenadier Regiment with about eight to twelve tanks. It was expected that the bridges had been prepared for demolition.

Eight glider pilot crews began specific LZ training at Tarrant Rushton with day and night releases from 6000 feet onto the airfield. Landing training then switched to RAF Netheravon, a small clump of trees - Holmes Clump, Figheldean Field, 700 yards south east of RAF Netheravon - had been chosen for practice LZs. Two LZs were marked out to simulate LZs X and Y.

The Horsas were towed off from Tarrant Rushton and climbed to 6000 feet then released six miles from the practice LZs. Three glider crew practised landing on the simulated canal bridge LZ and three on the river bridge LZ. Precision glider flying was called for with the glider pilots using stop watches and compass bearings to land in the dark on their LZS. After landing the Horsa gliders were manhandled by RAF Riggers using tractors, off the practice LZs onto

Netheravon airfield. No mean task as there is no roads - merely rutted tracks - to the airfield perimeter track. LZ landing training ended on the 30th May.

On the 5th June Howard's task force and the glider pilots had completed their final preparations at Tarrant Rushton. All the Horsa gliders were overloaded at 7300lbs each. It had been intended for each Horsa to carry a canvas assault boat weighing 180lbs for use as a personnel ferry in case the bridges were blown but this was reduced to four of the gliders carrying one boat each. Every glider to be used in the Normandy invasion was allocated a chalk number - the Deadstick Operation gliders were allocated numbers 91 to 96.

Caen Canal bridge force. LZ X.
Horsa 91. serial Number PF800. Pilots: Staff Sergeants J. Wallwork and J. Ainsworth, MM.Tug pilot W/C Duder.
Troops. A (Able) Platoon under Major Howard and Lieutenant D. Brotheridge.
Horsa 92. Pilots: Staff Sergeants O. Boland and P. Hobbs.
Troops. B (Baker) Platoon under Lieutenant D. Wood. with Captain J. Neilson, OC. Royal Engineer Sappers. Tug pilot WO Berry.
Horsa 93. Pilots: Staff Sergeants G. Barkway and P. Boyle.
Troops C (Charlie) Platoon. OC. Lieutenant R. Smith. Tug pilot WO Herman.

River Orne bridge force. LZ Y.
Horsa 94. Pilots: Staff Sergeants A. Lawrence and H. Shorter.
Troops. D (Dog) Platoon OC Captain B. Priday (2 i/c to Major Howard) and Lieutenant C. Hooper. Tug pilot F/O Clapperton.
Horsa 95. Pilots: Staff Sergeants S. Pearson and L. Guthrie.
E (Easy) Platoon. OC Lieutenant H. Sweeney. Tug pilot WO Bain.
Horsa 96. Pilots: Staff Sergeants R. Howard and F. Baacke.
Troops. F (Fox) Platoon OC Lieutenant D. Fox.Tug Pilot F/O Archibald.

Because of the uncertainty of the precise time and place of landing at night, every platoon had to be prepared to do any of the other platoon's tasks according to the order in which they reached the bridges.

During the morning and afternoon of the 5th June 1944, the six gliders and tugs were marshalled on the runway at Tarrant Rushton. At 2256 hours Horsa glider No.91 was towed off from Tarrant Rushton by Halifax LL355 piloted by W/C Duder - to be followed at one minute intervals by WO Berry piloting Halifax LL335 and WO Bain in Halifax LL406, all from 298 Squadron. 644 Squadron glider tugs followed with Halifax LL350 piloted by F/O Archibald,

Halifax LL344 piloted by F/O Clapperton and Halifax LL218 piloted by WO Herman.

Flying at 7000 feet over the Channel the stream crossed the French coast at 0007 hours and cast off their gliders at 6000 feet over Cabourg. The Halifax tugs continued on to bomb a cement factory at Caen as a cover and diversionary raid. Silently gliding over Normandy the glider pilots steered 187° with their second pilots checking stopwatches. At 1500 feet the passenger troops opened the sliding doors ready for a quick exit. Horsas 95 and 96 turned starboard on 270° for thirty seconds then back on 187° for the River Orne bridge. Horsas 91, 92 and 93 glided on past the LZ then turned back on reciprocal 187° and headed for the canal bridge. Horsa 94 was mistowed and landed south east of Cabourg by a road running east from Varaville near two bridges by the River Dives - which from the air looked like the intended target.

Staff Sergeant Wallwork put Horsa 91 down right on target using the arrester gear to reduce his landing run on skids. The Horsa came to a stop entangled in barbed wire forty-seven yards from the canal bridge at 0016 hours. The first fighting men to land on D-Day had arrived. Horsa 92 came in one minute later with Staff Sergeant Boland using the arrester gear and flaps to swerve and avoid colliding with Horsa 91. The violent skid landing and swerve broke the Horsa's fuselage and it came to rest by a pond. Horsa 93 landed at 0018 hours on skids and arrester gear - the platoon commander, Lieutenant Smith, was thrown forward and out of the glider by the impact which buried the nose in the pond. Six men were trapped inside the badly damaged fuselage and one soldier drowned in the pond. This was the only fatal casualty of the landing. The noise of the Horsa landings had been heard at the canal bridge by a German sentry Private Wilhelm Furtner who thought they were an RAF aircraft crashing.

There was no enemy fire from the canal bridge garrison - surprise had been effected. Lieutenant Brotheridge assembled Able Platoon and led it across the bridge through the defences, with his platoon firing their Sten guns, Bren guns and rifles in a spirited assault. A vicious fire fight developed on the far side of the bridge during which Lieutenant Brotheridge was hit in the neck by enemy machine-gun fire as he ran forward. He died an hour later of his wounds, leading from the front.

Baker Platoon under Lieutenant Wood engaged the enemy's inner defences of trenches and gun pits. A fierce battle ensued and both Lieutenant Wood and the Platoon Sergeant were wounded leaving Corporal Godbold in command of the Platoon. Charlie Platoon under Lieutenant Smith was ordered by Major Howard to reinforce Able Platoon and mop up enemy resistance. Before many minutes had passed the canal bridge was in British hands. The Sappers under Captain Neilson

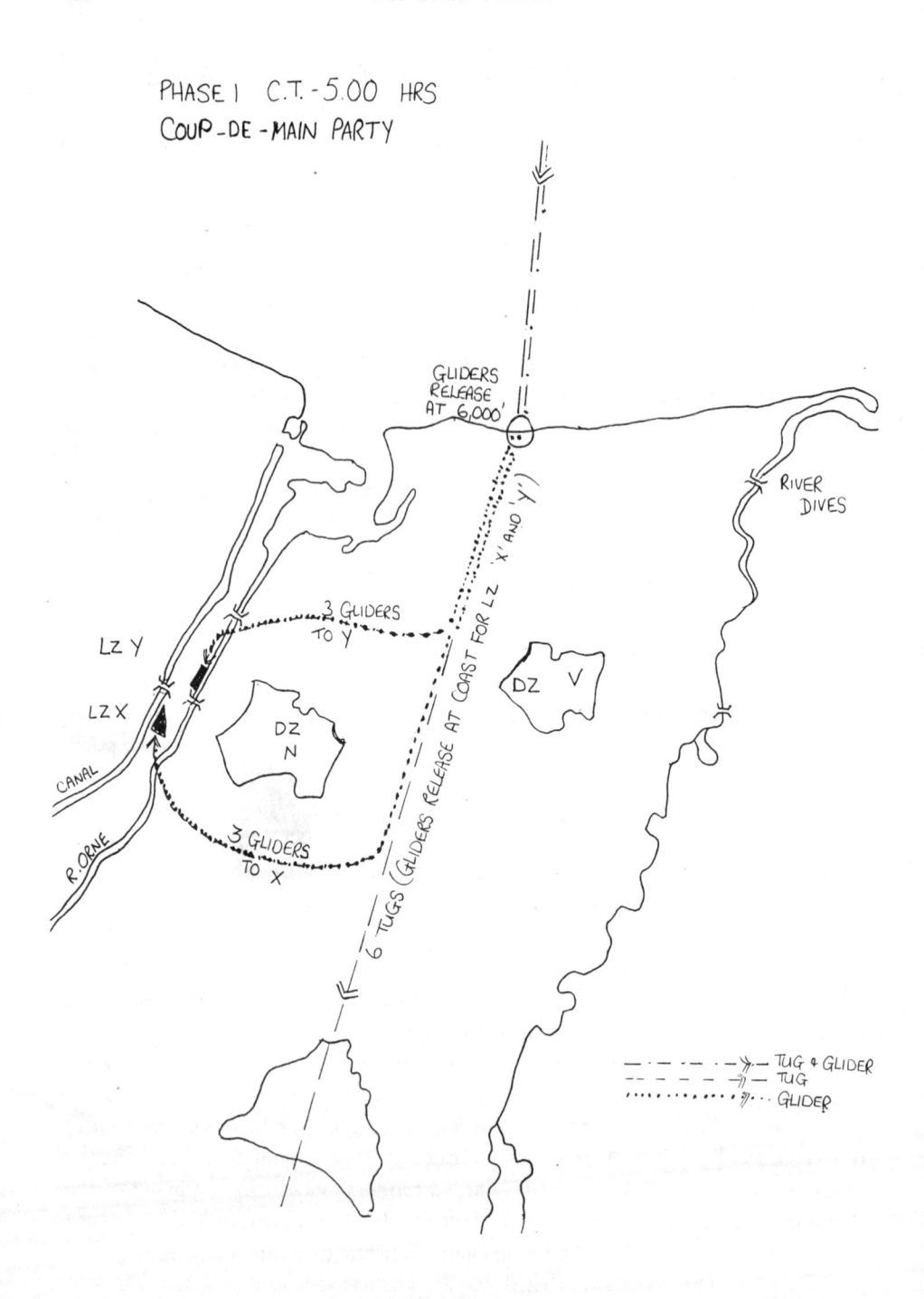

and Lieutenant Bence, removed the demolition charges and occupied a defensive position at the bridge.

Overhead aircraft of the RAF were dropping paratroops on their DZ nearby - the paratroops coming under fire from the now alerted Germans - as they descended. Meanwhile, Horsa 95 piloted by Staff Sergeant Pearson was coming in to LZ Y. At 3000 feet the Horsa crew saw the battle begin at the canal bridge - at 1000 feet an inrush of air through the opened doors caused the Horsa to swing violently. Descending rapidly, Pearson and Guthrie put on half then full flap, the arrester gear line was pulled and the Horsa was down on the LZ some four hundred yards from the bridge. Easy Platoon under Lieutenant Sweeney exited rapidly and made for the river bridge at the double.

Horsa 96 piloted by Staff Sergeant Howard made a precision approach and when at 1200 feet Howard saw the target bridge. Lining up the Horsa he took off the flaps for a moment to slow the descent then put them on again as the glider came up to a line of trees they had to pass over at just the right height. Passing over the trees Howard put the Horsa down and deployed the arrester gear to shorten the landing run. The Horsa came to rest close to the river bridge and Fox Platoon under Lieutenant Fox disembarked quickly and stormed the bridge. The defenders ran away leaving their weapons in their gun pits. Easy Platoon reinforced Fox Platoon at the river bridge and the position was consolidated. The prearranged code words for notification of the successful capture of the river bridge - Ham and Jam - were sent by Lance Corporal Tappenden by radio to Major Howard at the canal bridge with great gusto.

The 2nd Oxford & Bucks coup de main parties had been put down on target on time by the glider pilots in a brilliant display of flying skills. To land an engineless aircraft weighing some seven tons, heavily loaded, in the dark without landing aids, alongside bridges guarded by enemy troops in a foreign land, was a superb achievement. The senior RAF Officers who had, at the beginning, stated that flying an aircraft was a job for RAF pilots, had to change their minds.

Both bridges were now in British hands and the enemy alerted. At the river bridge Easy Platoon came into action against the enemy approaching from Ranville. A motor-cycle and staff car were engaged with Bren gun fire and either killed or captured. Tanks were then heard approaching. Fox Platoon took out one German tank with a PIAT and the others retreated quickly. At 0300 hours 7th Parachute battalion arrived and moved out to positions west of the canal bridge which lessened the threat of enemy counter attack to the bridges. At first light a German gunboat came up the canal from the seawards direction and opened fire on the British positions. Able Platoon under Corporal Godbold took it out with one PIAT round and captured the crew. Soon after first light the bridges were visited by 6th Airborne Divisional Commander General Gale, 5th Parachute Brigade Commander Brigadier Poett and Brigadier Kindersley, Commander 6th Air Landing Brigade.

The enemy mounted several counter-attacks which were repelled but the pressure was becoming greater on the airborne bridgehead and it was with relief that at 1330 hours the bridge defenders heard the sound of bagpipes and knew that 1st Special Service Brigade, Commandos, led by the Lord Lovat with his piper Bill Millin ranting the "Black Bear" on the pipes, was approaching to reinforce 6th Airborne Division east of the River Orne. The pilots and passengers of Horsa 94 - Capt. Priday, Lieut. Hooper and Dog Platoon - fought their way back to the 2nd Oxford & Bucks at Ranville, having been on the move for 24 hours through enemy occupied territory, losing four men in the process. Casualties on the Deadstick operation were one officer killed and two wounded with one soldier killed and twelve wounded. By French Government Decree the Caen Canal bridge is now known as Pegasus bridge and the area immediately east of the bridge has been named Esplanade Major John Howard. Marker stones have been erected to show the position of the Horsa glider landing points. In 1989 the River Orne bridge was renamed Horsa bridge in commemoration of the assault. For their part in the operation the following were decorated:

Distinguished Flying Medal:
Staff Sergeant Wallwork.
Staff Sergeant Howard.
Staff Sergeant Pearson.
Staff Sergeant Barkway.
Staff Sergeant Hobbs.

Croix de Guerre:
Staff Sergeant Guthrie.
Staff Sergeant Baacke.
Staff Sergeant Boland.

Distinguished Service Order:
Major Howard.

Military Cross:
Lieutenant Hooper.
Lieutenant Sweeney.
Lieutenant Smith.

The author wishes to thank Major John Howard, DSO, commander of the Deadstick Operation, and Staff Sergeant Roy Howard, DFM, for their unstinting help in the preparation of this account.

## THE TAKING OF THE RIVER ORNE BRIDGE

Staff Sergeant Roy Howard, DFM, recalls his part in Operation Deadstick:

I was lucky enough to be teamed up with Squadron Leader Emblem as my tug pilot. He was Commanding Officer of 297 squadron and as such all his aircrew including his navigator, were leaders in their various fields. During training we were to do a night landing of thirty gliders on Netheravon. My second pilot was Fred Baacke who was nine years my senior. I was by far the most junior person in the combination, yet when the message came from the tug 'down you go this is it', I replied, 'I'm sorry but you have got the wrong airfield, we have been circling Upavon not Netheravon', ( RAF Upavon is several miles north east of RAF Netheravon) 'Steer 180° and I will go when I am ready'. As a result the exercise was a success - but what I did not know was that our own Squadron Commander Major Toler, DFC, was also in the tug - so I had a very good audience. It was all a matter of luck really.

There followed more successful exercises and on the 21st April 1944, Fred and I were told that we were to start some special training. Apart from gathering that it had something to do with D-Day we did not otherwise have the slightest idea at that stage of what we were ultimately to be required to do. The training started in daylight with a 6000 feet tow from Brize Norton to Netheravon where a very small area had been marked out with white tape. 'Now we want you to get in there' we were told. This went quite well and we repeated it several times until it was decided that our Albemarle tugs did not have sufficient power for the 6000 feet climb with a full load and we transferred to RAF Tarrant Rushton, Dorset, with Halifax II tugs.

For the next phase a formation of trees close to the east side of Netheravon airfield had been selected and two small fields side by side were created. Each day the six chosen glider crews - three from B Squadron and three from C Squadron, Glider Pilot Regiment, were towed from Tarrant Rushton on the same height, course and pull off point to simulate the operation's requirements, of which we still knew nothing. Three gliders would land in each of these very small fields. RAF ground crews were there each day to somehow get the Horsas back onto

Netheravon airfield and service them. This meant that we could only do one landing each day.

The operation required that the three gliders which were to attack the River Orne bridge had to shed their 6000 feet as quickly as possible, whereas the three gliders attacking the Caen Canal bridge were to carry out a longer and more orthodox approach. Our three gliders had about half the distance to fly although from the same cast off height of 6000 feet, so to lose so much unwanted height in sufficient time we had to apply full flap as soon as we released. This would make navigation extremely difficult but it had been decided by those formulating this brilliant and audacious plan that the height was necessary to deceive the Germans into thinking it was a bombing raid. As soon as we cast off the Halifax tugs were to continue straight on to drop bombs on Caen.

By this time we were training at night. At first with a few lights on the ground and as our landings became more precise these lights were removed and we were told to do spot on landings in those small fields with no lights or aids of any kind. At first I thought that it could not be done, but after one or two hairy missions we found out it could. On the 28th May we met our load of Major Howard and his Oxford & Bucks Light Infantry and in my case Lieutenant Fox and his men. There followed the most intensive briefing on the military side of the operation, greatly aided by an elaborate sand table (now on view at the Airborne Forces Museum at Aldershot). This showed every detail of the terrain with all the trees and of course the River and canal with its bridges. We did not know where it actually was until we were told two days before D-Day.

At 2100 hours on 5th June we assembled on the runway and our load of troops under Lieutenant Fox. As glider 96 Fred and I were last off and we staggered off into the air with a very heavy load at approximately 2235 hours (Double British Summer Time). Later I was to suspect that every man probably took a few more grenades and rounds of ammunition etc because the weight proved to be greater that we had allowed for.

We crossed the coast near Worthing and set a direct course for Normandy. About three miles from the French coast the tug navigator gave us a compass check and told us we were on course. Because of the very steep angle of descent of a Horsa with full flap applied (about 45°) our standard P4 compass - which could have become inoperative - had been supplemented with a gyro direction indicator (GDI) for we were required to do what had never before, nor to the best of my knowledge was ever required again in the later airborne landings at Arnhem and the Rhine, namely to navigate various courses on a 45° angle of descent, dropping at a rate of 2000 feet per minute.

'Good luck! cast off when you like' came the tug navigator's message through the wire in our tow rope. Whether I liked it or not was at this stage academic. The culmination of all my training and indeed of the short 21 years of my life had reached a point of no return and I cast off immediately at the 6000 feet height which we had practised more times than I could remember. I reduced speed and applied full flap but to my horror I could not get the speed below 90mph even with the stick fully back. The extra weight was going to ruin all our calculations. I turned my head to the right towards the door between the cockpit and my load and shouted, 'Mr. Fox, sir, two men from the front to the back - quickly!' This manoeuvre corrected our trim and the Horsa was under proper control again

What a load there was behind me! It seemed so crowded behind that to this day I wonder whether in addition to extra stores and ammunition a few more men had slipped aboard unobserved at the last minute before take off. As well as the gyro compass Fred had been supplied with a special light strapped to his hand so as not to spoil my night vision - which in the next few minutes was going to be so vital for all of us.

So far we had seen nothing not even the coast line when we cast off. Suddenly, bright as day we were illuminated by a German parachute flare. Thankfully we entered a cloud and when we emerged all was dark again. But we were falling like a spent rocket and steering a course at the same time of 212° - to be held for 90 seconds as Fred checked the map and his stop watch. This covered the first two miles and we turned again onto 268° which we held for 2 minutes 30 seconds covering a further 3.3 miles. Still not seeing anything of the ground but continuing our half way to the vertical dive with only the hiss of the slipstream to be heard among all the now silent men, we turned on our third course of 212° for the final run in.

We were now at 2000 feet and there below us the Canal and River lay like silver - instantly recognisable. Orchards and woods lay as darker patches on a dark and foreign soil. 'It's all right now Fred, I can see where we are', I said, as I thought that it all looked so exactly like the sand table that I had the strange feeling that I had been there before. I took off the flaps for a moment to slow our headlong descent and ensure we had enough height. I put them back on as we shot towards the line of trees over which I had to pass, not by fifty feet or we would overshoot and be crushed by the load weight as we hit the embankment which I knew was at the end of the field. I had to just miss and scrape over the tree tops as we deployed the parachute brake specially fitted to the rear of the glider in order to shorten our landing run to the minimum. Up with the nose and the heavy rumble of the main wheels as we touched down a few minutes after midnight close to the River Orne bridge. 'You are in the right place, sir,' I shouted to Lieutenant Fox - who seemed both surprised and happy at the same time - as with a drumming and crash of army boots along the floor of the glider, he and his men disappeared into the night to shoot up the Germans guarding the bridge.

It was up to Fred and I to unload the rest of the stores but now we received a shock as we climbed out through the door of the glider into the field. Apart from a herd of cows which had panicked in front of us as we landed, we were quite alone. Alone in Occupied France. Separated from our load. Alone in front of the whole invasion force which was not to land on the beaches six miles away until daybreak, and ahead of the earliest parachute drop by one hour. Where were the other two gliders? We had been number 96 and should have been the third to land in our field. It was only much later that we learned that number 95 had undershot by some 400 yards whilst number 94, due to its tug navigator's error was ten miles away with its load busy capturing a bridge on the wrong river. But they realising the error were later to orientate themselves and fight their way through the night to liase at our bridge. An astonishing feat of arms and determination in itself. At 0100 hours we saw paratroops dropping in the Bois de Ranville and shortly afterwards a wave of gliders followed.

The night was full of noise and alarms and I was glad when dawn came. Soon afterwards the Naval and aerial bombardment preceding the seaborne landings began. The volume of noise was past anything in my experience and as the barrage lifted and came nearer we prayed that someone knew when to stop it. At 1300 hours we heard a hunting horn and Lord Lovat appeared complete with walking stick and Piper leading his Commando over our bridges: ignoring the fact that a sniper was methodically knocking out one in twelve of his men. This same sniper had already taken out a man who was standing between Fred and I earlier in the day.

At 2100 hours the main glider force came into the Ranville area. Our task was complete and we decided to go home - our orders being to return to UK as soon as practicable in order to be ready to fly in a further load if necessary. We took our leave of Major Howard and his men who with the other three gliders had successfully landed on the Canal Bridge. We walked along the road to Ouistreham snatching as much fitful sleep in a field of cabbages as the 15" shells which HMS Warspite was pumping into Le Havre would allow. As we arrived at the beach early on D+1 a JU88 was shot down crashing some thirty yards from us and it continued to explode and burn for some time. Later Colonel Murray and the glider pilots from the main glider landing force arrived. We all waded out to Infantry Landing Craft and arrived back at Newhaven on 8th June.

# THE MERVILLE BATTERY ASSAULT

In April 1944, Lieutenant Colonel T.B.H. Otway of the Royal Ulster Rifles, although seconded to the Parachute Regiment and Commanding 9th Battalion, of that regiment, received orders from Major General R.N. Gale to plan for the assault and elimination of a German coastal gun battery at map reference 155776 near Merville, some one and a half miles from the Normandy coast of France.

The gun battery was believed to consist of four 150mm calibre guns capable of firing on Sword Beach - the planned landing area of the British 3rd Division on D-Day. (It was later confirmed that they could do this). General Gale stressed that the neutralisation of the battery was vital to the success of the seaborne troops: it had to be taken at whatever cost.

The four guns in the battery were thought to be in concrete emplacements with six feet six inches thick walls and roofs covered with thirteen feet of earth. Surrounding the four hundred diameter complex were minefields - one a hundred yards deep and barbed wire, fifteen feet thick and five feet high, plus an electrified wire perimeter.

A garrison of 150 men of the 176th Artillery Regiment manned the battery and had a 20mm automatic cannon in the centre of the complex for defence against air and ground attack. Interconnecting trenches, tunnels and foxholes gave the defenders overlapping fields of fire from machine-guns over the approaches. A deep and wide anti-tank ditch had been dug in front of the battery on the seaward side.

It was a most difficult and deadly position to attack and eliminate but it had to be done to prevent the Germans firing on the seaborne assaulting troops. The RAF had attempted to eliminate the battery by bombing in March 1944, but although over 1000 bombs had been dropped only two had landed on target but they did not cause any damage to the well protected battery.

Colonel Otway decided to use a battalion group consisting of the 9th Parachute Battalion supported by Signallers of the Royal Navy and detachments of the Royal Artillery, Royal Engineers and Royal Army Medical Corps, a total of 750 officers and men.

The assault plan was for the main body - 600 paratroops of 9th Parachute Battalion - to drop on DZ V early on the morning of D-Day and, equipped with anti tank guns, mine detectors, flame throwers, explosives and bridging ladders, carried in two Horsa gliders which would also land on DZ V, move to and assault the battery.

At the same time (0430 hours) as the main body attacked three Horsa gliders piloted by volunteers from the Glider Pilot Regiment and carrying a coup de main party of fifty paratroops of A Company, 9th Parachute Battalion and eight Royal Engineers from 591 Parachute Squadron, would crash land on the battery complex, guided in by Eureka beacons and 3-inch mortar star shells fired by the attacking ground paratroops.

Just before the ground assault the RAF would bomb the battery with 99 Lancaster bombers for ten minutes. Three hours later another 100 bombers would bomb nearby Ouistreham to reduce another battery and flak positions. It was hoped that the bombing of the Merville battery would stun the defenders and blow gaps through the minefields and barbed wire defences. The Merville battery had to be taken by 0515 hours as a fall back plan was for the Royal Navy to bombard the complex unless otherwise ordered.

In May 1944, a complete mock up of the battery was constructed at West Woodhay, Newbury, Berkshire, and Colonel Otway and his men practised day and night simulated assaults. Live ammunition was used for test night practice, which was co-ordinated for timing of the attack with RAF aircraft towing gliders overhead. On the 25th May the 9th Battalion moved to RAF Broadwell, Oxfordshire, where they were given their final briefing and sealed in camp.

The Horsa glider force for the assault and supply landings assembled at two RAF airfields, with the three Battery assault gliders at RAF Brize Norton and the supply gliders (two for the Merville battery assault party) at RAF Down Ampney. The battery gliders order read:

Method.
1. Three crews of B Squadron.
   Selection by Commander - Glider Pilots. (every pilot in the
   Squadron volunteered).
2. Albemarle/Horsa combination detailed below.

| Base | serial Nos. | Load. | LZ. |
|---|---|---|---|
| Brize Norton | 27, 28 & 28A | 9 Para. Bn. RE. | Bty. |

Release.
Height 5000 feet or as high as practicable with Albemarle/Horsa combination.
Release points at glider pilot's discretion. Navigators will check wind speed and direction, and pass information to glider crews before release.
Gliders will be individually navigated after release on courses given at briefing and corrected by navigators..

**Ground Aids.**
Immediately before landing at a height of approximately 500 feet the second pilot of the glider will flash three dots on the landing light. On this signal the ground forces will illuminate the landing area.

**Landing Plan.**
Direction of final approach and landing - west to east. Pilots will select the clearest available area for landing.

**Action after landing.**
Military operation orders for glider pilots to be issued by 3 Para. Bde.

At 2249 hours on Monday, 5th June 1944, the seven Horsa gliders of E Squadron, Glider Pilot Regiment, began to lift off from Down Ampney towed by Dakota aircraft of 271 Squadron, 46 Group, Royal Air Force, bound for DZ V, two of the Horsas (266 & 267) being loaded with equipment for the Merville battery assault paratroops, with the last glider being airborne at 2254 hours.

Glider Number 266     Dakota KG 516      P/O William 2253 hrs
       "           267         "      KG 387      W.O Wood   2254 hrs

Load: Gliders. nos, 266 & 267    4th A/L A/T Battery.
                                 2 x 6 pdr a/t guns plus equipment

The four Horsas of A Squadron, Glider Pilot Regiment, lifted off from RAF Harwell towed by Albemarle aircraft of 295 and 570 Squadrons, 38 Group, Royal Air Force, between 2310 and 2316 hours carrying 9th Parachute Battalion troops, assault and supporting medical personnel for DZ V.

Glider No.66 towed by Albemarle V1620 pilot S/L Grice 2315 hrs
   "       67                   V1746       F/O Lawson 2316 hrs
   "       68                   V1757       F.L Unwin  2310 hrs
   "       69                   V1647       P/O Yull   2310 hrs

**Glider pilots.**
S/Sgt. Marfleet  Sgt Haines.
S/Sgt. Bramah    Sgt Bartley.
S/Sgt. Ockwell   Sgt.Hellyer.
S/Sgt. Thorpe    Sgt.Hardie.

Load: Glider 66 - 68.   Equipment for 9th Para. Battalion coup de main party.
      Glider 69        Equipment for 224 Para. Field Ambulance

At 2310 hours on the 5th June the Dakota aircraft of 512 Squadron, 46 Group, Royal Air Force, began to take off from Broadwell carrying the main body of 9th Battalion, The Parachute Regiment. Led by the squadron commander - Wing Commander Coventry - the thirty-two aircraft took off at intervals until 2336 hours when all were airborne.

Weather was bad requiring instrument flying in almost continuous cloud cover and both paratroops and glider troops had a bumpy ride. RV was made for the three groups over Worthing, Bognor and Littlehampton on the south coast - the course was set for DZ V and into military history.

The three Horsa gliders scheduled to land on the Merville battery lifted off from Brize Norton between 0230 and 0231 hours on the 6th June towed by Albemarle aircraft of 297 Squadron, 38 Group, Royal Air Force.

| Glider No. | Glider pilots | Tug Pilot. |
|---|---|---|
| 27 | S/Sgt Kerr & Walker | F/Lt Thomson. |
| 28 | S/Sgt Bone & Dean | F/O Garnett. |
| 28a | S/Sgt Baldwin & Michie | F/Sgt Richards. |

Load: 9th Parachute Battalion coup de main party & Royal Engineers.

Officer Commanding Glider assault party Major R. Gordon Brown.

Glider No.27  i/c   Lieutenant H. Pond.
Glider No.28  i/c   Major R. Gordon Brown.
Glider No.28a i/c   Lieutenant H. Smythe.

Horsa glider Number 28a was towed off by an Albemarle piloted by Flight Sergeant Richards but the tow rope broke soon after take off and the glider had to land at RAF Odiham - the Albemarle returned to Brize Norton. The 9th Para. Battalion in No.28a under Captain Smythe, made their own way to Portsmouth, 'cadged a lift' in an assault landing craft and landed on the beaches on D-Day: they joined up with the 9th Parachute Battalion later at Chateau St. Come. The other two Horsas were towed on to Normandy in adverse weather conditions.

On the ground in Normandy only some 150 paratroops had assembled at their RV point by 0215 hours - with the assault planned for 0330 hours. To make matters worse Colonel Otway had none of his essential equipment for signalling the Merville battery assault gliders or his guns, mine detectors, explosives, radio sets or support aids for the ground assault, and only one heavy machine-gun.

99 RAF Lancaster and Halifax heavy bombers dropped three hundred and thirty-nine tons of bombs - including some two ton bombs - from 9000 feet on what they thought was the Merville battery, but was in fact the nearby hamlet of Gonnerville. The bombs missed their target and only narrowly missed the paratroops recce party near the battery. Furthermore they made large craters on the 9th Battalion's route to the battery, making the going very difficult. Unfortunately for the incoming stores and assault gliders this bombing raised clouds of dust and smoke which drifted across the intended landing zones making map reading impossible in the run in and approach.

Nevertheless the crews of the stores gliders cast off their tow at 0045 hours at 1500 feet with a patchy cloud base of 1000 feet and a wind speed of 25 knots from 310 degrees. Struggling to navigate and fly in the appalling conditions the Horsa pilots began to land their gliders as best they could south east of DZ V amid anti glider poles which caused casualties and heavy damage. Six glider pilots were killed and all the Horsas badly damaged - all the 9th Battalion's support equipment was out of reach of Colonel Otway and his paratroops.

Undaunted, Colonel Otway decided to attack with his depleted force armed with but one Vickers machine-gun, three PIATs and light weapons only. As 9th Battalion reached the outer defences of the battery the defenders opened up with six heavy machine-guns firing waist high, to which the paratroops answered with their one machine-gun - the German machine guns were silenced by two parties of paratroopers.

Working their way through the defences the paratroopers began to take casualties. Regardless, two gaps were blown in the wire and the paratroopers stormed through hurling grenades and firing their weapons in a valiant assault. Savage hand-to-hand fighting raged through the battery but the superbly trained paratroopers swiftly gained control, with some Germans surrendering when they realised who it was they were up against. The Red Devils reputation had gone before them.

As the ground attack began the two remaining Horsa assault gliders appeared overhead, having flown the Channel in almost continuous cloud cover. Staff Sergeants Bone and Dean in glider 28 - together with their paratroop load had had a bumpy ride over the sea. The glider's parachute arrester gear had streamed over the Channel - the combination stalled and lost height but the jettison gear was operated, releasing the arrester parachute and flying control was regained. The arrester parachute drag had strained the glider's tail plane and the flying controls became sloppy - the starboard undercarriage had also been carried away.

German flak opened up on both gliders as they crossed the French coast wounding four troops in the glider piloted by Staff Sergeants Kerr and Walker. Staff Sergeant Bone released tow at 1800 feet - his tug Albemarle piloted by Pilot Officer Garnett had circled the area four times under fire trying to pin point the battery without landing aids. Bone descended to 500 feet thinking that the bombed village of Gonnerville was his target, realising his error Bone banked his Horsa and landed successfully about three miles away from the battery at 0424 hours.

The other Horsa - number 27, flown by Staff Sergeants Kerr and Walker - - had also been towed four times round the area trying to locate the battery. Casting off tow at 1200 feet Kerr attempted to land on the battery but could not make it so streamed his arrester parachute and landed at 0425 hours under German anti- aircraft fire which hit the tail plane, only fifty yards from the target in an orchard. No sooner had the paratroops, with skull and crossbones painted on their helmets, and commanded by Lieutenant Hugh Pond - exited from the glider than they were in action against sixty Germans from the 736th Infantry, who were rushing to reinforce the battery garrison. This part of the assault played an important role by preventing reinforcements assisting the battery defenders. For their part in the Operation Staff Sergeants Bone and Kerr were awarded the Distinguished Flying Medal.

By 0500 hours the battery was in British hands and the bloody fighting ceased. Only twenty-two German troops, all of them very frightened, were left. The remainder, about one hundred, were dead. The sixty Germans who had been engaged by the glider party were dead or wounded.

The battery guns were found to be 75mm not 150mm as believed and were spiked by the paratroopers using grenades and explosives. Two were destroyed and the other two put out of action. Lieutenant M. Dowling reported to Colonel Otway that he had carried out the destruction of his objective - one of the guns- a few minutes later Colonel Otway found the gallant officer dead.

The price of victory was high - 9th Battalion took seventy-five casualties, killed, wounded and missing plus another one hundred and ninety-two para-troopers missing before the battery assault - some drowned in the swamps of Normandy.

Colonel Otway fired his "success" signal to prevent the Royal Navy opening fire on the battery, which was acknowledged by an RAF aircraft observed waggling its wings and his Signals Officer Lieutenant J. Loring, released a dishevelled homing pigeon to fly to England with news of their success. As Colonel Otway did not know for certain that his "Success" signal was known by the Royal Navy ships - he withdrew his men for safety.

Later the same day the battery was recaptured by the German 736th Grenadier Regiment but next day was again taken by 3rd Commando. It changed hands several times before being finally taken by British forces.

From the 7th to the 13th June when 9th Parachute Battalion was surrounded by the enemy in defensive positions at the Chateau St. Come, members of the Glider Pilot Regiment who had flown the battalion and other units, fought with great bravery in an infantry role, alongside 9th Parachute Battalion.

The concrete emplacements of the Merville battery are still there today and have become a tourist attraction. When the author visited the battery he spoke - somewhat in awe - to one of the surviving assault party, CSM' Dusty' Miller, of 9th Battalion, and marvelled that anyone could survive crossing the open ground surrounding the battery under fire. Rightly, the Merville battery assault has gone down in military history as an example of the valour and courage of the British airborne soldier.

The author is obliged to Colonel T.B.H. Otway, DSO. for his help in writing this account of the Merville battery epic assault.

# OPERATION MALLARD

The air lifting on the evening of D-Day, 6th June 1944, of 6th Air Landing Brigade as reinforcements for 6th Airborne Division, holding the left flank on the Normandy invasion bridgehead, by 38 and 46 Groups, Royal Air Force, in Phase Four of airborne operations for D-Day.

Army Forces to be air lifted:
6th Air Landing Brigade. CO. Brigadier H.K.M. Kindersley. comprising:
1st Battalion, Royal Ulster Rifles. CO. Lt. Col. Carson.
2nd Battalion, Oxford & Bucks. Reg. CO. Lt. Col. Roberts.
'A' Company, 12th Devons. Regt. CO. Lt. Col. Stevens.
195th Field Ambulance, RAMC. CO. Lt. Col. Anderson.
6th Airborne Recce. Regt. RTR. CO. Major Barnett.
Divisional troops:
53rd Air Landing Light Regt. RA.
249th Field Company, RE.
286th Field Park Company, RE.
63rd Company, RASC.
398th Company, RASC.
716th Company, RASC.
Ordnance Field Park, ROAC.
Divisional Signals, RCS.
Workshops, REME.
317th Field Security Section, Intelligence Corps.
Divisional Provost Company, CRMP.

Only 'A' Company of the 12th Devons under command of Major J. Rogers would be transported by glider on D-Day, the remainder of the regiment under Lieutenant Colonel G.R. Stevens would be seaborne, landing on "Queen" Beach at 1000 hours D+1.

'A' Company would be part of a special task force "Parkerforce" under command of Colonel R.G. Parker, DSO. Deputy Brigade Commander, consisting of 6th Airborne Recce Regiment, a Battery of the 53rd Light Regiment, Royal Artillery and one Troop of the 3rd Air Landing Battery. Their task would be to form a firm base with the artillery near Cagny so that the Recce Regiment could carry out reconnaissance south and south east of the 6th Airborne Divisional area of operations.

Landing Zones for Operation Mallard:
"N" Immediately north of Ranville to the east of the River Orne.
"W" Immediately south of Ouistreham on the west bank of the Caen Canal

Royal Air Force:
38 Group

| Squadron | Aircraft | Airfield | Glider | Nos. | LZ. |
|---|---|---|---|---|---|
| 190 | Stirling | Fairford | Horsa | 18 | W |
| 196 | Stirling | Keevil | Horsa | 17 | W |
| 295 | Albemarle | Harwel | Horsa | 20 | W |
| 296 | Albemarle | Brize Norton | Horsa | 20 | N |
| 297 | Albemarle | Brize Norton | Horsa | 20 | N |
| 298 | Halifax | Tarrant | Horsa | 1 | N |
| 298 | Halifax | Rushton | Hamilcar | 15 | N |
| 299 | Stirling | Keevil | Horsa | 18 | W |
| 570 | Albemarle | Harwell | Horsa | 20 | W |
| 620 | Stirling | Fairford | Horsa | 18 | W |
| 644 | Halifax | Tarrant | Horsa | 1 | N |
| " | " | Rushton | Hamilcar | 15 | N |

46 Group.

| 48 | Dakota | Down Ampney | Horsa | 22 | N |
|---|---|---|---|---|---|
| 271 | Dakota | Down Ampney | Horsa | 15 | N |
| 512 | Dakota | Broadwell | Horsa | 18 | N |
| 575 | Dakota | Broadwell | Horsa | 18 | N |

Glider Pilot Regiment:
1 & 2 Wings.
Squadrons. A, B, C, D, E, F, & G.
512 First and Second Pilots.

MALLARD

Between 1840 and 1935 hours on the evening of D-Day 256 tug/glider combinations began to take off from seven airfields in southern England, carrying troops of 6th Air Landing Brigade and 6th Airborne Divisional troops, including for the first time in history tanks of the Royal Tank Corps ( 6th Airborne Armoured Reconnaissance Regiment). One Horsa glider crashed on take off and three force landed in England due to tow rope breakage.

Weather conditions were good as the armada converged on the exit points on the English coast and steered for their two landing zones in Normandy. Some

274    The Glider Soldiers

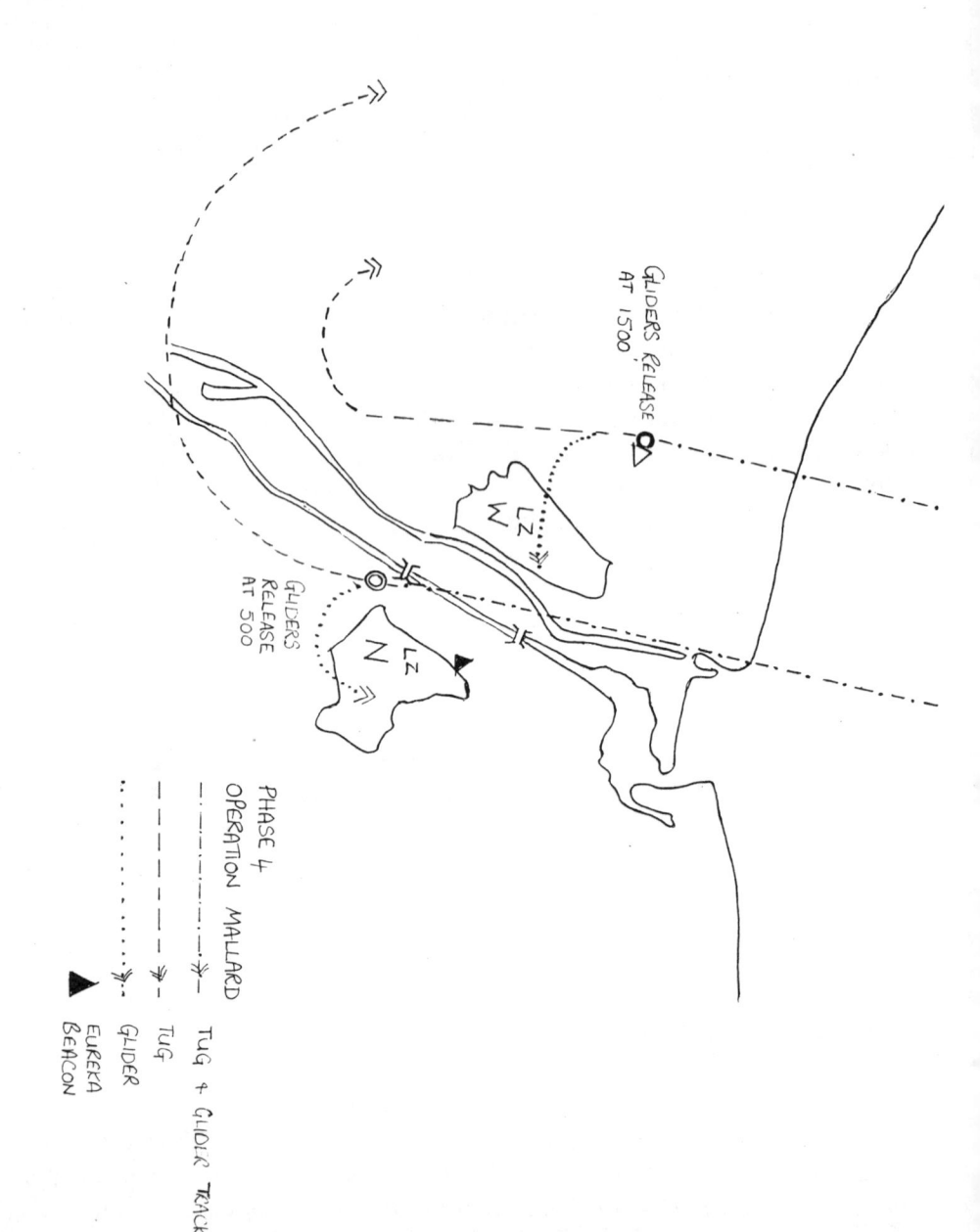

gliders were towed at 130mph five hundred feet over the Channel to avoid enemy radar as long as was possible. Half way across squadrons of Spitfire and Mustang fighters joined the armada, weaving a protective screen around it. Three Horsas and one tug ditched in the Channel - the remainder flew on in two loose streams - one stream for LZ W passed north west of Ouistreham, the other for LZ N over the mouth of the Caen Canal with weather conditions still good. As the combinations passed over the French coast they saw below Royal Navy ships bombarding the enemy with 16-inch guns. There was little or no cloud over the LZs with a wind of 10-15 knots from 320 degrees at the 1500 feet cast off point.

At 2051 hours the first of 142 gliders began to land under mortar and shellfire on LZ N. Thirty-two minutes later all had landed amid the 15 foot high anti-glider poles.

All thirty Hamilcars landed safely - the first tanks in history had been landed by air to the battlefield. Their engines had been started whilst airborne and the moment the gliders came to rest the tanks were driven out of the gliders and into action regardless of damage to the Hamilcars. The original tank plan was to form an Armoured Group with the 12th Devons but this had to be discarded as they were required elsewhere. Many of the twenty tanks and nine carriers became immobilised by discarded parachute canopies being caught up in and winding round the tank sprockets. An unforeseen development which was resolved during the night by burning the parachutes off with blow lamps. At dawn the Recce Regiment joined 8th Parachute Battalion in the Bois de Bavent and set up a series of Observation points (OPs) overlooking the Troarn - Caen - Escoville area. Motor cycle patrols were sent deep into German held ground from which much valuable information was gained which resulted in very successful air strikes and naval bombardment by HMS Mauritius on German vehicle parks and armoured units.

Captain B. Murdoch of the Glider Pilot Regiment who had flown his Horsa loaded with three gunners, a jeep and a 6-pounder gun, safely onto the LZ found himself acting as loader on the 6-pounder gun which went into action against German Mark IV tanks - armed with long barrel 75mm guns - of the 22nd Panzer Regiment. When the gun layer on Captain Murdoch's gun was killed he took command and with the remaining gunners knocked out four tanks. The Germans, due to tank losses, were unable to break through the British defences and halted their attack but the battle continued.

Meanwhile on LZ W 104 Horsa gliders began to land at 2052 hours. Considerable aerial bunching occurred and at one stage six combinations arrived line abreast. At 2120 hours all were down with the lead gliders having landed in the wrong direction which caused the following gliders to do the same.

## UK AIR MOVEMENT TABLE – "MALLARD"

| Load | RAF Unit | Aircraft | GPR Unit | Glider | Airfield | Take/Off | LZ | Remarks |
|---|---|---|---|---|---|---|---|---|
| 1st R.U.R. & 195th Air Land. Ambulance | 48 Sqdn 46 Grp | C.47 Dakota | 'E' Sqdn | Horsa (22) | Down Ampney | 1852-1902 | N | Down 2103-2109 |
|  | 271 Sqdn 46 Grp | C.47 Dakota | 'E' Sqdn | Horsa (15) | Down Ampney | 1840-1850 | N | 2106 |
|  | 512 Sqdn 46 Grp | C.47 Dakota | 'F' Sqdn | Horsa (18) | Broadwell | 1840-1950 | N |  |
|  | 575 Sqdn 46 Grp | C.47 Dakota | 'F' Sqdn | Horsa (19) | Broadwell | 1855-1910 | N |  |
| 33 Jeeps 29 Trailers 11 Motor Cycles | 190 Sqdn 38 Grp | Stirling | 'C' Sqdn & G | Horsa (18) | Fairford | 1938-2000 | W |  |
| 211 A/L Bty. R.A. 8 x 75mm Guns | 620 Sqdn 38 Grp | Stirling | 'C' Sqdn & G | Horsa (18) | Fairford | 1910-1935 | W |  |
| 716 Coy. RASC Part HQ A.L. Bdge | 296 Sqdn 38 Grp | Albemarle | 'B' Sqdn | Horsa (20) | Brize Norton | 1908-1946 | N | Down 2113-2115 |
| 'A' Coy. 12th Devons | 297 Sqdn 38 Grp | Albemarle | 'B' Sqdn | Horsa (20) | Brize Norton | 1850-1907 | N | Down 2112 |
| 2nd Ox & Bucks | 196 Sqdn 38 Grp | Stirling | 'D' Sqdn | Horsa (17) | Keevil | 1930-1945 | W |  |
|  | 299 Sqdn 38 Grp | Stirling | 'D' Sqdn | Horsa (16) | Keevil | 1903-1926 | W |  |
| 2nd Ox & Bucks | 295 Sqdn 38 Grp | Albemarle | 'A' Sqdn | Horsa (21) | Harwell | 1850-1905 | W | Down 2052-2055 |
|  | 570 Sqdn 38 Grp | Albemarle | 'A' Sqdn | Horsa (20) | Harwell | 1907-1917 | W | Down 2052-2055 |
| 3 Men. 1 Jeep. 1 Gun. | 298 Sqdn 38 Grp | Halifax | 'C' Sqdn | Horsa (1) | Tarrant Rushton | 1925 | N |  |
| 5 Tanks 62 Men 12 Trailers 9 Carriers 16 Motor Cycles | 298 Sqdn 38 Grp | Halifax | 'C' Sqdn | Hamilcar (15) | Tarrant | 1935-1950 | N | Armoured Recce Regiment |
| 3 Men. 1 Jeep 1 x 6 PDR Gun | 644 Sqdn 38 Grp | Halifax | 'C' Sqdn | Horsa (1) | Tarrant Rushton | 1925- | N | Pilot of Horsa Capt. Murdoch |

| Load | RAF Unit | Aircraft | GPR Unit | Glider | Airfield | Take/Off | LZ | Remarks |
|---|---|---|---|---|---|---|---|---|
| 15 Tanks and 60 Men | 644 Sqdn. 38 Grp | Halifax | 'C' Squadron | Hamilcar (15) | Tarrant Rushton | 1925-1940 | N | Armoured Recce Regiment |
| TOTALS | 14 Squadrons | 74 C.47s<br>69 Stirlings<br>81 Albemarles<br>32 Halifax's | 7 GPR Squadrons | 256 Gliders | 7 Airfields | | 2 LZs | |

On both LZs 246 gliders out of the 256 which had lifted off landed successfully - a magnificent achievement in the short period of landing which reflected the high flying skill of the Glider Pilots.

The 195th Air Landing Field Ambulance (formed 1st October 1943, from the 195th Field Ambulance) which had been carried in ten Horsas, established its Medical Dressing Station (MDS), which had been carried in six Horsas, at Ranville complete with two operating theatres and carried out treatment on casualties despite shellfire which struck the Station. The Medics collected casualties from the Regimental Aid Posts and brought them to the MDS day and night. For ten weeks the MDS was the main and almost the only medical aid unit east of the River Orne. Over 2500 casualties were treated and almost four hundred surgical operations carried out with the Germans only a mile away. Total medical staff was eleven officers, one hundred and two other ranks, using nine jeeps and five trailers. No.3 Section, RAMC moved with the Royal Ulster Rifles and No.4 Section with the Oxford & Bucks. A section consisted of one officer and twenty-one other ranks, (nineteen RAMC Medics and two RASC drivers), with two jeeps and one trailer. The Medics took 195 casualties all ranks, with three officers and twenty-eight other ranks killed.

1st Battalion Royal Ulster Rifles - 864 all ranks strong - were landed in the correct place at the correct time and immediately grouped at their appointed RV - a small village. At dawn next day C Company led by Major Hynds occupied a small strategic feature 'Hill 30' from which they gave covering fire with anti-tank and machine-guns whilst the remainder of the RUR attacked and captured Longueval. C Company on 'Hill 30' took heavy casualties from German mortar and self-propelled gun fire as the RUR made its attack. For two days the RUR were officially 'cut off' when engaged in the capture of Longueval, a position known as the 'Anzio beachhead'. The Germans put in strong attacks with self-propelled guns on the RUR and even the Regimental Aid Post, marked with Red Crosses, came under fire causing further wounds to already wounded troops. Not until the 14th June was the battalion relieved. Major Hynds and Captain Wheldon were awarded the Military Cross for the 'Hill 30' action.

The RUR suffered casualties of six officers and forty-five other ranks killed, one officer and thirty-three other ranks missing, and eighteen officers and three hundred and eighty-five wounded during the Normandy campaign.

The 2nd Battalion Oxford & Bucks. Regiment began to land in their gliders at 2130 hours having descended through enemy flak. All but four gliders landed on or near LZ W and casualties were slight. The Commanding Officer Lieutenant Colonel M.W. Roberts was injured when the glider in which he was in collided with another glider when landing.

After clearing the enemy out of Benouville with a battalion of 3rd Infantry Division the regiment assembled as planned at the RV point just west of the River Orne and moved out at 2215 hours to the intended concentration point east of the Orne. Passing over Pegasus Bridge the regiment located at Ranville chateau where they set up a defensive perimeter in the grounds. There they were joined by the Coup de Main troops from the Caen Canal and River Orne bridges assault party and Captain B. Priday and his men from a Coup de Main glider, which had been mis navigated by its tug, landed some miles away from its LZ. C Company sent a fighting patrol into the village of Herouvillete but found it deserted.

At 0430 hours next day (7th June) the regiment moved off towards Herouvillete with C Company in the lead. Entering the village they found an injured glider pilot who had been locked up by the enemy all day without food or water.

With the village clear of Germans the regiment moved off at 0830 hours towards their prime objective, Escoville, which lay 1000 yards to the south.
A and B Patrols were sent out and reported German snipers in the village but by 1100 hours the regiment was dug into defensive positions. German resistance increased and Regimental Headquarters could not reach its intended position - the chateau at Escoville. At 1500 hours the enemy attacked supported by armour and it became clear that Escoville could not be held without anti-tank guns. The Commanding Officer obtained permission to withdraw to Herouvillete as Escoville was dominated by enemy held high ground to the south and east.

During this withdrawal to better positions at Herouvillete A, B and D Companies were heavily engaged in house to house and close quarter combat. C Company moved to a covering fire position forward of Herouvillete and the forward companies of the regiment withdrew through their positions. Elements of A and D Companies were cut off at Escoville but Major J.S.R. Edmunds led a counter attack which enabled the two companies to withdraw. The regiment then occupied defensive positions but had taken eighty seven casualties. The Commanding Officer Lieutenant Colonel Roberts was now unable to walk and was evacuated and his place as CO was taken over by Major M. Darrel Brown.

During the period till the 10th June the regiment took casualties of fifteen killed, ninety seven wounded and eighty-nine missing. The regiment remained in the line and advanced to the River Seine taking more casualties of six all ranks killed and forty-two wounded. On the 31st August orders were received to return to England and on the 3rd September the regiment was in barracks at Bulford.

'A' Company 12th Devons landed on LZ W at 2130 hours without serious mishap although the LZ was mined and obstructed by anti-glider poles. The seven Horsa gliders were widely dispersed and some difficulty was experienced in removing the tails of the Horsas for off loading the Jeeps, trailers and 300lb of ammunition carried in four of them. Some of the tails were hacked off with axes and it was 2300 hours before the company finally assembled.

The company moved out to the "Parkerforce" assembly area south of Breville but on reaching Ranville at 2359 hours found it occupied by the enemy so a halt was made. At 0300 hours "Parkerforce" was disbanded and the company was put under the command of 13th Parachute Battalion and engaged in clearing German snipers of which five were dealt with. At noon on the 7th June the company occupied the village of Herouvillete - clearing it of snipers and booby traps. Later that afternoon the 2nd Oxford & Bucks. who had been in position at Escoville, were attacked and withdrew to the 'A' Company positions. A line was then taken up with the Oxford & Bucks. and the Germans held. At 2100 hours the company rejoined 12th Devons at Le Bas de Ranville.

By the 7th July the 12th Devons had been in the Line in close contact with the enemy for a month so handed their positions over to the 2nd Oxford & Bucks. and went into battalion reserve. On the 18th August they were back in action under 5th Parachute Brigade and so continued until the 27th August when they were withdrawn. On the 2nd September the Devons embarked on the LSI Princess Astrid for Southampton then Bulford.

Operation Mallard had been an outstanding success - 256 tug/glider combinations had been detailed of which 256 lifted off and were escorted to their LZs by 15 Fighter Squadrons of No.11 Group, Royal Air Force. 246 gliders reached the LZs in daylight carrying troops and equipment. German morale was reduced to a low ebb by this display of overwhelming power and by the end of D-Day 6th Airborne Division had achieved its objectives, thanks to brilliant planning and the courageous actions of the aircrews of 38 and 46 Groups, Royal Air Force, the soldier airmen of the Glider Pilot Regiment and the gallant soldiers they carried by air to battle.

## OPERATION 35A (DINGSON)

The landing behind enemy lines of ten Hadrian gliders carrying French SAS troopers and jeeps near Lorient, France, on the 5th August 1944.

By the beginning of August 1944, US Armoured columns were thrusting into Brittany with their objectives the deep water ports of Lorient, Brest and St. Nazaire on the French coast, the capture of which would enable the United States to bring men and materials direct from the USA to France. Under their flamboyant leader, General George S.Patton, the US Armies raced towards the ports bypassing any resistance offered by the enemy.

Active in the Brittany area were 20,000 men and women of the French Resistance under the overall command of a French officer Albert M. Eon. Also active in the area were 150 troopers of the 4th Battalion French SAS centred on Vannes near Lorient, whose prime objective was cooperation with the Resistance and causing mayhem to German communications and troop movements fifty miles ahead of the Allied front lines. On the 3rd August 1945, the British Broadcasting Corporation broadcast coded messages to the Resistance to increase their activity against the Germans short of open warfare.

In order to aid further both the Resistance and the US Army advance it was decided to send in more French SAS troopers and jeeps to attack German strongpoints, some by held by Russians who had joined the German Army. As this was to be a small clandestine operation the smaller US Waco CG4A (Hadrians) gliders were selected instead of the large British Horsa glider. Fourteen Hadrian gliders were gathered at RAF Tarrant Rushton, Dorset, and 298 and 644 Squadrons of RAF 38 Group equipped with Halifax aircraft were detailed to be the towing squadrons.

Operation Dingson itself was one of four SAS Operations which had been established near Vannes with 150 SAS troopers from 4th Battalion French Parachute Regiment and almost 3000 armed French Resistance whose mission was to operate fifty miles in front of the Allied front lines and cause havoc to the German's lines of communication thereby disrupting troop movement and tying down large numbers of German troops who tried to deal with them. On the 18th June 1944, the Germans had attacked the Dingson force at Vannes but the SAS and resistance melted away into small groups who continued to wreak havoc on the enemy.

Dingson Air Movement Chart - Planned. Tarrant Rushton.

| Load | RAF Unit | Aircraft | Glider |
|---|---|---|---|
| Jeep/3 men | 298 Squadron | Halifax | Hadrian No.2 |
| " | " | " | No.4 |
| " | " | " | No.5 |
| " | " | " | No.7 |
| " | " | " | No.9 |
| " | " | " | No.11 |
| Jeep/3 men | 644 Squadron | " | No.1 |
| " | " | " | No.3 |
| " | " | " | No.6 |
| " | " | " | No.8 |
| " | " | " | No.10 |

Twenty two glider pilots of the of the Glider Pilot Regiment under the command of Captain 'Peggy' Clarke, were to fly eleven Hadrian gliders on tow from RAF Tarrant Rushton, Dorset, across the English Channel to a release point eight miles ENE of Lorient to land at an LZ near St. Helene, four miles south of Lorient with with their loads of French SAS troopers. Each glider would carry three troopers and one heavily armed jeep together with their ammunition and equipment. One glider - No.8 - would carry in addition Brigadier McLaren as a Liaison Officer.

With all men and aircraft assembled at Tarrant Rushton the operation was scheduled for August 5th 1944, and radio messages were sent to the Resistance in Brittany to expect a small force of gliders to land at St. Helene at 2200 hours on that date.

At 2005 hours on the 5th August the operation got under way when Squadron Leader Norman of 644 Squadron with Major Dale as passenger, towed off glider No.1 piloted by Captain Clarke and his co-pilot Staff Sergeant James from Tarrant Rushton, to be followed in rapid succession by five more Halifax tugs piloted by F/O Blake, F/Lt Egerton F/O Calverley and S/Ldr. Rymills all of 644 Squadron.

A few minutes later at 2010 hours six Halifax tugs of 298 Squadron piloted by F/Lt Ensor, F/O Lee, F/Sgt Cunliffe, W/O Smith, W/O Bain and F/O Doughill towed off six more Hadrian gliders.

All eleven combinations set course for France in a loose stream but almost immediately the Hadrian glider towed by F/O Lee went unserviceable and had to be brought back to Tarrant Rushton. The remaining combinations continued on over the Channel at 800 feet towards France.

Ten Hadrians were now being towed in two loose streams over the Channel escorted by two squadrons of Spitfires. Each glider carried an armed jeep weighing over 3250lbs plus the weight of a twin Vickers K machine-gun mounted at the front and a single one at the rear of the eleven foot long vehicles. The French SAS crew of three - one driver and two gunners - either sat strapped in the seats of the jeeps or crouched behind it. Each trooper was heavily armed with a sub machine-gun, pistol, fighting knife, grenades and phosphorous bombs specifically for use in attacking enemy strong points. They were hard tough troops who gave nor expected any quarter - they bitterly resented the German occupation of their country and the fact that White Russians were serving with the Germans in the area.

As the first of the combinations arrived over the LZ at St. Helene the light was failing. The Resistance had marked the LZ with small fires and purple smoke indicators but additionally the Germans had coincidently and unwittingly set fire to a house near the LZ which also acted as a marker. Glider No.1 flown by Captain Clarke and Staff Sergeant James cast off tow on their own initiative and landed safely one and a half miles north of the intended LZ. Their tug pilot, Squadron Leader Norman flew over the correct LZ and his aircrew which included Major Dale, GPR, fired green Very lights to indicate the intended LZ to prevent a wholesale landing on the wrong field.

The remaining nine gliders cast off their tow at 2200 hours at 1000 feet and began to make their landings. Five landed on the correct LZ and the other four nearby. The landing went well apart from Hadrian No.5 piloted by Staff Sergeants Rossdale and Newton which made a heavy landing in an orchard and went into a hedge. Both pilots were badly cut and shaken by the impact and were spirited away by the Resistance to receive medical attention.

On landing the SAS troopers unloaded their jeeps and equipment and with the remaining eighteen glider pilots crammed into the jeeps and made for the local Resistance HQ located in a farmhouse. There the glider pilots were confined as the Germans had put a price of 20,000 francs - dead or alive - on their heads. ided by the weapons, ammunition and jeeps brought in by the gliders the Resistance attacked and took the airfield at Vannes. Shortly afterwards the US 4th Armoured Division, commanded by General John S. Wood, took Vannes intact and the Germans retreated into Lorient which they had turned into a fortress.

With the glider pilots unable to return to England they had to live in the Resistance farmhouse with the SAS troopers and shared in their sparse fare. Chafing at being confined to the HQ some glider pilots explored the local countryside and on one occasion Sergeant Beezum and Staff Sergeant May almost walked into a patrol of renegade Russians fighting for the Germans, and had to be led back to the Resistance HQ by an elderly Frenchman. The main duty of the glider pilots was guarding the very few prisoners the French SAS brought in and some Frenchmen accused of being collaborators. The standing order for the glider pilots was that if the Germans attacked they were to lob a few grenades into the pig sty where the prisoners were held but to try and avoid harming the other occupants of the sty - the pigs.

The glider pilots stayed with the Resistance for a week until the US 4th Armoured Division entered the town of Aurai a few miles away - they were then taken by the Resistance to Aurai and then the airfield at Rennes. There the enterprising glider pilots managed to get a message back to England requesting transport home and two days later a Dakota aircraft arrived at Rennes and the eighteen glider pilots embarked - landing at RAF Netheravon three hours later. The two casualties Staff Sergeants Rossdale and Newton stayed in Brittany in the care of the Resistance and returned later.

Operation 35A (Dingson) had been successfully carried out with no fatal casualties to the glider pilots or the aircrews of the towing squadrons.

Operation Dingson - Actual glider/tugs involved:

### 298 SQUADRON

| | | | |
|---|---|---|---|
| Halifax LL347 F/L Ensor | 2010 t/o | Hadrian 2. Pilots. | Perkins & Crockford |
| Halifax LL346 F/O Doughill | 2035 t/o | " 5. | Rossdale & Newton |
| Halifax LL361 F/Sgt Cunliffe | 2010 t/o | " 7 | May & Bunpeal |
| Halifax LL271 W/O Smith | 2010 t/o | " 9 | Cason & Carr |
| Halifax LL401 W/O Bain | 2010 t/o | " 11 | Walter & King |

### 644 SQUADRON

| | | | |
|---|---|---|---|
| Halifax LL326 S/L Norman | 2005 t/o | " 1 | Clarke & James |
| Halifax LL402 F/O Blake | 2005 t/o | " 3 | Mullholland & Redbreast |
| Halifax LL301 F/L Egerton | 2005 t/o | " 6 | Thomson & West |
| Halifax LL218 S/L Rymills | 2005 t/o | " 8 | Glover & Critchett + Brig. McLaren |
| Halifax LL400 F/O Calverley | 2005 t/o | " 10 | Bayley & Beezum |
| Halifax LL406 F/O Lee | 2010 t/o | " 4 | Took off but glider went u/s and was brought back to base, landing at 2050 hours. |

The author is obliged to Staff Sergeant Denis Cason, Dingson glider pilot, for his assistance in writing this account of Operation Dingson.

# OPERATION ANVIL/DRAGOON

The invasion by Allied airborne and ground forces of the South of France on the 15th August 1944.

The airborne landings - though largely by US Forces - did contain a British element landing by glider and parachute. As in Sicily it was found that the smaller US Waco CG4A (Hadrian) gliders could not carry the support equipment needed by the parachute troops. It required two Wacos to carry a gun and jeep - accordingly the much larger Horsa gliders were needed.

The basic airborne landing plan was for teams of US and British Pathfinder paratroops to drop during the early hours of the 15th August and mark LZs for the landing of gliders and paratroops inland of the seaborne forces assault beaches. The airborne forces would seize and hold ground to prevent German reinforcements counter attacking the Allied beachhead and also harry the rear of the enemy positions.

Specifically formed for the operation was the 1st Airborne Task Force under the command of Major General Robert T. Frederick, US Army. The British forces under his command were:

2nd Independent Parachute Brigade Group CO Brigadier C.H.V. Pritchard
3rd Independent Squadron, Glider Pilot Regiment.CO Major R. Coulthard.
64th Light Battery, Royal Artillery.
300th Air Landing Anti-Tank Battery, Royal Artillery.

GLIDERS:
Horsa 36.

British forces would land on LZ O - a four hundred yards square area some three miles north of the village of Le Muy. 1st Independent Parachute Platoon would drop at 0330 hours as Pathfinders to be followed at 0410 hours by 2nd Parachute Brigade Group. The gliderborne artillery would land at "H" Hour - 0800 hours - as the seaborne forces assaulted the beaches.

Take off airfield for the British gliders would be Tarquina on the Italian coast north-west of Rome and the flight path would be the island of Elba, the northern point of Corsica then landfall just east of Cannes on the French coast. The glider tugs would be C47 Dakotas of the USAAF 9th Troop Carrier Command, commanded by Brigadier Paul L. Williams. The 75th, 76th 77th and 78th Squadrons of the 435th Troop Carrier Group, 53rd Troop Carrier Wing,

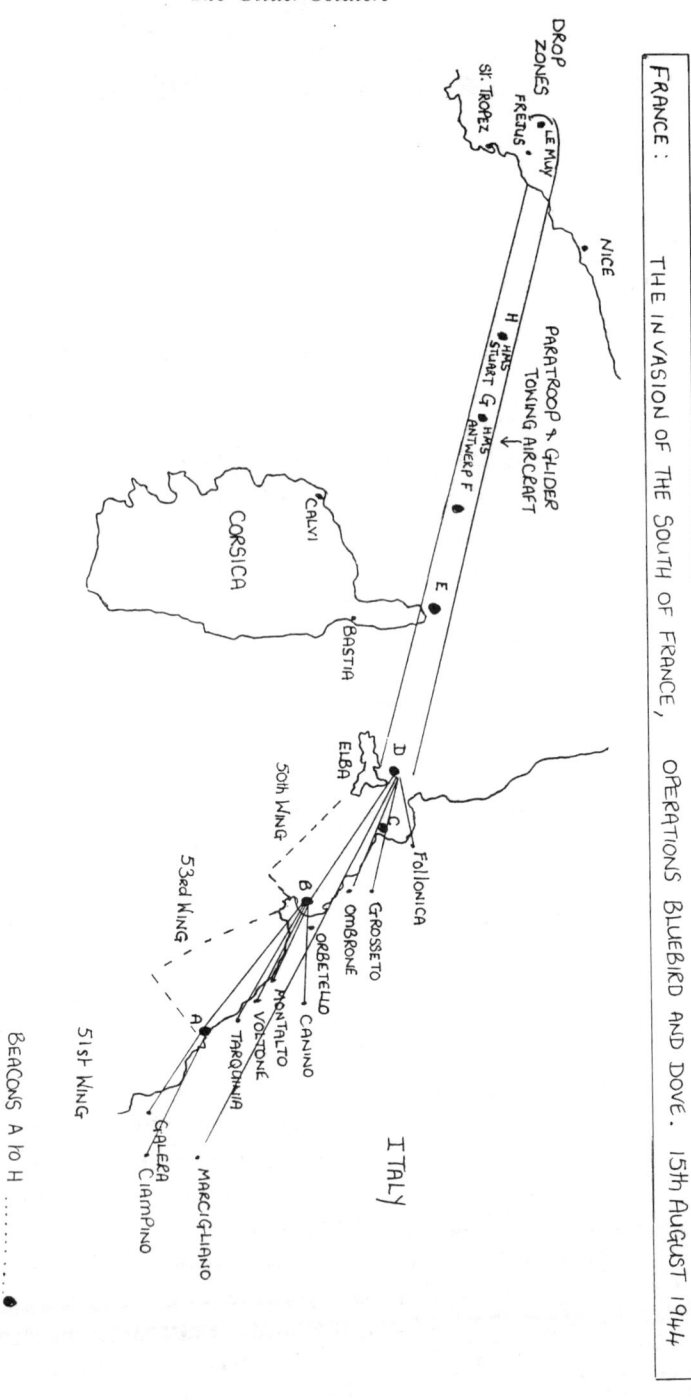

FRANCE: THE INVASION OF THE SOUTH OF FRANCE, OPERATIONS BLUEBIRD AND DOVE. 15th AUGUST 1944

DROP ZONES
ST TROPEZ
LE MUY
FREJUS
NICE
PARATROOP & GLIDER TOWING AIRCRAFT
H HMS STUART G
ANTWERP F
CORSICA
CALVI
BASTIA
E
ELBA
50th WING
D
C FOLLONICA
GROSSETO
OMBRONE
ORBETELLO
MONTALTO
VOLTONE
CANINO
TARQUINIA
53rd WING
B
A
51st WING
GALERA
CIAMPINO
MARCIGLIANO
ITALY

BEACONS A to H ●
G HMS ANTWERP UNTIL DUSK D day
H HMS STUART PRINCE

would tow thirty-six Horsa gliders, piloted by aircrews of the Glider Pilot Regiment and four hundred and fifty Waco gliders piloted by US pilots. The Wacos would be on double tow and the Horsa gliders on single tow with the whole glider operation codenamed Bluebird.

Before dawn on D-Day - Tuesday, 15th August 1944, the glider operation began. At 0530 hours the first combinations began to lift off from Italy and head for France via Elba and Corsica. One glider was forced to return to base with unserviceable ailerons but the remainder flew on in brilliant sunshine towards Corsica.

Off the southern French coast Allied warships began bombarding the invasion beaches between Saint Raphael and Cavalaire at 0730 hours. At 0800 hours the seaborne US 7th Army began to land on the beaches.

The Bluebird glider mission flying over Corsica received a radio message from General Williams instructing that due to mist blanketing the LZS, all Horsa were to return to base - the Waco gliders however were to fly on to France. The lead Horsa combination turned over Corsica and the rest of the Horsa mission followed suit in radio silence. The pilots unaware of the reason for returning to base. Two of the towing Dakotas developed engine trouble and had to cast off their Horsas - both of which had to land in Corsica.

The Waco combinations flew on towards their LZ and on reaching it found it shrouded in mist making landing impossible. For an hour the Waco mission orbited the area waiting for the sun to burn off the mist. At 0926 hours the mist had cleared enough to locate the LZs and the Wacos cast off and began to land. The LZ had been largely cleared of anti glider poles and German troops by the paratroops and the Wacos were able to land without fatality - although eight pilots were injured in heavy landings. The Waco loads of guns and jeeps were offloaded and soon in action.

Meanwhile the Horsa mission were flying back to base - the glider passengers unaware of what was happening or where they were. As the Horsas cast off their tow ropes and began landing some of the passengers thought they were in France. In one glider the Royal Artillery gunners prepared to drive out with jeep and gun through the wooden tail fuselage without worrying about damage. They were stopped in the nick of time from driving out and rendering the Horsa to wreckage.

Tarquina airfield became a hive of activity with the tow planes having to be refuelled and the Horsas re-marshalled for another lift off. By 1430 hours the first Dakota/Horsa combination lifted off - en route once again for France - within thirty minutes all were airborne.

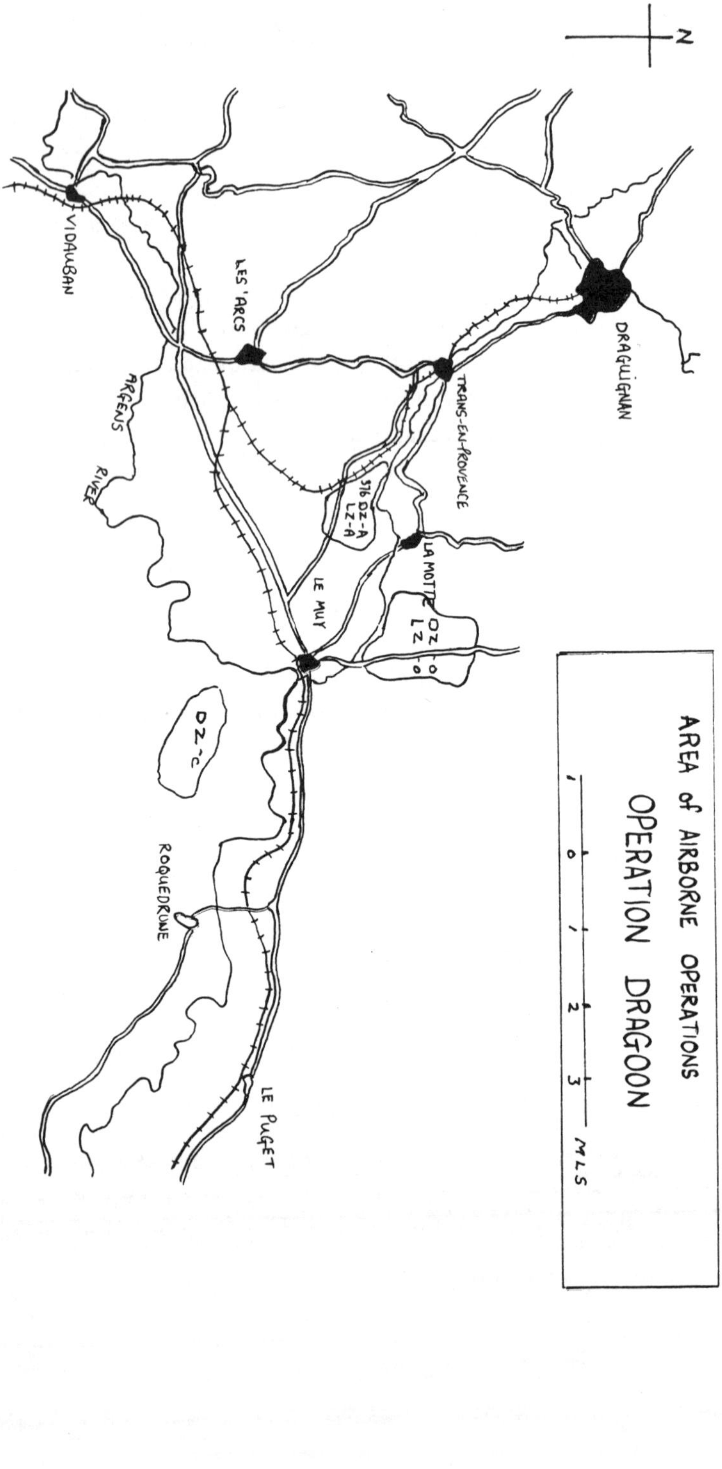
AREA of AIRBORNE OPERATIONS
OPERATION DRAGOON
1 0 1 2 3 MLS
N
VIDAUBAN
LES 'ARCS
DRAGUIGNAN
TRANS-EN-PROVENCE
ARGENS RIVER
516 DZ-A LZ-A
LA MOTTE
DZ-O LZ-O
LE MUY
DZ-C
ROQUEDRUNE
LE PUGET

This time there was no recall instruction and at 1745 hours the Horsa mission arrived over LZ O. Casting off at 1200 feet they began landing in echelons of three in fields and vineyards with no enemy opposition.

The lead Horsa - flown by the Squadron Commander Major R. Coulthard - overshot the LZ and landed heavily. Major Coulthard suffered serious injuries but his cargo was undamaged. The glider loads of thirty guns, jeeps, ammunition and gun crews were soon unloaded and driven off. The Glider Pilot Regiment took one fatal casualty - Sergeant W.R. Jenner- who died as the result of injuries received on landing and was later buried at Frejus.

Operation Dragoon/Bluebird was an eventual success with light casualties to the British glider borne force. The Independent Glider Squadron had displayed great flying skill and in spite of the mid operation recall - re-mounted a classic glider borne support role.

## DRAGOON

by Captain Corey Turner, Second in Command, Independent Glider Squadron.

We had already guessed that our D-Day for the invasion of France could not be far away. All the time we had continued the steady stream of gliders up from African ports, Horsas and Wacos, packing them in where we could like cars in a car park. The Paras and Gliders had done well in Normandy but there had been lessons to learn and we set to work to show what the veterans could do. In take off practice we had been getting the trains into the air - one every two minutes - then we halved the time and experimented to halve it again. By August we had three trains rolling down the runway at one time, thirty seconds apart, with the Yanks competing with us stop watches and all, a new record every day.

By now we had moved up once more from Salerno to an airfield 10 kilometres north of Rome called Marcigliano and by the first week in August we knew we were bound for France, the Cote d' Azur, Monte Carlo and all that. Our exact target was a road, rail and river bridge junction ten minute flight time inland from Cannes, a little town called Le Muy.

Our squadron was to head the operation, flying thirty-six Horsa gliders to be followed by four hundred and fifty American Wacos. Over 200 jeeps, 200 guns, bulldozers and scrapers for airfield construction, explosives, ammunition and rations. They asked us how much landing space we needed and we happened on a tattered copy of Picture Post with an aerial photo the most crowded corner of the Normandy landings they could find. Scaled up we counted thirty gliders in an area 300 yards square. On the premise that what has been done can be done better we asked for an area 250 yards square for our thirty-six Horsas.

The 1st Independent Glider Squadron - to give its Army description, commanded by Major Robbie Coulthard - was divided into three Flights led by me (also acting 2 i/c), Johnny Mockridge and Wally Masson. In addition, I had a Flight second in command - Teddy Hain. Robbie was to head the whole armada as number 1 in an echelon of 9. Thirty seconds behind I came with the second echelon - numbers 10 to 18. Then John with 19 to 27 and Wally with 28 to 36. That was the theory. You have a landing plan even though you know that in the event - for a hundred obvious reasons, it will not work. After all the first one to land has a nice area to himself, while number 20 will in theory find 19 gliders scattered all over the place in front of him. Not only that but if you stray outside your target you are getting under the wheels of the other four hundred, desperately looking for a place to put down. The photos showed our area to be covered with small trees and we hoped they were young fruit trees which would not seriously affect the Horsas.

So far as we were concerned Operation Dragoon went off as near perfection as you are ever likely to get in a turn out of this size. We were off to the second, having been up most of the night. We'd been in the air well over an hour and were already in our minds picking the Riviera coast out of the morning mist when the lead tow ships suddenly banked round and the whole shebang headed back to Italy and by 0800 hours we were landing back at our starting point at Tarquina. There was a rumour that the Navy had scrubbed the whole thing, that they had got nervous as they had Churchill on a battleship somewhere watching the affair like a football match. What a let down! But wait, here comes the Base Commander. How long would it take to set up the gliders again? you tell us - Two hours? Yes, we'd be ready in two hours. And then the pandemonium. Re-testing of tug engines and release gear. Gliders being dragged back from every corner of the airfield. Controls to check, ropes to snake out, maps to check. By mid afternoon we were airborne once more, steering fair for France, course 300° in a cloudless sky! Elba down there under the starboard wing, the northern tip of Corsica dim in the distance ahead.

This time it went like a dream. There was the coast, no imagination this time: white buildings, red cliffs, timber. There was the island Santa Marguerite and the glaring white front of Cannes and the timbered hills beyond. Ships. We'd never heard of rocket ships much less seen them, spouting their hundreds of missiles ahead of us. Then we were over the land. Ten minutes to go. I'd already drawn the track on my map, divided into ten one minute sections. One minute, two minutes, three minutes, all forest and rocky hills below - tracer like toy fireworks curving up and away. On my wing the other gliders rocking steadily along. Sergeant Harry Lansdell keeps his eyes rock steady ahead staring along the rope. Four minutes. Over my shoulder, over the bonnet of the jeep behind, the eyes of the Gunnery Sergeant Major stared past me as I gave him a thumbs up sign. Five minutes. Lots of smoke below the forest well alight but we were on track. Good old Peter Baker - his Pathfinders are guiding us bang on. Six minutes - whoops! that was a near one and the Horsa lurched for a moment but Harry gave no sign, his knuckles white on the control column. Seven - the craggy hills dead ahead and to port the flat cultivation in the river valley. Eight minutes and there was the town - Le Muy: there was the railway and on towards the north the river gorge. We were going to do it. Nine minutes, there is the LZ a square field, one corner cut off - the country road beyond. Time for Robbie dead ahead to let his rope go - there - well done Robbie. Their tow ships flying straight on, Robbie followed by his other eight gliders swing round to the left. My hand reached down for the rope release lever, a firm tug and away goes the rope. Now gently, all we have to do is to sit this old lady down.

'Dead ahead, you have got 1000 feet. 80 knots. 90 degrees to port.' Harry dipped the port wing as we came across track and there for the first time I saw the sky behind us, dark with a thousand aircraft, close packed as far as the eye could see. '700 feet, 75 knots, bring her round 90 degrees. Right. I've got her!' As I took the wheel Harry leaned back and took up the instrument readings without a break, '500, 70 knots, 400.' now round for the landing. Robbie's glider disappeared into the boundary hedge in a cloud of dust. 'Twenty seconds Sergeant Major - hold tight,' I called over my shoulder. We were hitting anti-glider poles as big as telegraph poles, knocking them over like dominoes as we came to a stop. I breathed out. 'Well done Harry!'

The gunners were out already, fanning out amid the vines, like on an exercise. I pulled the lever that should have blown the tail off with an explosive charge. Nothing!. So they set to work to hack it off with axes. I climbed onto the roof and looked about. John Mockeridge called across from thirty yards away, "OK Crash?" as I waved back I watched Wally settle beside him gentle as a feather. And suddenly the air was full of Wacos landing in all directions, at all speeds, crashing, stalling, cartwheeling. We kept our heads down for ten minutes and then it was over. By now our gunners had got their jeeps and guns away and the Yanks were picking themselves out of the wreckage, lighting cigars and shambling off down the road in the general direction of the war.

It took some time to cut Robbie out of his glider. He had two broken legs and as it turned out the war was over for him. Teddy Hain, our operatic tenor, finished his war here as well; he'd finished upside down with a jeep on top of him and was lucky to get away with a broken back. Sergeant Jenner had been hit in the air point blank as he was landing and was killed as he crashed straight into the German gun post wiping it out. Half of us had already flown over it at tree top height. This was the one and only time in the whole war that I got within a stones throw of the opposition. Within an hour all the Germans within a mile of us were behind barbed wire.

Finding myself for the first time in command of the squadron, I joined up with Peter Baker's Pathfinders and we made ourselves useful cutting out and clearing a light aircraft landing strip and collecting and organising the hundreds of containers that came down by parachute.

That first night - our first in France - we turned in like birds at dusk, tired out as much by the sheer excitement of it all as by our labours since reveille at 0400 hours at Tarquina. We purloined some wine from a nearby barn where the casks had come under fire; then we rigged parachutes overhead to keep off the dew and piled them up in dozens to make a bed of unimagined luxury - then slept like the dead. Hardships? I tell you!.

# OPERATION MOLTEN

The ferrying of Horsa glider reinforcements from England to Italy by the Glider Pilot Regiment and the Royal Air Force on the 9th October 1944.

In August 1944, 38 Group, RAF and the Glider Pilot Regiment were ordered to tow thirty-two Horsa gliders from RAF Fairford, Gloucestershire, to the Allied airfield at Chiampino, Italy.

Nos 190 and 620 Squadrons of 38 Group, equipped with Stirling aircraft, would tow the thirty-two Horsas of 22 Heavy Glider Conversion Unit based at Fairford and D Squadron, Glider Pilot Regiment under the command of Major J.F.Lyne would pilot the gliders.

On the 4th October 1944, D Squadron reported to Fairford to be briefed for the operation. Major Lyne tried to get his pilots included in the RAF aircrew briefing but was told that this was unnecessary - he was merely shown aerial photographs of Istres airfield on the south coast of France which was to be the first stop for the operation, and Chiampino airfield - the final destination. From these photographs Major Lyne had to decide where to land his Horsa gliders. He was also given a rough flight plan of the route to France and Rome which he passed on to his glider aircrews. It would appear that someone had decided that the glider pilots did not need detailed operational briefing as their gliders were being towed. It did not seem to occur to the RAF that if any tow ropes broke it would be helpful to the glider crews to know where they were if they had to make emergency landings.

Major Lyne asked that his glider pilot aircrews to be crewed up with particular tug crews but was told that this was not possible - another jarring fact was that the glider pilot's crew rations would be carried in the tug aircraft and issued on landing in France. The normal first class co-operation between the Royal Air Force 38 Group and the Glider Pilot Regiment did not seem to be in evidence on this occasion.

At 1000 hours on the 9th October 1944, the first of the thirty-two Stirling/Horsa combinations lifted off from Fairford and set course for France. Over France three glider tow ropes broke and the glider pilots had to make emergency landings. At 1600 hours the same day twenty-nine combinations arrived over Istres.

Two of the Horsas suffered damage to their wing tips on landing - the other twenty-seven being undamaged. The glider pilots marshalled their gliders into position for take off the next day.

After having flown for six hours they were hungry and tried to collect their flying rations from the tug crews but then discovered that the tug crews had not been told that the glider pilots flying rations had been included in their flying rations. The USAAF at Istres with their usual generosity came to the rescue and provided food and drink to those glider pilots who had none. The glider aircrews were not happy at this turn of events.

By 0600 hours the next day the glider pilots were back at work marshalling their gliders for take off. They had to collect their cast off tow ropes from where the RAF had dropped them and lay them out at the side of the runway between tug and glider. This was a task which - in Britain - was carried out by RAF Riggers. The author can testify that this is hard dirty manual labour for the Riggers.

By 1000 hours twenty-seven gliders were ready to go but had to wait until their tugs were refuelled. At 1200 hours the twenty-seven gliders began to be towed off for the next leg of the journey to Rome. The two damaged Horsas were left at Istres to be repaired and carry on their tow to Rome as soon as was possible.

Arriving at Chiampino the gliders cast off their tow ropes and landed successfully. The USAAF there were most helpful, collecting the cast off tow ropes and giving the glider pilots meals. No-one seemed to know what to do with the gliders - the USAAF not having received any instructions - the usual grit in the works situation which obtained in wartime (and peacetime). The USAAF did advise that the Horsas be placed under guard in case they disappeared via the local peasants as firewood. The glider pilots then found themselves acting as guards on their gliders until Major Lyne managed to arrange for the British 2nd Parachute Brigade troops to supply guards.

Major Lyne was now faced with the task of getting his glider pilots - over sixty in number - back to England. After much effort he managed to secure C47 Dakotas to fly his men back to England, but it was not until the 17th October that they were all back at their base in England.

Operation Molten was a success - twenty-seven of the thirty-two Horsa gliders which had been towed off on the 9th October had been delivered intact to Italy the next day, in a flight time of ten hours by the glider pilots of the Glider Pilot Regiment.

# OPERATION MARKET

The airlanding of 1st Airborne Division at Arnhem, commencing on the 17th September 1944.

In June 1944, General Eisenhower, Supreme Allied Forces Commander, Europe, approved the formation of an Allied Airborne Army with unified control of all Allied airborne troops in the European theatre of operations. On the 16th July 1944, US Lieutenant General Lewis H. Brereton was placed in command of the Allied Airborne Army and on the 2nd August received official notice of his appointment.

The British airborne commander Lieutenant General F.A.M. Browning was appointed Deputy Commander to Brereton on 4th August. On the 16th August the Airborne Army was designated 1st Allied Airborne Army, directly under Supreme Headquarters Allied Expeditionary Forces, Europe, (SHAEF). All Allied airborne forces came under its control and also operational control of all British and American troop carrying air forces. Command of the new army was exercised through Headquarters, 1st Airborne Corps under General Browning for British airborne forces and 18th Airborne Corps under US General Matthew Ridgeway for US forces.

By August 1944 Allied Forces had fought their way out from the Normandy beachead and were in pursuit of the German forces falling back towards Germany. Ahead of the Allies barring the way into Germany lay the formidable Siegfried Line - a chain of static defences - to which the Germans could retreat, occupy and hold.

The aggressive US General George S. Patton with his US 3rd Army were spearheading a rapid drive east and General Miles Dempsey's British 2nd Army were advancing eastwards through Belgium but both Armies were out running their chain of supplies, which stretched back 200 miles. Petrol, essential for a rapid advance, was in short supply.

The question arose as to which of the two armies should receive priority in supplies. General Patton with his plan to smash through the Siegfried Line with his armour or General Montgomery commanding 21st Army Group in the north who wanted to attack through Holland, outflank the Siegfried Line and punch into Germany. Berlin was the prize and a quick end to the war in Europe.

During August Montgomery recommended to Eisenhower that 21st Army Group and the US 12th Army Group be launched northwards through Belgium and Holland to take the port of Antwerp then wheel right to turn the Siegfried Line.

Eisenhower accepted Montgomery's plan and by the 4th September Montgomery's forces had driven through Belgium and into Holland, taking Brussels and Antwerp. But by the 8th September German resistance had stiffened and the Allied advance came to a halt on the Meuse-Escaut-Albert canal line.

On the morning of the 10th September Montgomery conferred with Eisenhower and obtained permission to use 1st Allied Airborne Army. The same day Major General Urquhart received his orders to carry out the airborne operation. Codenamed Operation Market the bold plan was to lay a carpet of US airborne troops from Eindhoven to Nijmegan by paratroop drop and glider landings - to take and hold vital bridges over canals and rivers for ground forces to advance over (Operation Garden). British airborne troops would parachute drop and glider land at Arnhem to take the bridges there.

The Arnhem bridges were the real prize but they were also the furthest away from Allied ground forces. When the Arnhem objectives had been taken British reinforcements would be flown in to the airhead there. The proposed plan gave an airhead from ten to sixty miles behind German positions and relied on the ability of the British 2nd Army - spearheaded by tanks - to punch along a single road through Eindhoven and Nijmegan to link up with 1st Airborne Division at Arnhem. D-Day was set for the 17th September.

At 1800 hours on the 10th September General Brereton held a Conference at his HQ at Sunninghill Park, Berkshire. General Browning was designated airborne forces commander and US General Paul L. Williams as air commander of troop, glider and supply aircraft. General Browning would fly in to the airhead by glider with a small staff to direct operations until contact was made with the advancing ground forces.

At 0900 hours on the 11th September another Conference was held to select the aerial routes to the airhead and landing zones. Two routes were chosen: a northern route which ran from the English coast at Aldeburgh, Suffolk, across the North Sea for ninety-five miles to the Schouwen Islands, then sixty miles to the Initial Point (IP) codenamed Ellis - three miles south of Hertogenbosch and thirty miles south of the Landing zones at Arnhem.

A southern route lay from Broadwell Bay, Essex, across the Thames estuary to North Foreland, Kent, then one hundred and fifty-nine miles to the IP code named Delos in Belgium on the Albert canal, then thirty-one miles north east to the Eindhoven landing zones.

Three glider landing zones were chosen - LZ S, LZ Z, and LZ L. 1st Air Landing Brigade would land on LZ S which was a mile long by half a mile wide, just north of the Amsterdam to Arnhem railway line and five miles from the Arnhem bridges - the main objectives. LZ Z was north of the village of Heelsum and south of the railway line - it was divided in two the eastern half being DZ X. LZ L was half a mile east of LZ S and was scheduled for use by the gliderborne element of 1st Polish Parachute Brigade and the US 878th Aviation Engineer Battalion who would land on D+2 to prepare landing strips to airland in British reinforcements. A supply dropping zone - SDP V - was chosen north of the railway line near Kopel.

Brereton decided that the airborne operation would be carried out in daylight to reduce landing losses but this increased the risk of casualties from German flak so the Royal Air Force and USAAF were detailed to attack and eliminate all known enemy positions before the airborne fleets were over the landing zones.

Beginning on the night of D minus 1 until the morning of D-Day, 404 RAF and 872 USAAF aircraft dropped 4191 tons of bombs on targets along the troop carrier routes and around Arnhem, Ede and Nijmegan. 100 RAF aircraft made a diversionary cover raid on Walcheren Island to conceal the real airborne assault points.

The Royal Air Force had 812 Horsa and 64 Hamilcar gliders available for the operation and seventeen squadrons of 38 and 46 Groups. But with 10000 troops to carry to the battlefield it was impossible to transport them all in one airlift so, of necessity, the operation had to be phased over three days.

First to land on D-Day would be paratroop Pathfinders to mark the landing zones, followed by 1st Parachute Brigade and 1st Air Landing Brigade plus half the gunners, engineers and divisional troops. The remainder of the division would follow on later lifts. A total of 8969 troops plus 1394 glider pilots would be involved.

Order of Battle - 1ST Airborne Division
General Officer Commanding: Major General R.E.Urquhart. DSO.

| Divisional HQ. | Divisional Troops. |
| --- | --- |
| CRA Loder Symonds | 1st Light Regt. RA. Thompson |
| CRE Myers | No.1 FOU. |
| Div. Signals Stephenson | 9 Fd Coy RE. Callaghan. |
| CRASC St.J. Paacke | 21 Independent Para Coy.Wilson |
| ADMS Warrack | 250 Coy RASC |
| ADOS Mobbs | 93 Coy RASC |
| REME Ewens | Ord.Fd. PKS. |
| SCF Harlow | REME Wshps. |
| Prov. Haig | 89 Fd Security Sec. |
| | Div. Pro. Coy. |

1 Wing GP Regt. Murray.
2 Wing GP Regt. Place.

1st Parachute Brigade
Brig. G.W. Lathbury, DSO.
Recce Squadron Gough
1st Para. Bn. Dobie
2nd Para. Bn. Frost
3rd Para. Bn. Fitch

1st Air Landing Brigade
Brig. P.H.W. Hicks, DSO.MC.
1st Border Regt. Hadden
7th KOSB. Payton Reid.
2nd South Staffs. McCardie
1st A/L Lt. Bty. Walker
181 Para. Fd. Amb Marrable

4th Parachute Brigade
Brig. J.W. Hackett, DSO. MBE. MC.
156th Para. Bn. des Voeux
10th Para. Bn. Smyth.
11th Para. Bn. Lea.

1st Polish Parachute Brigade
Major General S.Sosabowski

The basic battle plan for the operation was for 1st Parachute Brigade to drop and take the single span bridge over the Lower Rhine at Arnhem together with a pontoon bridge three quarters of a mile eastwards. By evening it was planned that a half circle bridgehead would be held with the ends anchored on the Rhine. When the remainder of 1st Airborne Division landed it was planned to enlarge this bridgehead. 1st Polish Parachute Brigade would paradrop south of the Rhine and land by glider on LZ L on the third lift and reinforce 1st Parachute Brigade both then acting as Divisional reserve.

    1st Air Landing Brigade, less half of the 2nd Battalion South Staffords who were to land on the second airlift, would land on LZ S north of the railway line and secure the LZs so that the second lift could land safely. 7th KOSB would cover to the north of the LZs, the Border Regiment - the south and west and the South Staffords the east towards Arnhem.

    D-Day - Sunday 17th September 1944, dawned fair in England. At 1010 hours 186 men of 21st Independent Parachute Company Pathfinders under Major B. Wilson took off in twelve Stirlings of 620 and 190 Squadrons, from RAF Fairford. Led by Squadron Leader Bunker in Stirling LJ930 the Pathfinder force set course for Holland and located LZ S and DZ X accurately. Arriving over the landing zones at 1240 hours, every one of the Pathfinders was dropped on the correct landing zones without casualties and, within fifteen minutes, had set out the landing aids of Eureka beacons, coloured panels and smoke pots. Only one aircraft had been fired on and damaged en route - no casualties were sustained.

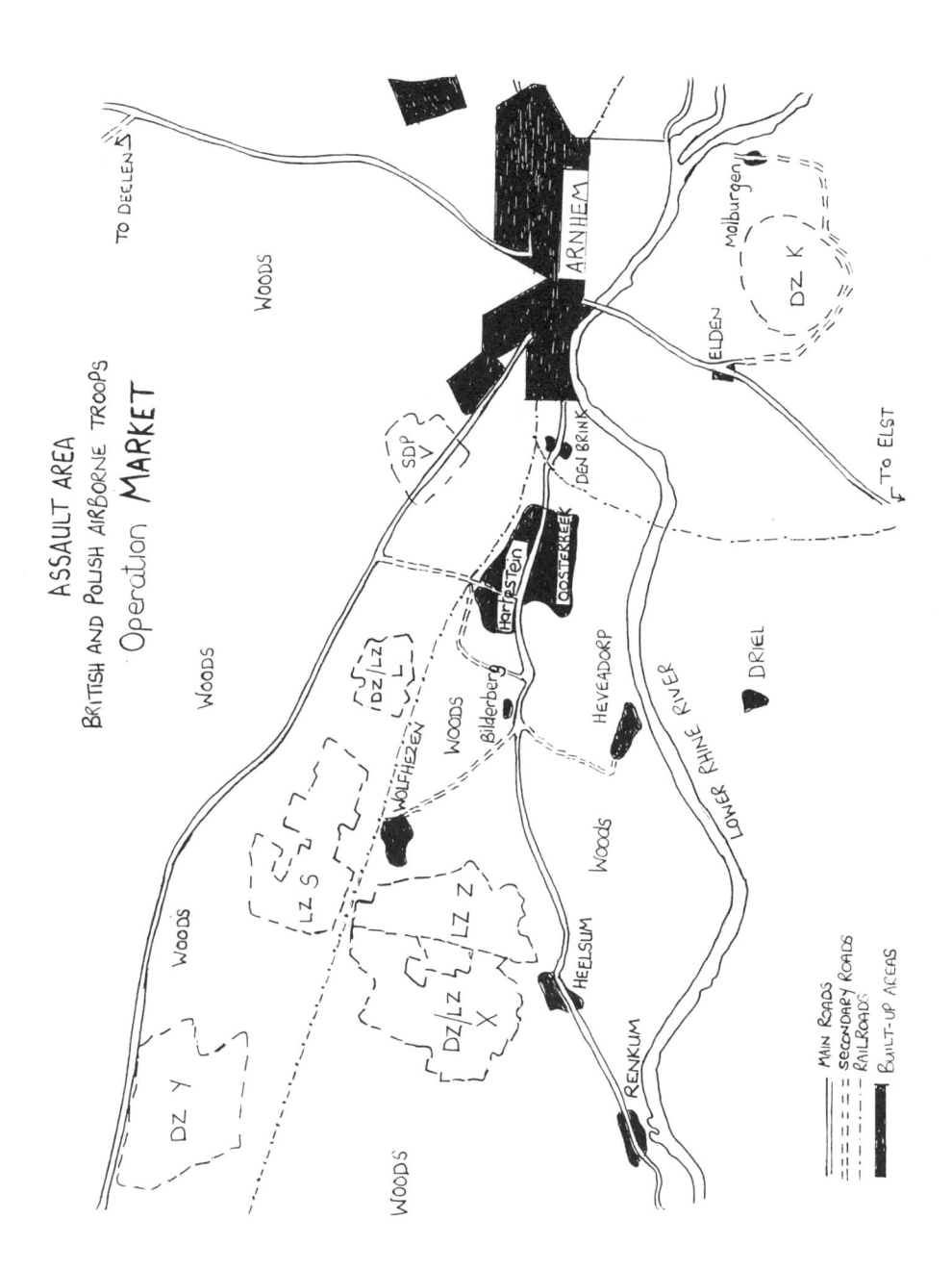

## The Glider Soldiers

**ASSAULT AREA**
**British and Polish Airborne Troops**
**Operation MARKET**

Immediately behind the Pathfinders flew 143 paratroop transport aircraft carrying 1st Parachute Brigade and 359 tug/glider combinations, a vast armada of 871 aircraft.

The gliders, 336 Horsa, 13 Hamilcar and 10 Hadrians, carried troops of 1st Air Landing Brigade. 7th Battalion KOSB, part of 2nd Battalion South Staffords and 1st Battalion Border Regiment were carried in Horsas and nine 17-pounder guns, five carriers and ninety troops were carried carried in the 13 Hamilcars. Thirty-two Horsa and six Hadrian gliders carried 1st Airborne Corps HQ under General Browning to LZ N near Nijmegan in the American sector. One Horsa had to force land in England, one ditched in the sea and one broke its tow rope over Holland. The remaining thirty-five gliders landed near Groesbeek at 1410 hours - twenty-eight managing to land on the actual LZ. By 1530 hours 1st Airborne HQ was functioning but was unable to make radio contact with 1st Airborne Division at Arnhem. Radio contact was established with HQ in England and 2nd Army, but General Browning had no information about the Arnhem situation until 0800 hours on the 19th September.

The Arnhem bound armada of transport and tug/glider combinations began to lose gliders - twenty three suffered tow rope breakage over England. Flying at 2500 feet in cloud the glider stream lost another glider over the sea and seven more over Holland. One combination had to return to base with tug engine trouble and three other tugs with engine trouble had to release their gliders. All The ditched gliders's crews and passengers were rescued by Air Sea Rescue. Thirty-nine gliders failed to reach the landing zones.

En route very little flak was encountered but on reaching the Arnhem area the glider stream came under small arms fire which damaged six glider tugs. Arriving over the landing zones at 1325 hours the glider pilots began to cast off their tow ropes and land in a light but variable breeze. 132 gliders landed on or near LZ S and 116 landed on LZ Z with another 27 very near.

7th KOSB under Lieutenant Colonel R. Payton Reid landed at 1330 hours amid slight enemy small arms fire. One glider crashed into a tree killing the pilot - this was the only fatal casualty on the LZ. Several of the gliders made heavy landings in the soft ground, which forced the undercarriages up through the bottom of the fuselages. To the strains of the pipes playing "Blue Bonnets over the Border", the Battalion assembled. 740 all ranks including 40 officers answered Roll Call and at 1500 hours the battalion moved off north in defence of the landing zones.

Encountering a German armoured car 'A' Company dealt with it but the other companies took up their defensive positions without opposition capturing several Germans including a female member of the Luftwaffe.

181st Air Landing Field Ambulance, RAMC, under Lieutenant Colonel A.T. Marrable and Major S.M. Frazer, landed in their gliders between 1315 and 1400 hours with ten officers and one hundred and four other ranks. By 1600 hours they had established a Dressing Station at Wolfhezen, two and a half miles north west of Osterbeek.

All the Hamilcar gliders managed to land but two got stuck in the soft ground killing the pilots and two 17-pounder guns were lost. One Hamilcar piloted by Staff Sergeants Jenks and Rathband was landed near the mental hospital at Wolfhezen. The two pilots stayed with their load - a 17-pounder gun and crew - and took part in the action that followed landing.

1st Parachute Brigade moved off their DZ to seize the bridges at Arnhem. 2nd Battalion reached the railway bridge but it was blown by the enemy. 'A' Company reached the main target the single span steel bridge between 2030 and 2100 hours and secured the northern end and houses nearby. An attempt was made to cross the bridge and secure the southern end by the attack was thwarted by strong enemy fire.

The first glider lift of the South Staffords consisted of Battalion HQ, B and D Companies and a platoon each of mortars and machine-guns, this went well and all except two gliders landed. One glider came down in German occupied territory and the other, with B Company's OC Major R.H. Cain aboard force landed in Kent. The Staffords landed amid German machine-gun fire and took nine casualties but silenced the opposition taking twenty prisoners - they then dug in and spent a quiet night apart from hearing the noise of battle at Arnhem.

On landing 1st Border Regiment moved off with 7th KOSB to take up their positions to defend the landing zones for the second lift due in next day. 1st Borders occupied all its objectives successfully without enemy resistance but came under enemy mortar fire during the night.

At dawn on the 18th September Lieutenant Colonel Frost's A Company at the Arnhem bridge numbered some 550 men - they had been reinforced during the night by Battalion HQ, B Company and men from other units. 3rd Parachute Battalion had followed Frost's troops but was heavily engaged by the enemy and came to a halt. 1st Parachute Battalion had fought their way towards the Arnhem bridge but came to a halt during the night north of the railway station due to strong enemy fire.

The German 9th SS (Hohenstauffen) and 10th SS (Frundsberg) Panzer Divisions had moved into the Arnhem area to refit and although this was reported by Dutch intelligence to the British it was not given credence. Present in the Arnhem area was Field Marshal Walter Model, commanding officer German Army Group B; at 54 years of age the youngest Field Marshal in the Wehrmacht, who

302  The Glider Soldiers

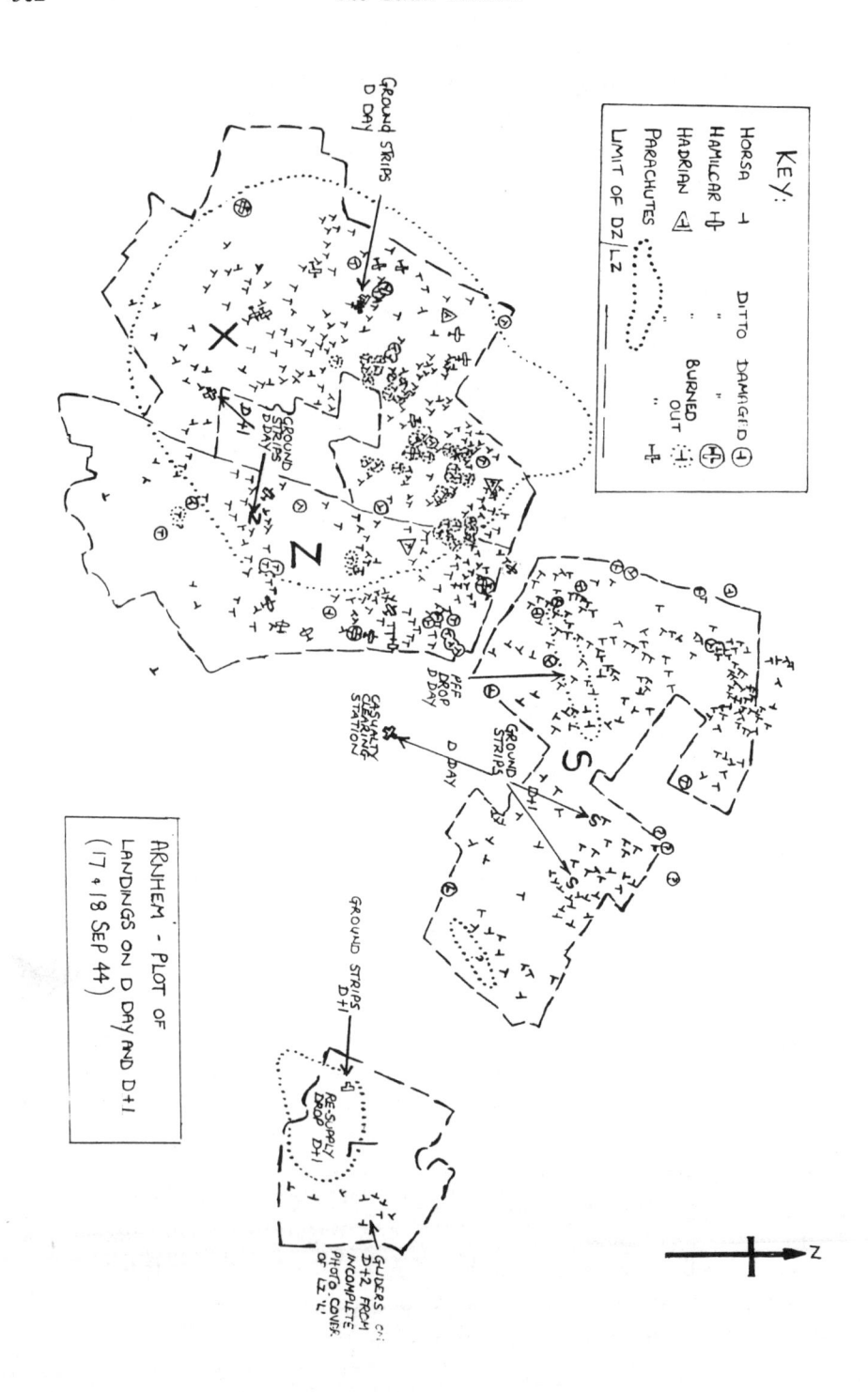

had his Headquarters at the Hartenstein and Tafelberg Hotels in Oosterbeek some three miles from the British landing zones. When Model had witnessed the British airborne troops descending he had ordered his Panzer Divisions into action - so the British troops were faced with numerically superior forces from the onset of the battle. On the afternoon of 17th September - D-Day - the Germans had found the Airborne Corps battle plan in a downed glider.

D+1 saw Colonel Frost and his men still fighting hard at Arnhem bridge. The 1st and 3rd Parachute Battalions were still valiantly fighting their way forward but could make little progress against strong German positions. Casualties began to mount and the two battalions were reduced to about one hundred able bodied paratroops each.

The Commander of 1st Air Landing Brigade, Brigadier Hicks, ordered Colonel McCardie and his South Staffords to get through to Arnhem bridge. Moving off at 1030 hours the South Staffords came under enemy air attack from fighters and ground attack from snipers. Oosterbeek was reached but the troops came under machine gun and sniper fire from high ground towards Mariedaal. D Company dealt with the snipers and remained in position to cover the remainder of the Staffords who reached the outskirts of Arnhem where they joined 1st Parachute Battalion under Colonel Dobie, who had but seventy men left. Rather than risk the small force in street fighting in the dark the advance was halted.

At 1123 hours on D+1 USAAF aircraft of the 314th and 315th Troop Carrier Groups took off from England with 2119 paratroops of 4th Parachute Brigade plus fifty one tons of supplies for dropping on Dz Y. Arriving over the DZ at 1406 hours 90% of the troops, jumping from 800 to 1000 feet, made a good drop under enemy fire. Twenty-four of the US aircraft were damaged by enemy fire and six were lost. Of the six aircraft lost five managed to drop their troops but the sixth went down killing all the US aircrew on board.

Low cloud and rain prevailed over the English take off airfields but at 1045 hours the first of the gliderborne reinforcements lifted off. By 1215 hours 279 Horsa and 15 Hamilcar were airborne and in stream to LZs X and S with the second airlift of 1st Air Landing Brigade.

The combinations had to fly in 8/10ths cloud with a base of 2000 feet. Seven gliders broke their tow ropes over England and two over the North Sea. Streaming over Holland with the now alerted enemy throwing up heavy fire - thirty of the tugs were damaged and several gliders. One tug was shot down but the glider released and came down near Arnhem. Thirteen gliders released over Holland and one over Belgium due to enemy flak.

Seventy-three gliders were intended for LZ S and sixty-seven landed on or near the landing zone. Two hundred and twenty-three were due on LZ X and one hundred and eighty-nine landed in the vicinity of the zone - of the two hundred and ninety-four which had lifted off two hundred and seventy had landed.

All the gliders carrying 2nd South Staffords under Major J.C. Commings, the second in command, landed safely - including one with Captain R.H. Cain aboard, whose glider had broken its tow rope over Kent the previous day. By 1530 hours all the gliders were down, some under enemy fire. One Platoon of C Company had to fight, under Lieutenant D.K. Edwards, to secure the load from a glider and became detached from the main body of South Staffords. Major Commings and his men moved off towards Arnhem with A Company in the van. They fought their way to the outskirts of Arnhem where they linked up with 11th Parachute Battalion at 0530 hours. Neither the Staffords nor the 11th Battalion could get further than near the St. Elizabeth Hospital, some distance from the all important Arnhem bridge.

After heavy fighting and amid confusion as to what was happening overall, the Border Regiment and 7th KOSB succeeded in reaching their objectives west and south of Arnhem, but were running out of ammunition and had taken many casualties.

By night fall on the 18th September 1st Airborne Division moved to positions near Hartenstein two miles west of Arnhem. Radio communications were bad, the Divisional command links to brigades were not capable of providing service over such a wide area at extreme ranges. The thick birch forest and built up areas blanketed radio transmissions and reception. The rear link to England was often unworkable and suffered interference from German radio stations. The rear link to Airborne Corps HQ at Groesbeek was not established and radio contact with 1st Parachute Brigade was lost on the Divisional Command Network frequency which was almost unusable and suffered interference from a British radio station. In spite of a change to reserve frequencies 1st Parachute Brigade could not be contacted. From the beginning there was a serious failure in radio links - both Divisional and Brigade Command radio links failed.

Pigeons had been issued at the take off airfields and 2nd Battalion - unable to get through on their radio from Arnhem bridge - released their pigeon William of Orange at 1030 hours of the 19th September he made it back to his loft in London at 1455 hours. He had covered 260 miles, of which 135 miles was over the North Sea, in four hours twenty five minutes, an average speed of 61mph. He was awarded the Dickin Medal - the animal VC - for the feat.

The glider pilots who had brought part of the division to battle now engaged the enemy as soldiers. The 1st lift pilots ringed the landing zones and fought off the Germans taking many casualties. When reinforced by the second lift glider pilots they fought with the 7th KOSB and the South Staffords, then later formed part of the defence of Divisional HQ at Hartenstein.

On D+2 the 19th September the South Staffords, followed by the 11th Parachute Battalion attacked at dawn along the road to Arnhem. A, B and D Companies of the Staffords moved off at 0430 hours and by 0500 hours reached the St. Elizabeth Hospital but had taken 40% casualties and called on 11th Parachute Battalion for assistance.

At 0800 hours strong German counter attacks began to develop and by 1050 hours the situation became serious causing the South Staffords to withdraw to the St. Elizabeth Hospital until the 11th Battalion attacked. A strong German attack with Tiger tanks overran the South Staffords positions, the Commanding Officer and second in command were wounded and taken prisoner. Captain (Acting Major) Cain the only senior officer left, took command of the remnants of the Staffords and ordered a withdrawal to form a defensive perimeter around Oosterbeek. This perimeter became known as the Station Oosterbeek position.

The Germans launched a ferocious assault - Tiger tanks attacked from the river direction and the Stafford's gun crews knocked out five of them. Lance Sergeant John Daniel Baskeyfield, in command of a gun crew, held his fire until the enemy tanks were within 100 yards. Opening fire he took out two Tiger tanks and a self-propelled gun. Baskeyfield was badly wounded in the leg and the rest of his gun crew were killed or wounded. Refusing to be evacuated he stayed at his gun alone. At 1430 hours the Germans attacked again and Baskeyfield, still manning his gun alone, stopped them in their tracks. His gun was put out of action by enemy fire but the lance sergeant dragged himself to another gun of his Section, the crew of which had been killed, opened fire and took out a self-propelled gun. As he prepared to fire another round he was killed. Lance Sergeant Baskeyfield was awarded the Victoria Cross for his actions in battle.

Back in England bad weather had prevented the airlift of 1st Polish Parachute Brigade by aircraft of the USAAF 52nd Troop Carrier Wing to DZ K - south of the Arnhem bridge.

Arnhem bridge the Germans began to reduce Colonel Frost's position by tank attack but the defenders still held out.

From seven airfields in England the third and final airlift of gliders began at 1130 hours. Forty three Horsa and one Hamilcar gliders lifted off with Polish troops, RASC, jeeps, and machine guns. Thirty five Horsas were scheduled for LZ L with the Poles and eight for LZ S and one (which had been left over from the second lift) for LZ S. Once airborne the small stream almost immediately lost four Horsas over England three due to tow rope breakage and one with a shifted load.

Two more Horsas ditched at sea and five more broke tow over Belgium. The Hamilcar had to force land at Ghent.

Heavy flak was encountered over the Arnhem area as the remaining gliders approached at 1600 hours. They had no fighter escort due to and error in timing. One glider was shot down and one was damaged so had to cast off.
Twenty eight Horsas were released over LZ L and landed while the battle was in progress. Heavy casualties were taken. Two gliders landed on LZ X and one landed on LZ S. The Polish troops carried reported to Roll Call but had lost many men. B Company of 7th KOSB helped the Poles to extricate their vehicles from the Horsas.

Also scheduled for the 19th September was a resupply drop by 38 and 46 Groups, Royal Air Force. The intended SDP V was in enemy hands and frantic visual efforts were made by the British airborne troops to inform the pilots of this to no avail. General Urquhart had sent a message to England informing that the SDP was not available but this message did not reach the Royal Air Force who were determined to aid their comrades on the ground.

The one hundred Stirlings of 38 Group and sixty-three Dakotas of 46 Group headed for the original SDP V. Crossing the enemy gun positions at 1000 feet the supply aircraft met an intense hail of German flak, which set several aircraft on fire. The Royal Air Force aircrews flew on unflinching into the flak. One pilot - Flight Lieutenant D.S.A. Lord, DFC 271 Squadron, 46 Group, out of Down Ampney, flying a Dakota - had his starboard wing hit twice by flak and the engine caught fire. The aircrew were uninjured and SDP V was coming up three minutes away. With his starboard engine blazing Lord let down to 900 feet and the aircraft became a prime target for the German gunners. Flight Lieutenant Lord dropped all but two of his supply containers then - determined to drop the last two - went round again with his Dakota still on fire. For eight minutes his aircraft was under enemy fire and finally he ordered his aircrew to bale out but did not do so himself. He stayed at the controls and his aircraft crashed in flames. So died a gallant pilot of 46 Group, Royal Air Force, striving to resupply the hard pressed airborne soldiers at Arnhem. He was awarded the Victoria Cross for Valour in action.

One hundred and forty-five aircraft dropped their loads on SDP V but thirteen aircraft were lost and ninety-seven damaged by German flak. 388 tons in total were dropped but only some 21 tons reached British ground forces - the rest fell into enemy hands.

Despite the odds the Royal Air Force 38 and 46 Groups continued to try and support the airborne troops on the ground but only 7.4% of the supplies dropped reached British hands. The two Groups lost fifty-five aircraft and had three hundred and twenty damaged by flak. At times the aircraft came down to 300 feet to drop their loads and the aircraft gunners engaged the enemy at what was - for them - point blank range.

By the 19th September 1st Airborne Division was running short of ammunition, food and water. They held an area less than two square miles around Oosterbeek and Hartenstein. Now there was no hope of linking up with 2nd Parachute Battalion at Arnhem bridge, who still doggedly fought on against numerically superior forces.

The Divisional Commander decided to form a perimeter around the village of Oosterbeek and hold out until relieved by 2nd Army. The western side of the perimeter was held by what was left of 1st Battalion Border Regiment, Polish troops, Royal Engineers and a detachment of Glider Pilots under the command of Brigadier Hicks.

The eastern side was defended by three detachments of Glider Pilots, some Borderers, Recce Squadron, 21st Independent Parachute Company, and elements of RASC, plus the remnants of 10th and 156th Parachute Regiment, and Londale Force commanded by Major R. Lonsdale, DSO. MC. which comprised the remaining men of 1st, 3rd and 11th Parachute Battalions and 2nd Battalion South Staffords - all under command of Brigadier Hackett. The south-east corner was held by the South Staffords with about 150 men under Major R.H. Cain. Three other parties of South Staffords were with 1st Border Regiment and the Pioneer Platoon defended Divisional HQ.

By the 20th September 7th KOSB strength was down to 270 men - the remnants of three rifle companies plus a Support Company and Battalion HQ staff. They fought on aggressively Lieutenant Hannah and Corporal Watson using an anti tank gun engaged and knocked out a 56-ton Tiger tank. CSM R.F. Tilley, Glider Pilot Regiment, found himself the ranking officer in a party of 7th KOSB when all the officers were either dead or wounded and fought with such gallantry that he was later awarded the Distinguished Conduct Medal. Corporal John Moir of 1st Airborne Provost Section went into a bayonet charge with five men from the Borderers - only Moir and two men returned.

Provost Sergeant Austin Roberts was last seen - one arm blown off - charging the enemy with a Bren gun under his remaining arm till he was killed. At Arnhem bridge Colonel Frost was badly wounded and command of the remaining defenders was taken by Major C.F.H. Gough, MC. Commander of the Recce Squadron. Incessantly raked by German fire and suffering mounting casualties the gallant defenders fought on now reduced to 116 men. Finally they were forced to make their final valiant stand - some underneath the bridge. Here Lieutenant J.H. Grayburn led a series of counter attacks and for his gallantry there and during the whole battle, was awarded a Victoria Cross which he did not live to receive being killed by tank gunfire.

With most troops wounded and out of ammunition, food and water the defenders of Arnhem bridge finally ended their epic struggle. Some tried to break out westwards towards British positions but came under enemy fire which killed several and wounded more. The bridge was once more in enemy hands.

1st Airborne Division in their defensive perimeter at Oosterbeek were still fighting on. Brigadier Hackett had been badly wounded and his command had been taken by Lieutenant Colonel I. Murray, Glider Pilot Regiment. Headquarters was at the Hartenstein Hotel which had been the enemy HQ till they were driven out. At his position north of Oosterbeek church, Major Cain and his South Staffords were repeatedly attacked by enemy tanks and self-propelled guns. Single handed, Major Cain attacked a Tiger tank with a PIAT and knocked it out. A self-propelled gun became a serious threat and Cain fired fifty projectiles at it finally knocking it out but was himself concussed by the rear blast of a PIAT projectile. Refusing to leave his command he fought on and when all the PIAT rounds had been expended used a two-inch mortar, firing it at a low angle. For his valour and command in battle Major Cain was awarded the Victoria Cross. The South Staffords had now earned two Victoria Crosses in one battle - the only battalion so to do in WWII.

By the 21st September the situation was going badly for 1st Airborne Division. The tanks of the British Guards Armoured Brigade on the road to Arnhem had been stopped by enemy anti-tanks guns three miles north of Nijmegan and could go no further. The road was the only way to Arnhem - the fields on either side were marshy and impassable to armour.

On the afternoon of the 21st September the USAAF 52nd Wing took off in almost impossible weather conditions over England. Cloud extended from 150 to 9000 feet but the pilots of the 314th and 315th Troop Carrier Groups somehow managed to get airborne with 1511 Polish paratroops and 100 tons of supplies and made for Arnhem. Meeting heavy German flak the two Groups dropped 998 paratroopers and 69 tons of supplies at Driel, south of the Rhine opposite Oosterbeek. That evening some 750 paratroops managed to assemble and by 2100 hours had reached the Rhine but found the enemy in position opposite so withdrew to a defensive perimeter at Driel. On the night of the 23rd September 250 Polish paratroops tried to cross the Rhine but only 150 managed to get through to 1st Airborne Division.

During the night of the 24th September 250 troops of the Dorset Regiment made an attempt to reach 1st Airborne but only elements of four companies made the other side of the Rhine. Led by Lieutenant Colonel G. Tilley the Dorsets strove to reach their beleaguered comrades - Colonel Tilley led a bayonet charge and was last seen engaging the enemy and shouting encouragement to his men. Some of the Dorsets and Poles managed to fight their way through to 1st Airborne but their numbers were too small to change the course of the battle.

Just before dusk on the 24th the Glider Pilots were forced out of a house they were holding by heavy German shellfire and took up new positions behind 7th KOSB. Both regiments continued to resist the enemy with rifles, machine-guns and mortars. The 64th Medium Regiment artillery of 2nd Army at Nijmegan had the range of Arnhem and 1st Airborne did not hesitate to call down their supporting fire close to and on occasion on their own positions.

Montgomery saw that it was impossible to hold a bridgehead over the Rhine and at 0930 hours on the morning of the 25th September ordered 1st Airborne Division to withdraw south of the river - the odds against them were too heavy.

Codenamed Operation Berlin the withdrawal began at 2200 hours on the 25th September. The Glider Pilots were stationed along the withdrawal route to the river bank as guides. The weather - rain and a high wind - for once was in favour of the airborne soldiers and covered the withdrawal of 1741 men of 1st Airborne Division plus 422 Glider Pilots, 75 Dorsets and 160 Poles.

Many airborne soldiers hid and evaded the Germans and during the next few weeks, assisted by the Dutch people, eventually managed to reach Allied lines. 10005 men had landed at Arnhem - 2163 came back. More than 1200 men of 1st Airborne Division died at Arnhem. Over 6000 were taken prisoner and many died en route to the German POW camps. Many were wounded and suffered from lack of care by their captors. It was estimated that the enemy lost over 7000 men in battle.

At Roll Call the 2nd Battalion South Staffordshire Regiment had only six officers and one hundred and thirty other ranks returned from Arnhem. Forty-seven officers and eight hundred and twenty other ranks had set out. Later, elements of B Company rejoined the regiment - they had been posted missing in action.

A mere thirteen soldiers of the Airborne Provost Company returned - others including the Provost Marshal, Major O. Haig although wounded, managed to escape. The Glider Pilot Regiment suffered two hundred and twenty-nine soldier pilots killed. Thirty-one officers and four hundred and thirty-eight were taken prisoner. The loss to the regiment of six hundred and ninety-eight glider pilots was shattering.

The Roll Call held by 7th Battalion Kings Own Scottish Borderers at Nijmegan showed only four officers, and seventy-two other ranks. Seven hundred and forty all ranks land landed on 17th September. Seventy-six returned.
38 and 46 Groups, Royal Air Force, lost two hundred and ninety-four aircrew. No.85 Group lost nine ground crew out of twenty, landed as radar operators, who fought as infantry. The survivors were taken prisoner.

Montgomery's offensive did not outflank the Siegfried Line and it was four months before the Canadian 1st Army attacked at Nijmegan. With hindsight it would be easy to list why the British part of Operation Market failed. Montgomery in a letter to 1st Airborne Divisional Commander Major General R.E. Urquhart said:

> In the annals of the British Army there are many glorious deeds. In our Army we have always drawn great strength and inspiration from past traditions and endeavoured to live up to the high standard of those who have gone before.
>
> But there can be few episodes more glorious than the epic of Arnhem and those who follow will find it hard to live up to the standards you have set.
>
> So long as we have in our Armies of the British Empire, Officers and Men who will do as you have done, then we can indeed look forward with complete confidence to the future. In years to come it will be a great thing for a man to be able to say 'I fought at Arnhem'.
>
> B.L.Montgomery.

There was no failure of 1st Airborne Division, or the Royal Air Force, at Arnhem.

## The Glider Soldiers

**U.K. AIR MOVEMENT TABLE**
**OPERATION "MARKET" — 17TH SEPTEMBER 1944**
**1ST LIFT**

| Load | RAF Unit | Aircraft | GPR Unit | Glider | Airfield | First Take/Off | LZ | Gliders landed & Remarks |
|---|---|---|---|---|---|---|---|---|
| 7th KOSB 1st Abn. Provost Coy. | 48 Sqdn. 46 Grp | C.47 Dakota | 'E' Sqadron | Horsa (23) | Down Ampney | 0957 | S | 292 Troops 19 landed |
| 542 Troops 19 Jeeps. 4 x 6 PDR Guns | 271 Sqdn. 46 Grp | C.47 Dakota | 'E' Squadron | Horsa (24) | Down Ampney | 0940 | S | 19 landed |
|  | 437 Sqdn. 46 Grp (RCAF) | C.47 Dakota | 'E' Squadron | Horsa (2) | Down Ampney | 1003 | S | 1 landed |
| 1st ALB. 130 Troops 17 Jeeps | 190 Sqdn. 38 Grp | Stirling | 'D' Squadron | Horsa (19) | Fairford | 1025 | Z | 18 landed |
|  | 620 Sqdn. 38 Grp | Stirling | 'D' Squadron | Horsa (19) | Fairford | 1045 | Z | 16 landed |
| 1st Abn. LT Regt RA Royal Engineers 1 Para Brigade | 196 Sqdn. 38 Grp | Stirling | 'D' Squadron | Horsa (25) | Keevil | 1040 | Z | 21 landed |
|  | 299 Sqdn. 38 Grp | Stirling | 'D' Squadron | Horsa (25) | Keevil | 1015 | Z | 21 landed Double Hills Crash |
| 7th KOSB | 233 Sqdn. 46 Grp | C.47 Dakota | 'F' Squadron | Horsa (22) | Blakehill Farm | 0956 | S | 21 landed |
| 308 troops 1st Border Regt. | 437 Sqdn. 46 Grp (RCAF) | C.47 Dakota | 'F' Squadron | Horsa (12) | Blakehill Farm | 1003 | S | 12 landed |
| 1st Airborne Corps HQ. | 295 Sqdn. 38 Grp | Stirling | 'A' Squadron | Horsa (25) | Harwell | 1120 | N | 22 landed 154 Men. |
| 1st A/L Lt. Reg RA | 570 Sqdn. 38 Grp | Stirling | 'A' Squadron | Horsa (20) | Harwell | 1108 | Z&N |  |
| 1st A/L A/Tk Bty & HQ 1st Airborne Co. | 296 Sqdn. 38 Grp | Albemarle | 'B' Squadron | Horsa (21) | Manston | 1055 | Z&S |  |
|  | 296 Sqdn. 38 Grp | Albemarle | 'B' Squadron | Hadrian (6) | Manston | 1100 | N |  |
| 2nd South Staffs | 297 Sqdn. 38 Grp | Albemarle | 'B' Squadron | Horsa (24) | Manston | 1040 | Z | 26 landed |
|  | 297 Sqdn. 38 Grp ORTU | Albemarle | Hampstead Norris | Hadrian (4) Horsa (2) | Manston Manston |  | Z |  |

## 1st Lift

| Load | RAF Unit | Aircraft | GPR Unit | Glider | Airfield | Take off | LZ | Gliders landed |
|---|---|---|---|---|---|---|---|---|
| 4 x 17 pounderguns 6 carriers. 45 Men. Recce Regt. 4 x 17 pounder guns. 2 carriers 42 men. | 298 Sqdn. 38 Grp 298 Sqdn. 38 Grp 644 Sqdn. 38 Grp 644 Sqdn. 38 Grp | Halifax " " " | 'C' Sqdn " " " | Hamilcar (7) Horsa (13) Hamilcar (6) Horsa (15) | Tarrant Rushton Tarrant Rushton Tarrant Rushton | 1020 " " " | N N | 7 landed 7 landed |
| 544 troops of | 512 Sqdn. 46 Grp | C.47 Dakota | 'G' Sqdn | Horsa (22) | Broadwell | 1000 | S | 22 landed |
| 1st Border Regt. | 575 Sqdn. 46 Grp | C.47 Dakota | 'G' Sqdn | Horsa (24) | Broadwell | 0945 | S | 19 landed |

16 Squadrons plus
2 a/craft from
Operational
Refresher
Training
Unit.

129 Dakotas
133 Stirlings
56 Albemarles
41 Halifaxs
359 Tugs

336 Horsas
13 Hamilcars
10 Hadrians
359 Gliders

## OPERATION "MARKET" – 18TH SEPTEMBER
### 2ND LIFT

| Re-inforcements | RAF Unit | Aircraft | GPR Unit | Glider | Airfield | Take Off | LZ | Gliders Down |
|---|---|---|---|---|---|---|---|---|
| 132 troops. 17 jeeps. 22 trailers | 48 Sqdn | C.47 Dakota | 'E' Sqdn | Horsa (25) | Down Ampney | 1100 | S | 24 landed |
|  | 271 Sqdn | C.47 Dakota | 'E' Sqdn | Horsa (24) | Down Ampney | 1113 | S | 24 landed |
| 92 troops. 18 jeeps 7 scout cars. 4 guns. | 190 Sqdn | Stirling | 'D' Sqdn | Horsa (21) | Fairford | 1152 | X | 17 landed |
|  | 620 Sqdn | " | " | " (22) | " | 1125 | X | 21 landed |
|  | 196 Sqdn | " | " | " (22) | Keevil | 1150 | Z | 19 landed |
|  | 299 Sqdn | " | " | " (22) | " | 1125 | Z | 21 landed |
| 84 troops. 15 jeeps. 8 x 6 PDR Guns. | 233 Sqdn | C.47 Dakota | 'F' Sqdn | Horsa (17) | Blakehill Farm | 1045 | X | 16 landed |
| 21 troops 4 x 6 PDRS 2 jeeps. | 437 Sqdn (RCAF) | C.47 Dakota | " | " (6) | " | 1045 | X | All landed |
| RAF stores 6 men | 295 Sqdn | Stirling | 'A' Sqdn | Horsa (3) | Harwell | 1215 | X | 2 landed |
| HQ AEAF 250 Coy RASC | 570 Sqdn | " | " | " (10) | " | 1207 | X | 9 landed |
|  | 296 Sqdn | Albemarle | 'B' Sqdn | " (20) | Manston | 1146 | X | 18 landed |
|  | 297 Sqdn | " | " | " (22) | " | 1140 | X | 22 landed |
|  | 298 Sqdn | Halifax | 'C' Sqdn | Hamilcar (8) | Tarrant Rushton | 1122 | X | All landed |
|  | 298 Sqdn | " | " | Horsa (8) | " |  |  | All landed |
|  | 644 Sqdn | " | " | Hamilcar (7) | " | 1125 | X | 5 landed |
|  | 644 Sqdn | " | " | Horsa (8) | " |  |  | 8 landed |
| 1st Border Regt. 235 troops of | 512 Sqdn | C.47 Dakota | 'G' Sqdn | Horsa (24) | Broadwell | 1045 | S | All landed |
| 2nd South Staffs. | 575 Sqdn | " | " | " (25) | " | 1047 | X | 24 landed |

```
121 Dakota
100 Stirling           Horsa      279
 42 Albemarle          Hamilcar    15
 31 Halifax            Gliders    294
294 Aircraft
```

U.K. AIR MOVEMENT TABLE
OPERATION "MARKET" - 19TH SEPTEMBER 1944
3RD LIFT

| Re-inforcements | RAF Unit | Aircraft | GPR Squadron | Glider | Airfield | First Take/Off | LZ | Gliders Landed |
|---|---|---|---|---|---|---|---|---|
| 6 Troops. 2 Jeeps 3 Trailers. | 190 Sqdn | Stirling | 'D' Squadron | Horsa (2) | Fairford | 1230 | X | 1 Landed |
| 6 Troops. 1 Jeep. 1 M.Gun | 620 Sqdn | Stirling LK 509 F/Lt. Jack | 'D' Squadron | Horsa (1) | Fairford | 1230 | X | |
| Polish Troops | 196 Sqdn | Stirling | 'D' Squadron | Horsa (9) | Keevil | 1210 | L | 5 Landed |
| 19 Troops. 9 Jeeps. 5 Trailers | 299 Sqdn | Stirling | 'D' Squadron | Horsa (7) | Keevil | 1213 | L | 6 Landed |
| 6 Troops. 1 Jeep. & Trailer. 1 M.Gun | 233 Sqdn | C.47 Dakota KE 448 F/Lt. Cody | 'F' Squadron | Horsa (1) | Blake Hill Farm | 1138 | X | Landed |
| Polish Troops | 296 Sqdn | Albemarle P 1851 F/Lt.Scott | 'B' Squadron S/S Proctor & McCulloch | Horsa (1) | Manston | 1320 | - | Returned to Manston. Glider Load shifted |
| Polish Troops | 298 Sqdn | Halifax | 'C' Squadron | Horsa (10) | Tarrant Rushton | 1208 | L | 9 Landed |
| Polish Troops | 644 Sqdn | Halifax F/O Blake | 'C' Squadron | Hamilcar (1) | Tarrant Rushton | 1215 | L | Forcelanded Ghent. |
| | 644 Sqdn | Halifax | 'C' Squadron | Horsa (10) | Tarrant Rushton | 1207 | L | 8 Landed 1 Shot Down |
| Admin. 4 Troop 250 Coy. RASC 1 Jeep & 2 Trailers | 570 Sqdn | Stirling V8L-LK 199 F/Lt. Brierly | 'A' Squadron | Horsa (1) | Harwell | 1250 | - | Glider released at Eindhoven |
| 17 Troops KOSB & 2 Trailers | 48 Sqdn | C.47 Dakota F/Lt. Whitfield | 'E' Squadron S/S Melrose & Sgt. MacDonald | Horsa (1) | Down Ampney | 1300 | S | Glider No.272 left over from 1st lift |
| TOTALS | Dakota - 2 Stirling - 20 Albemarle - 1 Halifax - 21 / 44 | | | Horsa - 43 Hamilcar - 1 / 44 | | | | |

| Re-inforcements | RAF Unit | Aircraft | GPR Squadron | Glider | Airfield | First Take/Off | LZ | Gliders Landed |
|---|---|---|---|---|---|---|---|---|
| GRAND TOTALS ALL LIFTS | | Dakota - 252<br>Stirling - 253<br>Albemarle - 99<br>Halifax - 93<br><br>TUG - 697<br>Aircraft | | Horsa - 658<br>Hamilcar - 29<br>Hadrian - 10<br><br>Gliders - 697 | | | | GRAND TOTAL<br><br>1394 Aircraft |

## MEGARA, GREECE

By September 1944, the continued occupation of Greece by the Germans had become untenable. In Italy the Allied Forces were advancing northwards and Russian forces were rolling forward on the Hungarian frontier. Both these advances would eventually cut off German forces in Greece and Yugoslavia, leaving them no choice but to withdraw, although in the Aegean islands several units still held out in obedience to Hitler's order of no surrender.

With the start of withdrawal northwards by the Germans a power vacuum developed in Greece with the various left and right wing factions seeking power. The British wished to install the exiled Greek Government in Athens as soon as was possible to stabilize the situation and prevent civil war.

On the 23rd September British airborne and seaborne forces captured the airfield at Araxos in the Pelopennese preparatory to capturing Athens. By the 10th October the dirt strip airfield at Megara, twenty miles from Athens, had been taken but was till under fire from German artillery. General Wilson, the British commander, decided to launch Operation Manna - a combined sea and air operation to take Athens. The British 2nd Parachute Brigade would drop on and secure Megara airfield then advance on Athens. The seaborne assault would commence at 0500 hours on the 15th October.

The USAAF 51st Troop Carrier Wing had one hundred aircraft to drop 2nd Parachute Brigade and Waco CG4A Hadrian gliders to carry ammunition, supplies and earth moving equipment to Megara - the gliders to be flown by pilots of the 1st Independent Squadron, British Glider Pilot Regiment.

At Tarquina, Italy, the Glider Pilot Regiment's base, a new commanding officer, Major McMillen, had arrived together with a draft of glider pilots, to take over 1st Independent Squadron, with Captain C. Turner who had been in command, reverting to second-in-command.

Scattered around the Rome area were about two hundred Waco Hadrian gliders rejected by the USAAF. Within a week, Captain Mockeridge of the Glider Pilot Regiment, with assistance from the 64th Troop Carrier Group engineers, had managed to salvage forty of the least forlorn looking gliders and they were flown down to Manduria on the toe of Italy, by the glider pilots.

The airborne operational plan was for the Pathfinder paratroops to land on D minus 1, D-Day being Friday 13th October 1944, to be followed next day by the main body of paratroops and six gliders with special loads including a bulldozer to level the cratered Megara airstrip. On D+1 the rest of the brigade and gliders would land with container drops to follow as required. On the 12th October the paratroops jumped onto Megara airfield in a strong wind which caused casualties. To add to the difficulties the Germans who were still dug in nearby, managed to shell the dropping zone causing more casualties.

Early on the morning of D-Day the six Megara-bound gliders, carrying a bulldozer and supplies, were being marshalled by Captain Turner on the airfield ready to be towed off by the USAAF. Major McMillen was in the lead Hadrian as glider Commander and ready to go, when the second-in-command of the Parachute Brigade arrived and instructed that Captain Turner was to take command at once and Major McMillen remain behind with the squadron. At the time Captain Turner was only wearing shorts and gym shoes as he was not detailed to fly on this part of the operation. Captain Corey Turner now relates the Operation from the glider pilots standpoint:

Harry Lansdell and I just had time to scramble aboard the Hadrian and we were on out way, rising into a fine still morning sky, eastward bound. As usual I left the flying to Harry as I sorted through someone else's maps then looked round the glider to see what we had got aboard. It all looked neatly stowed, secured and labelled, just wooden crates, 4000lbs of high explosives and demolition stores. Well, I was not going to waste any sleep over it now, but it would have been more comfortable for one and all if the crates had been marked Senior Service or Johnny Walker!

We left the Albanian coast and Corfu on the port quarter and an hour after take off we were approaching Patras at the western end of the Gulf of Corinth. We had a good tail wind and Waco. Harry as ever firm and steady as the Sphinx. Friday the 13th - 4000lbs of High Explosive? ah well. Whoever was in the C47 ahead of us was dead on track. We came up to the Corinth canal; a cleanly sliced wedge cut through the isthmus, it looked hundreds of feet deep - a proper engineering job. A burst of tracer fire cut short our admiration, curving up and away behind us. Not a bad position to be No.1; you get a good view! Ten minutes now from the Canal to Megara - lower hills now to port the sea to starboard. A white town half a mile inland left, and a high headland right with a large island beyond, pale grey on an inky sea. Salamis - we were there! The airstrip between the town and the sea. More ack ack! No, it's Peter's (the ground controller Captain Peter Baker of the Parachute Pathfinder Company) Very light signal and his smoke - what a wind - from the north too. We would have to go half way round again.

I hit the button and let the nose go bringing Harry, who was piloting, round left to our reciprocal, over the town, left again out over the foreshore and the sea four hundred feet below and the last 90 degrees to come over the headland. Down, down, perfect hairy one hundred feet over the strip and touch down, gentle as a gull. "Well done Harry, sorry I forgot to take over!"

There was no time for back slapping - a Jerry detachment was dug in at a culvert half a mile away and Peter was keeping their heads down with the help of a score of Partisans. He had half a dozen plane loads of 4th Parachute Battalion coming in an hour behind us and left me and my lads with Dumbo Willans to look after the Very lights while he went after the Jerries. It was blowing a full gale by the time the C47s came in with the paratroop drop and the thing was a bit of a disaster. Many of the paras who had not been able to get out of their harness (as the old hands did) were swept off the LZ like autumn leaves and dragged over the foreshore rocks and bashed to pieces. They lost a round dozen dead, including Lieutenant Marsh who had won the Sword of Honour at Sandhurst only months before.

Next day the wind had dropped and the rest of the Parachute Brigade and Major McMillen with our remaining gliders came in more or less without further calamity. There were parachute canopies everywhere and soon the local women began coming nervously down from the town begging for them. With no clothing materials for years but rough home spun wool the silk chutes must have looked like manna from heaven to them.

I'd found some uniform shoes among the dropped containers and a pair of battledress trousers to supplement my scanty rig out. We were gathering the containers into some sort of order when I felt an agonising knife stab of pain right on my tail! Staff Sergeant Tom Gillies was right beside me. 'For God's sake come and look what I've got in my pants!' I yelled, diving for the door of the nearest glider, dropping my pants on the way. 'Look out!' someone shouted, 'It's a scorpion'. But no help to me...they had me spreadeagled on my tummy and trouserless, opened a Red Cross container and dressed my swiftly swelling bum from a tube like toothpaste, with the local ladies present and watching offering no doubt the best Greek advice. My groans were genuine but lost on the sergeants who fell about laughing. For days afterwards as I limped about the town I could see the black clad matrons and giggling girls nudging each other and grinning behind(?) their hands as they sat, endlessly tatting beside the doors of their white shining cottages.

Within a couple of days the Germans were clear of Athens and on their way north, so the partisans judged it safe to come down from the hills, bearded desperadoes, bandoliers criss crossed over their chests.

A few days after our arrival at Megara Major McMillen was invalided home and once more I took over the squadron. John Mockeridge got a little crew of RAF Riggers to overhaul our gliders as I wanted to try and fly them out. A relief force arrived at Megara and within forty-eight hours we said goodbye to all our friends, called up our old tow ships from the 64th Troop Carrier Group and lined up the Wacos to await them at dawn on the 4th December.

Throughout the autumn we had enjoyed lovely weather and this day was no change. Megara was only a short runway but the Wacos were empty and everyone got off without incident. Harry Lansdell and I led off, circling the strip until all were airborne, except for the half dozen wrecked gliders we couldn't repair, then we were away. It was one of the worst glider flights I ever made, with great masses of black clouds which caused severe turbulence so we had to take ten-minute turns in flying the glider. After seven hours - first roasted then nearly frozen - we slithered to a stand at Tarquina. Five or six gliders came in during the next hour and over the next week all but three came home. Two crews crashed on the Italian mountains and one crew on an island off Albania where the Navy sent in a frigate to rescue them. Every man arrived in some shape eventually and we settled down into winter quarters once more.

The operation in Greece had been successful apart from the dropping of the paratroops onto Megara in a high wind and the Greek Government under Prime Minster Pappandrou was installed in Athens on the 18th October 1944.

# OPERATION VARSITY

The first Allied tactical airborne operation of WWII on the 24th March 1945, over the River Rhine, Germany, and the largest single lift airborne operation undertaken.

The harsh lessons of Operation Market/Garden at Arnhem had been well and truly learnt and the Planning Staff determined that Operation Varsity would be tactically different. 18th Airborne Corps, commanded by US General Matthew B. Ridgeway with General Richard N. Gale as Deputy, consisting of the US 17th Airborne division and the British 6th Airborne Division would carry out the airborne operation. 18th Corps was to be dropped and air landed over the Rhine some four hours after the start of the ground assault across the Rhine by the US 9th and the British 2nd Armies.

The re-supply of the airborne armies would be made six hours after their landing - not at a later date as at Arnhem. It was intended to transport and land by parachute and glider 21680 troops in a single air lift. The logistics of the plan were staggering; a total of 1591 aircraft and 1346 gliders were to be used to transport the airborne troops.

Their objectives were to capture the Diersfordter Forest on high ground overlooking the Rhine north east of the small town of Wesel and secure the bridges over the River Issel north of Wesel, to enable the main ground forces to thrust into heartland Germany.

Brigadier Chatterton, Commander, Glider Pilot Regiment, had in consultation with the Royal Air Force airborne groups and 6th Airborne Division, evolved a method of tactical landings by glider in which specific targets were chosen for specific glider landed troops. The gliders would be landed as near as was possible to the intended targets and not spread out en masse. This concentration of troops would reduce the chance of enemy fire disrupting the airborne attack before it had begun. Airborne troops are at their most vulnerable during the run in, landing and assembling after landing.

BRITISH VARSITY FORCES:
6th Airborne Division. GOC. Major General E.L. BOLS. DSO.
3rd Parachute Brigade. CO. Brigadier S.J.L. Hill. DSO.
5th Parachute Brigade. CO. Brigadier J.H.N. Poett. DSO.
Elements of 3rd and 5th Parachute Brigade would be landed in twenty-five gliders.
6th Air Landing Brigade. CO. Brigadier R.H. Bellamy. DSO.
2nd Oxford & Bucks. Regiment. CO. Lt.Col. M. Darrel Brown.

12th Devonshire Regiment. CO. Lt.Col. P. Gleadell. DSO.
1st Royal Ulster Rifles. CO. Lt.Col. R.J.H. Carson.
Royal Artillery. CO. Brigadier C.K.T. Faithfull.
3rd Anti Tank Battery, RA.
4th Anti Tank Battery, RA.
53rd Light Regiment, RA.
195th Field Ambulance, RAMC.
249th Airborne field Company, RE.
HQ. Staff. 6th Airborne Division.
6th Airborne Recce Regiment, RTR.
22nd Independent Parachute Company.
Glider Pilot Regiment. CO. Brigadier G.J.S. Chatterton, DSO.
A Squadron. Major H.T. Bartlett, DFC.
B Squadron. Major T.I.J. Toler, DFC.
C Squadron. Major J.A. Dale, DFC.
D Squadron. Major J.F. Lyne, MC.
E Squadron. Major P.H. Jackson, DFC.
F Squadron. S/Ldr V.H. Reynolds.
G Squadron

The strength of the Glider Pilot Regiment had been depleted by casualties at Arnhem so pilot reinforcements were obtained from the Royal Air Force to fly the gliders. They were given a short course of military training so that they could fight on the ground as soldiers after landing their gliders.

ROYAL AIR FORCE:
38 Airborne Forces Group. CO. AVM J.R. Scarlett Streatfield.

| RAF Unit. | Aircraft. | Duty. | Airfield. |
|---|---|---|---|
| 190 Squadron | Stirling | Glider tug | Great Dunmow. |
| 196 Squadron | Stirling | Glider tug | Shepherds Grove. |
| 295 Squadron | Stirling | Glider tug | Rivenhall. |
| 296 Squadron | Halifax | Glider tug | Earls Colne. |
| 297 Squadron | Halifax | Glider tug | Earls Colne. |
| 298 Squadron | Halifax | Glider tug | Woodbridge. |
| 299 Squadron | Stirling | Glider tug | Shepherds Grove. |
| 570 Squadron | Stirling | Glider tug | Rivenhall. |
| 620 Squadron | Stirling | Glider tug | Great Dunmow. |
| 644 Squadron | Halifax | Glider tug | Woodbridge. |

Supplying 120 Halifaxes and 194 Stirlings to tow 48 Hamilcar and 266 Horsa gliders. Operational Refresher Training Unit (ORTU) from RAF Matching would supply 20 Stirling aircraft to tow 20 Horsa gliders.

46 Group. CO. A/Com. L. Darvall, MC.

| | | | |
|---|---|---|---|
| 48 Squadron | Dakota | Glider tug | Birch. |
| 233 Squadron | Dakota | Glider tug | Birch. |
| 271 Squadron | Dakota | Glider tug | Gosfield. |
| 512 Squadron | Dakota | Glider tug | Gosfield. |
| 575 Squadron | Dakota | Glider tug | Gosfield. |

120 aircraft to tow 120 Horsa gliders.
Overall total: 440 tugs to tow 440 gliders.

The first stage of the operation was the bombing by RAF Bomber Command and the US Army Air Forces of all lines of communication in the Ruhr to prevent the German 15th Army and 5th Panzer Army - some twenty-two divisions in all - moving towards the River Rhine in counter attack. Railways in the Ruhr were attacked by Bomber Command, 2 Group, 2nd Tactical Air Force, (TAF) Royal Air Force, and the US 8th and 9th Air Forces. German troop concentrations and anti-aircraft guns were heavily bombed on the 22nd March 1945, by seven squadrons of 83 Group, 2nd TAF.

At 1530 hours on the 23rd March RAF Bomber Command sent seventy-seven Lancaster bombers to pound Wesel - the small town on the Rhine which would be the objective of 1st Commando Brigade, attacking across the river.
As soon as the bombing ended the artillery of 2nd Army commenced firing and continued all day on specific German target groups on the intended battlefield.

At 2235 hours the Royal Air Force bombed Wesel again with 212 bombers of 5 and 8 Groups, Bomber Command, dropping some 1100 tons of bombs on the town. At 2200 hours on the 24th March 1st Commando Brigade began Operation Widgeon - the crossing of the Rhine to take Wesel - preceded by a softening up barrage of two hours duration from ten medium regiments, four heavy batteries and one super heavy battery of 7th Armoured Divisional Artillery Group.

During the night Mosquito fighter bombers of 2 Group, 2nd TAF attacked German transport in front of the invading ground forces, dropping thirty tons of bombs on enemy positions causing heavy damage. A pall of smoke and dust - the "Fog of War" - arose from the devastated town, or what was left of the town, of Wesel and began to drift over the intended LZs and DZs of 1st Allied Airborne Army.

At 0600 hours on the 24th March 1945, 1st Allied Airborne Army began to take off. 6th Airborne Division from English airfields - the US 17th Airborne Division from Continental airfields. The first British and US paratroops were scheduled to drop at 1000 hours and the first British gliders at 1021 hours with the last glider landing at 1100 hours.

The British aerial armada formed over Essex, with the paratroop aircraft leading, in an eighteen minute time length stream. The glider combinations followed in a thirty-nine minute time length stream. The armada RVd over Hawkinge, Kent, and set course for Cap Gris Nez on the French coast with the paratroops aircraft flying at 1500 feet above sea level and the glider stream at 2500 feet at ground speeds of 115mph (Dakota/ Horsa) to 145 mph (Stirling/ Horsa).

Of the 440 British gliders scheduled for the operation, four had to abort the mission almost at once due to tow rope breakage or tug engine failure. Crossing the Channel two gliders fell into the sea and nineteen more suffered tow rope breaks over France. This was believed to have been due to severe air turbulence caused by the slipstream of the aerial armada.

The US and British air fleets RVd south of Brussels over the Field of Waterloo, and merged into a mighty morale boosting air armada flying north east the last ninety-two miles to the final RV - codenamed Yalta North and Yalta South - before peeling off to their respective LZs and DZs. As the armada was approaching the battlefield RAF Typhoon fighter bombers were attacking the German anti-aircraft batteries with rockets, cluster bombs and cannon fire, but due to the dust and smoke were unable to knock out the German defences.

With the Airborne Army arriving some seven minutes before their ETA the RAF fighters had to break off their attack to allow the landings to begin - but several squadrons remained over the battlefield all day to provide fighter cover and 'cab rank' attacks. (Attacks requested by the ground forces on specific targets). As the Airborne Army began to descend the enemy opened up with small arms and anti-aircraft fire causing casualties and damage. Of the 402 British gliders which reached the LZs only 88 landed without damage. Thirty-seven were burned out but 92% had reached the battlefield.

The battle plan called for 6th Air Landing Brigade to seize and hold the bridges over the River Issel near Hamminkeln and Ringenberg. The 3rd and 5th Parachute Brigade would drop on the northern flank and hold off enemy counter attacks. The divisional troops would land in the centre and the US troops further south and take other bridges over the Issel, north of Wesel.

Fifteen Horsa gliders of F Squadron, Glider Pilot Regiment, commanded by Squadron Leader Reynolds, RAF, carried the 'Coup de Main' force to take the Hamminkeln and Ringenberg bridges. Eight Horsas carried the 2nd Oxford &

Bucks. and seven the 1st Royal Ulster Rifles. These were to land as near as was possible to the bridges and seize them intact. This placed the 'Coup de Main' party in the van of the assault.

At 1025 hours the Horsa carrying Major A.J. Dyball, OC 'D' Company, 1st RUR, landed on LZ1 one hundred and fifty yards from the river bridge. The landing was a heavy one and some of the troops were thrown out through the nose of the glider and immediately came under enemy machine-gun fire which killed the wireless operator. 22 Platoon of 1st RUR landed nearby and went into action at once clearing houses near the river bridge. The Germans were still holding the bridge but some were seen to run away as the RUR, with a small number of glider pilots, a few men from the Oxford & Bucks. and some Royal Engineers went into the assault. The bridge was stormed and taken - twenty Germans were killed and twenty-five taken prisoner. By 1430 hours the fighting had died down but the RUR suffered sixteen officers and two hundred and forty-three casualties.

Twenty Horsa gliders carrying the 12th Battalion, Devonshire Regiment, had lifted off from RAF Matching towed by Stirlings of ORTU. One glider was lost near Folkestone another near Southend. One went down mid-Channel then another near Waterloo. One tug/glider had to return to base due to engine trouble. Landing on LZR the 12th Devons attacked and secured their objectives at Hamminkeln and prevented a flank attack from the west.

The other gliderborne 'Coup de Main' parties of the 2nd Oxford & Bucks. landed on the west side of their target bridge held by 200 German paratroops and secured it by 1100 hours. Glider number 1 piloted by Captain A.M.D. Carr and carrying 17 Platoon, B Company, 2nd Oxford & Bucks. sustained a direct 88mm flak hit at 2000 feet and all occupants were killed. Glider number 2 piloted by Staff Sergeants Rowland and Collins and carrying 18 Platoon, B Company, 2nd Oxford & Bucks. was also badly hit by flak which killed Staff Sergeant Collins and wounded Staff Sergeant Rowland. The glider crashed into a wood killing all but ten of the occupants. Glider number 3 piloted by Staff Sergeants Page and Elton, carrying 19 Platoon, B Company, 2nd Oxford & Bucks. and towed by an aircraft of 512 Squadron which had Air Commodore Darvall, MC, Air Officer Commanding, 46 Group, as second pilot, was landed under enemy flak close to its objective which was stormed by the glider troops with grenades and sten guns then held. The glider was later blown up as an anti-tank defence. The RAF glider pilots joined in the attack and acquitted themselves well - some went to battle proudly wearing the red beret, they were now soldiers and entitled to wear it.

Squadron Leader Reynolds, who was carrying the Commanding Officer of the Oxford & Bucks. landed his glider near an enemy flak battery - the second pilot firing a machine-gun from the Horsa cockpit as they were landing. On

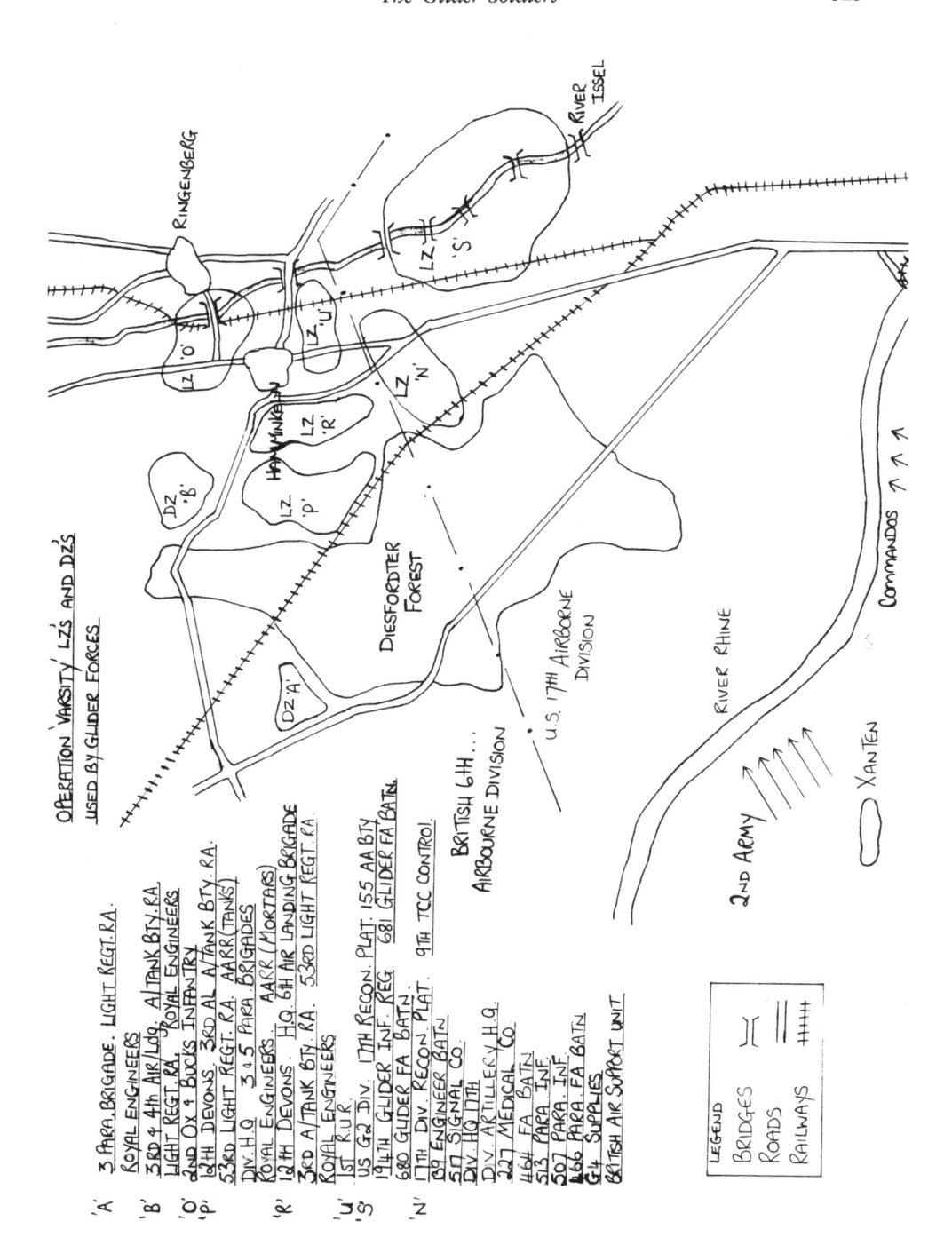

OPERATION 'VARSITY' LZ'S AND DZ'S
USED BY GLIDER FORCES

'A' 3 PARA BRIGADE. LIGHT REGT. R.A.
    ROYAL ENGINEERS
'B' 3RD & 4TH AIR LDG. A/TANK BTY. R.A.
    LIGHT REGT. R.A. ROYAL ENGINEERS
'O' 2ND OX & BUCKS INFANTRY
'P' 12TH DEVONS 3RD A/L A/TANK BTY. R.A.
    53RD LIGHT REGT. R.A. AARR (TANKS)
    DIV. H.Q.  3 & 5 PARA BRIGADES
'R' ROYAL ENGINEERS  AARR (MORTARS)
    12TH DEVONS  H.Q. 6TH AIR LANDING BRIGADE
    3RD A/TANK BTY. R.A.  53RD LIGHT REGT. R.A.
    ROYAL ENGINEERS
'U' 1ST R.U.R.
'S' US G2 DIV. 17TH RECON. PLAT. 155 AA BTY
    194TH GLIDER INF. REG  681 GLIDER FA BATN.
'N' 680 GLIDER FA BATN.
    17TH DIV. RECON PLAT.  9TH TCC CONTROL
    139 ENGINEER CO.
    517 SIGNAL CO.
    DIV. HQ 17TH
    DIV. ARTILLERY H.Q.
    224 MEDICAL CO.
    464 FA BATN.
    513 PARA INF.
    507 PARA INF.
    466 PARA FA BATN.
    G4 SUPPLIES
    GRITISH AIR SUPPORT UNIT

LEGEND
BRIDGES )(
ROADS   =
RAILWAYS +++++

landing the flak battery was taken but the position came under fire from other gun pits so Flying Officer Bailey, RAF. fired a PIAT round at the German firing position wiping it out. As was later said the RAF glider pilots, with but three weeks military training, acquitted themselves well fighting as soldiers. Fifty-one RAF glider pilots were killed in action.

6th Airborne Armoured Recce Regiment were carried to battle in Hamilcar and Horsa gliders. Twelve Locust tanks and a 4.2-inch mortar troop were brought in under flak when in the air and on landing. Only 50% of each survived but they gave a good account of themselves. One tank - though immobilised - was reported to have killed over a hundred of the enemy.

195th Airborne Field Ambulance landed in their gliders at 1030 hours in the midst of battle north-west of Hamminkeln. They were immediately at work aiding the wounded. Two of the Medics, Privates P.M. Lenton and T. Downey, engaged in rescuing wounded troops from wrecked gliders. Private Lenton was awarded the Military Medal and Private Downey was Mentioned in Despatches. Corporal F.G. Topham, Royal Canadian Army Medical Corps, was awarded the Victoria Cross for his conduct in rescuing wounded under fire, although wounded himself. RAMC records show 3000 casualties dealt with of the 14,000 troops in battle.

6th Air Landing Brigade Divisional Signals established their communications network without delay - Brigade Command Network being in use in twenty-five minutes. The unit lost three officers and sixty-three men killed in action but by late evening had established Divisional HQ in Kopenhof Farm.

By 1430 hours most enemy resistance had crumbled - German morale had been shattered by the preliminary bombardment and the sight of the airborne army approaching to do battle. Isolated pockets of resistance lingered and some German counter-attacks were made but repulsed. At 1500 hours the same day contact was made with the advancing forward elements of the ground armies from across the Rhine.

By 2359 hours Operation Varsity had ended - the greatest and most successful tactical air landing of WWII. The mightiest army ever to take to the air - the like of which was never to be seen again in war - had achieved its objectives. The way into Germany lay open for the Allied armies.

The cost in lives was heavy - 6th Airborne Division had 347 men killed and 731 wounded. The Glider Pilots Regiment lost 101 glider pilots, including the Royal Air Force glider pilots who died wearing their red berets. The Royal Air Force lost 43 killed, 153 wounded and 163 missing aircrew. All had flown and fought their way into military history in the largest airborne operation ever mounted.

## GLIDERBORNE - B COMPANY, 2ND OXFORD & BUCKS AT THE RHINE CROSSING.
### by
### Geoff Yardley.

In March 1945, 6th Airborne Division left England en route for Germany. Halifaxes, Dakotas and gliders took off in the darkness of the morning of the 24th. Gathering in great numbers they set course for Brussels, then east to the area of Wesel just across the Rhine.

Once again the 52nd Light Infantry - better known as the 2nd Oxford & Bucks were leading 6th Air Landing Brigade; right at the point of the flying sword were the gliders carrying B Company in numerical platoon order:

Glider Number 1. 17th Platoon. Lt. J. Cochrane, MC.
Glider Number 2. 18th Platoon. Lt. R. Preston.
Glider Number 3. 19th Platoon. Lt. H. Clarke, MC.
and so on.

I flew in No.2 glider as a member of Bob Preston's 18th Platoon, piloted by Staff Sergeant Bill Rowland and Staff Sergeant Geoff Collins of E Squadron, Glider Pilot Regiment.

Some three hours flying time passed uneventfully as many such flights had been in the past except that once again, in less than twelve months, this was for real. Darkness turned into a lovely morning clear sky and the promise of good weather. Now and again the sight of the escort fighters gave the feeling of some security against attack by the Luftwaffe.

At last the River Rhine came into view and as we approached it at about 3000 feet, the order was given to open the doors. One forward on the port side and one rear starboard. As I sat on the starboard side forward I watched Ginger Belsham pull the forward door upwards and at that precise moment flak burst under the port wing banking the aircraft over to starboard almost throwing Ginger out of the door - only to be pulled back by the Platoon Commander and Sergeant. This took perhaps two seconds and allowed this man to live for another few minutes - for he and sixty per cent of the Platoon were soon to die.

The dropping and landing zones were shrouded in smoke which must have made target identification very difficult for the pilots. The gentle jerk of the tow line being cast off was felt as the nose went down and the landing procedure began. Arms linked in each others and a silent prayer.

The enemy was waiting for us with a prepared concentration of ack ack guns and being the first gliders in our regiment we took the full weight of the defences as historical records were later to show. We descended through the heavy barrage of flak - many lives being lost during those first few minutes including one of the pilots, Geoff Collins while Staff Sergeant Bill Rowland was wounded. One chap by the name of Shrewsbury who sat opposite me got a burst of machine gun fire through the neck - the bullets then passing between the heads of myself and Ted Tamplin who sat on my right a gap of about eight to ten inches. (luck number one).

With some of the controls damaged and no compressed air to operate the landing flaps we flew across the landing zone, over the railway and the River Issel to crash head on into a wood at ground level. At a speed of over 70 knots a fully loaded glider - the size of a heavy bomber - becomes a pile of matchwood in about one second flat.

While all this was going on No.1 glider - 17th Platoon - had also been badly hit by flak and was breaking up, spilling men and equipment out, finally to crash as we had done - except for them there were no survivors. I was one of the lucky ones (luck number two) being the centre one of five men still sitting on one piece of seat with harness on. With the exception of a few cuts and bruises we five were Ok. I remember going over to Staff Sergeant Rowland wounded by the flak, and asking him silly questions like what speed we had been doing and what had happened to the brake parachutes. Several other chaps were alive but wounded, but most were dead including the Platoon Commander, Sergeant and two Corporals, leaving a Corporal, myself and another Lance Corporal and seven others unhurt.

The wounded were attended to by the Platoon Medic Lance Corporal Greenwood and Ted Noble, who did sterling work during the following few hours. During this time a recce patrol reported a tank at the west end of the next wood and large enemy concentrations in the area.

I took a compass bearing on artillery fire assuming it was our own firing according to plan, and established our position on the map (which I still have). From the information we had of the enemy strength and positions it was agreed that the best plan would be to try and link up with the nearest Allied unit which was the Royal Ulster Rifles at their objective on one of the two bridges over the River Issel. As the shortest distance between two points is a straight line this meant we had to run like hell over some 1000 yards of open ground to reach it.

There were about eight of us capable of doing this but one man - Ted Tamplin - had an injured ankle and offered to stay behind with the wounded, knowing he would probably be taken prisoner or maybe shot. He was taken but did however escape some days later and rejoined the regiment.

Bill Rowland recalls coming round and finding himself looking up at A German officer demanding whether they were English or American. Bill was convinced that had they been American they would have been shot - I wonder why? By the Grace of God they were allowed to live and were told they would be left to their devices as they would probably be picked up by our own side - they were - some forty-eight hours later.

The moment for our hasty departure was indicated by the sound of the enemy sweeping the wood from the other end and so with the old saying "he who fights and runs away (may) live to fight another day" we ran like bats out of hell. A line of bobbing red berets weaving across a large open field must have appeared easy targets to the enemy who promptly opened up on us from all angles. Either we had been very well trained or a lot of Germans were bad shots as no one was hit...or maybe we were very lucky (luck number three).

Fortunately the Royal Ulster Rifles had taken the bridge and the sound of a rich Irish voice shouting "Halt who goes there?" was a most welcome sound. We crossed the bridge between bursts of machine gun fire and reported to an officer with a request for stretcher bearers and some help to go back for our wounded. This request was denied coupled with an order to stay put. (40 years later I found that an artillery stonk was coming down on the spot where we had left our wounded. An artillery shell landed by Bill Rowland taking off an arm and leg...how many of our wounded died as a result of that shell?).

We rejoined our regiment the next day - the 25th March 1945, my 20th birthday.

AIR MOVEMENTS TABLE - OPERATION "VARSITY"

| Troop Unit | RAF Groups & Squadrons | Glider | Chalk Nos. | Airfield | LZ | Down | Remarks |
|---|---|---|---|---|---|---|---|
| 2nd Ox & Bucks 1st R.U.R. | 46 Grp. Dakota 271,512,575 | Horsa | 1-8 9-15 | Gosfield | O U | 1021 " | Coup de Main. Bridges 15 gliders. Major A.J. Dyball. 3 Mk2 Horsas. |
| 2nd Ox & Bucks | 46 Grp. Dakota 271,512,575 | " | 16-30 (30) | " | O | " | 9 Mk2 Horsas |
| 2nd Ox & Bucks | 46 Grp. Dakota 271,512,575 | " | 31-63 (33) | Birch | O | 1024 | 15 Mk2 Horsas |
| 2nd Ox & Bucks 1st R.U.R. | 46 Grp. Dakota 48,233,437 RCAF | " | 64-72 73-93 (30) | Gosfield | O U | 1027 " | 14 Mk2 Horsas |
| 1st R.U.R. | 46 Grp. Dakota 48,233,437 RCAF | " | 94-120 (27) | Birch | U | 1030 | 15 Mk2 Horsas |
| 1st R.U.R. 12th Devons 12th Devons | 38 Grp. Stirlings " " | " " " | 121-131 132-146 147-152 (32) | Rivenhall " " | U R P | 1033 " " | 4 Mk2 Horsas 10 Mk2 4 Mk2 |
| HQ 6th A/L Bge. 3rd A/Tk Bty 53rd Lt. Reg. RA 195th Field Amb. | 38 Grp. Halifax " " " | " " " " | 153-167 168-172 173-175 176-182 (30) | Earls Colne " " " | R R R R | 1036 " " " | 23 Mk2 Horsas |
| 12th Devons | 38 Grp. Halifax 296,297 | " | 183-206 (24) | Great Dunmow | R | 1039 | 11 Mk2 Horsas |
| 12th Devons | 38 Grp. Stirling 190,620 | " | 207-226 (20) | Matching | R | 1042 | 11 Mk2 Horsas |
| 12th Devons | 38 Grp. Stirling ORTU 295,570 | " | 227-238 (12) | Woodbridge | R | 1045 | 12 Mk2 Horsas |
| 4th Air Landing A/Tk Bty. RA | 38 Grp. Halifax 298,644 | " | | | B | | |

## The Glider Soldiers

| Troop Unit | RAF Groups & Squadrons | Glider | Chalk Nos. | Airfield | Down | LZ | Remarks |
|---|---|---|---|---|---|---|---|
| 3rd Air Landing A/Tk Bty RA | 38 Grp. Halifax | Hamilcar | 239-244 | Woodbridge | 1046 | R | 48 Hamilcars landing at three minute intervals. |
| " | " | " | 245-246 | " | | P | |
| " | " | " | 247-254 | " | | B | |
| 53rd Lt. Reg RA | " | " | 255-258 | " | | P | |
| A.A.R. Regt | " | " | 259-266 | " | | P | |
| Divisional HQ | " | " | 267-278 | " | | P | |
| 3 Para Brigade | " | " | 279-281 | " | | A | |
| 5th Para Brigade | " | " | 282-284 | " | | B | |
| Royal Engineers | 298,644 | " | 285-286 | " | | P | |
| 53 Lt. Reg RA | 38 Grp. Stirling 196,299 | Horsa | 287-314 (28) | Shepherds Grove | 1048 | P | 15 Mk2 Horsas |
| Divisional HQ | 38 Grp. Stirling 295,570 | Horsa | 315-342 (28) | Rivenhall | 1051 | P | 20 Mk2 Horsas |
| 53rd Lt. Reg. RA. | 38 Grp. Halifax 296,297 | Horsa | 343-372 (30) | Earls Colne | 1054 | P | 20 Mk2 Horsas |
| 4th A/L A/Tk Bty | 38 Grp. Stirling 190,620 | Horsa | 373-378 (6) | Great Dunmow | 1057 | B | 5 Mk2 Horsas |
| 3rd A/L A/Tk Bty | 38 Grp. Stirling | Horsa | 379-384 | Great Dunmow | 1057 | A | 27 Mk2 Horsas. |
| " | " | " | 385-393 | " | | P | 5 |
| 53rd Lt. Reg. RA. | " | " | 394-402 | " | | P | 8 |
| A.A.R. Mortars. | 190,620 | " | 403-408 (30) | " | | P | 8 |
| | | | | | | | 6 |
| 3 Para. Brigade | 38 Grp. Stirling | Horsa | 409-420 | Shepherds Grove | 1100 | A | 24 Mk2 Horsas |
| Light Reg RA | " | " | 421 | " | | A | 8 |
| Royal Engineers | " | " | 422-423 | " | | A | 1 |
| 5 Para Brigade | " | " | 424-435 | " | | B | 2 |
| Light Regt RA | " | " | 436-438 | " | | B | 8 |
| Royal Engineers | 196,299 | " | 439-440 (32) | " | | B | 3 |
| | | | | | | | 2 |
| | Dakotas 120 | Hamilcar 48 | | 8 Airfields | | 6LZ | |
| | Halifax 120 | Horsa 392 | | | | | |
| | Stirling 200 | —— | | | | | |
| | —— 440 | 440 | | | | | |

## CONCLUSION

The carrying of troops, tanks and equipment in military gliders did not last for long in WWII military history - a few years in wartime only - but the original German concept, adapted by British and American Forces, worked well after a faltering start. The main attribute of the glider - the ability to carry men and materials silently to the target en masse - has never been replaced by the noisy helicopter.

The men who designed the Horsa and Hamilcar gliders, the Royal Air Force tug crews who towed the gliders, the soldier pilots of the Glider Pilot Regiment and the fighting soldiers who flew in the fragile wooden aircraft served Britain well and deserve their unique place in British Military History.

The British military glider has gone, superseded by the helicopter, but its place in history is secure.

# BIOGRAPHIES - AIR LANDING FORCES

BASKEYFIELD, JOHN DANIEL, VC. Lance Sergeant, 2nd (Airborne) Battalion South Staffordshire Regiment. Awarded posthumous Victoria Cross for valour in action during the battle of Arnhem, September 1944.

BELLAMY, R.H. DSO. Commanding Officer 6th Air Landing Brigade. With effect from 19th January, 1945.

BRERETON LEWIS, H. USAAF Lieutenant General. Allied Air Commander, Operation Market, September 1944.

BRIODY, M.J. MBE. WOI. Instructor at Glider Pilot Regiment Depot, Tilshead. Awarded Dutch Bronze Lion at Arnhem.

BRITTEN, G.V. Lieutenant Colonel, Commanding Officer, 1st (Airborne) Battalion, Border Regiment.

BROWNING, F.A.M. (Boy). Sir, Lieutenant General, KBE. CB. DSO. MC. First General Officer Commanding, Airborne Forces. 4th November 1941. Airborne Forces Commander, Arnhem 1944.

CAIN, R.H. VC. Major 2nd (Airborne) Battalion, South Staffordshire Regiment. Awarded Victoria Cross for valour during Battle of Arnhem, September 1944.

CARSON, R.J.H. Lieutenant Colonel. Officer Commanding 1st (Airborne) Battalion Royal Ulster Rifles.

CHATTERTON, G.J.S. OBE. DSO. Brigadier. 1912-1987. Commander, Glider Pilot Regiment. Royal Air Force pilot from 1930 to 1935. Queen's Royal (West Surrey) Regiment 1939 to 1941. Glider Pilot Regiment 1942 to 1946. Awarded DSO Sicily, 1943. Second in command 1st Battalion, Glider Pilot Regiment. CO 2nd Battalion, Glider Pilot Regiment, CO 1st Battalion, Glider Pilot Regiment. Commanding Officer Glider Pilot Regiment. Devised tactical landing plan for gliders in battle. Retired 1962. Author 'The Wings of Pegasus'. Foremost figure in Glider Pilot Regimental history.

COOPER, T. Group Captain, DFC. 38 Wing/Group, Royal Air Force. Air Commander Operation Freshman, November 1942. Operation Beggar/Turkey Buzzard, Sicily 1943.

COULTHARD, G.A.R. Captain, Glider Pilot Regiment. Commander Independent Glider Squadron, Operation Dragoon, South of France, 1944.

DARREL-BROWN, M. DSO. Lieutenant Colonel, Commanding Officer, 2nd (Airborne) Battalion, Oxfordshire & Buckinghamshire Light Infantry, 1944.

DARVELL, L. MC. Air Commodore, Royal Air Force. Air Officer Commanding 46 Group. Royal Air Force, 1944.

DAVIES, N.A. Pilot Officer, Royal Australian Air Force, one of the four first operational glider pilots - killed on Operation Freshman 1942.

DOIG, P. Sergeant, Glider Pilot Regiment, one of the four first operational glider pilots - killed on Operation Freshman 1942.

FRASER, H.J. Pilot Officer, Royal Australian Air Force, one of the first four operational glider pilots killed on Operation Freshman 1942.

GALE, R.N. KBE. CB. DSO. MC. Sir, Major General, General Officer Commanding 6th Airborne Division 3rd May 1943, Operation Neptune, D-Day 1944. Deputy Commander 18th Airborne Corps 1945.

GALPIN, D. DFM. WOI. Glider Pilot Regiment. Pilot of only successful glider landed near Ponte Grande bridge, Sicily.

GOBEIL, F.M. Squadron Leader, Royal Canadian Air Force, co-pilot Operation Voodoo transatlantic glider tow 1943.

HADDON, T. Lieutenant Colonel, Commanding Officer 1st (Airborne) Battalion Border Regiment, 1943. Battle of Arnhem, September 1944.

HICKS, P.H.W. DSO. MC. Brigadier, Commanding Officer 1st Air Landing Brigade, Arnhem, September 1944.

HOLLINGHURST, L.N. CB. OBE. DFC. Air Vice Marshal, Air Officer Commanding 38 Group, Royal Air Force, 6th November 1943.

HOPKINSON, G.F. OBE. MC. Major General. First Commanding Officer of 1st Air Landing Brigade 10th December 1941. Commanding Officer 1st Airborne Division 1943. Killed in action by machine-gun fire Italy 1943.

KINDERSLEY, H.K.M. Brigadier The Honourable. Commanding Officer 6th Air Landing Brigade, D-Day June 1944.

HOWARD, R.J. DSO. Major 2nd (Airborne) Battalion, Oxfordshire & Buckinghamshire Light Infantry. Commander Operation Deadstick, Caen Canal and River Orne coup de main assault, D-Day 1944.

LORD, D.S.A. VC. DFC. Flight Lieutenant, 271 Squadron, 46 Group, Royal Air Force. Awarded posthumous Victoria Cross for valour in action during re-supply drops at Arnhem, September 1944. The only VC to be won by the Royal Air Force while engaged on airborne forces duties.

MCCARDIE, W.D.H. Lieutenant Colonel, Commanding Officer 2nd (Airborne) Battalion, South Staffordshire Regiment.

MURRAY, I.A. DSO. Lieutenant Colonel, Glider Pilot Regiment. Officer Commanding No.1 Battalion, Glider Pilot Regiment. Led the main glider assault Normandy D-Day 1944. At Arnhem took command of 4th Parachute Brigade after its commanding officer Brigadier J. Hackett was wounded. Commanded British glider pilots Operation Varsity and was awarded bar to DSO.

NORMAN, SIR NIGEL, CBE. Group Captain 38 Wing, Royal Air Force. One of the founders of British airborne forces at RAF Ringway 19th September 1940. Killed in air crash 1943 en route to North Africa.

OTWAY, T.B.H. DSO. Lieutenant Colonel, Royal Ulster Rifles. Officer Commanding 1st Airborne Reconnaissance Regiment 1941. Officer Commanding 9th Parachute Battalion, Parachute Regiment, 1944. Commander of the epic assault on the Merville gun battery D-Day 1944.

ROCK, J.F. Colonel, Royal Engineers. The founder of British airborne forces on the 24th June 1940, at RAF Ringway. Killed in Hotspur glider crash at Shrewton, Wiltshire, October 1942.

SCARLETT STREATFIELD, J.R. CBE. Air Vice Marshal, 38 Group Royal Air Force, 18th October, 1944. Killed in air crash in Norway May 1945.

SEYS, R.G. AFC. DFC. Squadron Leader, Royal Air Force, Commander of Operation Voodoo transatlantic glider crossing 1943.

STRANGE, L.A. DSO. MC. DFC. Squadron Leader, Royal Air Force, one of the founders of British airborne forces RAF Ringway, 1940.

STRATHDEE, M.F.C. Staff Sergeant, Glider Pilot Regiment, one of the first four operational glider pilots - killed on Operation Freshman 1942.

STUDENT KURT. Generaloberst Luftwaffe. Commander of German airborne troops. Foremost German exponent of gliderborne warfare.

TURNER, C. Captain, Glider Pilot Regiment. Commander of Operation Bunghole, Yugoslavia 1944.

URQUHART, R.E. DSO. Major General, General Officer Commanding 1st Airborne Division at the Battle of Arnhem.

WALLWORK, J.H. DFM. Staff Sergeant. Glider Pilot Regiment, pilot of first glider to land on D-Day, 1944.

WILKINSON, A.M.B. Squadron Leader, 38 Wing Royal Air Force. Pioneer of long distance towed glider flight. Operation Freshman November 1942, killed in action Sicily 1943.

WILLIAMS, P.L. USAAF Brigadier Officer Commanding USAAF 9th Troop Carrier Command.

WINGATE, O. Major General, Burma 1944. Leading exponent of airborne warfare in Far East theatre of operations WWII.

# APPENDIX

## THE MERVILLE BATTERY

## Lieutenant Colonel T.B.H. Otway, DSO. Commanding Officer 9th Battalion, Parachute Regiment.

The job of the 9th Battalion was to capture and destroy a German battery at Merville, near the mouth of the River Orne and a few miles inland from the coast. The battery contained four guns which were thought to be 150mm (in fact we found them to be 105mm) and each gun was in an emplacement made of concrete six foot thick, on top of which was another six foot of earth. There were steel doors in front and rear.

The garrison was believed to consist of between 150 and 200 men, with two dual purpose guns and up to a dozen machine guns. There was an underground control room and odd concrete pill boxes dotted about. The position was circular, about 400 yards in diameter and surrounded by barbed wire and mines. There was a village a few hundred yards away which might have held more German troops.

There were only two sides from which we could possibly attack. To the north there was a double apron barbed wire fence, outside which was a minefield about thirty yards deep. Outside this again was an anti-tank ditch fourteen feet wide and sixteen feet deep which we assumed would be full of horrors.

On the south side there was the same double apron fence and the same thirty yard mine field, but instead of the ditch there was another barbed wire fence some twelve to fifteen feet thick and five to six feet high. The whole battery was then surrounded by a mine field one hundred yards deep which was protected by a barbed wire cattle fence, possibly electrified. Such was the nut to be cracked. As we were to land to the south of the battery I decided to attack from the south.

The basis of my plan was surprise and the fact that I did not intend to allow the garrison to concentrate on any one point - they would have to look several ways at once. Briefly it consisted of a preliminary recce party of a major and two APTC WOs, a taping party to mark the way through the minefield, a breaching party to blow three gaps in the wire, and an assault party to destroy the guns. There were various fire parties to cover the flanks, a couple of anti tank guns to shoot up the rear of the emplacements and a diversionary party to try and force the main gates to the east. Synchronised with the main assault three Horsa gliders, containing fifty men of the battalion and eight sappers, were to crash land inside the battery to take the garrison in the rear and assist in destroying the guns. Guns and jeeps and special stores were to come in another six gliders.

The RAF who had already bombed the battery three times and only hit it once, were to use one hundred Lancasters carrying 4000lb bombs to paste it five hours before we attacked. The time and distance factor was such that we could not attack before 0430 hours on D Day, and yet if the Navy did not receive the success signal by 0515 hours they were going to shell the battery - and threatened to use HMS Rodney as well as three cruisers, five destroyers and a monitor.

The battery was sited to fire straight down the assault beaches of 3rd British Infantry Division, which included 2 RUR, on the other side of the River Orne. I was told that it must be taken at all costs, for if it was able to fire the whole seaborne landings on these beaches might be a failure. To do the job I had the 9th Battalion, a section of 6 pounder anti-tank guns, a troop of sappers, a section of a field ambulance, some naval telegraphists, some war correspondents and a war artist - a total of about 600 all ranks. I had quite a contingent from 1 RUR - Major Robert Gordon Brown who commanded the glider assault force, Lieutenant Mike Dowling, RSM Cunningham and several others who had volunteered for parachute duties. In May we built a complete replica of the battery near Newbury and went into camp there to practise. We did nine rehearsals, five by day and four by night, with live ammunition, so that by the time we had finished every man knew the task backwards. At the end of the month we went into a transit camp at Broadwell airfield which we shared with 1 RUR.

We took off at 2210 hours on 5th June, and as we marched out of camp we were given a rousing send off by 1 RUR and by our own glider assault party who were to follow a few hours later. The flight across the Channel was uneventful but when we crossed the coast there was quite a bit of light flak which increased as more planes came in. I was in the first aircraft and so it wasn't too bad, but even then there was enough to be unpleasant. I jumped at ten minutes past midnight and found that I was about 1000 yards away from the dropping zone and landed slap up against the wall of a house which was a German battalion headquarters. A corporal and a private soldier also landed there and my batman went through the greenhouse roof - though I didn't know this till later. The corporal, private and I beat a hasty retreat after the corporal threw a brick at the Jerries - we hadn't time to get our grenades out.

We made for the rendezvous but found that the whole area was flooded. What had been shallow ditches were wide streams anything up to six feet deep and on three occasions we had to swim, which wasn't much fun in full equipment. We saw two men come down by parachute and land in the marshes. We tried to pull them out by their parachute harness but it was useless. With their equipment and sixty pound kit bags they sank out of sight at once and were drowned in the mud and slush. I am afraid that many were lost like that.

We arrived at the rendezvous at 0130 hours after meeting two more Germans. Wet through and tired I discovered to my horror that there were hardly any men there at all. There was desultory firing going on but otherwise everything was quiet except for the moans of a sapper with a broken leg. What had happened was that the weather over France was not good and the planes had become split up, some navigators mistaking the mouth of the River Dives for the River Orne. A number of the more inexperienced pilots had taken evasive action when they ran into flak and this threw the troops onto the floor of the aircraft, as they were standing up waiting to jump, so the aircraft had to go round and try to drop them again. To do this they had to cut into the stream which caused further confusion. The result was a very scattered drop, a lot of men in the marshes, a number in the River Dives and one stick of twenty men under a sergeant over thirty miles away. They came in four days later with the pay books of eleven senior German officers they had killed - including some generals.

We were due to move off at 0230 hours from the rendezvous and by then I was a very worried man, despite whisky produced by my batman. There was no sign of the gliders carrying the jeeps, anti-tank guns and special stores. (One landed by the River Dives - the other five were shot down or lost in the Channel) and I had only 100 all ranks. However, I had another fifteen minutes up my sleeve so we waited on and in came another fifty men. Now I had 150 all ranks, one Vickers MG, three PIATS, a few wireless sets, no 3inch mortars whose flares were required to guide in the assault gliders, no anti-tank guns, no jeeps, no mine detectors, no special explosive stores, one doctor and five medical orderlies, no sappers and twenty lengths of Bangalore Torpedo out of 120 loaded in the planes and gliders. I learned that the Lancasters had missed the battery but nearly hit the recce party which had gone ahead all right, and that the taping party had moved off three short with no tape and no mine detectors. So off we went.

Half way to the battery the officer in charge of the recce party met me as arranged and confirmed the position of the garrison. To do this he had left his WOs outside the minefield while he crawled through it and sat listening to the Germans talking for half an hour. He told me that the taping party had found and neutralised the mines with their hands and marked the paths to the wire by digging their heels along the ground. I decided to blow two gaps only in the wire and reorganised accordingly, making four assault parties for each gun, each of an officer and fifteen other ranks. The remainder of the force was to be under my hand for mopping up. The last half of the journey was hell, as we had to lie doggo when Jerry patrols passed and also climb in and out of RAF bomb craters.

However, we made it. As we approached the battery six heavy machine guns opened up on us from outside the battery, three to the left and three to the right. I told our one machine gun to silence those on the left, which they did and sent an NCO and three men to deal with those on the right, which they did.

At 0430 hours there was a loud bang as the two gaps in the big fence went up. Men in the breaching party rushed forward through the inner minefield and flung themselves on top of the double apron, and the gun parties followed using their comrades as mats over the wire. At the same time the first glider appeared but as we had no flares he couldn't see the position so he turned and landed some distance away. The second one then arrived and ran into a hail of flak which set him on fire. He did a steep turn and came down in a minefield behind us, bounced out of it and landed on top of an orchard - just in time for the twenty occupants to deal with a patrol of sixty Germans who were about to attack us from the rear.

The Dante's Inferno was let loose. The Germans began to shell us and mortar us from neighbouring positions with complete disregard for their own troops, the garrison concentrated everything waist high on the gaps in the wire, booby traps and were going off all over the place, the battle in our rear was going full tilt and fierce hand to hand fighting was taking place inside the battery. By this time I was just inside the wire and it was getting light, so I sent in most of the few reserves I had to assist in the hand to hand stuff. Then, apart from the shelling and mortaring, it got gradually quieter and I heard four explosions clear and distinct - the battery guns going up. As I went forward Mike Dowling reported that his gun was destroyed. I few minutes later I found him lying on his face - dead. I remember RSM Cunningham taking on three Germans by himself successfully. I saw what I thought was a dog tied up outside a pillbox and went to investigate but an officer who was lying near by with a shattered leg shouted - 'Don't touch that, you bloody fool, it's a booby trap'

The success signal went up at 0500 hours luckily seen by the Navy and we sent a pigeon to the War Office. Of the officer and fifteen men in the party detailed to destroy the left hand gun only the officer and sergeant got as far as the gun - the others were hit on the way. The results of the attack were that two guns were destroyed completely, and two put out of action for forty eight hours (Bangalore Torpedoes and Hawkins grenades down the muzzle were the dose prescribed.) Twenty two prisoners were taken and the rest of the garrison killed or wounded, the sixty men who attacked from the rear were all killed or wounded. We lost sixty five killed, wounded and missing which included one officer killed and two company commanders, the adjutant and another officer wounded. To this day there are 192 men of the 9th Parachute Battalion missing from that first night.

# Index.

Aberdeen LZ, 207.
Ainsworth John. MM. GPR., 252.
Airborne Divisions;
British 1st, 8, 22, 26, 32, 35, 41, 212, 295.
British 6th, 8, 26, 33, 35, 40, 46, 245, 272, 320.
Indian 44th, 34.
Airborne Forces airfields, 135.
Airborne Task Force Provisional, France, 135.
Air Landing Brigade, British 1st, 21, 28, 35, 37, 212, 298.
Air Landing Brigade, British 6th, 35, 43, 272, 323.
Albemarle Aircraft. RAF, 125.
Aldergrove Airfield, N.Ireland, 200.
Alexander. H.L. British General, 210.
Algiers, North Africa, 210.
Alison John R. US Colonel. Burma, 205.
Allen A.C. Lt. RE. Operation Freshman, 180.
Allied Airborne Army, 40, 323.
All American Aviation Company, 171.
Antopoulous A. GPR pilot, 188.
Arcier A.F. US Glider designer, 89.
Army Air Corps, British, 34.
Army Cooperation Command, British, 23, 112.
Army Museum of Flying, Middle Wallop, 202.
Arnhem, 32, 295.
Athens, Greece, 316.
Atomic Bomb research, Germans, 25, 174.
Avro 504 glider tug, 20, 127.

Baacke Fred. GPR pilot, Deadstick Operation, 77, 256.
Bailey Ernest W. Operation Freshman, 180.
Baker, Lance Corporal, glider pilot pioneer, 20.
Baldwin A. Staff Sergeant GPR. Merville Battery, 265.
Barkway Geoff. GPR. Operation Deadstick, 260.
Barrie Captain. GPR, 226.
Baskeyfield J.D. Victoria Cross, 305, 333.
Baynes carrier Wing, 88.
Beggar Operation, British glider tow, 27.
Belfield John T.V. Operation Freshman, 180.
Bennett D.C.T. Group Captain. RAF, 200.
Bevan Howell, RE. Sapper. Operation Freshman, 180.
Bigot, codename, 253.

Birmingham Railway Company, glider builders, 92.
Blackburn James. F. Operation Freshman, 179.
Blackpool LZ, Burma, 207.
Blui West One airfield, 200.
Boland Olly. GPR pilot, Operation Deadstick, 252.
Bomber, Lancaster, 130.
Bone S.G. GPR pilot, Merville Battery, 265.
Bonner Frank, RE Operation Freshman, 179.
Border Regiment, 21, 35, 50, 212, 300.
Bouchier Giles A.F. Major GPR, 219.
Bourne Sir Alan. Royal Marines, 18.
Bowen Dr. Peter. Army Museum, 7.
Bray Frederick W. Lance Corporal, RE Operation Freshman, 180.
Bren light machine-gun, 109.
Brereton Lewis. USAAF General, 295, 333.
Briody, CSM, GPR, 24, 72, 333.
Broadway LZ, Burma, 207.
Brook David, Eagle Magazine. GPR, 7.
Browning F.A.M.Boy. General. British, 21, 25, 37, 295, 333.
Buckton Albert. F/Sgt. RAF, Freshman Operation aircrew, 179.
Bunghole Operation, 1944, 31, 228.
Burma Operations, 31, 205.
BBC FFI messages, 281.

Caen Canal, Normandy, 252.
Cain R.H. Major. Victoria Cross award, 308, 333.
Cairncross James. D. Operation Freshman, 179.
Calvert M. Brigadier. India, 205.
Carrier Wing, Baynes project, 88.
Central Landing Establishment, RAF, 20.
Chambers W. Lieutenant. GPR, 191.
Chatterton G.J.S. Commandant. GPR, 22, 27, 212, 246, 321, 333.
Chindits, Burma, 205.
Chindwin River, Burma, 206.
Chowringhee LZ, Burma, 207.
Churchill, Winston, 19.
Clarke Dudley Lt. Colonel, 18.
Cochran Phillip. US Colonel. Burma, 205.
Commandos, British, 18.
Coogan Jackie, Film Star. Us glider pilot, 208.

Cooper Alaister, Major GPR, 39, 188, 224.
Cooper Tom B. Group Captain. RAF, 174, 187, 227.
Coulthard A. Major GPR, 228, 285, 289.
Coup de Main, Deadstick. Normandy, 248, 252.
Crete, 21.
Curnock Private. RAMC. Sicily, 217.

Darvall L. Air Commodore. RAF. 46 Group, 30, 324.
D-Day, 1944, 232.
Deadstick Operation, 1944, 252.
Dean L.G. Sergeant. Gpr. Merville Battery, 265.
Denholm J.W.C. Captain. GPR. Sicily, 74, 217.
Devonshire Regiment. 12th Battalion, 47, 272, 279, 324.
Diersfordt Forest, Germany. Varsity Operation, 325.
Dill Sir John, British, 18.
Dingson Operation, British. 1944, 31.
Doig Peter. Sergeant. GPR. Operation Freshman, 177.
Dorset Regiment, 35, 295.
Dorval, Canada, 200.
Dragoon Operation, 32, 285.
Duden Lt. Colonel. USAAF, 229.
Dyball A.J. Major. RUR, 324.

Eben Emael Fort, Belgium. 1940, 18.
Edwards George. F/Sgt. RAF Operation Freshman, 179.
Eisenhower Dwight. US General, 210, 295.
Elaborate operation, 29, 194.
Elba, 287.
Emblem S/Ldr. RAF, 261.
Eon Albert. French Maquis Leader. 1944, 281.
Eureka homing device, 26.

Falconer James. Sergeant RAF. Operation Freshman, 179.
Fargo 1 and 2. GPR depots, 75.
Farrell Peter. RE. Operation Freshman, 179.
Faulkener Thomas. Sapper. RE. Operation Freshman, 180.
Feltham, GAL Company, 21.
Ferry Command. RAF, 200.
Fine Samuel. US glider pilot. Sicily, 219.
Fox Dennis, Lt. Ox and Bucks. Deadstick, 252.
Fraser H.J.P/O RAF Operation Freshman, 179.
Frederick Robert T. US General, 285.
French Maquis, 281.

Frejus, France, 289.
Freshman Operation, Norway, 1942, 25, 174.
Frost John. Colonel. Arnhem, 301.
Fustian Operation. Sicily, 28, 74.

Gale Richard British General, 26, 43, 240, 244.
GAL Company, 21.
Galpin Dennis. DFM GPR, 28, 39, 74, 217.
Gander airfield, 200.
Geschwader, Luftwaffe, 16.
Gliders, British;
  Baynes Carrier Wing, 88.
  GAL55, 87, 88.
  Hadrian, 27, 29, 31, 38, 87, 89.
  Hamilcar, 29, 87, 91.
  Hengist, 87, 96.
  Horsa, 24, 27, 33, 87, 97.
  Hotspur, 21, 24, 87, 100.
  Kirby Kite, 21.
  Miles 32 Project, 87, 104.
  Taylorcraft H glider, 87, 104.
Gliders, German;
  DFS 230, 21.
Gliders US Main types;
  CG4A, 27, 29, 31, 55, 89.
Glider Pilots, First British Army, 20.
Glider snatching, 171.
Glider Tugs, 125.
Gliders Groschev GN4, 18.
Glider Instructors School, British, 22.
Glider Pilot Regiment, British, formed, 23, 35, 71.
Glider Training Units, British, 165.
Glider Training Squadron, British 1st, 20.
Gobeil F.M. S/Dr. Operation Voodoo, 201.
Goose Bay airfield, 201.
Grayburn J.H. Victoria Cross award, 307.
Grini Concentration Camp, Norway, 182.
Gruppe, Luftwaffe, 16.

Harper Colonel Joseph H. US Army, 11.
Harrison .W.J.Lance Corporal, glider pilot, 20.
Harvey Group captain, RAF. Ringway, 19.
Haward Arnold. RAF aircrew. Operation Freshman, 179.
Hawker Hector glider tug, 21, 33, 129.
Healey F. Lance Sergeant. Operation Freshman, 179.
Heavy Water Plant, Norway, 25.

Hicks F.H.W. Brigadier, 26, 41, 212, 298.
Hitler Adolf, 21, 25.

Hooper A. Lieutenant. Deadstick Operation, 252.
Hopkinson G.F. Brigadier, 22, 25, 37, 58.
Howard John. Major. DSO. Deadstick Commander, 44, 64, 252.
Howard Roy. Staff Sergeant. GPR. Deadstick pilot, 45, 259.
Hunter John. Operation Freshman, 179.
Hurn, Bournemouth, 23.

Ibsley airfield, Hampshire, 172.
Independent Squadron, GPR, 76, 78, 290.
Issel River, Germany, Operation Varsity, 325.

Jackson Wallis Lance Corporal. Operation Freshman, 179.
Jacques William. Operation Freshman, 179.
Jenner W.R. Sgt, GPR. Buried south of France, 289.

Kairouan airfields, Tunisia, 189, 211, 222.
Kerr D. Staff Sergeant GPR. Merville Battery, 265.
Kirby Kite glider, 20, 21.
Knowles George. Operation Freshman, 180.
Korneyev Marshal, Russian. Operation Bunghole, 228.
KOSB, 35, 40, 300.
Kronfeld F/Lt. RAF Test Pilot, 88.
Kuriate Islands, Tunisia. RV, 223.

Ladbrooke Operation, 210.
Legate Herbert. Operation Freshman, 180.
Le Muy, France, 285.
Longhurst W.S. F/Lt. RAF Operation Voodoo, 201.
Lord D.S.A. RAF. Victoria Cross award, 306.
Lovat Lord. D-Day, 260.
Luftflotten, Luftwaffe, 16.
Lund Brigadier. British, 18.
Lysander glider tug, 130.

Mallard Operation. British, D-Day, 272.
Manna Operation, Greece, 316.
Maquis, France, 281.
Market Operation, British, 32, 295.
Masters T.L. Operation Freshman, 180.
Merville Battery Assault. British, 31, 78, 240, 265.

Methven Lieutenant. Operation Freshman, 179.
Michie Joe. GPR. Merville Battery pilot, 265.
Miles M32 glider project, 104.
Miller Dusty, Sgt Major. Merville Battery, 265.
Moir John. Airborne Provost Section. Arnhem, 307.
Molten Operation, British, 33, 293.
Morris L. RASC glider pilot 1st, 20.
Moscow Glider Factory, 18.
Mo 9, War Office, London, 18.
Mykitina air field, Burma, 209.

Neilson Jock. RE. Operation Deadstick, 44, 252.
Netheravon airfield, Wiltshire, 23, 25, 30, 175, 186, 255.
Newfoundland. Operation Voodoo, 200.
Noble Ted. Ox & Bucks Medic, 328.
Norman Robert. RE. Operation Freshman, 179.
Norman Sir Nigel. RAF, 19, 23, 25, 27.
North Africa, 26, 27, 55.

Operations, American;
    Thursday, Burma with British Army, 205.
Operations, British;
    Freshman, 25, 174.
    Beggar/Turkey Buzzard, 27, 186.
    Bunghole, 31, 228.
    Dragoon, 32, 285.
    Dingson, 31, 281.
    Elaborate, 29, 194.
    Fustian, 28, 74, 222.
    Ladbrooke, 28, 74, 210.
    Mallard, 31, 45, 272.
    Market, 32, 295.
    Manna, Greece, 33.
    Molten, 33, 293.
    Tonga, 30, 240.
    Varsity, 33, 320.
    Voodoo, 29, 200.
Operational Glider Airfields, British, 146.
ORTU, 114, 124.
Otway T.H.B. Colonel, 69, 265.
Overlord 1944, 232.
Ox & Bucks Light Infantry, 21, 26, 35, 37, 38, 43, 62, 262, 272.
Ox & Bucks, Varsity, 152.

Palestine gliders, 70.
Parkerforce, 272.

Pegasus badge, 37.
Pendlebury Ernest. RE. Operation Freshman, 180.
Peterson. German CID. Norway, 181.
Priday B. Captain Ox & Bucks. Deadstick, 256.
Project Nine, USAAF, 205.

RAF Group 38, 23, 29, 33, 34, 38, 41, 111, 222, 246, 273, 321.
RAF Group 46, 30, 33, 34, 41, 111, 246, 273, 322.
Rathband Harry, GPR. 301.
Recce Regiment, 6th Airborne, 35, 44, 83, 326.
Ringway airfield, 20, 23.
Rock John Frank. Colonel. Founder Airborne Forces, 19, 21, 22, 24, 336.
Rogoland, Norway, 174.
Royal Ulster Rifles, 21, 26, 35, 44, 46, 272, 321.
Russian gliders, 18.
Russian Military Mission to Tito, 1944, 31, 228.

Sale, North Africa, 189, 196.
SAS, French, 31, 281.
Seago E, Major, designer of Pegasus badge, 37.
Sewell de Gency. RAF. Operation Freshman, 179.
Seys R.G.S/Ldr. Operation Voodoo, 201.
Sicily, 28, 212, 223.
Simkins George. RE. Operation Freshman, 179.
Skitten airfield, Scotland, 73, 175.
Smallman Leslie. RE. Operation Freshman, 180.
Smith John RE. Operation Freshman, 179.
South Staffordshire Regiment, 21, 35, 37, 40, 57, 212, 300.
South Staffordshire Regiment. Victoria Crosses, 308.
Soya Link code name, Burma, 206.
Squadrons, RAF;
  47; 116.
  48; 30, 116, 273.
  190; 29, 112, 116, 122, 124, 153, 196, 200, 273, 293, 321.
  196; 29, 112, 116, 273, 321.
  233; 30, 116.
  271; 30, 116, 273.
  295; 23, 27, 29, 112, 116, 186, 273, 321.
  296; 23, 29, 112, 116, 273, 321.
  297; 23, 29, 112, 116, 273, 321.
  298; 30, 112, 116, 255, 273, 285, 321.
  299; 30, 112, 116, 273, 321.
  437 RCAF; 116.
  512; 116.
  570; 30, 112, 273, 321.
  575; 30, 116, 273.
  620; 30, 112, 116, 273, 293, 321.
  644; 30, 112, 255, 273, 321.
Staffel, Luftwaffe, 16.
Strange Louis. RAF. Ringway, 19.
Strathdee M.F. GPR. Operation Freshman, 174, 177, 336.
Student Kurt. German Airborne Commander, 18.
Syracuse, Sicily, 28, 211, 218.
Syrencot House. Wiltshire. Airborne HQ, 25, 43.

Tappenden Ted, Ox & Bucks, D-Day. Deadstick, 259.
Taylorcraft H glider British, 104.
Thompson C.W.H. F/Lt. RAF. Operation Voodoo, 200.
Thursday Operation, Burma. US, 205.
Tilley Colonel. Dorset Regiment, 308.
Tilley CSM GPR. DCM, 307.
Tilshead, Wiltshire. GPR Depot, 22.
Toler T.I.J. Major. DFC. TD, 246, 321.
Tonga Operation, British, 30, 240.
Trandum, Norway. Operation Freshman, 174.
Troop Carrier Groups US;
  61st; 60, 214.
  62nd; 214.
  64th; 228.
Turkey Buzzard Operation. British, 27, 186.
Turner C. Captain. GPR. Commander Operation Bunghole, 228, 289, 317, 336.
Turner K. F/O RAF Operation Voodoo, 200.

Urquhart, Major General, 297, 336.
US Troop Carrier Wing;
  50th; 212.
  51st; 222.
  52nd; 214, 308.
  53rd; 285.

Varsity Operation, 33, 320.
Vemork, Norway. Operation Freshman, 25, 174.
Versailles Peace Treaty, 18.
Victoria Cross. Awards;
  J.D. Baskeyfield, 60, 305.
  J.H. Grayburn, 307.
  D.S.A. Lord, 306.
  F.C. Topham, 326.

R.H. Cain, 60, 308.
Voodoo Operation, 29, 200.


Waco Hadrian glider, 27, 29, 31.
Wallwork Jim, Glider Pilot DFM D-Day, 45, 256, 336.
Walsh John. Operation Freshman, 174.
White Staff Sergeant, GPR Sicily, 29, 39, 224.
White Thomas W. Operation Freshman, 179.
Wilkinson A.M.B.S/Ldr RAF, 27, 179, 187, 226, 336.
Williams Gerard. Operation Freshman, 180.
Wingate Orde, Burma, 31, 205, 336.
Withers L, Lt. South Staffs, 217.
Wormington P/O. Operation Voodoo, 200.
Wright Len. Staff Sergeant. DFM. GPR, 195.


Yardley Geoff. Ox & Bucks, 327.
Yugoslavia glider operations, 31, 228.